Y0-DBX-218

SOCIETY OF BIBLICAL LITERATURE
1979 SEMINAR PAPERS
VOL. II

GOLDEN GATE SEMINARY LIBRARY

SOCIETY OF BIBLICAL LITERATURE
SEMINAR PAPERS SERIES
Edited by
Paul J. Achtemeier

Number 17

Society of Biblical Literature
1979 Seminar Papers
Vol. II
Edited by
Paul J. Achtemeier

SCHOLARS PRESS
Missoula, Montana

SOCIETY OF BIBLICAL LITERATURE
1979 SEMINAR PAPERS
VOL. II

Edited by
Paul J. Achtemeier

One Hundred Fifteenth Annual Meeting
15–18 November 1979
Statler-Hilton Hotel, New York, New York

Published by
SCHOLARS PRESS
for
The Society of Biblical Literature

GOLDEN GATE SEMINARY LIBRARY

Distributed by
SCHOLARS PRESS
PO Box 5207
Missoula, Montana 59806

SOCIETY OF BIBLICAL LITERATURE
1979 SEMINAR PAPERS
VOL. II

Edited by
Paul J. Achtemeier

Copyright © 1979
by
The Society of Biblical Literature

ISBN: 0–89130–358–x pbk
ISSN: 0145–2711

Printed in the United States of America

Printing Department
University of Montana
Missoula, Montana 59812

8000—UM Printing Services

TABLE OF CONTENTS

INTRODUCTORY NOTE

The various papers contained in the two volumes of *Seminar Papers, 1979*, will be discussed in the appropriate program units during the One Hundred Fifteenth Annual Meeting of the Society of Biblical Literature, 15-18 November, in New York City. The volumes are produced photographically, from the copy submitted by the authors of the papers. Both content and format are therefore the direct responsibility of the respective authors. Editorial work is limited to assembling the papers and preparing them for publication. Occasionally a title is recast to conform to the normal format of the papers, but there is no further editing.

The volumes are intended to aid the discussion carried on within the appropriate program units at the annual meeting. Since the papers are intended to foster and stimulate such discussion, in many cases they represent the first attempt to formulate the ideas they contain and the theses they propose. Only rarely do they represent the final product of scholarly reflection. Rather, they represent for the most part the first step in the process of scholarly debate and refinement. Publication of the papers in this volume is simply to aid in their distribution, and represents no claim on the part of the SOCIETY that they are representative of the mature theological work of these or other SOCIETY members.

The order in which the papers appear is dictated by their place within the Annual Program. The identifying number preceding each title refers to the program, and the Book of Abstracts. The letter *S* indicates they are presentations of the Society of Biblical Literature.

The editor happily takes this opportunity to thank the authors and the chairmen and chairwomen of the various Groups and Seminars, and the Conveners of the various consultations whose efforts resulted in the papers collected in these two volumes. Thanks is also due to Sally Hicks, who prepared the camera-ready copy of the introductory material.

"THE SON OF MAN WHO HAS RIGHTEOUSNESS"

John J. Collins
DePaul University

In 1 Enoch 46, Enoch sees in his vision "one who had a head of days" and with him another figure "whose face had the appearance of a man" and was like "one of the holy angels."/1/. When Enoch asks about this second figure he is told: "This is the Son of Man who has righteousness, and with whom righteousness dwells." This figure has given rise to a copious literature which has been mainly concerned with the evidence for a "son of man" figure in Jewish expectations prior to the New Testament./2/. Relatively little attention has been paid to the understanding of righteousness associated with this "son of man." There has been a tendency to subsume the Similitudes under "1 Enoch" as a whole and classify the lot as "covenant-keeping righteousness," /3/ despite the conspicuous absence of allusions to covenant or law./4/. In recent years the theory of J. T. Milik that the Similitudes are a late Christian work/5/ has dissuaded some scholars from taking them into account in studies of Judaism. /6/. However, those scholars who have examined Milik's theory have rejected it vigorously, and reaffirmed a date in the first or early second century CE. /7/. The Similitudes can no longer be left out of account, and the controversial "son of man" figure must be recognized as a significant representative of one Jewish ideal of righteousness.

I

The Similitudes of Enoch consist of three "Parables" (38-44, 45-57 and 58-69) each of which is introduced by a chapter indicating the subject of the parable proper, which is visionary in form. The final two chapters, 70 and 71, fall outside the parables themselves and constitute a double epilogue. /8/. The "son of man" figure first appears in chap. 46, in the second parable. The manner in which he is introduced does not presuppose that "son of man" is a well-known title: Enoch sees a figure who had "the appearance of a man" and this figure is subsequently referred to as "that son of man." /9/. The expression "son of man" then is a periphrastic way of referring to the figure with "the appearance of a man" in 46:3. On the basis of these data M. Casey has argued that "son of man" is not a title and "would naturally be read as the equivalent of 'man.'"/10/. He proceeds to take it as established that a man is meant. This conclusion is too hasty, and neglects some important considerations. First, a figure with the appearance of a man is quite commonly found to be an angel in apocalyptic literature./11/. Whether the figure is in fact a man depends on whether he should be identified as Enoch throughout the Similitudes, a problem to which we shall return below. Second, as Casey also recognizes, the expression "son of man" is an allusion to Daniel 7(especially in the context of the vision of the head of days in chap. 46)/12/. Therefore, whenever the expression "that son of man" is repeated it is not simply equivalent to "the figure you saw" but also implies that this figure carries the eschatological associations of Daniel 7. While the Similitudes do not assume that "son of man" is a well known title, the expression serves to establish an identity that is more than just "a human figure."

The identity of this "son of man" figure does not depend entirely on its association with Daniel. The "son of man who has righteousness" cannot be distinguished from the "Righteous One" of 38:2 and 53:6./13/. It is also generally agreed that "the Chosen One," who appears in all three parables is the same being since he exercises the same functions as the "son of man" and the two expressions are interchanged in such a way that the identification is not in doubt./14/. Both the Righteous One and the Chosen One are used in association with the broader categories of "the righteous" and "the chosen" and these are also described as "the holy" (e.g. 48:1,4). These terms have several layers of reference. Besides the holy on earth there are "the holy

1

ones who dwell in the heavens,"(47:2) primarily the angelic host, but also transformed human righteous ones after their death, since we are told that they "all will become angels in heaven" (51:4) and they have "their dwellings with the angels and their resting-places with the holy ones" (39:5)./15/. When "the chosen will begin to dwell with the chosen" (61:4), the human, earthly, chosen ones will begin to dwell with the heavenly. In short, the human community of the elect and righteous stands in very close association with the angelic world and will be ultimately merged with it./16/.The Righteous, Elect "son of man" figure is directly related to both the human and the heavenly righteous./17/. The association does not lie only in "the fact that the son of man figure and the elect and righteous have in common certain basic qualities, those of election and righteousness."/18/. His entire function is defined in relation to the human righteous ones: "He will be a staff to the righteous and the holy, that they may lean on him and not fall"(48:4); "the wisdom of the Lord of Spirits has revealed him to the holy and the righteous, for he has kept safe the lot of the righteous"(48:5) and after the judgment "with that Son of Man will they dwell and eat and lie down and rise up for ever and ever"(62:14). His function as eschatological revealer and judge is to vindicate the righteous and condemn their enemies.

This close connection between the individual "son of man" and the community of the righteous has led some scholars to invoke the allegedly Hebrew conception of corporate personality./19/. This idea has rightly been criticized in so far as it implies "psychical unity" and rests on outdated anthropological theories which have been widely discredited./20/. There is no room for doubt that the Similitudes present the "son of man" as an individual figure distinct from the community. However, the communal dimension of the figure does not stand or fall with corporate personality. Mowinckel put the matter well: "Representative unity and a corporate conception of the leader as the bearer of the whole, and of the individual as a type of the race, is not the same as literal and actual identity. The fact that in the cult a person represents the whole, or in a symbolic sense is the whole, means that there is an intimate community of destiny between them..."/21/. The relation of the king to his people illustrates the point. The unity involved in the Similitudes is evidently closer to Mowinckel's "representative unity" than to corporate personality. Yet the relation of the king to his people is not the closest analogy we can find. Throughout the parables the "son of man"/Chosen One is located in the heavenly sphere in the presence of the Lord of Spirits: "For from the beginning the Son of Man was hidden and the Most High kept him in the presence of his power and revealed him (only) to the chosen"(62:7, cf. 48:6). As Sjöberg has remarked, he is not a man, at least in the usual sense of the word, but is rather a heavenly being./22/. A closer analogy is found with the patron deities of nations in Near Eastern mythology./23/. These deities have a representative unity with their peoples, although they are definitely distinguished from them. While "the gods of Hamath and Arpad" (Isa 36:19) cannot be conceived apart from the nations they represent, there is no doubt that any divinity was assumed to have greater power than his people and to be able to act independently over against them. The heavenly counterparts of nations played an important part in apocalyptic literature, most notably in Daniel 10 where the angelic "princes" of Persia and Greece do battle with Michael, "the prince of your people."/24/. I have argued elsewhere that the "one like a son of man" in Daniel 7 should be understood in this sense, as the heavenly counterpart of the faithful Jews./25/. The Similitudes differ from Daniel in so far as the human community is not identified in national terms but is designated as the "righteous" or the "chosen." Correspondingly, its heavenly counterpart is not identified as Michael, the patron of Israel, but as "the son of man who has righteousness" or the "Chosen One."/26/. The difference in terminology is at least potentially significant and may suggest that the community which produced the Similitudes did not find its basic identity in membership of the Jewish people but was sectarian in character./27/. Yet the correspondence between "the Chosen One" and the community of the chosen is analogous to that between Michael and Israel or any other mythological counterpart of a group or nation./28/.

There is a parallelism of action, or "structural homologue"/29/ between the earthly and heavenly counterparts. George Nickelsburg has noted the similarity between the Similitudes and Daniel in this respect. In Daniel "the son of man stands parallel to the (people of) saints (of the Most High). His exaltation means their exaltation."/30/. Similarly in 1 Enoch the manifestation of the son of man figure entails the triumph of the righteous. Nickelsburg has further argued that both the Similitudes and Wisdom 1-5 reflect a common exegetical tradition based on Isa 52-53./31/. In Isa and Wisdom a single figure, the servant and the righteous man, suffers, dies (at least in Wisdom, the interpretation of Isa is disputed) and is exalted.In the Similitudes the "son of man" stands parallel to the persecuted community and is finally exalted. However, even if we agree with Casey that the "son of man" is an "exalted man"/32/ there is no suggestion that he suffers or dies /33/. In view of this difference we may question whether Wis and 1 Enoch necessarily draw on a common exegetical tradition. Yet the parallels between them and Isa 53 are significant. In Isa and Wis the true nature and destiny of the servant and righteous man are hidden until the time of the judgment and cause consternation when they are revealed. In 1 Enoch the "son of man" is hidden until the judgment and also causes panic on his appearance. The hiddenness of the "son of man" corresponds to the sufferings of the righteous community and the hidden character of their destiny./34/. The "structural homologue" between the son of man and the community is thus complete. While he does not share their suffering, the pattern of hiddenness and revelation is common to both. The fact that he is preserved from their sufferings makes him a figure of pure power and glory and an ideal embodiment of the hopes of the persecuted righteous. The efficaciousness of the "son of man" figure requires that he be conceived as other than the community, since he must possess the power and exaltation which they lack.

In short, the "son of man" is not a personification of the righteous community, but is conceived, in mythological fashion, as its heavenly Doppelgänger. Now it is characteristic of mythological thinking that such a Doppelgänger is conceived to be more real and permanent than its earthly counterpart and prior to it in order of being./35/. However, from a modern critical perspective, it is clear that, in the words of André Lacocque, "it is a question of men before it is a question of angels."/36/. The human community is the datum of our experience and knowledge. The heavenly counterpart is posited on the basis of this datum. While the "son of man" is conceived as a real being he symbolizes the destiny of the righteous community both in its present hiddenness and future manifestation./37/.

II

When we turn to examine the idea of righteousness associated with this "son of man" figure, we find that it can only be approached through the righteousness of the human community. The statements about the righteousness of the "son of man" do not provide a clear model of conduct. He "has righteousness" and righteousness "dwells" with him (46:3). His "lot" surpasses all in uprightness (46:3). Righteousness is entailed in his "election" and is one of his defining characteristics. Righteousness is, of course, also an attribute of the Lord of Spirits (63:3). The righteousness of both Lord of Spirits and "son of man" is manifested especially in the judgment where the human "righteous ones" are vindicated and their enemies condemned. The righteousness of the "son of man" then confirms and vindicates that of the human community and so corresponds to theirs in the same way that the "son of man" figure corresponds to the community.

Most of the statements about the human righteous ones also lack reference to specific conduct. As David Hill has pointed out the term "righteous" is used as a quasi-technical term or even title for the community./38/. There are, however, a few specific references. In 43:4 we read of "the names of the righteous who dwell on the dry ground and believe in the name of the Lord of Spirits for ever and ever." Chap. 47 refers to the "blood of the righteous" - thereby implying that they are persecuted. In 48:6 the righteous "have hated and rejected this world of iniquity, and all its works and its ways they have hated in the name of the Lord of Spirits, for in his name they are saved." The picture of the righteous ones can be filled out from the more frequent descriptions of their opponents, "those who commit sin and evil"(45:5). They are "the kings and the powerful"(46:4, cf. 38:4, 48:8, 53:5, 54:2, 62:9, 63:1). They are also the ones "who have denied the name of the Lord of Spirits"(38:2, cf. 41:2, 45:1). These two characteristics are related. They deny the name of the Lord of Spirits because "their power rests on their riches, and their faith is in the gods which they have made with their hands"(46:7) and their "hope has been on the sceptre of our kingdom and of our glory"(63:7). The issue which divides the righteous and the wicked is belief in the heavenly world of the Lord of Spirits and "son of man," and in the judgment where they will prevail. Those who lack such a belief put their trust in such power as is available in the present. Those who enjoy power in the present, the kings and the mighty, are especially prone to such an attitude. Conversely, those who are powerless are more likely to "hate and reject this world of iniquity." Yet powerlessness in itself is no virtue and does not constitute righteousness. Righteousness is rather an attitude of rejecting this world and having faith in the Lord of Spirits and "son of man." Faith here involves both belief in their existence and trust and dependence on them for salvation. We should note that the Similitudes do not explicitly refer to keeping the law or distinguish between Jew and Gentile. It is probably true that the law is presupposed, and that the "kings and the powerful" who trust in the gods they themselves have made are gentile rulers, but the opposition is not formulated in terms of Jew and Gentile, and the possibility is left open that the division does not fall exactly along those lines.

The faith of the righteous, then, entails wisdom and knowledge. This in itself is not surprising since righteousness and wisdom go hand in hand, not only in OT wisdom but also in the mythology of the Ancient Near East./39/. However, in the Jewish tradition wisdom had come to be identified with the law of Moses (Sir 24:23) and was said to have made its dwelling in Israel (Sir 24:8)./40/. This identification is not apparent in the Similitudes. In chap. 42 we read that "Wisdom went out in order to dwell among the sons of men, but did not find a dwelling; wisdom returned to her place and took her seat in the midst of the angels." This passage is in direct contradiction to Sir 24. /41/. While the passage is enigmatic and may be out of context here it is quite in keeping with the general attitudes of the Similitudes. Wisdom is said to abound in the presence of God (48:1, 49:1). The spirit of wisdom dwells in the Chosen One who stands before the Lord of Spirits (49:3). This wisdom is not readily available. Righteousness and faith involve secrets (38:3, 49:2, 58:5) which are known only by revelation. This revelation is never related to the Mosaic covenant. Most obviously it is given to and through Enoch himself ("until now there has not been given by the Lord of Spirits such insight as I have received in accordance with my insight"[37:4]). The Similitudes themselves are the revelation of the wisdom disclosed to Enoch in his heavenly journey in which he sees "all the secrets of heaven" including the judgment (41:1). Yet the revelation of the Similitudes presupposes an antecedent revelation of the "name" of the "son of man" and expects a further definitive revelation in the future. In 48:7 we are told that the wisdom of the Lord of Spirits has revealed the "son of man" to the holy and the righteous (cf. 62:7) and in 69:26 the righteous rejoice "because the name of that Son of Man had been revealed to them." The "son of man" or his "name" is then a fundamental object of revelation, but he in turn "will reveal all the treasures of that which is secret" (46:3) and "judge the things that are secret" (49:4). The final and definitive revelation of the "son of man" is still in the future, on the day of judgment, and that is when he will judge the things that are secret. For the present faith in "that son of man" provides assurance that there will indeed be a judgment over which he will preside. This faith presumably undergirds righteous actions, but it also seems to be constitutive of righteousness in itself, since it involves not only belief but also the attitude of trust, in contrast to the self-sufficiency of the wicked.

The righteousness of the human community, then, comes through faith rather than the law. Unlike Paul, the Similitudes do not formulate an antithesis between faith and law. It is quite probable that fidelity to the law is presupposed, but it does not establish the distinctive identity of the righteous. That identity comes from their acknowledgement of the Lord of Spirits, the "son of man" and the heavenly world they represent.

The question how such a faith may have arisen cannot be answered fully without more definite information on the provenance of the Similitudes. On one level the conception of the "son of man" figure may be explained as an exegetical development of Daniel 7 in the light of other scriptural passages. /42/. More broadly, belief in a heavenly world and eschatological judgment had been part of apocalyptic tradition from the third century BCE./43/. The fact that the self-styled righteous were persecuted or oppressed by the kings and the mighty (cf. the "blood of the righteous" in chap. 47) was surely conducive to otherworldly beliefs. It is not clear, however, whether the persecution gave rise to the beliefs or was caused by them./44/. We simply do not have enough information on the provenance of the work to account for the genesis of its views.

III

Up to this point we have not considered the disputed question of the precise identification of the "son of man." The question arises because of two passages in the epilogues. The first, 70:1, is a disputed reading. The editions of Charles and Knibb read that Enoch's name was lifted up "to the presence of that Son of Man _and_ to the presence of the Lord of Spirits." However, a few mss. U, V and W, support a different reading: "the name of that son of man was raised aloft... to the Lord of Spirits."/45/. The second passage is 71:14, where an angel tells Enoch: "You are the Son of Man who was born to righteousness..." The problem, then, is that throughout the Similitudes Enoch has observed "that son of man" with no indication that he is seeing himself. Then in 71:14 (and possibly in 70:1) he is identified with the figure in his visions. The solution of Charles was to emend 71:14 to read "this is the Son of Man..." and change "you" to "him" in the following verses. /46/. This procedure has no basis in the text and is clearly unacceptable. Three possible solutions deserve serious consideration. The first is that of Mowinckel: "it is clear that 'son of man' is used, not in the technical sense, 'that Son of Man,' but in the ordinary sense, as a common noun, 'that man who' etc. It then follows that lxxi conveys the same meaning as lxx: the exaltation of Enoch to a conspicuous position in the presence of the Lord of Spirits, but not his exaltation to be the Son of Man."/47/. We must distinguish this view from the related theory of Manson and Russell that "the Son of Man idea, purposed from the beginning, finds its realization first in Enoch, then in the company of the elect and righteous of whom he is the 'firstborn,' and finally in the Messiah himself."/48/. As formulated by Manson and Russell this solution is flawed by its reliance on the discredited theory of corporate personality and its view of the Son of Man as an "idea." However, the formulation of Mowinckel does not involve these features. If "son of man" is not a title, but simply means "man", then 71:14 does not necessarily identify Enoch with the eschatological judge. In support of this solution we might point to 60:10 where Enoch is directly called "son of man" "after the manner of Ezekiel"/49/ and no eschatological function is necessarily implied, but this passage is part of a Noachic fragment and presumably from a different author. Against this theory, however, we must note that 71:16 (all... will walk according to your way,...with you will be their dwelling and with you their lot") strongly suggests an identification with the "son of man" of 48:7,and 71:14 corresponds closely to 46:3. Also the phrase "son of man" is used throughout the actual Similitudes (apart from the Noachic 60:10) if not as a title, at least with specific reference to a single figure. A distinction in 71:14 strains probability and must be considered unlikely.

The second possible solution might seem at first glance to be the most straightforward: the identification with Enoch is intended throughout./50/. In support of this view Morna Hooker has argued that chap. 71 "forms the climax and logical conclusion to the whole section by revealing that the 'name' which has been disclosed to the elect (69:26)is the name of Enoch himself."/51/. However, we cannot say that such a conclusion is required or that the Similitudes would be incomplete without it. Hooker herself has entertained the possibility that the "name" revealed is simply "Elect One." More basically, as U. B. Müller has noted, the "name" is not necessarily a title or proper name, but the person himself - as is clearly shown in 70:1 where Enoch's name is lifted up to heaven./52/. Hooker does not adequately address the difficulties that her view involves.

Three main problems confront the view that the identification with Enoch is intended throughout. The first concerns the disputed reading in 70:1, which, in the manuscripts followed by Charles and Knibb, shows a clear distinction between Enoch and the "son of man." Casey objects that "Charles' reading will have been determined by his conception of the Son of Man." However, this is even more blatantly true of Casey's own textual preference for the reading of U, which implies the identification./53/. On purely textual grounds, Charles' reading seems better. The disagreement of the manuscripts requires us to suppose that some copyists emended the reading of 70:1. If the text followed by Charles and Knibb is the original, then it would appear that the reading in U, V and W was changed to conform to 71:14. If the reading of U is original, as Casey holds/54/, then the copyists presumably changed the text because they wished to distinguish Enoch from the "son of man." In that case, however, we are at a loss to explain why they did not also change 71:14 but, in effect, introduced a contradiction into the text. In short, the reading of U is more easily explained as a scribal alteration. Accordingly, it seems more plausible that the reading followed by Charles and Knibb is the original, and so that Enoch was distinguished from the "son of man" in 70:1.

A second problem with the view that the identification is intended throughout is that it requires us to believe that Enoch does not recognize himself in his vision. Caquot has tried to counter this objection by pointing to T. Levi, where Levi sees himself in a vision./55/. There is, however, a crucial difference. Levi recognizes himself from the start. I know of no case in Jewish apocalyptic literature where the visionary fails to recognize himself.

A third problem might be raised by the alleged pre-existence of the "son of man" in 1 Enoch 48/56/. In 48:2 his name was named even before the sun and the constellations were created, and in 48:6 he was chosen and hidden before the world was created. Manson has questioned whether pre-existence is necessarily implied "except as a project in the mind of God" and points to the pre-mundane election of Israel and the name of the messiah in Rabbinic literature/57/. It is at least noteworthy that while the "son of man" is hidden since before the creation he is known only by special revelation to the chosen ones, and revealed to others only in the eschatological judgment. There is no question of his being revealed in the "historical" life of Enoch. This consideration is problematic for the view that the identification of Enoch with the "son of man" is an original element in the Similitudes.

In support of the identification with Enoch, scholars point to the later development of the Enoch figure in the Metatron of 3 Enoch/58/. There is no doubt that at some point Enoch was identified with the heavenly "son of man." /59/. The issue is whether this identification was already presumed in the Similitudes or was developed later and merely added in chap. 71 by a redactor.

The third possible solution is that Enoch was not originally identified with the "son of man" figure but that chap. 71 is a later addition./60/. This view is not an <u>ad hoc</u> solution to the "son of man" problem but arises independently from literary considerations. As we have noted above, chaps. 70 and 71 constitute a double epilogue to the Similitudes. Each tells how Enoch was carried up to the heavens./61/. Now redundancy and duplication is not in itself surprising in a work such as the Similitudes, but is in fact a common feature of apocalyptic literature./62/. However, we usually find such redundancy in the visions, not in the narrative framework. Accordingly, the repetition here strongly suggests the hand of a redactor. Of course this argument is strengthened if we follow the reading of Charles and Knibb at 70:1, which makes a clear distinction between Enoch and the Son of Man, in contradiction to 71:14.

The main objection to this view has been expressed by Hooker: that it "is merely to push the problem one stage further on, and to leave unexplained how an editor or translator was able to make the identification."/63/. This point is not entirely valid. It is a well-known fact that ancient redactors did not consistently revise the documents to which they made additions. The view that chap. 71 is an addition can explain why other passages stand in tension with that chapter and does not require us to read the other chapters in the light of 71./64/. The redactor presumably intended that other statements about the "son of man" should now be applied to Enoch, but since he did not systematically revise the other statements some of them may now be anomalous. Hooker is quite right to pose the question how the redactor was able to make the identification at all. However, the balance of probability inclines to the view that the identification of Enoch with the "son of man" is a secondary addition.

The question whether the identification with Enoch is original to the Similitudes is not so crucial for our purpose as it might appear. Even if the identification is original, it is clear that "that son of man" refers to Enoch in his exalted state. No reference is made to the earthly life of Enoch. For all practical purposes he is treated as a heavenly being. Even when the identification is clearly made in chap. 71 there is no attempt to provide an example for human, earthly life through the figure of the "son of man." Accordingly, the conclusions of the first two parts of this essay can still stand even if the identification with Enoch is accepted. Further, as we have seen in the first part of this study, there is continuity between the "son of man" and the earthly righteous ones. Now Enoch is in any case pre-eminent among the righteous ones and shares to some degree in the "son of man's" role as revealer. The figure of Enoch was widely used as a paradigm of righteousness. This does not prove that no distinction between Enoch and the "son of man" is possible, but it shows how the identification could be suggested by the Similitudes apart from the epilogues. It is the destiny of all the righteous to be with "that son of man" in the heavenly resting places (62:14). Enoch has already attained that destiny and so is distinguished from other humans. However, Enoch is a model for the earthly righteous ones in a way that the "son of man" in the actual Similitudes is not. He has made the transition from the earthly world to the heavenly. This is the source of his wisdom and confirmation of his righteousness. There can be little doubt that the status of Enoch as a revealer rests on the tradition that he had been taken up (Gen 5:24). It is this fact, rather than any specific conduct on earth, that gives him significance. Like the "son of man" he symbolizes the destiny of the righteous. Accordingly his identification with the "son of man" is not as drastic an innovation as it may at first seem.

IV

Two concluding reflections may serve to relate the Similitudes to other literature of their time. First, righteousness in the Similitudes is attained through faith in a heavenly world, God as Lord of Spirits and an eschatological judge referred to as "son of man." Faith here means both belief and trust and leads to an attitude of rejection of this world. While faith is not conceived in antithesis to law, it involves a revelation which goes beyond the Mosaic covenant, which is simply passed over in silence. We should not exaggerate the analogy with Pauline Christianity. The nature and implications of faith are evidently modified when focused on the death and resurrection of Jesus, and Paul's idea of faith is developed in far greater explicit detail. Yet the Similitudes are closer to Paul's "pattern of religion" than to any form of "covenantal nomism," the pattern which E. P. Sanders finds to be typical of Palestinian Judaism./65/. We should not conclude too hastily that the Similitudes are anomalous in Judaism. The entire Enoch tradition is based on the revelation of heavenly and eschatological mysteries,/66/ and claims in Enoch an authority older than Moses. The terminology of election and righteousness, which plays a prominent part in the Similitudes can also be traced to the earliest stages of the tradition./67/. Since the need for a higher revelation is a basic postulate of apocalyptic literature,/68/ it would seem that Sanders' argument that this literature conforms to "covenantal nomism" might bear re-examination./69/.

The second reflection concerns the relation of the "son of man" in Enoch to the Son of Man in the NT. The origin of the belief in Jesus as the Son of Man who would come on the clouds of heaven can be adequately explained as an adaptation of Daniel 7 in conjunction with other OT texts, without reference to the Similitudes./70/. However, J. Theisohn has argued strongly that a few passages in Matthew show the influence of the Similitudes in the way the Son of Man is conceived, specifically Matt 19:28 and 25:31 where the Son of Man sits as judge upon his glorious throne (compare 1 Enoch 61-62)./71/. Specific cases of literary influence would seem to be rare; at least, few have been demonstrated. Barnabas Lindars has argued that "the connection between this literature and the New Testament is to be seen in the community of ideas rather than in direct links." While apocalyptic texts "do not refer to a single, universally accepted personality entitled the Son of Man," they do frequently refer to a "celestial Messiah" (Michael in 1QM, Melchizedek in 11QMelch etc.)./72/. The community of ideas between the Similitudes and the Son of Man Christology is noteworthy, though not complete. We have argued in Part One above that there is a "structural homologue" or parallelism between the "son of man" in 1 Enoch and the earthly righteous. Recently Gerd Theissen has argued that "many sayings about the attitude of the Jesus movement display an unmistakeable parallelism to sayings about the Son of Man" and suggested that the early Christians "identified themselves with the destiny of the Son of Man."/73/. In fact the parallelism is closer in the NT, since the Son of Man has an earthly career and suffers and dies like his followers. The NT Son of Man is a model for human conduct in a way that the Enochic "son of man" is not. The analogy between the Similitudes and Christianity becomes closer when Enoch is identified as the "son of man." The identification with Enoch is intelligible as an inner Jewish development, arising from the pre-eminence of Enoch as righteous man and revealer and the tradition of his translation to heaven. However, we may also wonder whether this development in the Enoch tradition was not a reaction to the Christian appropriation of the phrase "son of man" for another who was believed to have made the transition from earth to heaven.

Notes

/1/. The text and translation followed here is that of M. A. Knibb, with the
assistance of E. Ullendorff, The Ethiopic Book of Enoch. A New Edition
in the Light of the Aramaic Dead Sea Fragments (2 vols.; Oxford:
Clarendon, 1978).

/2/. For bibliography see C. Colpe, "ho huios tou anthrōpou," TDNT 8(1972)
423-427; J. Theisohn, Der Auserwählte Richter (SUNT 12; Göttingen:
Vandenhoeck & Ruprecht, 1975); U. B. Müller, Messias und Menschensohn
in jüdischen Apokalypsen und in der Offenbarung Johannes (Gütersloh:
Mohn, 1972) 36-60; M. Casey, "The Use of Term 'Son of Man' in the
Similitudes of Enoch," JSJ 7(1976) 11-29.

/3/. So J. A. Ziesler, The Meaning of Righteousness in Paul. A Linguistic
and Theological Enquiry (Cambridge: Cambridge University, 1972) 95-96.

/4/. A. Jaubert (La Notion d'Alliance dans le Judaïsme aux abords de l'Ere
Chrétienne [Patristica Sorbonensia 6; Paris: Seuil, 1963] 261-267) finds
only one reference to a covenant in 1 En 60:6, which she refers to the
Noachic covenant. Yet she comments: "Il n'est guère possible d'admettre
une indifférence à l'égard de la doctrine même de l'Alliance" (262) and
assumes that the adversaries in the Similitudes are considered unfaithful
to the law (264).

/5/. J. T. Milik, "Problèmes de la littérature hénochique à la lumière des
fragments araméens de Qumrân," HTR 64(1971) 333-378; The Books of Enoch
(Oxford: Clarendon, 1976) 89-107.

/6/. So E. P. Sanders (Paul and Palestinian Judaism [Philadelphia: Fortress,
1977] 347-348) in his important study of the "patterns of religion"
which provide the framework for understanding righteousness, concludes
that "It would be premature to accept any one reconstruction for the
date of the Similitudes, but it now seems the better part of wisdom to
regard the section as probably post-Christian in origin." In Sanders'
view all the documents of Palestinian Judaism conform to the pattern
of covenantal nomism.

/7/. J. C. Greenfield and M. E. Stone, "The Enochic Pentateuch and the Date
of the Similitudes," HTR 70(1977) 51-65; M. A. Knibb, "The Date of the
Parables of Enoch: A Critical Review," NTS 25(1979)345-359. Greenfield
and Stone argue for a first century date. Knibb prefers a date in the
period 70-135 CE (after the destruction of Qumran) despite the lack of
any reference to the destruction of the temple. J. H. Charlesworth,
"The SNTS Pseudepigrapha Seminars at Tübingen and Paris on the Books of
Enoch," NTS 25(1979) 315-323, reports that M. Black, who formerly
shared Milik's view, now sees the Similitudes "as Jewish and post-
Christian, perhaps a Jewish reaction to Christianity from about A. D.
100." Charlesworth also reports that no scholar at the SNTS seminars
seemed persuaded by Milik's dating. C. L. Mearns, "Dating the Similitudes
of Enoch," NTS 25(1979) 360-369, argues for an early date on the basis
of very dubious analogies with the stage "Christian eschatology had
probably reached in the late forties AD." D. W. Suter, Tradition and
Composition in the Parables of Enoch (unpublished diss. Chicago: Univ.
of Chicago, 1977) 50, argues for a date before 70 CE.

/8/. See the outline by M. D. Hooker, The Son of Man in Mark (Montreal:
McGill University, 1967) 36-37. The Noachic passages in 54:7-55:2; 60;
65:1-69:25 are recognized as intrusive.

/9/. Casey, "The Use of Term 'Son of Man,'" 14-18. In all but four instances
the expression "son of man" is used with a demonstrative. While it is
conceivable that the demonstrative could represent the Greek definite
article (as Charles had argued) the fact that it never occurs with
the expression "Chosen (Elect) One" makes this unlikely. As many scholars
have noted, three different Ethiopic expressions are used for "son of
man": walda sab'e; walda be'esi and walda 'eguala 'emmaheiaw. Distinct
Aramaic equivalents were proposed by N. Schmidt in 1908 but convincingly
refuted by E. Sjöberg, Der Menschensohn im Äthiopischen Henochbuch (Lund:
Gleerup, 1946) 43-44. The Ethiopic expressions can most easily be
understood as translation variants, irrespective of whether the original
was in Greek or Aramaic (Casey, 18). We should note that at

62:5 some manuscripts read "son of a woman" (walda be'esit) but others read "son of man" walda be'esi or walda sabe'. The feminine be'esit could easily be a scribal error.

/10/. Casey, "The Use of Term 'Son of Man,'" 23.

/11/. E.g. Dan 8:15; 9:21; 10:5; 12:6. See J. J. Collins, The Apocalyptic Vision of the Book of Daniel (HSM 16; Missoula: Scholars Press, 1977) 142.

/12/. Casey, "The Use of Term 'Son of Man'" 20-22. Casey refutes the arguments of K. Müller("Menschensohn und Messias. Religionsgeschichtlichen Vorüberlegungen zum Menschensohnproblem in den synoptischen Evangelien," BZ 16[1972] 161-187) who argues that the Similitudes preserve an older conception of the "son of man" which is adapted in Daniel.

/13/. Some manuscripts read "righteousness" instead of Righteous One at 38:2.

/14/. Hooker, The Son of Man in Mark, 38-40.

/15/. The ambiguity of the term "holy ones" in apocalyptic literature is well known from the Qumran scrolls. See C. W. Brekelmans, "The Saints of the Most High and their Kingdom," OTS 14(1965) 305-329; S. Lamberigts, "Le sens de qdwšym dans les textes de Qumrân," ETL 46 (1970) 24-39; L. Dequeker, "The 'Saints of the Most High' in Qumran and Daniel," OTS 18(1973) 133-162.

/16/. This is a common conception in apocalyptic literature. See J. J. Collins, "Apocalyptic Eschatology as the Transcendence of Death," CBQ 36(1974) 21-43.

/17/. Müller, Messias und Menschensohn, 45.

/18/. So Casey, "The Use of Term 'Son of Man,'" 13.

/19/. T. W. Manson, "The Son of Man in Daniel, Enoch and the Gospels," Studies in the Gospels and Epistles (Manchester: Manchester University, 1962) 123-145 (originally published in BJRL 32[1949-50] 171-193), N. A. Dahl, Das Volk Gottes (Darmstadt: Wissenschaftliche Buchgesellschaft, 1963) 90; D. S. Russell, The Method and Message of Jewish Apocalyptic (Philadelphia: Westminster, 1964) 350-352.

/20/. J. W. Rogerson, "The Hebrew Conception of Corporate Personality - A Re-examination," JTS NS 21(1970) 1-16. See also the criticism of Dahl by S. Mowinckel, He That Cometh (Nashville: Abingdon, 1955)381.

/21/. Mowinckel, He That Cometh, 381.Mowinckel's discussion is flawed by his reliance on a theory of Primordial Man and anima generalis, which can not be maintained.

/22/. Sjöberg, Der Menschensohn, 50: "Die hier geschaute Gestalt ist tatsächlich kein Mensch - wenigstens nicht im gewöhnlichen Sinn des Wortes. Sie ist vielmehr ein himmlisches Wesen, der ganz besondere himmlische Mensch." This remains true despite the use of OT motifs and passages associated with the royal, Davidic messiah (Theisohn, Der Auserwählte Richter, 53-99) and the fact that he is called messiah (48:10).

/23/. P. D. Miller, The Divine Warrior in Early Israel (HSM 5; Cambridge: Mass: Harvard, 1973) 156-159; P. D. Hanson, "Jewish Apocalyptic Against Its Near Eastern Environment," RB 78(1971) 39-40.

/24/. Collins, The Apocalyptic Vision, 108-116.

/25/. Ibid., 144-146. So also U. B. Müller, Messias und Menschensohn, 28; K. Müller, "Der Menschensohn im Danielzyklus," in R. Pesch and R. Schnackenburg, eds., Jesus und der Menschensohn (Für Anton Vögtle; Freiburg: Herder, 1975) 37-80. Compare also A. Lacocque, The Book of Daniel (Atlanta: John Knox, 1979) 122-134.

/26/. Michael appears independently in the Similitudes as one of the archangels.

/27/. Analogies with the Qumran Scrolls are instructive at this point. There such designations as "Sons of Light" are used to express the identity of the community, and its heavenly counterpart is the "Spirit of Light." Qumran, however, continued to use national designations as well - e.g.

1QM 17:7: "to raise up among the angels the authority of Michael and the dominion of Israel among all flesh." See J. J. Collins, "The Mythology of Holy War in Daniel and the Qumran War Scroll," VT 25(1975) 596-612. For further analogies between the Similitudes and Qumran see further Greenfield and Stone, "The Enochic Pentateuch," 56-57. They also point out that the Similitudes would have been unacceptable to the Qumran sect because of the treatment of the sun and moon in chap. 41.

/28/. The suggestion of Manson ("The Son of Man," 140) that the Son of Man is an idea in the mind of God imports a Hellenistic category which is foreign to the Similitudes although it may be appropriate for some later Rabbinic conceptions. Manson fails to do justice to the concrete vitality of mythological thinking. E. Schweizer, "Menschensohn und eschatologischer Mensch im Frühjudentum," in Pesch and Schnackenburg, Jesus und der Menschensohn, 109-112, draws analogies to portrayals of the ideal man in Philo but fails to note the significant differences between the philosophical and mythological modes of thought.

/29/. For the phrase, see G. Theissen, Sociology of Early Palestinian Christianity (Philadelphia: Fortress, 1978) 121, who uses it with reference to the Son of Man in the NT.

/30/. G. W. Nickelsburg, Resurrection, Immortality and Eternal Life (HTS 26; Cambridge, Mass: Harvard, 1972) 77.

/31/. Ibid., 70-78. The influence of the Isaianic servant songs has also been noted by J. Jeremias, "pais theou," TDNT 5(1967) 687-688; Müller, Messias und Menschensohn, 38-39 and Theisohn, Der Auserwählte Richter, 114-126.

/32/. Casey, "The Use of Term 'Son of Man,'" 20.

/33/. Sjöberg, Der Menschensohn, 116-139.

/34/. Ibid., 102-115 for the hiddenness of the "son of man" and its apocalyptic connotations.

/35/. See M. Eliade, The Myth of the Eternal Return (New York: Pantheon, 1954) 3-6.

/36/. Lacocque, The Book of Daniel, 131.

/37/. Compare the remarks of Theissen (Sociology, 101)on the function of the Son of Man in the NT.

/38/. D. Hill, "Dikaioi as a Quasi-Technical Term," NTS 11(1965) 296-302.

/39/. See H. H. Schmid, Gerechtigkeit als Weltordnung (Tübingen: Mohr, 1968) 96-98.

/40/. The classic text is Sirach 24. See Sanders, Paul and Palestinian Judaism, 329-346, and, with a somewhat different interpretation, J. Marböck, "Gesetz und Weisheit. Zum Verständnis des Gesetzes bei Jesus Ben Sira," BZ 20(1976) 1-21.

/41/. On the contrast between the apocalypses and the wisdom books on the nature of wisdom see U. Luck, "Das Weltverständnis in der jüdischen Apokalyptik," ZTK 73(1976) 283-305 and J. J. Collins, "Cosmos and Salvation: Jewish Wisdom and Apocalyptic in the Hellenistic Age," HR 17(1977) 121-142.

/42/. See Nickelsburg, Resurrection, 70-78; Theisohn, Der Auserwählte Richter, 1-148.

/43/. M. E. Stone, "The Book of Enoch and Judaism in the Third Century B.C.E.," CBQ 40(1978) 479-492.

/44/. Compare Wis 2:12-20, where the righteous man is persecuted because he is righteous.

/45/. Casey, "The Use of Term 'Son of Man,'" 25-26. The reading in V is slightly different from U and W.

/46/. Charles, APOT 2:237.

/47/. Mowinckel, He That Cometh, 443.

/48/. Russell, The Method and Message, 352. Compare Manson, "The Son of Man," 140-142.

/49/. Charles, The Book of Enoch (Oxford: Clarendon, 1893) 156. Even Casey,

who notes that the Ethiopic phrase is not the one used in the translation of Ezekiel, agrees that it is used after the manner of
Ezekiel ("The Use of Term 'Son of Man,'" 24).

/50/. So Hooker, Casey and, most recently A. Caquot, "Remarques sur les
chap. 70 et 71 du livre éthiopien d'Hénoch," Apocalypses et Théologie
de l'Espérance (Lectio Divina 95; ed. H. Monloubou; Paris: Cerf, 1977)
111-122.

/51/. Hooker, The Son of Man, 41-42.

/52/. Müller, Messias und Menschensohn, 59. So also Manson, "The Son of Man,"
136.

/53/. Casey, "The Use of Term 'Son of Man,'" 25. Casey takes it as "given that
a man is being described here"(21-22), an assumption which, as we have
seen above, is unwarranted. He then appeals to "considerations of
inherent probability."

/54/. See also M. Black, "The Eschatology of the Similitudes of Enoch,"
JTS NS 3(1952)4.

/55/. Caquot, "Remarques," 121.

/56/. Sjöberg, Der Menschensohn, 83-101; Mowinckel, He That Cometh, 370-373.

/57/. Manson, "The Son of Man," 136.

/58/. Black, "Eschatology," 6.

/59/. Sjöberg, Der Menschensohn, 169-174, argues that 2 Enoch and at least
some of the Metatron passages in 3 Enoch involve the translation of
a human being who was not in any sense pre-existent. See also
Mowinckel, He That Cometh, 437-440.

/60/. Müller, Messias und Menschensohn, 54-59; Colpe, "ho huios tou anthrōpou,"
426.

/61/. In fact there are three statements of the translation of Enoch: 70:1-2;
71:1 and 71:5. Müller defines the addition as 71:5-17.

/62/. On redundance in the Similitudes see Suter, Tradition and Composition,
passim. Compare A. Y. Collins, The Combat Myth in the Book of Revelation
(HDR 9; Missoula: Scholars Press, 1976)43-44.

/63/. Hooker, The Son of Man, 42. Compare Sjöberg, Der Menschensohn, 165 and
the critique by Müller, Messias und Menschensohn, 56.

/64/. Black, "Eschatology," 8, recognized the tension between chap. 71 and
the main body of the Similitudes, but suggested that 70-71 is the older
stratum, because of its similarity to the elevation of Enoch in 1 En
14. Despite the fact that it is often cited with approval, this
suggestion has not been supported by any compelling argument, since,
as Black himself admits, chaps. 70-71 may simply be influenced by
the older visions. Against Black's theory is the fact that the
Similitudes do not betray the identification of the "son of man" with
Enoch.

/65/. Sanders, Paul and Palestinian Judaism.

/66/. M. E. Stone, "Lists of Revealed Things in Apocalyptic Literature," in
F. M. Cross, W. Lemke and P. D. Miller, eds., Magnalia Dei. The Mighty
Acts of God (Essays in memory of G. E. Wright; New York: Doubleday,
1976) 414-452 and "The Book of Enoch," 479-492.

/67/. F. Dexinger, Henochs Zehnwochenapokalypse und Offene Probleme der
Apokalyptikforschung (Studia Post-Biblica 29; Leiden: Brill, 1977)
145-181.

/68/. See Luck, "Das Weltverständnis," 283-305 and compare the definition of
apocalypse in J. J. Collins, ed., Apocalypse, The Morphology of a Genre
(Semeia 14 [1979]) 9.

/69/. Sanders is definitely right in arguing that there is no essential
incompatibility between apocalypticism and legalism (Paul and Palestinian Judaism, 423-424). It is also true that most, perhaps all, of the
apocalypses presuppose the importance of the law. What is questionable
is whether the law and the covenant were the most important factors
in their world-view.

/70/. The identification of Jesus as eschatological "son of man" has been best explained by N. Perrin, _A Modern Pilgrimage in New Testament Christology_ (Philadelphia: Fortress, 1974) 34-36, 57-93, although his remarks on the Jewish material are less than satisfactory.

/71/. Theisohn, _Der auserwählte Richter_, 175-182. Compare G. W. Nickelsburg's review of Milik, _The Books of Enoch_ in CBQ 40(1978) 417-418.

/72/. B. Lindars, "Re-enter the Apocalyptic Son of Man," NTS 22(1976) 60.

/73/. Theissen, _Sociology_, 25,27.

Dennis Berman

University of Pennsylvania

Preface. This is a summary of the hasid traditions in
rabbinic literature,[1] based in part upon my dissertation research. In general, I have given emphasis to those materials
and aspects which are most relevant to the seminar theme:
Profiles of the Righteous Person. The tentative results of
my investigation of the sources lead me to differ with general scholarly opinion on a number of interpretations and conclusions. Though many points could not be discussed in this
brief presentation, the notes provide references to most of
the primary and secondary sources. By way of introduction the
hasid traditions in pre-rabbinic sources are mentioned as well.

Hasid in the Bible.[2] The word hasid (plural: hasidim)
appears 32 times in the Hebrew Bible, exclusively in religious
poetry.[3] It is related to hesed, an act of kindness or generosity flowing from faithfulness to a relationship. God is
hasid when He lovingly forgives Israel's past faithlessness.[4]
The hasid is one who performs hesed for God and man and is
thereby the deserving recipient of divine hesed.[5] Often hasid
is synonymous with "righteous (zaddik), upright, faithful."[6]
The hasidim love and praise God.[7] David is called a hasid.[8]
Sometimes the people of Israel or the priests are ideally
spoken of as hasidim.[9]

Bible Translations. The Aramaic targums often retain
hasid, but sometimes they render it "righteous, good, pure."[10]
The old Greek renders hasid by hosios throughout Ps. and in Dt.
33:8 and 2 Sam.22:26; elsewhere it uses several other Greek
words.[11] The few fragments of Aquila, Symmachus and Theodo-
tian render hasid with hosios.[12] But while hosios regularly
renders hasid, the word itself represents a much wider lexical group and it is very often used to render a number of
other terms. Hence, it would be precarious to assume that
whenever hosios appears in Jewish-Greek translation literature
it represents hasid in the original Hebrew.[13] The Latin
renders with sanctus.

The Hasideans.[14] About 167 BCE a group, apparently
calling themselves the Hasidim,[15] joined the Maccabean forces,
along with all those fleeing the persecutions (1 Macc.2:42f.).
It is unclear whether they were originally a religious organization or a revolutionary band. The former seems more likely
in light of 1 Macc.7:12ff. where the Hasideans are foremost
among those anxiously seeking peace. Their representatives
are scribes,men learned in the Torah, whose naive trust in
Alcimus simply because he is a priest probably reflects their
great reverence for the priesthood.[16] In 2 Macc.14:6 Alcimus
tells Demetrius (162 BCE) that the Hasideans and their leader
Judah are warmongers and revolutionaries who must be destroyed.[17] Since Alcimus is attempting to protect himself and
regain power, his charges must be viewed with suspicion. After
betraying and murdering many of their leaders, he undoubtedly
counted the Hasideans among his bitterest enemies, along with
his arch-rival Judah. In any case, his accusations seem to
have proven false.[18]

Nothing is known concerning the origins or eventual fate of the Hasideans, or even about their size and influence during the brief five years for which their activity is documented. Josephus ignores the Hasideans in his account of the Maccabean revolt; perhaps he considered them too insignificant to single out for mention.[19] There is no reference to the Hasideans in rabbinic literature, nor is there any basis for identifying them with either the Pharisees or the Essenes.[20] Nor is there any solid evidence for identifying them with the hasidim in certain post-exilic Psalms.

Rabbinic Literature.[21] In the Bible the hasid is a pious, saintly person. Hasid is rarely found in rabbinic literature in this general sense outside of a few occasions when its use is influenced by biblical exegesis. The hasid in rabbinic literature is kind and merciful, but still more he is completely selfless, sinless and devout. He is not simply pious, for in his zeal to fulfill the Law he goes beyond the norm. A quality of exuberance and extreme piety pervades the rabbinic hasid traditions. However, the hasid is never characterized as a martyr or an ascetic.[22]

Related Concepts. The abstract noun hasidut (literally, hasid-ness) represents that quality which the hasid embodies.[23] In various contexts it has the sense of kindness, mercifulness, total honesty and scrupulous regard for the Law.[24] In R. Pinhas b. Yair's (beg.iii) progression of virtues hasidut ranks near the top, after diligence, cleanliness, purity, abstinence, holiness, humility and fear of sin (M. Sota 9.15). One version even ranks it above the spirit of holiness,[25] only one step below the resurrection of the dead (TY Shab.3c), while another insists that hasidut is the greatest of them all.[26]

Gemilut hasadim is a comprehensive term for all Jewish social virtues, although originally it was limited to acts of piety in which one fulfilled the ethical or cultic commandments. But such "acts of lovingkindness" were considered a normative and fundamental part of the value system of rabbinic Judaism. Like any pious Jew the hasid would undoubtedly perform them, but there are no hasid traditions explicitly connected with gemilut hasadim.[27]

Hasid and Zaddik.[28] In addition to its rare meaning "lovely"[29] hasid is sometimes used in rabbinic literature in the generic sense of "pious, good, righteous."[30] In such cases there is an occasional interchange between hasid and zaddik.[31] But usually the rabbis carefully distinguish between the two.[32] Thus an aphorism (ca. ii CE) states that the hasid burns his nail parings, the zaddik buries them and wicked man throws them away.[33] In general, the zaddik is a good man who does his best to avoid sin and obey the moral and ritual commandments: the ideal average man. However, the hasid goes beyond the bounds of duty. He passionately strives for absolute perfection and complete devotion. Of course, being a perfect zaddik the hasid shares the reward of the righteous in the hereafter.[34]

Methodological Observations. The primary sources for a study of the hasid must be those texts which explicitly refer to hasid or hasidut.[35] Rabbinic interpretations of hasid in Scripture are important and traditions which describe attitudes or conduct very similar to those found in the primary hasid traditions are also significant, especially when they concern figures who are called hasidim. However, not every idea or practice attributed to an identified hasid should automatically be considered essentially characteristic of the hasid, but only those which actually appear in the primary hasid traditions.

Several scholars (Büchler, Baer, Sarfatti, Safrai, Urbach, Vermes) sometimes argue that a certain figure would have been called a hasid, then proceed to use that person as a kind of archetypical hasid, subjectively emphasizing some attributes for which parallel traditions are adduced. Such an approach runs the risk of turning every pious man into a hasid and every form of Jewish piety into hasidut. It is important to realize that the same man who is a hasid can function in various roles, e.g. friend, rabbi, zaddik or even miracle-worker. In dealing with the sources it is necessary to carefully distinguish those qualities and activities which characterize the hasid qua hasid from those which probably reflect other such roles.

Misconceptions. In light of these strictures several scholars (Büchler, Sarfatti, Urbach, Vermes) appear to have placed undue emphasis on the relationship between hasidim and miracle-workers. There is only one tale of a hasid who is asked to bring rain and then halt it (T. Taan. 2.13) and here it is not this activity but rather the exceptional righteousness of the man that is underscored by calling him a hasid.[36] While Hanina b. Dosa (end i-beg.ii) may well have been a hasid,[37] he was also considered a miracle-worker ("a man of deed") par excellence (M.Sota 9.15). Indeed, the sources carefully distinguish between hasidim and "men of deed."[38]

Despite the contention of several scholars (Baer, Safrai, Falk) there is no evidence that the hasidim created a separate legal tradition which informed rabbinic law. The sources speak only about the practices of pious individuals; there is no reference to an autonomous community of hasidim or their teachings.[39] A work called the Scroll of the Pious (megillat hasidim) is mentioned several times (ca.ii-iv), but it appears to have been an ethical treatise.[40]

Jewish Law. A number of rabbinic teachings in the Mishna and elsewhere are characterized by an attitude of such extreme piety that they are better suited for the hasid than the average man. But these need not be attributed to a hasidic legal corpus. Presumably the same rabbis who advocate such teachings are perfectly capable of creating them. In their interpretation of the Bible and formulation of the Oral Law the sages were guided by a view of Torah as the revelation of God's ideal for human conduct and character. This spirit of piety and idealism which pervades Jewish law inspired R. Judah's (d.299) suggestion that whoever wishes to become a hasid should strive to fulfill the rabbinic precepts concerning social responsibility, honesty in business,concern for the property and well-being of others. Another sage recommends heeding the teachings of the religio-ethical tractate Avot. Still others suggest the tractate on divine worship, prayer and blessings.[41] But all three are complementary. The hasid is zealous in ritual observance and scrupulous in his conduct; he is intensely devout and perfectly righteous.

Early Hasidim. There are a few traditions (most stemming from ca. ii CE) about the early hasidim, the pious men of yesteryear (ḥasidim harishonim). They would wait an hour before prayer to direct their minds to God.[42] They affixed the fringes to their garments as soon as three handbreaths were woven, instead of simply waiting until they were ready to wear.[43] R. Judah (mid.ii) states that since God did not allow them to fall into sin, in their eagerness to bring a sin offering they took a nazirite vow which necessitated one. However, R. Simeon b. Gamaliel (mid.ii) denies that the early hasidim made a nazirite vow, which he considers sinful, and claims instead that they brough a free-will offering whenever they wished.[44] R. Judah also relates that shortly before death they were afflicted with intestinal illness, which purged them so that they entered paradise in purity.[45] The early hasidim engaged in conjugal relations only on Wednesdays, believing that thereby their wives would not give birth on the Sabbath and so avoid any desecration of the holy day.[46] They would bury thorns and glass deep in their fields where it could never cause any harm.[47] And they gave precedence to visiting the mourner's home before attending the wedding feast.[48]

Neither the name itself nor the character of these traditions suggests that the reference is to an organized group of pietists. The expression "early hasidim" apparently refers to the pious folk of times past in general, from biblical times up to the destruction of the Temple (end i CE), whose great piety had become legendary. The rabbis considered many biblical figures hasidim.[49] One tradition (ca.ii) numbers Abraham and Hanina b. Dosa (end i-beg.ii) among the pious men of yesteryear.[50] If the rabbis pictured biblical saints acting in such ways they were largely projecting back the practices of the hasidim of their own day and recent memory.[51] By distinguishing between the "early hasidim" and contemporary hasidim (ii CE) the rabbis seem to endow the former with an aura of superiority. The tendency to glorify the past, especially the period up until the destruction of the Temple, is common in rabbinic circles.[52] This tendency probably underlies the hyperbolic lament: "When R. Yose Katonta died, hasidim disappeared."[53] The oldest known figures who might be considered among the early hasidim are Bava b. Buti (end i BCE)[54] and Yose b. Yoezer (first half ii BCE).[55]

The Tales. The over two dozen tales of "a certain hasid" (maʿaseh beḥasid eḥad) constitute an important body of hasid traditions. While most of the tales beginning with this formula stem from ca. ii CE Palestine, their popularity continued on into the middle ages, when new tales sprang up. The hasid tales usually function as exempla, that is, anecdotes which point to a moral, illustrate a Scriptural verse or sustain an argument. Stories about the hasid's miraculous reward would inspire piety,[56] while tales decrying his guilt of an incredibly trivial sin admonished diligence in the minutiae of rabbinic law.[57] The rabbinic conception of the hasid runs through these tales. Indeed, it is unthinkable to relate such stories about "a certain man."[58] Structurally, the core of the tale is the test to which the exceptional piety of the hasid is put. He usually emerges successfully, but not always. For no man is perfect, not even the hasid.[59] Several amusing tales inject an element of hyperbole[60] or irony.[61] Some have a legendary or supernatural touch, while others may well be "historical" with a bit of embellishment. However, the historical importance of these tales lies primarily in their accurate portrayal of the image of the hasid held by the Jews who

created and retold them. The character of the hasid that
emerges from the tales corresponds with that found in the
other hasid traditions.

Paragon of Virtue. Because of his urge to completely
fulfill the Law and even go beyond it the hasid is inherently
a perfectly righteous man. The notion that the hasid leads a
totally blameless life is reflected in several tales[62] and
midrashim[63] and also underlies a group of traditions about
Yose b. Yoezer and R. Judah b. Bava (end i-beg.ii).[64] It is
significant that the latter is depicted as fulfilling the dictum that all one's deeds should be for the sake of heaven,
whose author, R. Yose (end i-beg.ii), is called a hasid by his
teacher, R. Yohanan b. Zakkai.[65] The hasid strives to serve
God in his every activity.[66] In addition to the tales about
the hasid's remarkable honesty and faithfulness even to Gentiles,[67] there are a number of aphorisms (ca.ii) in which the
hasid epitomizes the virtuous man, in contrast to the average
and wicked man.[68] But while the hasid often serves as the
model of ethical perfection, there are also many traditions
praising his zealous observance of the ritual laws. The
hasid's exuberance extends to both the moral and cultic precepts of the Torah.

Protests. Although the hasid is generally touted as
the ideal Jew, there are a few traditions critical of particular hasidim.[69] R. Joshua (end i-beg.ii) condemns the idiotic
hasid whose excessive piety occasions unnecessary loss of
life.[70] In a similar vein Rabba b. R. Huna (d.322) says that
the sages were displeased with those hasidim (ca.ii) who were
peeved by the killing of snakes and scorpions on the Sabbath
(TB Shab. 121b). Several statements disparage the piety of
the 'am haaretz, the Jew who does not meet with the rigorous
rabbinic standards of religious education and observance.
The sages considered dedicated study and observance of Scripture and all the minutiae of the Oral Toral indispensible for
the attainment of religious perfection.[71] So Hillel (end
i BCE-beg.i CE) remarks: "The 'am haaretz is not (apt to be) a
hasid."[72] But even those ignorant men who were hasidim were
despised by some sages because of their enmity for the 'am
haaretz.[73]

Anonymity. Although there are hundreds of rabbinic
traditions extolling the piety of numerous sages, most hasid
traditions are related about anonymous hasidim. There is one
story which was originally told in Palestine about R. Judah b.
Bava but in later Babylonian circles was related as "a tale of
a certain hasid."[74] It may be that a confusion of this tradition underlies the puzzling Babylonian claim: "Everywhere it
says 'a tale of a certain hasid' it refers to R. Judah b. Bava
or R. Judah b. Ilai."[75] There are a few Babylonian traditions
(ca.iv-v) which also suggest that stories told about specific
sages were soon popularized about anonymous hasidim.[76] This is
largely because the hasid traditions often function as exempla.
They are primarily didactic; they extol the virtue rather than
glorify the particular saint.

Society. It is only natural that hasidim in rabbinic
literature often appear as sages. Yet the sources refer to
hasidim among all segments of society: men and women, rich and
poor, townsman and farmer, scholar and am haaretz, priest and
layman.

People were very conscious of the piety of their contemporaries. The conferred the epithet hasid only upon those rare
individuals who deserved it.[77] They even distinguished levels
of greatness among the hasidim.[78] People had great pride in
and respect for hasidim.[79] Special burial caves were set aside
for them.[80] Indeed, one of the highest honors was to be eulogized as a hasid.[81]

Role Model. Rabbinic Judaism developed three distinct
ideal types of piety. The scholar who studies, develops and
transmits the revealed Law is the highest aim of Jewish education and the ideal of intellectual perfection. The zaddik, the
just and virtuous man who fulfills the Torah, is the ideal of
the active life and ethical perfection. Although the two are
not exclusive of each other, they represent the embodiments of
fundamentally different values. The hasid is also an ideal of
the active life, but he is distinguished by his radicalism,
spiritual fervor and zeal for the Law. In principle, though,
not everyone could be educated to become a hasid; it is basically a matter of gift and character.[82] Nevertheless, the hasid
was held up as a model to emulate before the common man as well
as the sage, who was expected to set an outstanding example of
piety in his own right.[83] This may be attributed to the idealistic nature of Judaism in general and also to the concept of
the "joy of the Law," that every Jew perform the commandments
lovingly and enthusiastically, which was a fundamental tenet
of rabbinic Judaism.[84]

NOTES

1. I have focused here on those traditions which probably date between ca.i-vi CE; cf. n.58. Note the following abbreviations: ARN=Avot de-Rabbi Natan; EJ=Encyclopedia Judaica
(1972); M=Mishna; T=Tosefta; TB=Babylonian Talmud; TKF=S. Lieberman, Tosefta Ki-fshutah (1955-); TY=Palestinian Talmud.

2. See M.H. Pope, "Hasidim," IDB 2:528f.; J. Morgen-
stern in HUCA 38 (1967):59-73; K.D. Sakenfeld, The Meaning of
Hesed in the Hebrew Bible (1978); I. Heinemann, "Hesed; Hasidim," Encyclopedia Biblica (Hebrew) 3:221-25.

3. Mainly in Psalms (25 times) It may have been a poetic
convention. Most of the attestations are post-exilic.

4. Jer.3:12; cf. Ps.145:17; Ex.34:6; Sakenfeld, pp.
193ff.; TB R.H. 17b.

5. Cf. 2 Sam.22:26=Ps.18:26. Man/Israel performs
hesed for God by faithfully upholding the high moral and cultic
standards of the covenant; cf. Sakenfeld, pp.175ff. Already in
the Bible (but perhaps not until the post-exilic period) hesed
has the sense of "pious acts;" see Sakenfeld, pp.151-58; cf.
n.27; TY San.29c. Note the frequent use of the possessive suf-
fix to indicate "God's hasidim" (16 times); this never occurs
with zaddik. In its secular as well as theological (cf.n.4)
sense hesed denotes an act of succor freely done beyond the
bounds of strict obligation. Perhaps, then, already in the
Bible the hasid is one whose piety exceeds the norm.

6. Prov. 2:8; Mic.7:2; 1 Sam.2:9; Ps.12:2; 18:26;
31:24; 32:6; 37:28; 43:1; 50:5; 79:2; 97:10. Note the similar
expression "man/men of hesed" in Isa.57:1 and Prov.11:17; cf.
Sira 44:1,10. It is considered equivalent to hasid in TB Taan.

llb; cf. "men of ḥasidut" instead of hasidim in TY Sota 24c.

7. Ps.30:5; 31:24; 145:10,17; 149:1,5; cf. 97:10.

8. Ps.16:10; 52:11; 86:2; 89:20.

9. Ps.85:9; 145:10; 148:14; 149:1,5,9. Perhaps Ps. 132:9,16 and 2 Chr.6:41 refer to the Israelite laity, in synthetic parallelism with the priests; but cf. Dt.33:8.

10. So in 1 Sam2:9; Jer.3:12; Prov.2:8; Ps.4:4; 12:2; 16:10; 43:1.

11. The old Greek uses eulaboumenos in Prov.2:8; there are double readings in Jer.3:12 (eleemōn and eleōn) and Mic.7:2 (eulabēs and eusebēs).

12. So for Ps. fragments and Sym. and Aq. to Jer.3:12; Mic.7:2; Sym. to Dt.33:8.

13. The old Greek uses hosios to render a number of Hebrew terms for "pure, clean, upright" in Dt.32:4; Amos 5:10 (and Theod.); frequently in Ps., Prov. and also Sira. See Hatch-Redpath, Concordance to the Septuagint (1906),II,1018; Hauck, "Hosios," TDNT 6:489-93. Mr. Benjamin Wright, who is studying the lexical group hosios in Jewish-Greek translation literature, informs me that he would agree with my conclusions.

14. See W.R. Farmer, "Hasideans," IDB 2:528; Schürer-Vermes-Millar, The History of the Jewish People in the Age of Jesus Christ (1973),I,157,169; M. Mansoor, "Hassideans," EJ 7:1468 and "Essenes" EJ 6:899-902.

15. The Greek Asidaioi probably renders the Hebrew hasidim; cf. old Greek to Job 39:13; Hexaplaric fragment to Ps.29:5 in Hatch-Redpath, Sup.III,200c. The name itself implies only that they were staunch traditionalists; they may not have been more devout than the other Jews fighting with the Maccabees; cf.n.55. Note the play on their name in 1 Macc. 7:16f. which quotes Ps.79:2 in the style of a midrashic fulfillment text.

16. Cf. Josephus, Life 192; Ant.12.395.

17. Of course, there may have been both militant and pacifist factions within the Hasideans. The identifications of the Hasideans with the entire force under Judah (or perhaps only the most fanatical element is intended here) may be due to some ulterior motive on Alcimus's part.

18. Cf. 2 Macc.14:18ff.; Ant.12.382.

19. Ant.12.272,395,401; cf.12.391f.

20. There is no connection between the Hasideans and the early hasidim, nor is there any evidence of a hasidic legal corpus (see below). L.Finkelstein, The Pharisees (1962[3]) simply assumes without any justification that the Hasideans are identical with the plebeians. It is certainly possible that the Hasideans were a small group of pietists who had no connection with or influence upon the Pharisees (who were active by mid.ii BCE according to Ant.13.171) or the ascetic communities in the Dead Sea area; cf.J.T. Milik, Ten Years of Discovery in the Wilderness of Judaea (1959), pp.59,81. It is significant that the word hasid never appears in the DSS except incidentally in a few Bible quotations (4Q 174,175; 11Q Ps[a] 6,17,26; cf. 4Q Ps[q]; 4Q 176). Milik (p.80 and DJD 2:163f.) would identify the so-called "[fortress of the] pious" in Mur. 45.6 with Qumran, however the text of this letter fragment

(dated ca.134 CE) actually reads ḤSDYN not ḤSYDYN! It is
difficult to argue that the yod is omitted here; it was usually added as matres lectiones even when unnecessary. Nor is
the use of mitnadev, "volunteer" in 1Q S 5.1ff. related to
1 Macc.2:42 where the Hasideans are described as "mighty war-
riors of Israel, each a volunteer for the Law." The Hebrew
mitnadev, which probably underlies the Greek hekousiazomenos,
appears to be used here as in Jud.5:9,17 for those who readily
sacrifice their lives in battle. It has other uses, such as
the cheerful giving of free-will offerings to God (1 Chr.29:5,
9; cf.n.44), or for an "initiate," as in the DSS.

21. See A. Büchler, Types of Jewish Palestinian Piety
(1922); L. Gulkowitsch, Die Bildung des Begriffes Hasid (1935);
L. Jacobs, "The Concept of Ḥasid in the Biblical and Rabbinic
Literatures," JJS 8(1957):143-54; S. Safrai, "Teachings of
Pietists in Mishnaic Literature," JJS 16(1965):15-33; S.
Schechter, Studies in Judaism 2(1908):148-81; E.E. Urbach,
"Hasidim," EJ 7:1383-88 (rev. version of his article in
Encyclopedia Hebraica 17:750-52); G. Vermes, "Hanina b. Dosa,"
JJS 23(1972):28-50 and 24(1973):51-64; and in Hebrew: Y. Baer,
"The ancient hasidim in Philo's writings and in the Hebrew
tradition," Zion 18(1953):91-108; Z. Falk, "On the Mishna of
'the Pious,'" in Benjamin De Vries Memorial Volume (1968),
pp.62-69; G.B. Sarfatti, "Pious men, men of deeds, and the
early prophets," Tarbiz 26(1957):126-53.

22. The killing of hasidim in TB A.Z. 18a need not be
referring to martyrs, and the par. read zaddikim (see n.31).
The midrash in TB San.110b; TY San.29c on Ps.50:5 seems to dis-
associate hasidim from martyrs. In TB San.47a Abaye argues
that Ps.79:2 refers to martyrs only to defend his position in a
debate. And note the subtle tension between the tale of R.
Judah b. Bava as a hasid (see n.64) and the stories of his
death as a martyr.

The one tale which depicts a hasid who becomes an ascetic explicitly distinguishes his asceticism from his ḥasidut,
which seems to refer to his generosity (Ruth Zutta 1.2). A
hasid would fast to atone for his sins (cf. Gen.R.94.9) and
therefore Adam is called a great hasid for his exemplary efforts in this regard (TB Erub.18b); cf. Büchler, pp.74,139f.
The statement in TB Taan.11b is unclear (see ed. Malter, p.40
and notes). Cf. E.E. Urbach, "Ascesis and suffering in talmudic and midrashic sources," in Yitzhak F. Baer Jubilee Volume
(1960), pp.48-68 (Heb.).

23. Cf. TB Hul.63a; B.M. 52b; Shab.120a; A.Z. 20b;
M.Sota 9.15 and T. Sota 15.5; TY Sota 23b.

24. TB Hul.63a; San.110b; T.B.K. 11.14; and "manner of
piety" (midat ḥasidut) in TB Hul. 130b; B.M. 52b; Shab. 120a;
TY Shev. 39d, which is similar to going "beyond the line of the
law" (lifnim meshurat hadin) = equity in modern law.

25. On the idea that ḥasidut is the stage right below
prophecy cf. n.81. In light of the rabbinic view of the sage
as superior to the prophet (TB B.B. 12a) it is not impossible
that ḥasidut would deliberately be ranked above the spirit of
holiness.

26. Note the distinction here between humility and
ḥasidut; R. Joshua b. Levi (cf. n.39) argues that humility, not
ḥasidut, is the greatest (TB A.Z. 20b). The hasid can certainly be humble, but apparently this virtue is not a fundamental

characteristic of the hasid; cf. nn.69,80; Tanhuma Vayera 22.
The interchange between the two in Midrash Ps.86.1 and TB Shab.
88b is due to hasid in the proof text; ARN A 40 and TB Ber. 57b
are simply referring to Psalms in its double stress on humility
and devotion.

27. Explicit connections, however, should not always be
expected in rabbinic literature. There are several cases in
which a hasid is portrayed performing acts which would certainly be considered gemilut hasadim, such as ransoming captives
and visiting mourners. The point is that doing such pious acts
is not the essence of the hasid. The were expected from and
often performed by all Jews. See EJ 7:374-76; J. Goldin in
PAAJR 27 (1958):43ff.; cf. n.5 on hesed as "pious acts."

28. See G. Scholem, "Three Types of Jewish Piety,"
Eranos Jahrbuch 38 (1969):331-48; R. Mach, Der Zaddik in Talmud
und Midrasch (1957); EJ 14:180-83; 16:910f.; M. Kadushin, The
Rabbinic Mind (1952), pp.39f.; S. Lieberman, Greek in Jewish
Palestine (1965), pp.68ff.

29. Job 39:13, punning on the bird's name (cf. Zach.
5:9); see N.H. Tur-Sinai, The Book of Job (1967), pp.544f.;
Eccl.R.7:19=Song R.4:4 (cf. Midrash Ps.1.6). Cf. hasudah ,
"lovely," in Num.R.12.4 (Song R.3:9 reads hasidah); TB Ket.
17a; and hesed, "favor, beauty," in Est. 2:9,17 and perhaps
Isa.40:6; cf. TY Sota 24c and par.

30. In TB Yoma 38b R. Hiyya (beg.iii), probably taking
his cue from the Targums, equates hasid with "good" and "righteous." This usage is often an imitation of Scriptural idiom:
Sifre Dt.49; TB San.47a; cf. ARN A 36; Midrash Ps.119.1; 149.1;
3 Enoch 48.5. See Sifre Num.92 and par.

31. M. Kid. 4.14 (perhaps alluding to sailors' kindness
to shipwrecked persons) and TB Nidda 14a; TB A.Z. 18a and San.
64a; Yoma 69b; also Tanhuma Hukkat 25 and Tanhuma ib. 55 (ed.
Buber IV,130); Yalkut I #765; note variants in Lev.R.2.1 (ed.
Margulies, p.35); cf. TY Sota 24c. Homilists, probably aware
of the general sense of hasid in the Bible, could easily expound it in reference to the zaddik: TB San. 110b; Midrash
Ps.116.8; 149.5; cf. Gen.R.86.3.

32. Cf. ARN A 8 (see n.50); Num.R.18.9; Sifre Dt.49,
306 (ed. Finkelstein, pp.114,339); M. Avot 6.1; ARN A 3; and
Thirteenth Benediction of the ancient (ca.i CE) Tefilla.

33. TB Nidda 17a; M.K.18a. According to popular super-
stition stepping over nail parings could be harmful to pregnant
women.

34. Midrash Ps.16.11; 86.1; 149.5; Eccl.R.1.11; Tanhuma
Shemini 11; 3 Enoch 18.22; 23.18; A. Jellinek, Bet ha-Midrasch
(1967³) 3:29.

35. There are roughly a hundred traditions referring to
hasid and two dozen to hasidut (excluding parallels) from which
to determine what people meant when they used these words. In
light of the very consistent picture that emerges it seems reasonable to conclude that only those elements which find clear
expression in the primary hasid traditions are actually characteristic of the hasid.

36. God hearkens to the prayers for rain of the righteous (TY Taan.67a; TB ib.23a); cf. Mach, pp.110ff. The story
told about Honi the circle-drawer (first half i BCE) has the
same bare outline as the hasid tale, but it differs in nearly

every detail (M. Taan.3.8; TB ib. 23a; TY ib. 66d). The
hasid's prayer for rain is answered immediately, presumably
because of his great righteousness. However, Honi's prayer
is not fulfilled (in TY one sage explains that he did not pray
with humility), which prompts him to display rather imperious
behavior; cf. J. Goldin in HTR 61(1963):233-37. No hasid would
act this way. Indeed, one native Babylonian sage living in
Palestine (ca.mid.iv) once remarked (apparently quoting a popular saying) to a visiting countryman, "come and see the difference between the cocky/imperious ones of the land of Israel and
the hasidim of Babylonia," for the latter approached God with
much more humility than the former (TB Taan.23b). In a later
gloss (see ed. Malter, p.102 note) these hasidim are identified
as R. Huna (d.296) and R. Hisda (217-309); cf. TB M.K. 28a
which relates that the prayers for rain of the zaddikim Rabba
(beg.iv) and R. Hisda were always answered. Note that in TB
Taan. 8a (ed. Malter, p.25) Mss. Munich, London and the printed
eds. add that if "the whisperer's" prayer for rain fails, the
(greatest) hasid of the generation (hasid shebador) should be
asked to pray.

37. See n.50; cf. TY Sota 23b where Hanina is accidentally but quite readily added to the hasid tradition in M.
Sota 9.15. Hanina is called a perfect zaddik (TB Ber.61b) and
is said to be zealous in Sabbath observance, scrupulous regarding tithes and extremely concerned for the welfare of his
fellow man (Gen.R.10.8; TB Taan.25a; TY Dem.22a), all of which
are characteristic of hasidim according to the primary hasid
traditions.

38. M. Sukka 5.4 states that the hasidim and men of
deed would entertain the crowds in Jerusalem during the Sukkot
carnival (i CE), enthusiastically fulfilling Dt.16:14f. In
addition, both groups would say: "happy is the one who has not
sinned and whoever has sinned will be forgiven" (T. Sukka 4.2;
TY ib. 55b; TB ib. 53a). In reporting the hymns of praise and
adulation sung by the men of deed (who seem to be sinless) and
the penitent (cf. TB Ber.34b) it is unclear whether both groups
are sub-groups of the crowds in general or of the hasidim and
men of deed. The hasidim and men of deed appear in TB San.97a;
they are quite distinct from each other in M. Sota 9.15; cf.
Seder Eliahu Zutta 16. It is more likely that men of deed
(anshei ma'aseh) refers to miracle-workers than humanitarians.
Note that TB Yev. 121b recounts a miracle tale about Hanina in
defining a "miraculous event" (ma'aseh nisim)! Cf. Safrai,
pp.16f.; Vermes, pp.38f.

39. The so-called Mishna of the Pious (mishnat hasidim)
occurring in a legend about R. Joshua b. Levi (first half iii)
does not refer to a hasidic legal code (Gen.R.94.9; TY Ter.
46b). When the rabbi justifies his actions by pointing to the
ruling in a mishna, Elijah (see n.76) rebukes him for not following a saintlier code of conduct; that ruling was not a
mishna suited for pious men like him; cf. Jacobs, pp.150f.;
The expression "laws of the pious" has also been miscon-
strued. A tale relates that R. Joshua (end i-beg.ii) went to
speak with a hasid and they were engaged in studying the
hilkhot hasidim until mealtime (ARN B 27; cf. n.61). In rabbinic Hebrew hilkhot never means "the laws propounded by" but
only "the laws concerning." What would be "the laws about
hasidim"? However, hilkhot also is used in the sense "the
practices/customs of" which perfectly suits this context: the
rabbi went to the hasid to learn pious manners. For this usage

see M. B.M. 7.8; TB ib.93a; Kid.38b; M. Orla 3.9; TY ib.63b;
M. Avot 5.7f.; cf. J. Goldin in HUCA 19(1945/6):115.

It is not impossible that hilkhot ḥasidim is the name of
an ethical treatise, like the work (ca.ii-iii) entitled hilkhot
deretz eretz, "the ways/manners of proper deportment" (TB
Ber.22a; TY Shab.8a); cf. TY Shab.6a; TB San.65b; ib.67b.
Though hilkhot ḥasidut would be the more proper title, it
should be noted that sometimes the two interchange easily; cf.
n.23; Derekh Eretz Zutta 9.

40.   Two quotations of this work are preserved.   One is:
"(If) you leave me for a day, I will leave you for two days."
This is used by an anonymous homilist (ca.ii) to warn that
one's learning rapidly fades without diligent study (cf.ARN A
24) in Sifre Dt.48 (ed. Finkelstein, p.112 and see variants)
and similarly used by R. Simeon b. Lakish (end iii) in TY Ber.
14d; Midrash Song 4.15; 5.12 (ed. Grunhut, pp.91, 101) and
R. Samuel b. Isaac (beg.iv) in Midrash Samuel 1.1; cf. Safrai,
p.27.

Another is: "If you want to secure a friend for yourself, do business in his favor" (ARN B 26).   An almost identical statement is found in Derekh Eretz Zutta 2 and a similar
one in Kalla Rabbati 4.10.   This suggests that the Scroll of the
Pious was an ethical treatise similar to M. Avot, ARN and the
abovementioned works.   It was probably so entitled because
those who studied and followed its teachings would become
pious, somewhat like the later work Sefer Hasidim (beg.xiii).

41.   TB B.K. 30a (cf. Dikdukei Soferim a.l.) where the
discussion is prompted by an idealistic ruling (see n.47); cf.
the cases where the rabbis enacted "a manner of ḥasidut" (n.
24).   On the tractates Nezikin, Avot and Berakhot see EJ
12:1132; 3:983f.; 4:585ff.

42.   M. Ber. 5.1 where it exemplifies the proper attitude in prayer and is followed by two hyperbolic exhortations
in this regard (see n.60).   The version in TY Ber.8d and TB ib.
32b (which connects it with Ps.84:5) has the early hasidim
waiting another hour after prayer and this exemplifies the
teachings brought there demanding that one wait both hours (see
n.51).   The practical impossibility of spending nearly nine
hours a day in prayer is raised in the Talmuds and it is explained that since they were hasidim the little work and study
they did received God's blessing (cf. Lev.R.15.3).   However,
the Hebrew shaʿah, "hour," could also be rendered simply as "a
while," which may well have been the original meaning here.

43.   TB Men.41a where it is discounted as a valid example for establishing the norm since "hasidim are stricter upon
themselves."

44.   T. Ned.1.1 where it justifies R. Judah's opinion
that one who uses the formula "as the vows of the worthy" is
legally bound to a nazirite vow.   According to the rabbinic interpretation of Num.6:11 taking a nazirite vow is sinful (see
EJ 12:909).   In the parallels (TB Ned.10a; TY Nazir 51c; TY
Ned.36d) this exegesis is stressed by R. Simeon (b.Yohai?)
who rejects Judah's claim since the early hasidim would surely
not be guilty of taking nazirite vows, which meant sinfully
abstaining from wine.   M. Ned.1.1 rules that the formula "as
the vows of the worthy" is not valid; presumably the worthy do
not make such vows.

The notion that the hasidim were anxious to atone for an
any tiny sin they may have inadvertently committed is also

reflected in M. Ker.6.3 where R. Eliezer (end i-beg.ii) teaches
that one can freely make a guilt offering for a suspected sin
whenever desired and this was called "the guilt offering of
hasidim." Since this concerns the pious folk of the Second
Temple period it should be included among the early hasidim
traditions; see n.54.

45. Gen.R. 62.2 and par. (commenting on Gen.25:8;
Semahot 3.11 connects it with Prov.17:3). According to the
Akiban doctrine their suffering atoned for any minor sins so
that they would receive a full reward in the hereafter. The
midrash seems to imply that Abraham is considered one of the
early hasidim, as well as Isaac, Jacob and Job.

46. TB Nidda 38a-b where this tradition (ca.ii) arises
in a discussion about when conception occurs. A later sage
connects it with Ruth 4:13.

47. T. B.K. 2.6; TB ib.30a; TY ib.3c where it exemplifies the ruling that one who discards his trash in a wall is
held responsible for damages. In a way the practice of the
hasidim is turned into an idealistic norm; cf. n.41.

48. Semahot 12.5 (which connects it with Eccl.7:2).

49. Several figures are actually called hasidim: Adam
(TB Erub.18b); Jacob (Num.R.14.2); Abraham, Jacob and Moses
(Tanhuma Hukkat 25); David (TB Ber.4a; Lev.R. 1.4; midrash Ps.
16.11; 86.1 - often based on Scriptural use; cf.n.8); Esther
(Mekhilta Amalek 2, ed. Lauterbach 2:157); the people Israel
(Midrash Ps.149.1 - based on Scriptural use); and Job (TB B.B.
15b), the only Gentile called a hasid (cf.Ps.43:1); cf. Midrash
Tadshe 21 end which lists nine hasidot women converts. The
concept of the pious Gentiles (hasidei umot haolam) is medieval, based on T. San.13.2 which speaks of zaddikim. The
rabbis also interpreted Scriptural verses about hasidim in
reference to biblical saints: Abraham and Moses (Lev.R.1.4;
11.5); Joseph (Gen.R.86.3); Moses and Aaron (ARN A 36); the
generation of the exodus (M.San.10.3; ARN A 36; Midrash Ps.
119.1).

50. ARN A 8 (ed. Schechter, p.38) states: "Just as the
righteous men of yesteryear (zaddikim harishonim) were pious
(hasidim), so were their beasts pious." Two examples are
given: Abraham's camels would not set foot in a house containing idols and Hanina b. Dosa's donkey would rather starve than
touch food served by his captors. In both cases the beasts
went beyond the requirements of the law (cf. M.Dem.1.3). The
expression hasidim harishonim is not employed simply on stylistic grounds. It is probably significant that the equally pious
donkey of R. Pinhas b. Yair (beg.iii) is not mentioned here;
cf. Gen.R.60.8; TB Shab.112b; Midrash ha-Gadol to Gen.24:31.
In fact, one medieval author could not resist adding it here
(cited in Schechter, p.139). But Pinhas b. Yair could not be
considered an "early hasid."
Note that elsewhere zaddikim harishonim refers to the
righteous men of times past in general (TB Ket.103a) or the
patriarchs (Seder Eliahu Rabba 6; Lev.R.2.10); cf. Safrai,
p.20.

51. There are certainly no explicit Scriptural references to such behavior which could serve as a model for these
traditions. Cf. I. Heinemann, Darkhei ha-Aggadah (1950[3]), pp.
35ff. Note the artificial and exegetical character of several
traditions.

There are many examples of practices similar to those
of the early hasidim being reported about figures of the early
rabbinic period. Note the anonymous teaching (ca.ii), reiter-
ated by R. Joshua b. Levi (cf.n.39), that one should wait a
while/hour before and after prayer (cf.n.42). On the hasid's
enthusiasm for performing commandments and readiness to make
free-will offerings see the tale in T. Peah 3.8 and par.; cf.
Safrai, p.17 n.12. After the Temple was destroyed the hasidim
could atone for their sins by fasting; cf. n.22. Dying of intestinal illness was long considered a good sign, for, as R.
Yose (mid.ii) said, most of the righteous die from it (TB Ket.
103b; Shab.118b); cf. Mach, pp.156ff. The hasid R. Yose (see
n.65) would never send his letters via Gentiles, lest they
carry his mail on the Sabbath (TY Shab.4a). One tale mentions
a hasid who is greatly concerned for public safety (T B.K.
2.13 and par.). And like the early hasidim R. Ishmael (beg.
ii) gave precedence to visiting mourners (T.Meg.4.15); cf. TKF
4:1187ff.

52. M. Sota 9.12,15 and par.; TB Shab.112b; Erub.54b;
Yoma 9b; San.11a-b; cf.Eccl.7:10.

53. M. Sota 9.15 and par.; cf. TKF 8:762f.; n.65. It
is said that he was the quintessential hasid, playing on the
name Katonta. He appears in a section which lists sages from
the end i CE. Note the tenor of this entire passage is one
of lost grandeur.

54. In illustration of R. Eliezer's statement (see
n.44) an anecdote is told about Bava b. Buti who made such
offerings daily, a practice which some of his colleagues felt
that at times he carried to extremes (M.Ker.6.3). On Bava's
gracious disregard of an insult (TB Ned.66b) cf. the statement of R. Alexandri (end iii): "Whoever hears himself reviled
and remains silent is called hasid" (Midrash Ps.16.11; 86.1;
cf.n.26).

55. In M.Hag.2.7 he is called the (greatest) hasid in
the priesthood (hasid shebakehunah), apparently in reference
to his scrupulous observance of the purity laws; cf.M.Eduy.
8.4. Yose b. Yoezer also appears in a tradition about perfectly righteous men (see n.64). Due to the presence of Yohanan b. Gudgada (end i-beg.ii) in the following statement in M.
Hag.2.7, this tradition must be dated ca.ii CE. Hence, while
the rabbis probably considered Yose one of the early hasidim,
there is no evidence that his contemporaries (beg.ii BCE) would
have called him a hasid. The earliest attestations of hasid
in its "rabbinic sense" date ca.beg. i CE.
M. Sota 9.9 states that after Yose b. Yoezer the
"clusters" ceased (based on Mic.7:1; cf. 7:2), but there is no
basis for Baer's identification of the "clusters" with the
early hasidim. The term seems to refer to distinguished
scholars (TB Sota 47b; Tem.15b; Hul.92a; Lev.R.36.2; Song R.
1:14; Sifre Dt.323); cf. TY Sota 24a.

56. Miraculous rewards are given for extraordinary
Sabbath observance (Lev.R.34.15 and par.), for being especially charitable (ARN A 3; TB Ber.18b) and merciful (Eccl.R.9:7
about Abba Tehina the hasid); cf. Lev.R.15.3.

57. The hasid who mocks the superstitious prohibition
of uncovered liquids has to sip water during his sermon on the
Day of Atonement due to severe fever (TY A.Z.41a; Ter.45c); cf.
Safrai, pp.30f. Another tale relates how a sick hasid had
medical need of freshly weaned milk and so ties a goat to his

bedstead. His colleagues are shocked, but both they and he
himself are certain that his only sin in life was violating
the rabbinic prohibition against raising "small cattle" in
Palestine (TB B.K.80a; Tem.15b); though many, including the
pious Hanina b. Dosa, felt that goats could be raised without
their damaging neighboring property; see Vermes, pp.43f. The
stories in ARN B 27 and ARN A 12 also appear to fall into this
category.

58. This explains why there are no tales of "a certain
zaddik." In the post-talmudic period the opening formula "a
tale of a certain hasid" was used by story-tellers indiscrim-
inately for any tale about a good person. Its popularity
caused it to be prefixed to tales whose original hero was a
simple Jew. For example, see Lev.R.37.2 and Rashi to TB Sukka
46b; Pesikta Rabbati 14 (ed. Friedmann, 56b-57a) and Midrash
Decalogue, Forth Commandment (perhaps under the influence of
ARN A 8), where after the opening the man is called a zaddik
(note that ed. Verona 1647 omits the hasid formula). This
phenomenon was apt to occur when the hero of the tale performs
an act of exceptional piety For example, see Midrash Decalogue, Forth Commandment (ed.Verona 1647) which prefixes the
hasid formula to the famous story in TB Shab.119a; Pesikta
Rabbati 23 (ed. Friedmann, 119a) and Gen.R.11.4; cf. Büchler,
p.111 n.1. This formula even affected a tale of a bad Jew
(Eccl.R.6:11; cf. T B.K. 2.13), who is ironically transformed
into a hasid.

In four stories about hasidim the standard opening is
not used. But this may not be significant. In one case (ARN
A 8) the formula does appear in a parallel account (TB Shab.
127b).

59. Cf. n.57; Eccl.7:20. In one tale an elderly hasid
disdainfully considers himself beyond sin, but he is taught by
a demon in the guise of a woman that he is still subject to
sin; though he never actually is brought to sin (TY Shab.3b;
Tanhuma Bereshit 27 (ed. Buber I,20); Bet ha-Midrasch 6:95f.).
Cf. the ruling (ca.ii) that even the supreme hasid (hasid
shebahasidim) is not appointed a guardian against unchastity
(TY Ket.25d); and R.Aha's (mid.iv) statement that even the
supreme hasid cannot engage in sexual intercourse without
some selfish pleasure (Lev.R.14.5). (Underlying this is the
notion that the hasid always strives to serve God; here he
tries his best to single-mindedly fulfill the commandment in
Gen.1:28; cf.n.66.)

60. For example, see Lev.R.15.3; TY San.23b-c; Lam.R.
1.3; cf. n.57. In illustration of the idealistic ruling "Even
if the king greets him he should not respond (while in the
midst of prayer)" (M.Ber.5.1) a story is told of a hasid who
ignores an officer's greeting while praying in the road. After
being rebuked for risking his life, he conciliates the officer
with a parable (TB Ber.32b-33a); cf. Vermes, pp.34f.

61. In Midrash Ps.12.1 the hasid is cursed for his
honesty. In ARN B 27 the rabbi who comes to learn pious manners from an apparently well-known hasid, a priest (cf. ARN
A 12: an important priest), has the gall to ask his pious host
if the stove is ritually clean. When Pinhas b. Yair is shocked
by a hasid's grief (cf.Sira 38:17-23) he remarks to the townspeople, "This is your hasid!?" (TY Dem.22a; Shek.48d). Several
tales illustrating the maxim: "Give everyone the benefit of the
doubt" revolve around the surprisingly strange and suggestive

behavior of a hasid (ARN A 8; TB Shab.127b; cf. ARN B 19).
In the tale of the hasid with the goat tied to his bed (see
n.57) the sages jokingly refer to the "bandit" in his home
(alluding to the destructiveness of goats) and consider his
action sinful. Yet under such restraint the goat could not
possibly cause damage to other people's property, not to mention the compelling medical reasons for his keeping the goat.
Note R. Gamaliel's joking remark in TB B.K. 80a.

62. Cf. nn.57,64. There is a legend about a hasid living in Ashkelon in the days of Simeon b. Shetah (first half i
BCE) whose only sin was once donning his head before his arm
phylacteries (BY Hag.77d; San.23c). Such minutiae were taken
quite seriously by the pious; see TB Men.35a-b; M.K.25a.

63. TB Yoma 38b; Tanhuma Vayeshev 14 (ed. Buber I,185).
Any sins commited were unintentional (Tanhuma Shemini 11); cf.
nn.44,54. Even the wicked Jews are called hasidim once punishment has atoned for all their sins (Midrash Ps.79.4; cf. Yalkut
II #429); cf. n.22. In Numb.R. 18.9 Aaron's hasidut consists
of his extraordinary fear of sin. Also see n.38; Jacobs, p.154
n.60.

64. A Palestinian tradition (ca.ii) states that it was
impossible to find fault with the "clusters" (see n.55) from
Moses until Yose b. Yoezer, but since then it was possible to
find fault with them until R. Judah b. Bava, of whom it is said
that all his deeds were for the sake of heaven except that he
raised "small cattle," for once he had to keep a goat tied to
his bed for medical reasons (T. B.K.8.13; TY Sota 24a). However
in later Babylonian circles (end iii) this tradition apparently
became confused. R. Judah (d.299) in the name of Samuel
(d.254) cites a tradition that it was impossible to find any
fault with the "clusters" from Moses until Yose b. Yoezer, but
since then it was possible to find fault with them. An objection is raised from the tale of a certain hasid who led a
blameless life except for keeping a goat tied to his bed.
Since "We hold that everywhere it says 'a tale of a certain
hasid' it refers to R. Judah b. Bava or R. Judah b. Ilai (mid
ii)," this proves that even later sages were blameless (TB
Tem. 15b); see n.75.

Although the passage in T/TY does not explicitly refer
to hasidim, the statements about Yose and R. Judah apparently
fall into the general category of hasid traditions (cf.n.65).
The rare quality of perfect righteousness seems to be a basic
characteristic of the hasid. This underlies the bringing of a
hasid tale in connection with the Yose tradition in TB. Indeed, the "tale of a certain hasid" in TB (see n.57) is identical word for word with the story told about R. Judah. And both
Yose and R. Judah are actually called hasidim elsewhere (see
nn.55,81).

65. M. Avot 2.8,12; ARN A 14 and B 29 call him "the
(greatest) hasid of his generation" (cf.n.36). In M. Avot 2.8
and elsewhere in rabbinic literature he is called R. Yose the
priest. No doubt Yose was fully deserving of the appellation;
cf.n.67; J. Goldin in Traditio 21 (1965):11. The piety of R.
Yose the priest is mentioned in TY Shab.4c (see n.51). However
in TB Shab.19a this tradition appears with a gloss inserted:
"R. Yose the priest - and some say R. Yose the hasid." One
ancient witness (cited in Dikdukei Soferim a.l.) reads: "R.
Yose the priest the hasid." Note the tradition in TY Sota 24c:
"When R. Yose the hasid and R. Yose Katonta died, the men of
hasidut disappeared." But Ms. Rome omits R. Yose the hasid and

he does not appear in the par. (see n.53). Probably R. Yose
the priest was sometimes called R. Yose the hasid. But he
and R. Yose Katonta might be two distinct contemporary sages;
cf. TY B.K. 3d; TB Pes.113b and par.

66. Cf. J. Goldin in HUCA 19(1956/7):99f. on ARN A 17
and B 30; Büchler, pp.18f. In one tale a man and his wife,
both hasidim, seek divorce because they are not serving God by
bearing children (Gen.R.17.7); cf. n.59; D.M. Feldman, Marital
Relations, Birth Control, and Abortion in Jewish Law (1968),
pp.65-71.

67. Midrash Ps.12.1; TB B.K. 103b; cf.Büchler, p.36.
The hasid is also concerned for animals (TY San.23b-c; Yalkut
II #688). Note that R. Yose, a hasid, urges utmost regard
for the property of others(M.Avot 2.12) and thinks that the
summum bonum is for every human being to strive to be a good
neighbor (M.Avot 2.9); cf.Prov.27:10.

68. The hasid is praised as a generous, altruistic person, unconcerned with material needs: M.Avot 5.10,13; TB B.M.
70a; cf. tales in Gen.R.29.2; Lev.R.15.3; and David's selfless
devotion to God and man in TB Ber.4a. He is slow to anger and
easily appeased: M.Avot 5.11; cf. Sifre Dt. 323; n.54. He both
studies and puts to practice: M.Avot 5.14; cf. ib.2.17; 3.9,17;
J. Goldin in Traditio 21(1965):7f.
Probably these three basic groupsings are equivalent to
the frequent division of humanity into the perfectly righteous,
the average and the wicked (cf. TB Ber.7a-b; R.H.16b).

69. There never seems to be any condemnation of the
hasid qua hasid in rabbinic literature; cf. nn.54,57,59. Mention should be made here to the two passages in which the pious
behavior of the Palestinian R. Simeon b. Lakish (d.275) is
sharply contrasted under nearly identical circumstances with
that of the Babylonian sages R. Nahman (d.ca.320), who once
acted quite disrespectfully (TB Meg.28b), and R. Zeira (end
iii-beg.iv), who once acted rather grouchy and insultingly (TB
Hul.122a). In both cases a self-critical Babylonian tradition-
ary or editor sarcastically appended the popular saying: "Come
and see the difference between the cocky/imperious ones of the
land of Israel and hasidim of Babylonia." Cf.n.36; TB San.
11a-b and Rashi a.l.

70. R. Joshua said: "An idiotic hasid, a cunning knave,
an abstinent wife and the 'plagues of the Pharisees' -- these
are the wreckers of the world" (M.Sota 3.4). The later rabbis
provide examples: one idiotic hasid lets a woman drown rather
than sinfully look upon her (TB Sota 21b); another piously re-
moves his phylacteries before jumping into the river to save
a drowning child -- meanwhile the youth breathes his last;
another one decides to generously give away a ripe fig to the
first person he meets, then the fool goes dashing after a be-
trothed maiden and thereby courts death (TY Sota 19a). The
rabbis strongly felt that nearly all of the commandments should
be violated in order to preserve human life; see T. Shab.15.17;
TKF 3:262; EJ 13:509f.

71. M. Avot 6.1; TB Kid. 40b; cf. n. 41.

72. M. Avot 2.5; this statement is attributed to R.
Akiba (beg.ii) in ARN A 26 and B 33 (which reads: "...a Phari-
see hasid"); cf. J. Goldin in JR 26 (1946):276.

73. R. Simeon b. Yohai (mid.ii) says: "An 'am haaretz,
even if he is pious (hasid), even if he is holy, even if he is

upright -- cursed be he to the Lord God of Israel" (Pirke Rabbenu ha-Kadosh 6 end); cf. S. Lieberman in JBL 7 (1951): 204f. R. Abba in the name of R. Simeon b. Lakish states that one should cling even to a vindictive and begrudging scholar, but one should not live in the neighborhood of even a hasid 'am haaretz (TB Shab.63a).

74. See n.64. Note that TY prefaces the tale with: "And such was a tale (ma'aseh), one time (he became ill), etc." It is entirely possible that the tradition cited as a baraita (Tannaitic teaching) in TB actually reflects an early Palestinian version of this story which began with the hasid tale formula.

75. It first appears ca.end iii (see n.64) and then is later invoked by Rava (d.352) in connection with the tale of the scrupulously honest hasid who went to R. Tarfon and R. Akiba. In the course of convoluted argument over the interpretation and resolution of several rabbinic dicta, the theoretical possibility is raised that R. Akiba would have demanded an oath in certain cases where this would have involved an element of perjury. Rava tries to prove from the tale that R. Akiba did not require such an oath by arguing that presumably the hasid would never have compromised his honesty. Rava then counters the possible objection that this story refers to someone who had not yet become a hasid by pointing out that such tales always refer either to R. Judah b. Bava or R. Judah b. Ilai (mid.ii), both of whom were hasidim throughout their entire lives (TB B.K.103b).

It is not clear how seriously this identification was taken. Note that in both cases it is used in a clever and artificial way. Furthermore, in light of their arguments, the Babylonian rabbis could never have maintained this identification for the tales where a hasid sins with a spirit, falls dead at the sight of a demon, divorces his wife and becomes wicked, or digs cisterns for a living in the days of R. Pinhas b. Yair (beg.iii)! However, since none of these tales occurs in TB, it may be that they were unaware of them.

It is probably significant that this statement first occurs in connection with a confused recollection of a baraita (see n.64). Perhaps a vague memory persisted that this tale was somehow connected to the Yose b. Yoezer tradition and that it was about a "Rabbi Judah," possibly Judah b. Bava the famous hasid, or perhaps, if some doubt remained, it could refer to Judah b. Ilai, the Rabbi Judah in Tannaitic literature. But there is little in our sources to suggest that R. Judah b. Ilai was a hasid; cf. A. Hyman, Toldoth Tannaim ve-Amoraim 2:540f.; EJ 10:337-39. True, to turn this vague identification into a general rule would require taking a great deal of liberty with the traditions, but the rabbis were capable of doing this; cf. TB Yoma 9b bottom. Note the rather far-fetched explanation R. Joseph offers as an alternative in TB Tem.16a.

76. Cf. n.36. While describing several evasive practices employed by very respectable scholars to get around the law forbidding a Jew to keep an ox which had been castrated by Gentiles while in his possession, the rabbis (ca.mid.v) point out that even the eminent "Meremar(beg.v) and Mar Zutra (see n.77) -- and some say 'there were two hasidim'" -- simply exchanged animals (TB B.M. 90b).

Among a number of similar stories the rabbis (ca.beg.v) related that "There were two hasidim -- and some say 'R. Mari and R. Pinhas (end iv) the sons of R. Hisda'" -- one fed his

servant first while the other gave him his food after dinner
and Elijah conversed with the former but not the latter (TB
Ket.61a). Elijah is quite particular about his company and he
ceases to converse even with hasidim when they act improperly;
see TB B.B. 7b; Gen.R.94.9.

77. While scores of pious rabbis and saintly folk are
mentioned in rabbinic literature, there are not even twenty
sages who are clearly identified as hasidim. Of these, six are
actually given the cognomen "the hasid": cf. Simeon the ẓaddik,
R. Benjamin the ẓaddik and the designation "our holy (kadosh)
rabbi" for R. Judah the Patriarch. The little said about the
Palestinian sages Abba Tehina (see n.56), R. Yose (see n.65)
and R. Simeon (end iii), a noted aggadist (cf. TB Men.35b; Ket.
67b; San.22a) suggests that they deserved this designation. Of
the Babylonian sages nothing is known about R. Sala (first half
iv) except that he outshone his brother, who was pious enough
in his own right to merit visits from Elijah (TB Ber.29b; on
the significance of his designation as "the brother of R. Sala"
cf. TB Pes.117b). Mar Zutra (d.ca.414), the pious Babylonian
Exilarch, is called "the hasid" in a few places; cf. H. Albeck,
Mevo le-Talmudim (1969), pp.436f. There are several traditions
testifying to the great piety of R. Amram (beg.iv); see TB
Shab. 139a; Suk.11a; Kid.81a; B.B.151a; Git.67b and Rashi a.l.

78. Cf. nn.35,59,65,76; Midrash Ps.12.1; Lev.R.36.2
which similarly speaks about the perfect ẓaddikim and the
average ẓaddikim.

79. Note the deep regard the townspeople have for
their hasid in TY Dem.22a; cf. Safrai, p.33 who notes a variant reading in TB Erub.86a: "R. Jacob honored hasidim."

80. In TB M.K. 17a the rabbi whose moral character left
something to be desired is refused admittance to the burial
cave of hasidim, so he is interred in the burial cave of the
judges. On not burying the wicked with the righteous see TB
San.47a; cf.B.M.85a; EJ 5:275. Perhaps an example of such a
burial cave is that in which the pious R. Huna(cf.n.36) was
permitted to be interred along with R. Hiyya and his two
sons (TB M.K.25a; TY Kil.32b), for R. Judah and R. Hezekiah
the sons of R. Hiyya are explicitly called hasidim (Eccl.R.
1.11; see commentary of R. David Luria a.l.).
     Incidentally, while hosios occasionally appears on Jew-
ish tombstones, hasid never does. Scholem (n.344) reports that
even in the heyday of German Hasidism hasid rarely appears on
tombstones.

81. Legend has it that once a divine voice announced
that someone was indeed worthy of prophecy, but his generation
was not worthy, and all eyes alighted on Hillel (end i BCE-
beg. i CE). At his funeral they said: "Woe humble one! Woe
hasid! The disciple of Ezra." A similar story is told about
Samuel the Little (end i-beg.ii) who was eulogized: "Woe humble one! Woe hasid! The disciple of Hillel." The sages also
ordained that R. Judah b. Bava would be eulogized: "Woe humble
one! Woe hasid! The disciple of Samuel the Little," but the
times were troubled (T. Sota 13.3-4; TY Sota 24b; TB ib.48b;
San.11a). Evidently this particular eulogy (cf.Jer.22:18) was
reserved for the rare individual in a generation who combined
deep humility, great piety and outstanding contributions to
the study of Torah. The traditions about these three men suggest that this high praise was in fact well-deserved.

Mimicking this famous eulogy R. Helbo said in the name of R. Huna (d.296): "Whoever fixes a place for his prayer, the God of Abraham helps him,and when he dies, they say over him, 'Woe humble one! Woe hasid! One of the disciples of Abraham'" (TB Ber.6b). Of course, this is pure hyperbole (cf.TB Ber.7b); it is not suggesting that this formula would actually be used at his funeral.

82. I am basically following Scholem (see n.28), though many of his observations are applicable only to the medieval sources.

83. Cf. EJ 14:648f.,652.

84. See S. Schechter, Aspects of Rabbinic Theology, (1961[2]), pp.148-69. A good example of the "normative" extremism in Jewish piety is the practice in regard to the lighting of the Hannuka candles; cf. TB Shab.21b. This character of Jewish piety and the role of the hasid in rabbinic exempla is apparently misunderstood by Y. Dan, "Exemplum", EJ 6:1020-22.

Problems in Late Rabbinic "Biography":
         The Case of the <u>Amora</u> Rabbi Yohanan

Reuven Kimelman, Brandeis University

The problematics of rabbinic biography have deservedly been
the subject of recent scholarly inquiry. It is not my intent here
to present another rabbinic biography or to offer a single theory
for such presentations.(1) Instead, I propose to discuss some of
the issues involved in handling contradictions in statements about
the rabbis through several illustrations from the material about
Rabbi Yohanan (henceforth RY) - the major figure of third century
Palestinian rabbinic Judaism.

The Relationship Between RY and Resh Laqish

The alleged marriage of RY's sister to Resh Laqish is problematic. The relationship is principally reported in a series of
strange agadic accounts about RY

> One day while RY was bathing in the Jordan, Resh Laqish saw
> him and leapt into the Jordan after him.
> (RY) said to him: Your strength should be for Torah.
> He replied: Your beauty should be for women.
> (RY) said: If you will repent, I shall give you my sister
> in marriage who is more beautiful than I.
> He resolved (to repent). Then he wished to collect his
> equipment, but could not. Subsequently, (RY) taught him
> Bible and Mishnah, and made him into a great man.

This story is replete with elements of interest for one depicting how the rabbis are presented in rabbinic literature. Our
present purpose, however, is to weigh the factors for establishing
its historicity. W. Bacher pointed out that this romanticized
encounter appears only in Babylonian sources. Its purpose, he
contends, is to highlight the contrast between Resh Laqish's former and latter life. Nonetheless, Bacher considered the essential
kernel to be historical including the fact that RY influenced
Resh Laqish's return to a life of Torah study, and that Resh Laqish
married the sister of RY. (2) I. Halevy, however, noted that these
two conclusions are faced with chronological problems. Unable to
resolve these discrepancies, he concluded, "It is impossible to
know the order of events from agadic material alone...for the ancient rabbis were not exact in nonhalakic matters." The difficulties arise from other sources from which it is clear that RY and
Resh Laqish were student companions from their youth while here
RY appears as Resh Laqish's first teacher since he is teaching him
the elementary school subject of Bible. Halevy is of the opinion
that all these event occurred in their youth when RY was about
twenty-five and Resh Laqish about fifteen. He then arrives at the
dubious conclusion that RY's sister, also about twenty-six, married the then fifteen-year-old Resh Laqish. (3)

The crux of the issue is the conflict between two sources.
According to one source, Resh Laqish studied in his youth with
R. Judah HaNasi; indeed a source (B Shab 119b) ponders the possibility that Resh Laqish had received traditions from his forebears. According to another source, Resh Laqish appears as a
Jewish illiterate, innocent of even the Bible, when meeting RY.
Tosafot, trying to resolve the contradiction, suggested that this
reflects different stages in his life. Resh Laqish had indeed
studied in his youth, leaving it and turning to crime, later returning. (4) Halevy rejected this solution, because it assumes
that it all transpired after RY had already succeeded to the
position as head of the academy, and thus conflicts with those

sources which speak of Resh Laqish and RY being companions from their youth. (5)

The other objection to Bacher's conclusion is with regard to the marriage of Resh Laqish and RY's sister. There are, supposedly, two other notices of this relationship. The first is in a story which concludes with Resh Laqish falling ill after offending RY. (6) Whereupon, the story continues, אחתיה, came to seek forgiveness from RY for the sake of her son. The Aramaic word is thought to denote "his sister" that is RY's sister, the wife of Resh Laqish. With the addition of a curlicue to the second letter ח , however, it becomes a ת and would read אתתיה (his wife). This reading would smooth out the sentence, since it is self-evident that the subject is the wife of Resh Laqish (7) In contrast, by reading אחתיה "RY" has to be supplied as the antecedent of "his" since "RY" is not the nearest antecedent.

The second source is B Taan 9a. RY meets the young child of Resh Laqish and asks him to explain several Biblical verses. The young child gave several startling responses upon which –

> RY lifted his eyes and looked at the boy. The boy's mother then came in and took him away saying: Get away from him, that he may not do to you as he did to your father.

It is assumed by the commentators that this alludes to the story in which RY precipitated Resh Laqish's premature death, and that the woman is RY's sister.

This interpretation faces several difficulties. Since RY was born an orphan, his sister must have been at least a year older (if not a twin). (Unless we accept the gratuitous assumption that she is from a second marriage.) Resh Laqish died a year before RY who, according to all accounts, was at least eighty years old. Resh Laqish was probably then in his late seventies. Even if we accept Halevy's position that Resh Laqish was ten years RY's junior, he would be about ninety according to Halevy's calculations, or about seventy according to more conservative calculations. At the very least, we have an octogenarian and a septuagenarian – who according to Halevy have been married over three score years – with a child of Bible school age (about five to ten). (8) Yet, the literature makes no mention of this Abraham-Sarah-like wonder! Another difficulty with this interpretation is the fact that in the meeting between RY and the son of Resh Laqish, the mother is not mentioned as being RY's sister.

The inability to resolve these problems lends credence to I. H. Weiss' judgement: "Except for some startling agadot we have no sources for the youth of Resh Laqish." (9). Consequently, it is likely that these passages reflect, as S. Safrai, noted, "the tendency, so common in the Babylonian Talmud, of connecting prominent, historical personalities by family ties." (10)

In conclusion, any claim that the encounter between RY and Resh Laqish, as portrayed above, is historical has yet to be substantiated. The two major considerations for the rejection of its historicity are the contradictions in the literature itself, and the disclosing of a motive in the creation of the story. The next example reflects similar difficulties.

R. Kahana at the Academy of RY

This story relates how Rab advised R. Kahana to flee to
Palestine to avoid punishment for a crime he committed. He
also suggested that R. Kahana refrain from asking RY questions
for seven years. Upon arriving in Palestine -

> He went and found Resh Laqish who was sitting, completing
> the academic session for the rabbis,   but did not
> realize that this was Resh Laqish. He said to them:
> Where is bar Laqisha? They replied: Why? He posed
> several questions and suggested several solutions. They
> told Resh Laqish. Resh Laqish went and said to RY:
> A lion has come up from Babylonia. Let the master prepare
> well tomorrow's session. The next day they seated
> (R. Kahana) in the first row (before RY who) recited
> a tradition, but (R. Kahana) did not raise any difficulty.
> (He recited) another tradition, but he (R. Kahana) did
> not raise any difficulty. They moved him back seven rows
> until they seated him in the last row. RY said to Resh
> Laqish: The lion you mentioned has turned into a fox.
> (R. Kahana) said: May it be (God's) will that these seven
> rows substitute for the seven years which Rab mentioned.
> He rose on his feet and said to him: Let the master return
> to the beginning. (So) he recited a tradition, and
> (R. Kahana) raised an objection. They raised him to the
> first row. (RY) cited another tradition and again he
> objected.
>
> RY was sitting upon seven cushions.   Whenever he
> made a statement against which there was an objection,
> one cushion was pulled out from under him until all were
> pulled out and he remained seated on the ground. RY was
> then a very old man and his eyelashes were overhanging,
> he said to them: Lift up my eyelashes for me as I want
> to see him. So they lifted them up with silver pincers.
> (RY) saw that his (R. Kahana's) lips were parted and
> thought that he was smirking at him. (RY) felt aggrieved
> and (R. Kahana) died. On the morrow, RY said to the rabbis:
> Did you see how that Babylonian acted? They replied:
> That was his manner. (RY) went to the cave and saw a
> snake coiled around it. He said: Snake, snake, open your
> mouth and let the master enter to the disciple. But it
> did not open. He then said: Let one colleague enter to
> the other colleague. But it did not open. He then said:
> Let the disciple enter to the master. It opened. He
> then prayed for mercy and raised him. (RY) said to him:
> Had I known that that was your (natural) manner I would not
> have been so aggrieved. Now let the master return to the
> academy. (R. Kahana) replied: If you are able to pray
> for mercy that I should never die again, I shall go; if
> not, not, for once the moment has passed it is passed.
> Thereupon (RY) awakened and restored him and would consult
> him on doubtful points and he (R. Kahana) would solve them
> for him. And this is what is meant when RY says: Yours
> is theirs. (11)

This story which allegedly takes place in Palestine is found
only in a Babylonian source (B Babba Qama 117a-b). The question for the historian is whether the miraculous and folklor-
istic elements indicate the lack of a historical kernel.(12) On their
own they probably do not. In this case, however, caution is
urged since it meets two other criteria for suspecting its historicity, namely, general improbablity in the light of more
reliable data (i.e., data not derived from fantastic stories),

and an explanation which accounts for the creation of the story.

With regard to the criterion of improbability, several elements of the story have difficulty with cohering with other matters known about Rab and RY from other Babylonian sources. First Rab was RY's senior by quite a few years (see B Hullin 54a, 137b) and was addressed by RY as Master (ibid. 95a). Moreover, Rab left Palestine (ca. 219) long before RY achieved prominence. It is unlikely that RY headed the academy of Tiberias before 240 (13) and probably somewhat later. Rab, on the other hand, is thought to have died about 247. It is unlikely that Rab would be sufficiently knowledgeable to advise R. Kahana on proper behavior in RY's presence. Moreover, at the time of Rab's death RY was in his prime (ca. 200-280) while here he appears senescent. Finally, in the light of these difficulties, a normally inadmissible argument from si-lence may be justified. Although R. Kahana's stay is mentioned both in Palestinian sources (J Berakot 2,8 5c) and in Baby-lonian sources (B Pesahim 49a) there is no other mention of his one-upmanship of RY, an event which was bound to have reverberated through the halls of the academy heralding the arrival of a Babylonian upstart who turned the tables on the greatest living master. (14).

If so, why was this story told? and why of all the Baby-lonians who went to Palestine was R. Kahana selected to show up RY? According to M. Tannenblat, the story's _Tendenz_ is formulated with the purpose of influencing Babylonians "that there is no longer anything to seek in Palestine, for Torah scholarship...is already concentrated in Babylonia." If a Babylonian upstart can outwit the venerable and aging RY there is no need to leave Babylonian academic centers for those of Palestine. (15) There are several reasons for R. Kahana's role in the story. He is one of the few Babylonian students who did not go to Palestine willingly seeking out an enhanced intellectual life. On the contrary, he described his flight to Palestine as being "exiled" from Babylonia (B Pesahim 49a with Rashi ad loc.). Secondly the Palestinian source (J Bera-kot 2,8 5c) has him literally mocked out of Palestine. (16) What could be a more fitting revenge than having Palestine's pride and joy as the butt of mockery in Babylonian academies? The story was probably intended to serve the interests of the academy of R. Judah, the very R. Judah (b. Yehezkel) who tried unsuccessfully to enjoin his students from leaving Babylonia for Palestine. It is to the academy of this R. Judah that R. Kahana returned in Babylonia! (17)

In this case a story is used to discredit a teacher. Such usage parallels A. Momigliano's findings in his study of Greek biography, to wit, that biographies were used "by philosophers at large as a weapon against hostile schools."(17)

RY's Tenth Son

In the following case we have found no reason to deny a historical kernel even though subsequent embellishments are quite noticeable.

Mention of RY's tenth son appears only in Babylonian sources. Once while paying a sick-call to R. Eleazar he noticed him weeping. RY thought that R. Eleazar was weeping over his own childnessness. Supposedly to comfort him, RY said, "This is the bone of my tenth son" (Berakot 5b). The

other mention of this is where (Babba Batra 116a) RY and R.
Joshua b. Levi disputed the meaning of the verse: <u>Such as have
no replacements and fear not God</u> (Psalms 55:20) -
> One says: Whosoever does not leave behind a son. And
> the other says: Whosoever does not leave behind a dis-
> ciple. It may be proved (that it was RY who said 'a
> disciple') for RY said: This is the bone of my tenth
> son. (18)

The conclusion is based on the assumption that RY having no
son would not have stigmatized himself as one who is not God-
fearing. Regardless of the conclusion, it is clear that the
source is dependent on RY's statement in the first source.
Hence, there is only one independent mention of RY's sons and
that, as we shall see, in a highly stylized story. Still,
there are several statements of RY which are appropriate for
a bereaved or childless father. RY said, "It is grievous to
the Lord when the children of a righteous man have to die
during their father's lifetime." (19) He was also anxious to
find the Biblical basis for the teaching - "Whosoever is occu-
pied with Torah, acts of kindness, and buries his children all
his sins are forgiven him"(B Berakot 5a-b). A later Midrash
has RY lamenting his childlessness: (20)

> His students said to him (RY): If you our teacher are
> crying, what will be with us?
> He replied to them: My sons, how can I not cry? They
> will stand me in judgement and show me my deeds and
> judge me for them. Moreover, they will say to me: Why
> did your sons die in your lifetime? since I had not
> succeeded, thusly, in contributing to the betterment
> (or to the population) (21) of the world. As if it were
> not enough for a man that his sons should die in his
> lifetime, must he also be judged on account of them?!

In the later Geonic literature, the fate of RY's last son
received extensive treatment. The upshot of these traditions
if that after nine of his sons had died the tenth fell into a
boiling cauldron. His flesh rotted leaving RY to take up the
bone of the small finger which he would wrap in a cloth with
which to comfort mourners. There is also the tradition that
there remained one son, a R. Matnah, who was sent to Babylonia
to study with Samuel. (22)

Despite the variety of sources which deal with the above
information, they are all apparently dependent upon the Talmudic account and not of independent historical worth. The
added embellishments serve to resolve difficulties which arise
out of the original story. The mention of the cauldron is
necessary in order to explain how a bone remained when according to Jewish law all parts of the body are to be interred.
The small finger was a result of an attempt to find a bone
that was sufficiently small that it would not impart impurity.
With the same consideration in mind other medieval sources
claim that it was a tooth. As the medieval rabbinic dictionary
the <u>Aruk</u> wrote, "How could a holy man such as RY carry the
bone of a dead person which constantly imparts impurity, rather, the bone was a tooth of the dead person which does not
impart impurity." (23) In fact, one source avoids the whole
issue by arguing that the bone was a left over from the post-
burial repast.(24)

Whatever the explanation, RY presumably did bear a bone
of his son. The commentators assume that he bore it for the

sake of consoling others. (25) Nonetheless, it is not clear
from the context why he showed the bone at all to R. Eleazar
The text from where RY notices R. Eleazar weeping reads as
follows:

> Why do you weep? Is it perhaps because you did not (study)
> much (Torah)? We have already learnt: It is the same
> whether one does much or little as long as he directs his
> heart to God
> Is it perhaps because of (lack of) sustenance? Not
> everybody merits two tables.
> Is it perhps because of (lack of) sons? This is the
> bone of my tenth son.

What is the force of RY's last comment? Tosafot said that
since RY used to console others with it, it is obvious that
these chastisements are ones of love. (26) This interpretation
has two difficulties. Above on the same page of the Talmud,
RY says the lack of sons cannot be considered chastisements
of love. (27) Furthermore, it does not fit the literary structure which has each of RY's responses oriented towards consoling R. Eleazar with what he already has. This obviated any
need to lament any deficiency. In the first case, he tries to
dissuade him from mourning over the lack of quantity by pointing out the quality of his learning. In the second case, he
tries to console him over the lack of one table by pointing out
that he has achieved the other table. (28)

What about the third case? The structure demands something like 'do not mourn over the lack of sons, what you have
suffices.' (Note he has not yet asked R. Eleazar what he thinks
of suffering; only why he is weeping, which as seen from the
conclusion of the story has nothing to do with sufferings.)
But R. Elezar has no sons; so how can that suffice? Precisely, RY had ten sons and look what remains - a bone. There
is, therefore, no call for self-pity on R. Eleazar's part. (29)

In conclusion, in examining the historicity of rabbinic
stories, it is insufficient to establish verisimilitude.
Questions of textual reliability, probability, and congruence
must be raised   In addition, the text must be subjected
to literary analysis. Finally the question cui bono? must be
factored into any question of historicity.

1. For some reflections on rabbinic biography, see the
Association for Jewish Studies Newsletter 24(March, 1979) 26b.

2. Agadot Amore Eres-Yisrael I,2 (Tel Aviv, 1925) 134.

3. Dorot HaRishonim III (Frankfurt, 1901) 317-320, followed
by A. Hyman, Toledot HaTannaim VeHaAmoraim (Jerusalem, 1964)
660a.

4. B Babba Mesia 84a, s.v. אי,

5. Dorot HaRishonim III, 320. This was previously noticed by
I. H. Weiss, Dor Dor VeDorshav III (Vienna, 1871) 71f.

6. B Babba Mesia 84a

7. Following Hyman, Toledot 671a, who cited the reading
דביתהו אתאי = his wife. He gratuitously proposed that
this is Resh Laqish's second wife. If this reading is correct,
then there exists only one unambiguous mention of such a relationship - and that in the midst of that fantastic encounter
between RY and Resh Laqish; the details of which do not square
with all else known about the two.

8. See Abot 5:22; and B Babba Batra 21a

9. Dor Dor VeDorshav 71. A. Kaminka, Mehqarim BaTalmud (Tel
Aviv, 1951) 209, also rejected the historicity of the meeting
between them. He argued that the story of Resh Laqish's youth
as a brigand is based on a folk-expression recorded in Qohelet
Rabba 7,26,1: לקיש לסטים בכיר לצלובים =(the last of
brigands is the first of the hanged). Thus Resh Laqish's
patronym or just cognomen was associated with   and the
Babylonian agada viewed his youth as a sinner to sage conver
sion transformation which was triggered by the impact of the
great RY. On the other hand, the report (B Gittin 47a) that
he sold himself as some type of circus performer or gladiator
(ludarius) does reflect an economic reality of the time. The
raw material for this creation may have been the Palestinian
material that reports his readiness to fight off robbers, his
guarding of orchards (J Terumot 8,10 46b; Moed Qatan 3,1 81d; cf.
B Moed Qatan 17a), and his comments on selling oneself to
ludarii (J Terumot 8,5 45d = Abodah Zarah 2,3 41b following S.
Lieberman, Greek in Jewish Palestine [New York, 1965] 148, n.
20).

10. "Tales of the Sages in the Palestinian Tradition and the
Babylonian Talmud," Scripta Hierosolymitana III (Jerus., 1971)
229, see, ibid., 231.

11. The meaning of the last phrase is unclear, see M. Tannenblat, Peraqim Hadashim LeToledot Eres-Yisrael UBabel BeTequfat
HaTalmud (Tel Aviv, 1966) 127. The obscurity relegates to the
hypothetical historical conclusions based on it.

12. See L. Ginzberg, Commentary on the Palestinian Talmud I
(New York, 1941) 393; J. Neusner, History of the Jews in Babylonia II (Leiden, 1967) 32; Tannenblat, Peraqim 124ff.; and D.
Goodblatt, Rabbinic Instruction in Sasanian Babylonia (Leiden,
1975) 254.

13. See R. Kimelman, "Third Century Tiberias. The Alliance Between the Rabbinate, the Patriarchate, and the Urban Aristocracy," Supplement Volume to Aufstieg und Niedergang der romischen Welt II,8, ed. H. Temporini (forthcoming).

14. Tannenblat, Peraqim 125.

15. Ibid. 122.

16. Indeed, it was RY who insinuated there that he would be better off returning to where he was respected, see Ginzberg, Commentary 393f.

17. See B Yebamot 17a, 101b; Shabuot 36a; Ḥullin 19b. A later date is unlikely since the Babylonian heads of the next generation were not threatened by RY's success, indeed were already partisans of his, see Z. M. Dor, Torat Ereṣ-Yisrael BeBabel ((Tel Aviv, 1971).
17a. The Development of Greek Biography (Cambridge, 1971) 84.
18. The parallel in Midrash HaGadol Genesis, ed. Margoliot, 827 reads בידי instead of ביר , see ibid., n. 16. For an appreciation of the concinnity of the whole story, see E. Bin-Gurion, Shbile HaAgadah (Jerusalem, 1970) 180.

19. Leviticus Rabbah 20,10, ed. Margoliot, 467 and parallels and Midrash HaGadol Numbers, ed. Rabinowitz, 16.

20. Seder Eliyahu Zutta 24, ed. Friedman, 43.

21. תיקונו של עולם , see Isaiah 45:18.

22. The literature is collated in Oṣar HaGeonim, ed. Lewin, Berakot HaPerushim, p. 6, #18. For a R. Matnah who studied with Samuel, see Ḥ. Albeck, Mabo LaTalmudim (Tel Aviv, 1969) 204.

23. S. v. גרש . Cf. Rashbam to B Babba Batra 116b

24. This rests on the difficult assumption that such a repast consisted of meat, see R. Margoliot, Niṣoṣe Or (Jerusalem, 1965) to B Berakot 5b.

25. Cf., however, Z. Chajes in the Lewy Jubilee Volume: Tife ret Yisrael, Hebrew section, 174; and L. Finkelstein, Akiba (New York, 1936) 179, and 337, n. 3.

26. B Berakot 5b, s.v. והאמר ר"י , On such chastisements, see E. Urbach, Ḥazal Emunot VeDeot (Jerusalem, 1969) 392ff.

27. Tosafot followed the later Talmudic discussion there which itself is based on the assumption that RY's mention of the bone is to exemplify afflictions of love - petitio principii. The later Talmudic distinction between one who never had sons and one who had, but lost them, is an effort to resolve a contradiction which the Talmud sees between RY's dictum and a baraita. This is insufficient reason to argue that RY actually had in mind such a distinction when he originally said that the lack of sons cannot be considered as chastisements of love.

28. The two tables may be wealth and learning, or, as Midrash HaGadol Genesis 828 has, this world and the next world.

29. Seneca said it best: "No man goes into mourning for its own sake...There is an element of self-seeking even in our sorrow" (Epistle 63.2). Cf. his advice in Epistle 74.

CHRONOGRAPHY IN

HELLENISTIC JEWISH HISTORIOGRAPHY

Lester L. Grabbe

Ambassador College

The term "chronography" may be synonymous with "chronology" according to one definition. However, I use "chronography" as a technical term clearly distinguished from "chronology" as this latter is normally used in biblical and historical scholarship today. "Chronology" generally implies the attempt to work out a scientific and accurate dating of historical events. In this sense, modern chronology can be said to have begun with Eusebius who laid the framework in his *Chronicle*.[1] On the other hand, much of ancient chronological writing made use of stylized or stereotyped schemes of history and often overly concerned itself with the mythical or legendary period of the history of nations. Further, the mythical or legendary period in question may have possessed a sacred or semi-sacral character which vitiated critical historical methods which might otherwise have been applied. Thus, chronology, rather than arising from the historical data, was often superimposed on them.

It is to such stereotyped, stylized, frequently periodized, pre-scientific chronology that I apply the term "chronography," and distinguish it from "chronology" as used in its modern sense. In this way, "chronography" is an aspect of ancient writings which can be given a place alongside other schematic devices such as cosmology, theogony, arithmology,[2]

---

[1] The original text of Eusebius' *Chronicle* has not survived except in fragments. For Jerome's Latin edition, see R. Helm (ed.), *Die Chronik des Hieronymus* (GCS 47; Eusebius Werke, 7er Band; 2nd edition; Berlin: Akademie, 1956). The Armenian edition is available in the German translation of J. Karst, *Die Chronik* (GCS 20; Eusebius Werke, 5er Band; Leipzig: Hinrichs, 1911). For a study of Eusebius' *Chronicle* for its value for modern chronology, see J. Finegan, *Handbook of Biblical Chronology* (Princeton, NJ: University, 1964) 147-87.

[2] On the definition of this term in relation to such terms as "number symbolism," "number mysticism," and the like, see H. R. Moehring, "Arithmology as an Exegetical Tool in the Writings of Philo of Alexandria," *Society of Biblical Literature 1978 Seminar Papers* (SBLSPS 13; Missoula, MT: Scholars, 1978) 1.192-4.

etiological genealogy, just to name a few.[3]

Chronography has not been a popular subject for research for many years. Many of the definitive studies on
various early Jewish and Christian writers are half a century
or more old. Up-to-date studies are sporadic and often non-
existent for broad areas. With the current revival of interest
in apocalyptic literature and intertestamental studies in
general, scholars will no doubt apply themselves to some of
the major chronographers and chronographs as a matter of
course as time goes on. However, one major researcher who
already stands out is Ben Zion Wacholder. Professor Wacholder
has already produced a number of studies on various aspects of
early Jewish chronography.[4] It is on the base laid by
Wacholder and his predecessors that any future work must proceed; my indebtedness to Professor Wacholder and many others
in this paper will be readily apparent.

The question of how narrowly to define "Hellenistic
Judaism" is a problem, since all Judaism--whether rabbinic,
Palestinian, or diasporan--had been Hellenized to a greater
or lesser extent.[5] A major feature of Hellenism was the

---

[3]The origin of the term "chronography" naturally lies
in the popular title *Chronographia(i)* for the chronological
writings of such individuals as Eratosthenes, Julius Africanus,
Syncellus, and John Malala. Whether I am using the term
"chronography" in a slightly new way, I cannot say, though I
do not recall seeing it specifically defined as I have done
so here.

[4]Most of Wacholder's individual articles have been
collected in his *Essays on Jewish Chronology and Chronography*
(New York: Ktav, 1976). Not reprinted in this collection is
his very interesting "Chronomessianism, The Timing of Messianic Movements and the Calendar of Sabbatical Cycles," *HUCA*
46 (1975) 201-18. His monograph, *Eupolemus, A Study of Judaeo-
Greek Literature* (Monographs of the Hebrew Union College 3;
Cincinnati: Hebrew Union College, 1974), discusses chronographical matters at a number of points, especially in chapter
4, "Hellenistic Biblical Chronologies," 97-128. (The bulk of
this chapter appeared earlier in *HTR* 61 [1968] 451-81 and was
also reprinted in *Essays* 106-36.)

[5]See especially M. Hengel, *Judaism and Hellenism* (tr.
J. Bowden; 2 vols.; London: SCM, 1974); also S. Lieberman,
Hellenism in Jewish Palestine (Texts and Studies 18; New York:
Jewish Theological Seminary, 1950) and *Greek in Jewish
Palestine* (2nd edition; New York: Feldheim, 1965); M. Smith,
"Palestinian Judaism in the First Century," *Israel: Its Role
in Civilization* (ed. M. Davis; Jewish Theological Seminary
Israel Institute; New York: Harper, 1956) 67-81, especially
67-71; J. A. Fitzmyer, "The Languages of Palestine in the First
Century A. D.," *CBQ* 32 (1970) 501-31, especially 507-18; V.
Tcherikover, *Hellenistic Civilization and the Jews* (tr. S.
Applebaum; 1959; reprinted New York: Atheneum, 1975).

combination of Greek and native elements into a cultural and intellectual synthesis.[6] Much of the intertestamental Jewish literature falls under this category, not least because most of these writings circulated in Greek translation at some stage in their history. I doubt whether a proper picture of chronography can be drawn from using only the Hellenistic Jewish sources in their narrowest sense. Therefore, I have chosen to use all sources which seem helpful. Yet the true historians of the period are Hellenistic Jewish writers in the narrower sense, with the result that the focus of this paper is still ultimately on *Hellenistic* Jewish historiography.

Topical Aspects of Chronography

In his study of Eupolemus, Professor Wacholder presents a three-stage development in the use of biblical chronology by Hellenistic Jewish historians: Stage 1, reconciling biblical dates; Stage 2, fusion of biblical and Greek myth; Stage 3, fusion of the biblical chronology with world chronicles.[7] This is an ingenious theory of development which deserves further study. I doubt that Wacholder feels it adequate to take into account all the chronographical sources of the period even for biblical chronology alone; a more complex theory will ultimately be required. Nevertheless, it is a very useful start and the basis for developing a more comprehensive theory.

Yet at this stage of study--my own study, at least!-- it is still too early to advance a theory to replace that given by Wacholder. Instead, I propose in this paper to consider several features of chronography without attempting as yet to work out a comprehensive scheme. Not all of these are found in every chronographical writing, nor does the brief list here exhaust the major features of chronography. But they should serve as a means of beginning to see the schematic nature of chronography and some of the various possible elements which a chronographer might incorporate.

1. Resolution of Real or Imagined Scriptural Difficulties

One of the first chronological difficulties to be noted by chronographers was the 400 years of Gen 15:13 and the 430 years of Exod 12:40-1. Simple addition made it clear that the Israelites could not have spent 430 years in Egypt alone. The LXX is possibly our earliest Greek source to resolve the problem by stating that the Israelites spent 430

---

[6]This is very well discussed for the one aspect of Hellenistic religions by J. Z. Smith, "Hellenistic Religions," *Encyclopaedia Britannica* (Chicago: University of Chicago, 1974) *Macropaedia* 8.749-51.

[7]Wacholder, *Eupolemus*, sub-headings in chapter 4.

years "in the land of Egypt and in the land of Canaan."[8] However, some date the chronographer Demetrius to approximately
the same time as the translation of the Pentateuch in Greek.[9]
Demetrius is quite explicit about the length of time from
Abraham's coming to Canaan until Jacob entered Egypt: 215
years.[10] No specific total for the time in Egypt is given in
the fragments of Demetrius preserved, yet it is clear from his
figures that the time in Egypt was the same figure[11]:

Levi in Egypt before fathering Kaath	17 years
Kaath fathered Amram at age	40
Amran fathered Moses at age	78
(Moses' age at the Exodus	80)
Total	215 years

---

[8]Until the completion of the Göttingen volume on
Exodus, the best critical edition is still A. E. Brooke and
N. McLean (eds.), *The Old Testament in Greek, Vol. I. The
Octateuch, Part II. Exodus and Leviticus* (Cambridge: University, 1909). In the past it has often been assumed that the
phrase "in the land of Canaan" was a Hellenistic addition by
the translators. However, recent LXX research cautions one
against assuming this since many such deviations from the MT
have turned out to be faithful translations of a different
Hebrew *Vorlage*. The phrase, "in the land of Canaan," is also
found in the Samaritan Pentateuch: A. von Gall (ed.), *Der
hebräische Pentateuch der Samaritaner* (1918; reprinted Berlin:
Töpelmann, 1966) 140. Cf. also R. W. Klein, "Archaic
Chronologies and the Textual History of the Old Testament,"
HTR 67 (1974) 255-63.

[9]Demetrius flourished perhaps shortly before 200 B. C.
The consensus of Septuagintal scholarship is still that the
Pentateuch was translated before 250 B. C. Cf. S. Jellicoe,
The Septuagint and Modern Study (Oxford: Clarendon, 1968) 55.
Wacholder, *Eupolemus* 102-4, suggests that it is "possible,
even likely, that the chronological alterations adopted in the
Septuagint version of the Pentateuch were a product of
Demetrius' chronographic schemes." This is admittedly specu-
lative but is, of course, within the realm of possibility
under our present knowledge.

[10]F. Jacoby, *Die Fragmente der griechischen Historiker*
(IIIC, 2er Band; Leiden: Brill, 1958) 722 F 1.16 (= Eusebius,
P. E. 9.21.16). Jacoby's work is henceforth abbreviated *FGH*.

[11]*FGH* 722 F 1.19 (= Eusebius, *P. E.* 9.21.19). For a
discussion of the time Israel spent in Egypt in rabbinic and
other literature, see J. Heinemann, "210 Years of Egyptian
Exile," *JJS* 22 (1971) 19-30, though Demetrius is not mentioned
in this article.

Josephus gives essentially the same information: "They left Egypt . . . 430 years after the coming of our forefather Abraham to Canaan, Jacob's migration to Egypt having taken place 215 years later." He does not mention a source though it is very likely Demetrius.[12]

The 400 years of Gen 15:13 seems to have been ignored in the earlier chronographic works and is not dealt with until the time of Pseudo-Philo (= LAB, generally dated about 100 A.D.). LAB 8.14 states that Israel spent 210 years in Egypt.[13] LAB 9.3 states that Israel had been in bondage 130 years about the time of the birth of Moses, which was after 350 of the 400 years had passed. The 430 years is not mentioned but seems to be assumed. That is, if 350 years had passed at the birth of Moses, 430 would be gone by the time of the Exodus when he was 80. This implies that the 400-year period and the 430-year period began at the same time, but that the former ended 30 years before the Exodus. This seems to be the most straightforward reading of the text. However, this produces a difficulty since no special event is stated as taking place 30 years before the Exodus. Thus, it seems that the author is connecting the 350 years with the implicit 430 rather than the explicit 400 years he has just mentioned. If that is the case, then he probably begins the 430 years with the immigration of Abraham into Canaan while beginning the 400 years with the birth of Isaac.[14]

---

[12]Ant. 2.15.2 § 318. Translation from H. S. J. Thackeray, Josephus (LCL; London: Heinemann, 1930) 4.305; all English translations of Josephus in this article are from the LCL edition.

[13]For critical text and French translation, see D. J. Harrington, J. Cazeaux, C. Perrot, and P.-M. Bogaert, Pseudo-Philon, Les antiquités bibliques (SC 229-30; vols. 1-2; Paris: Editions du Cerf, 1976). An English translation, though sometimes based on an inferior text is M. R. James, The Biblical Antiquities of Philo (1917; reprinted with a new "Prolegomenon" by L. H. Feldman, New York: Ktav, 1971).

[14]C. Perrot in his commentary in Pseudo-Philon 2.103 (on LAB 9.3) assumes the latter suggestion, i.e., both periods beginning at different times but ending with the Exodus. As already stated, this is probably correct, but he may have been too much influenced by the Targum Pseudo-Jonathan on Exod 12:41 which gives the same explanation. One cannot automatically assume that traditions in this or other targums go back as early as the 1st century. Cf. L. L. Grabbe, "The Jannes-Jambres Tradition in Targum Pseudo-Jonathan and its Date," forthcoming in JBL (Sept. 1979) and the references given there. Although Perrot's explanation is probably the most compelling from an overall point of view, one must be willing to reckon with the possibility of a different counting in Pseudo-Philo.

One other example falls partly into the area of
chronography. This is the ancestry of Zipporah which is not
made clear in the MT or LXX. Demetrius traces Zipporah back
to Abraham through Keturah. By his reckoning there are seven
generations from Abraham to Moses but six from Abraham to
Zipporah. A difference of one generation for these two
contemporaries would, of course, be quite credible. However,
there seems to be more at stake than just tracing a genealogy;
Demetrius ends his account in this particular fragment by
asserting that the "Ethiopian" woman whom Moses had married
(Num 12:1) was none other than Zipporah. She was called an
Ethiopian because Keturah's sons had been sent to the East to
live. Thus, genealogy (and therefore indirectly chronography)
was called upon to resolve another difficulty which other
exegetes also labored over.[15]

2. Dating the Undated

Many events of the OT are naturally not dated precisely. This was usually of no concern until the intertestamental writers began to attempt to work out a chronographical
scheme of biblical history. Sufficient data are found
within the tradition itself to work out (or to give the
illusion of working out) an overall outline. But vast periods
of time with many important events are sometimes marked off
only with beginning and ending dates but no internal dates.
Sometimes dates could be inferred for undated events though
often they could not; irregardless, it occasions no surprise
to find the Jewish historians beginning to reason out or--if
necessary--to invent dates for the dateless.

Demetrius gives the specific time of birth for each of
Jacob's children (*FGH* 722 F 1.3-5 = Eusebius, *P. E.* 9.21.3-5).

---

[15]*FGH* 722 F 2.1-3 (= Eusebius, *P. E.* 9.29.1-3).
Exegetes had essentially two choices: (a) the "Ethiopian"
wife of Moses was Zipporah; (b) she was some other woman,
with the result that some explanation was required for how he
had acquired her. The alternative that she was Zipporah was
also taken by Ezekiel the tragedian (Eusebius, *P. E.* 9.28.4),
the *Targum Onqelos* on Num 12:1, and *Siprei* on Num 12:1. For
the other choice, Artapanus gives a long explanation of how
Moses fought the Ethiopians while a military leader before he
was forced to flee Egypt (*FGH* 726 F 3.1-10 = Eusebius, *P. E.*
9.27.1-10); yet nothing is said about marrying one of the
Ethiopian women. But Josephus also gives an account of an
expedition against the Ethiopians (with considerable differences from Artapanus) and includes a marriage to an Ethiopian
princess (*Ant.* 2.10.1-2 §§ 238-53). The *Targum Pseudo-
Jonathan* and the *Fragmentary Targum* on Num 12:1 both state that
the Ethiopian woman was not Zipporah though they do not otherwise identify her. The *Targum Neofiti I* states in the original
hand that the woman of Num 12:1 *was* Zipporah, though a marginal
note has been added stating she was *not* Zipporah.

Exactly why this was important to him is not completely clear,
though he seems concerned to show that 12 children were born
in 7 years. Doubtless, this had some symbolic value for him.
Needless to say, none of this information occurs in Genesis.
The previous section has already discussed the problem with
the 430 years of Exod 12. This figure is also important here
in that the Bible gives no other chronological data for the
time between Israel's entering Egypt and the Exodus. By
dividing the 430 years in half, Demetrius was able to provide
some information on the total length of time the Israelites
were in Egypt even if further precision was not attempted.

As the first king of Israel, Saul surely deserved to
have a clear length of reign but such an unambiguous figure
was not available. Although some sort of information was
apparently intended in the MT at 1 Sam 13:1, the present text
is meaningless. But the Hellenistic writers were not at a
loss though the origin of their figures is not clear. Eupolemus gives 21 years to Saul, an interesting number since it is
not a round one (*FGH* 723 F 2b.2 = Eusebius, *P. E.* 9.30.2).
Josephus assigns him 20 years in one place (*Ant.* 10.8.4
§ 143) but may give him 40 in another.[16] Considering the
lengths of reign of David and Solomon, one is not surprised to
see the figure 40 given to Saul as well (cf. also Acts 13:21).
The length of Solomon's reign is not given in the OT, but it
is also made clear that he was quite young when he came to
the throne (1 Chr 22:5; 29:1). Eupolemus gives Solomon's age
at his coronation as 12 (*FGH* 723 F 2b.8 = Eusebius, *P. E.*
9.30.8). Exactly where Eupolemus came up with that figure is
uncertain, but it also agrees with that of the *Seder Olam
Rabbah* which computes the figure by an elaborate piece of
deduction.[17]

A Semitic Jewish work which assigns many dates to
undated events is the Book of Jubilees. Even events not in
the Bible are given dates, such as the time Abram sat up to
observe the stars and God's word came to him (12:16-7). While
the times of these events are fitted into a schematic dating
by jubilee cycles, they are hardly more arbitrary than the
dating given by some of the historians.

---

[16]*Ant.* 6.14.9 § 378 says that Saul reigned 18 years
while Samuel was alive and another 22 after his death. This
is the text preferred by B. Niese, *Flavii Iosephi opera* (1885-
95; vols. 1-7; reprinted Berlin: Weidmann, 1955) 2.87, and
Marcus (LCL 5.356). The only variant is the Old Latin reading
of 18 plus 2 years. Marcus cites Rappaport's opinion that the
preferred text may be the result of a dogmatic change by a
Christian scribe to bring Josephus in harmony with Acts. However, Wacholder, *Eupolemus* 108 n. 47, assumes that this is
only another example of chronological inconsistency in
Josephus.

[17]Wacholder, *Eupolemus* 108-10, discusses the question
in some detail. For information on the printed editions
of the *Seder Olam Rabbah*, see note 47 below.

3. *Antiquity and Priority of the Hebrews*

Various discoveries and inventions were ascribed
to patriarchal figures. According to Pseudo-Eupolemus,
Abraham taught astrology to the Egyptians but the first to
discover astrology was Enoch.[18] Discoveries of various kinds
are credited to Joseph by Artapanus (*FGH* 726 F 2.1-4 = Eusebius, *P. E.* 9.23.1-4). These are all patent attempts to show
the priority--and thus the intellectual superiority--of the
Hebrews to other peoples such as the Egyptians or Greeks. In
this task, chronography was not neglected.

Since the time of Herodotus and before, the Greeks
accepted the antiquity of the Egyptians and certain other Near
Eastern peoples. Therefore, the Jewish writers had two means
of demonstrating their antiquity. They could tie their own
history into the older history of Egypt or Babylon. Or they
could synchronize their history with the legendary early
history of Greece itself. Both methods were used.

In *Contra Apionem* Josephus assembles a number of non-
Jewish authors in support of the long history of his people.
He expressly identifies the Israelites of the Exodus with the
Hyksos of Manetho (1.14 §§ 75-90). Josephus goes on to show
that the Israelites/Hyksos settled in Jerusalem long before
the time of the famous king Ramesses or Sethosis (1.15 §§ 93-
102). Finally, Josephus ties the Exodus to Greek history: "it
is clear that the so-called shepherds, our ancestors, left
Egypt and settled in our country 393 years before Danaus came
to Argos. Yet the Argives regard him as one of the most
ancient of men" (1.16 § 103). Josephus further asserts that
the Israelites left Egypt "at a date so remote in the past
that it preceded the Trojan War by nearly a thousand years"
(1.16 § 104). Josephus then moves on to the records of Tyre
to show that the temple was built by Solomon almost a century
and a half before the founding of Carthage (1.17 § 106-8).

Josephus is certainly not alone in this. Justus of
Tiberius, a contemporary of Josephus, also made a synchronism
with Greek history. Although his work on Judaean history has
by and large perished, two of the preserved fragments date
Moses according to Greek history. One makes Moses a contemporary with Inachus, the legendary ancestor of the Argives.
The other synchronizes him with Phoroneus and Apis, the first
two kings of Argos, and Amosis king of Egypt. These two data
are themselves contradictory on the surface though Justus may
have harmonized them to his own satisfaction. But the important thing is that Jewish history was tied to the Greek world
histories, to the obvious advantage of the Jews.[19]

---

[18]*FGH* 724 F 1; see Wacholder, *Eupolemus* 313-4, for
an English translation. Artapanus also has Abraham's teaching
astrology to the Egyptians (*FGH* 726 F 1 = Eusebius, *P. E.*
9.18.1). Josephus gives a similar story, only for him Abraham
teaches both astrology and arithmetic (*Ant.* 1.8.2 §§ 167-8).
Josephus does not ascribe the discovery to Enoch but only the
descendants of Seth in general (*Ant.* 1.2.3 §§ 69-71).

4. *World Millennial Week*

The concept of a world week, in which the whole of
human history is encompassed in seven 1000-year days, is well
known from early Christian writings. It was closely tied to
the belief in the millennial rule of Christ who would return
after the world had continued 6000 years. The earliest explicit Christian statement on the subject is found in the Epistle
of Barnabas 15:4: "Pay attention, children, to what he says:
'He finished in six days.' He is saying this, that in six
thousand years the Lord will finish everything. For with him
the 'day' signifies a thousand years."[20] However, the same
belief seems to underlie NT statements such as 2 Pet 3:8 and
Rev 20:1-7.[21]

The phenomenon of the world week is also well known
from later rabbinic literature.[22] But the question is, What
is the earliest reference to it in Jewish literature? Jubilees
4:30 from the mid-2nd century B. C. speaks of a day's being
as 1000 years in the sight of heaven but does not otherwise
indicate how long the world was supposed to last.[23] The

---

[19]*FGH* 734 FF 2-3. For more general bibliography on
Justus, see note 33 below. Wacholder, *Eupolemus* 123-4, discusses the possible confusion of Justus or those who preserved
him at this point.

[20]English translation from R. A. Kraft, *Barnabas and
the Didache* (The Apostolic Fathers 3, ed. R. M. Grant; New
York: Nelson, 1965) 128. Barnabas is usually dated 70-135 A.D.

[21]Other Christian writers who mention the concept of
the world week or imply it by a belief in the Millennium include the following: Irenaeus, *C. haer.* 5.28.3; Clement of
Alexandria, *Strom.* 4.25.158-9; Gospel of Nicodemus 2.12; Papias
(quoted in Eusebius, *H. E.* 3.39.11-3); Justin, *Dial. Tryph.*
80.4; Hippolytus, *Com. in Dan.* 4.23.5; Tertullian, *Adv. Marc.*
3.24; Methodius of Olympus, *Symp.* 9.5; Commodian, *Instruc.*
1.35.6; *Carmen.* 791; Pseudo-Cyprian, *De mont.* 4; Victorinus of
Pettau, *De fab. mun.* 6; Lactantius, *Div. instit.* 7.14; Didasca-
lia 26 (6.18). See also A. Luneau, *L'histoire du salut chez
les Pères de l'Eglise* (Théologie historique 2; Paris: Beauches-
ne, 1964) 37-45, 81-5; J. Daniélou, "La typologie millenariste
de la semaine dans le Christianisme primitif," *VC* 2 (1948) 1-
16. On Julius Africanus, see notes 34-5 below.

[22]See, for example, *b. Sanh.* 97a-b which quotes a
number of statements by various figures about the world week.
Also *Peseq. R.* 4a and *b. ʿAbod. Zar.* 9a.

[23]On the dating of Jubilees, see J. C. VanderKam,
Textual and Historical Studies in the Book of Jubilees (HSM 14;
Missoula, MT: Scholars, 1977) 207-85. On the chronological
system(s) of Jubilees, see E. Wiesenberg, "The Jubilee of
Jubilees," *RevQ* 3 (1961-2) 3-40; M. J. Krüger, "Die Chronologie
im Buche der Jubiläen," *ZDMG* 12 (1858) 279-99.

Testament of Abraham is generally dated before the fall of the
temple in 70.[24] But there is a complication in that this work
exists in two recensions, and the question of the relationship
between the recensions is still disputed in contemporary
scholarship. *T. Abr.* 7 (recension B = short recension) states:
"Michael said to Abraham, 'Your son Isaac has spoken the truth,
for it is you, and you will be taken up into the heavens, but
your body will remain upon the earth until seven thousand ages
are fulfilled, for then all flesh will arise.'"[25] Recension
A (= long recension) also has a statement which may presuppose
a world week (*T. Abr.* 19): "And Death said, 'Hear, O righteous Abraham. For seven ages I devastate the world and lead
all men down into Hades . . . .'"

Even more exact statements can be found elsewhere;
unfortunately, just like the ones in the Testament of Abraham
there are literary problems associated with them. The Book of
Adam and Eve 42, also evidently a 1st-century work, speaks of
"5500 years." This statement undoubtedly presupposes the
concept of the world week but is likely part of a Christian
interpolation.[26] Similarly, the Slavonic Enoch is a work considered pre-70 by a significant number of current researchers.
The long version (= version A) of it states (33:1-2): "Then
also I established the eighth day. Let the eighth be the
first after My work, and let the days be after the fashion of
seven thousand. Let there be at the beginning of the eighth
thousand a time when there is no computation, and no end; neither years, nor months, nor weeks, nor days, nor hours."[27]
However, more recent scholarship has tended to favor the short
version (= version B) which does not have this particular
passage.[28]

[24]J. H. Charlesworth, *The Pseudepigrapha and Modern
Research* (SBLSCS 7; Missoula, MT: Scholars, 1976) 70.

[25]For a general discussion of dating and recensional
problems in this work, see G. W. E. Nickelsburg (ed.), *Studies
on the Testament of Abraham* (SBLSCS 6; Missoula, MT: Scholars,
1976). My English citations from this work are from M. E.
Stone (tr.), *The Testament of Abraham* (SBLTT 2; Missoula, MT:
Society of Biblical Literature, 1972).

[26]Part of this passage refers specifically to Jesus
Christ and is thus unquestionably Christian. The statement
about "5500 years" does not appear to be inseparable from the
Christian interpolation. On the other hand, 5500 A.M. is a
commonplace date for the birth Jesus in later Christian chronographers. Also the passage is similar to *Gosp. Nicod.* 19.

[27]Translation from R. H. Charles and W. R. Morfill,
The Book of the Secrets of Enoch (Oxford: Clarendon, 1896) 45-
6. The best critical text, with French translation, is A.
Vaillant, *Le livre des secrets d'Hénoch* (Textes publiés par
l'Institute d'Etudes slaves 4; Paris: Institute d'Etudes
slaves, 1952).

[28]Vaillant labels the passage in question a product

Two further statements are problematic in that they may but do not clearly presuppose the world week. The Testament of Moses was probably given its final redaction sometime before 30 A. D.[29] In 1:2 the death of Moses is stated to occur in the year 2500 A. M. Further on in the book (10:12) it is stated that from Moses' death until the coming of God for judgment would be 250 "times" (*tempora*). The exact meaning of "times" is not clear; a number of commentators feel it means 250 weeks of years or 1750 years.[30] However, it may well be that there were to be 2500 years from Moses' death to the end of the world just as there were 2500 years from its beginning to his death.[31] In either case--whether the age was thought to last 4250 years or 5000 years--a world week is not clearly visible. Yet we cannot rule out that the writer may have assumed another figure after the time of God's coming which would fill out the remaining time to 7000 years.

Pseudo-Philo also has passages which have been taken to refer to the world week: 19:15 (4½ "times" have passed and 2½ remain) and 28:8. In the latter passage some MSS indeed have "7000 years," but the text preferred in the most recent edition is "4000."[32] Of some interest here is the statement of Eupolemus that from the creation of Adam to the 5th year of Demetrius (I Soter) and of Ptolemy XII (c. 158 B. C.) was 5149 years (*FGH* 723 F 4 = Clement of Alexandria, *Strom.* 1.141.4). Whether or not he believed in a world week, his figures are remarkably close to those of later Christian writers who put the birth of Jesus in 5500 A. M.

---

of "the second reviser" (pp. 102-5) whom he dates to about the 15th century. For a summary of the arguments in favor of the short recension (recension B) and current scholarship in general, see U. Fischer, *Eschatologie und Jenseitserwartung im hellenistischen Diasporajudentum* (BZNW 44; Berlin/New York: de Gruyter, 1978) 37-41.

[29] On the dating, see G. W. E. Nickelsburg (ed.), *Studies on the Testament of Moses* (SBLSCS 4; Missoula, MT: Scholars, 1973), especially the essays by Nickelsburg and Collins. The most recent transcription of the Latin text, with introduction and French translation, is E.-M. Laperrousaz, *Le testament de Moïse* (Semitica 19; Paris: Adrien-Masonneuve, 1970). The Latin text and an English translation are given by R. H. Charles, *The Assumption of Moses* (London: Adam and Charles Black, 1897).

[30] Laperrousaz (previous note) 131; Charles 44.

[31] H. Rönsch, "Xeniola thelogica, 3. Chronologisches und Kritisches zur Assumptio Mosis," *ZWT* 17 (1874) 542-62, especially 543-4; W. Bousset, "Das chronologische System der biblischen Geschichtsbücher," *ZAW* 20 (1900) 136-47, esp. 139.

[32] Harrington, *Pseudo-Philon* (note 13 above) 1.164, 228, gives the text; in his commentary to the two passages (ibid. 2.134-5, 163-4) C. Perrot argues that the world week of 7000 years is not in view here.

The concept of a world week is certainly as old as
the 1st century A. D. One is not likely to encounter much
resistance if he also asserts that the concept is Jewish and
pre-70 in origin. But despite a number of promising statements
the sad fact is still that the concept cannot be pushed back
further in time by any means known to me at the present. The
powerful symbolic value of the seven-day week would not be lost
on the fertile imagination of intertestamental Jewish interpreters, one would surely think. Yet hard evidence for an
early origin of the idea is still needed.

On the other hand, the idea seems to have influenced
one--if not both--of our major 1st century Jewish historians.
Josephus twice mentions that the world was about 5000 years
old (*Ant.* Proem. 3 § 13; *Ag. Ap.* 1.1 § 1). As already mentioned, this may but does not certainly indicate that he
believed in a total history of 7000 years. His contemporary
and rival Justus of Tiberius may have been more explicit in
this.[33] There are many problems associated with trying to get
at Justus' history of the Jews since his work has almost
entirely perished. Nevertheless, there are good indications
that later Christian writers, especially Julius Africanus,
depended heavily on Justus.[34] Africanus specifically tied his
history to the concept of the world week. According to him
Jesus was born in the year 5500 A. M., and world history would
continue only for another 500 years after his birth.[35] It
seems likely that the figure of 5500 years for the age of the
world at the turn of our era was taken over from Justus (with
perhaps a minor adjustment of a few years to make it fit
Christian chronology!). In this regard one should note a
statement in the Apocalypse of Ezra, which was probably
written about the same general period as Justus and Josephus.

---

[33]General treatments of Justus are E. Schürer, *The
History of the Jewish People in the Age of Jesus Christ* (new
English edition revised and edited by G. Vermes, et al.; vols.
1- ; Edinburgh: T. & T. Clark, 1973-) 1.34-7; A. Schalit,
"Josephus und Justus," *Klio* 26 (1933) 67-95; F. Rühl, "Justus
von Tiberias," *Rheinisches Museum* 71 (1916) 289-308; H.
Luther, *Josephus und Justus von Tiberias* (Inaugural-
Dissertation; Friedrichs-Universität Halle-Wittenberg, 1910).

[34]Wacholder, *Eupolemus* 123-4, 298-306; H. Gelzer,
Sextus Julius Africanus und die byzantinische Chronographie
(1885-98; reprinted New York: Burt Franklin, n. d.) 1.20, 258-
65; A. von Gutschmid, *Kleine Schriften* (ed. F. Rühl; 5 vols.;
Leipzig: Teubner, 1889-94) 2. 196-203.

[35]Gelzer, *Africanus* 1.24-6. For the text of the
fragments, see M. J. Routh, *Reliquiae sacrae* (2nd edition,
1846; reprinted Hildesheim: Olms, 1974) 2.221-512. An English
translation of some, but by no means all, of these fragments
is found in ANF 6.130-8. Statements on the birth of Jesus
in 5500 A. M. occur in Routh, fragments X (p. 246) and L
(p. 306).

4 Ezra 14:48 states that the world had lasted for 5042 years to
the time of Ezra.[36] If one assumes that the writer of this
statement really meant it to refer to Ezra's time and not his
own, he would be extremely close to the Christian figure of
5500 A. M. for the turn of the era. Perhaps Justus only
provided the hints, more or less accidentally, which Africanus
and others developed into a full-blown scheme of world history.
But that Justus himself built his history with a 6000- or
7000-year history in mind is a tantalizing suggestion and not
all that improbable.

5. *The Seventy-Weeks Prophecy of Daniel 9:24-7*

These four verses of Daniel became very important in
later writings for two reasons. For the apocalyptists and
others interested in predictive prophecy, they apparently
provided an exact timetable to the hoped-for deliverance. The
Seventy-Weeks Prophecy thus played an important role in
Judaism to the fall of the temple and later and, not surprisingly, was picked up by Christians to enjoy some prominence
for many centuries. But the predictive side of this passage
was not its only appeal. Historians even today have to wrestle
with a poverty of data for the Persian period in Jewish history. For the ancient historian, the problem was many times
worse. Between the end of the OT record in Ezra and Nehemiah
and the Macedonian conquest, there was almost no information.
This blank period had somehow to be bridged. The prophecy of
the 70 weeks was a means of doing so.

It has been the native Persian and especially the
Babylonian and Assyrian texts which have filled in the picture
largely blank to the ancient historians. True, they were not
without some account in Greek; unfortunately, most put their
bets on the wrong horse. Though far from complete, Herodotus
gave a surprisingly accurate account of the Median and Persian
kings of this period.[37] But Herodotus' account was not the one
used, by and large. Rather it was the mendacious Ctesias who
provided the basis most widely used by the classical historians.[38] His influence continued even down to the sober

---

[36]This is the figure in the Syriac version. It is
absent from the Latin and varies slightly in some of the other
versions. The classic commentary on 4 Ezra is G. H. Box, *The
Ezra-Apocalypse* (London: Pitman, 1912); a recent commentary is
J. M. Myers, *I & II Esdras* (AB; Garden City: Doubleday, 1974).

[37]A. R. Burn, *Persia and the Greeks* (London: Edward
Arnold, 1962) 11, states: "The decipherment of Darius' *res
gestae* at Behistun, . . . with the lists of peoples, confirms
the soundness (not the infallibility) of Herodotus' information
on Persia . . . ." See also R. Drews, *The Greek Accounts of
Eastern History* (Center for Hellenic Studies; Cambridge, MA:
Harvard, 1973) chap. 3.

[38]The most recent thorough study of Ctesias, with
the Greek text and a German translation of the fragments, is

Eusebius who was also misled by him.[39] Perhaps the Jewish
historians who used their interpretation of Daniel were not
much worse off than those who used Ctesias. Nevertheless, the
result was an elastic Persian period which went all the way
from 34 years in length--far too short--to 254 years, a figure
much too long.

Josephus seems to incorporate a number of earlier
interpretations of the 70 weeks.[40] The earliest seems to be
his source in *Ant*. 20.10.3 § 237 which gives a seven-year
interregnum between Alcimus and Jonathan. This statement contradicts Josephus' own earlier statements in *Ant*. 12.10.6 §§
413-14 (in which Judas is appointed high priest and holds the
office three years, 12.11.2 § 434) and 13.2.3 § 46 (Jonathan
succeeds to the post four years after Judas' death). It may
be that the interregnum between Alcimus and Jonathan was meant
to correspond to the last heptad of the 70 in Daniel. A later
reinterpretation which made the last week begin with Alexander
Jannaeus' rule in 103 B. C. appears to be reflected in *Ant*.
13.10.1 § 301. This states that Aristobulus I began to reign
481 years and some months after the end of the Exile. Since
Aristobulus ruled only one year and was succeeded by Alexander,
it seems more than coincidence that Alexander took the priesthood just about the beginning of the last heptad. But counting 481 years from Cyrus to Aristobulus makes the period half
a century longer than it actually was.[41]

F. W. König, *Die Persika des Ktesias von Knidos* (AfO Beiheft
18; Graz: Archiv für Orientforschung, 1972). Cf. also Drews,
Greek Accounts 103-16.

[39]R. Drews, "Assyria in Classical Universal Histories," *Historia* 14 (1965) 137, notes that Eusebius combined
the Berossian and Ctesian Assyrian histories; even then the
Ctesian tradition remained prominent. Eusebius' compromise
continued to hold sway until the 19th century when native
records became available.

[40]For these interpretations I am primarily dependent
on F. F. Bruce, "Josephus and Daniel," *ASTI* 4 (1965) 148-62.

[41]Eusebius, *Dem. evang.* 8.2, gives a number of interpretations of the 70-weeks prophecy. Among them is an opinion
which seems to be Eusebius' own contribution but also appears
to end the 70 weeks with "the death of Alexander Jannaeus. Yet
he goes on to state that "the first seven weeks must be reckoned from Cyrus to Darius, and the remaining sixty-two from
Darius to Pompey the Roman general." Either there is confusion on Eusebius' part or he has not expressed himself clearly.
The English translation of this passage comes from W. J.
Ferrar, *The Proof of the Gospel* (Translations of Christian
Literature, Series I; vols. 1-2; London: SPCK, 1920)
2.129.

Another early interpretation, according to a certain scholarly consensus, is found in CD 1:5-11.[42] This reckons 390 years from Nebuchadnezzar to the first gropings of the sect, which lasted 20 years until the Teacher of Righteousness. Elsewhere are statements indicating 40 years were expected to elapse between the death of the Teacher and the end of the age (CD 20:14-5; 4QpPs[a] 2:6-8). These figures add up to 450 years. If one adds a stereotyped 40 years (= 1 generation) for the life of the Teacher, the 490 years of Dan 9 is reached.

Josephus also gives two intriguing oracles which *may* have Dan 9:24-7 behind them. The first is found in *J. W.* 6.5.4 § 311: "Thus the Jews, after the demolition of Antonia, reduced the temple to a square, although they had it recorded in their oracles that the city and the sanctuary would be taken when the temple should become four-square." Although most commentators have been reluctant to name specific scriptures behind this, Bruce suggests the wording of Dan 9:25 is too similar to be ignored.[43] A second oracle of interest follows immediately in §§ 312-3:

> But what more than all else incited them to the war was an ambiguous oracle, likewise found in their sacred scriptures, to the effect that at that time one from their country would become ruler of the world. This they understood to mean someone of their own race, and many of their wise men went astray in their interpretation of it. The oracle, however, in reality signified the sovereignty of Vespasian, who was proclaimed Emperor on Jewish soil.

Various proposals have been made as to the source of this oracle. Yet a goodly number of recent commentators have seen Dan 9:24-7, in whole or in part, behind it.[44] One of the main reasons is that only the 70-weeks prophecy gives a specific terminal date. Furthermore, there are indications that the Zealot movement promoting the war leaned heavily on Daniel for its belief in imminent deliverance.[45] The cessation of the

[42]This interpretation, from what I can determine, originated with F. F. Bruce, *The Teacher of Righteousness in the Qumran Texts* (London: Tyndale, 1957) 16-7. It has been picked up and now appears widely in the literature. E. g., S. Hahn, "Zur Chronologie der Qumran-Schriften," *Acta Orientalia* 11 (1960) 181-9.

[43]Bruce, "Josephus and Daniel" (note 40 above) 155.

[44]Bruce, "Josephus" 157-8; Str.-B. 4.1002-4; U. Fischer, *Eschatologie* (note 28 above) 158-9; I. Hahn, "Josephus und die Eschatologie von Qumran," *Qumran-Probleme* (Deutsche Akademie der Wissenschaften 42; Berlin: Akademie, 1963) 167-72; H. Lindner, *Die Geschichtsauffassung des Flavius Josephus in Bellum Judaicum* (AGJU 12; Leiden: Brill, 1972) 72.

[45]M. Hengel, *Die Zeloten* (AGJU 1; 2nd edition; Leiden: Brill, 1976) 244-5.

daily offering was evidently very significant, and one prophet
led 6000 to their death on a firm belief in the fulfillment
of this scripture.[46] Regardless of how Josephus himself viewed
such prophecies, he is nevertheless a witness to widespread
belief that the 70-weeks prophecy was being fulfilled in the
Jewish war.

Despite the dashed hopes, the termination of the 70
weeks with the destruction of the temple was still a common
interpretation in post-70 times. The *Seder Olam Rabbah* (chaps.
28 and 30) reckons 490 years from the destruction of the First
Temple to that of the Second Temple.[47] As has already been
mentioned, this requires the artificial shortening of the
Persian period to 34 years. A similar reckoning occurs in *b.*
ʿAbod. Zar. 9a. Christian writers on the whole saw the 70
weeks pointing, in some manner or other, to Christ.[48] But
several seem to reflect Jewish interpretation or a close
parallel. Clement of Alexandria gives a somewhat confused
account but appears to end the 70 weeks with the destruction
of Jerusalem (*Strom.* 1.21.125-6). Similarly, Jerome speaks of
a "view which the Hebrews hold concerning this passage" (*Heb-*
raei quid de hoc loco sentiant).[49] This also ends the 70 weeks
essentially with the fall of the temple, yet the last week is
divided between Vespasian and Hadrian, 3½ years to each.

Much more research on the subject is desirable.
Nonetheless, the statement of F. F. Bruce is clearly established: "The history of the exegesis of the seventy heptads in
Jewish and Christians circles is largely the history of this
further reinterpretation."[50] The importance of the 70 weeks to
chronography, despite the constant reinterpretation, is clear.

---

[46]*J. W.* 6.5.2 §§ 283-7. Cf. Hengel, *Zeloten* 248-9.

[47]See the standard printed editions. The critical
edition and German translation of A. Marx, *Seder ʿOlam*
(Inaugural-Dissertation der Albertus-Universität zu Königsberg,
Berlin, 1903) covers only chapters 1-10. English translation
in J. Williams, *Seder Olam Rabba* (Chronological Institute of
London; London: Strangeways and Walden, 1861).

[48]A survey of patristic interpretation is given by
L. E. Knowles, "The Interpretation of the Seventy Weeks of
Daniel in the Early Fathers," *WTJ* 7 (1944-5) 136-60.

[49]The text is in *Commentariorum in Danielem* (S. Hier-
onymi presbyteri opera, pars I,5; CChr, series latina 75a;
Turnhout: Brepols, 1964) 886-9. For an English translation,
see G. L. Archer, *Jerome's Commentary on Daniel* (1958; reprinted Grand Rapids, MI: Baker, 1977) 108-10. A recent study of
Jerome's comments is J. Braverman, *Jerome's Commentary on
Daniel* (CBQMS 7: Washington, DC: CBA, 1978) 103-12.

[50]F. F. Bruce, "The Book of Daniel and the Qumran
Community," *Neotestamentica et Semitica* (Studies in honour of
Matthew Black; eds. E. Ellis and M. Wilcox; Edinburgh: T. & T.
Clark, 1969) 231.

Periodization

Periodization, dividing history into schemes with
discrete divisions or ages, is well known from literature of
this time, especially Jewish apocalyptic literature. These
schemes are often presented with some sort of symbolic representation such as metals, clouds, shepherds, animals, and the
like. In its ultimate aim periodization often seems to have
the same goal as chronography: the determination of the
future (whether real or only *vaticinio ex eventu*).

Whereas the aspect of chronography which attempts to
predict the future ties future events into some sort of chronological scheme, periodization is less exact. What is important
to it is the sequence of events (succession of empires, rulers,
human events, miraculous phenomena, etc.) Exact timing is not
given. Yet one easily comes to the hypothesis that there may
be some sort of connection between chronography and periodization. It is the purpose of this section to explore some of
the major periodization schemes and the possible nexus with
known chronographical constructions.

Four Metalic Ages/Empires

Perhaps one of the earliest examples of periodization
is the representation of some aspect of human history by the
four metals, gold, silver, bronze, and iron. Our earliest
source in chronological age is undoubtedly Hesiod (*Works and
Days* 106-201), from about 700 B. C.[51] Hesiod's ages represent
a general decline in human existence from age to age, and
there seems to be no tie to chronology except in a very general
sense. The gold and silver ages are in the dim past. The
bronze age seems to represent the heroic age, though the
heroic age has its own place--without metalic symbolism. The
author identifies his own time with the arduous iron age.

The origin of Hesiod's symbolism is still a moot
point,[52] though a good *prima facie* case has been made for seeing it as a scheme borrowed from the East.[53] A similar
scheme of four successive empires represented by the same four
metals is, of course, found in Daniel 2. Again, the dating of
sources is a problem, but there is reason to believe that the
concept of four empires represented by four metals was known

[51]See, e. g., A. Lesky, *A History of Greek Literature*
(tr. J. Willis and C. de Heer; New York: Crowell, 1966) 91.

[52]Cf. J. J. Collins, "The Place of the Fourth Sibyl
in the Development of the Jewish Sibyllina," *JJS* 25 (1973-4)
365-80, especially 371 n. 35.

[53]D. Flusser, "The Four Empires in the Fourth Sibyl
and in the Book of Daniel," *Israel Oriental Studies* 2 (1972)
148-75, especially 165-74.

in early Persian sources and had its origin there.[54]   But,
regardless of its ultimate origin(s), the scheme was extremely
influential in the last couple of centuries B. C. and
thereafter.

The sequence Assyria, Media, Persia, Macedonia was
the frequent identification for the four successive empires in
the earlier sources.[55]   However, with the rise of Rome it was
not surprising that this new power was eventually fitted into
the older scheme.   Sometimes Rome was made a fifth empire after
the other four, but this was not frequent in non-Roman sources.
These generally reinterpreted the older symbolism to make
Rome equal the fourth empire.[56]   This reinterpretation is often
patently obvious in some of our extant sources.[57]

The scheme of four empires seems to have arisen for
purely historical reasons.   At least, symbolism connected with
the number four was probably of minimal significance, if any,
in the origin of the tradition.   However, arithmology seems
to have played an important part in some other schemes.   The
number seven has already been discussed in connection with the
concept of the world week and the seventy weeks of Daniel.   The
numbers ten and twelve also figure in various sources.

Ten Periods

One of the earliest sequences of ten is the Apocalypse of Weeks in the Ethiopic Enoch (93:1-10 and 91:12-7).
These may well have arisen from Jeremiah's 70 years (Jer. 25:

---

[54]Ibid., 165-74.

[55]E. g., Ctesias gave the sequence Assyria, Media,
Persia (Diodorus Siculus, book 2).   Velleius Paterculus quotes
a certain Aemilius Sura (probably from early or middle 2nd
century B. C.) who gives the sequence Assyrians, Medes, Per-
sians, Macedonians (1.6.6).   See also Polybius 38.22.2; Diony-
sius of Halicarnassus, *Ant.* 1.2.1-4; Tacitus, *Hist.* 5.8.   For
a full discussion, see J. W. Swain, "The Theory of the Four
Monarchies, Opposition History under the Roman Empires,"
Classical Philology 35 (1940) 1-21; Flusser, "Four Empires."

[56]The 4 Sibylline Oracle (see next note), Josephus
Ant. 10.11.7 §§ 276-7), and 4 Ezra (12:10-1)--all toward the
end of the 1st century--are the earliest known sources to make
Rome the fourth.   For further discussion, see Flusser and
Swain.   On the various interpretations of Daniel, see H. H.
Rowley, *Darius the Mede and the Four World Empires in the Book
of Daniel* (Cardiff: University of Wales, 1935).

[57]This is very clear in the 4 Sibylline Oracle in
which Assyria is called the first empire; Media, the second;
Persia, the third; but when Macedonia comes up, no number is
given; finally, Rome is called the fourth.

11; 29:10).[58] It has also been suggested that each of the
weeks represents a fixed period of time, such as 700 years.
However, this suggestion has been rejected for the most part.[59]
More probable is the suggestion that the Apocalypse is made
up of two parts, a seven-week period and then three additional
eschatological weeks. The first seven weeks represent actual
history while the last three are still future to the writer.

The figure ten is also found in the Apocalypse of
Ezra 14:11 but in the Ethiopic version only. The other versions have the number twelve which is most likely the original
figure (see below). But the presence of "ten" in the Ethiopic
translation shows the continued importance of that number in
periodization.[60] 4Q Melchizedek is another document in which
ten is important. Unfortunately, the text is very broken, but
in line 7 the "last jubilee year" is evidently equivalent to
"the tenth jubilee" in the same line.[61] The ten jubilees or
490 years in this text seem to come from the 70-weeks prophecy
of Dan 9:24-7.[62]

The most interesting text with the figure ten is the
Fourth Sibylline Oracle (c. 80 A. D.). In it history is
divided into ten generations; the text is intriguing in that
these ten generations are also divided up among the (original)
four empires which were discussed above. A further point of
considerable interest is that the core of this work is a Hellenistic oracle which probably had its ultimate roots in
Persia.[63] The oracle as it stands is, of course, eschatologi-

---

[58]Str-B. 4.996, 1001 connects the Vision of the
Seventy Shepherds with the 70 years of Jeremiah. However, it
seems just as likely that the 10 weeks of the Apocalypse of
Weeks could have arisen from Jeremiah's figure.

[59]See F. Dexinger, *Henochs Zehnwochenapokalypse und
offene Probleme der Apokalyptikforschung* (SPB 29; Leiden:
Brill, 1977), especially 119-29 and the literature cited
there.

[60]Other unique readings in the various versions
sometimes seem to represent the innovations of the translator.
E. g., the 400 years of 7:28 are given as 1000 years by one of
the Arabic versions and 30 years by the Syriac version. Both
seem to be Christian assimilations.

[61]M. de Jonge and A. S. van der Woude, "11Q Melchizedek and the New Testament," *NTS* 12 (1965-6) 301-26; text
and translation on 302-3.

[62]De Jonge and van der Woude, "11Q Melchizedek" 304;
J. A. Fitzmyer, "Further Light on Melchizedek from Qumran Cave
11," *Essays on the Semitic Background of the New Testament*
(1971; reprinted SBLSBS 5; Missoula, MT: Scholars, 1974) 259.

[63]Collins, "The Fourth Sibyl" (note 52 above)
370-6; cf. Flusser, "The Four Empires" (note 53 above) 162-74.

cally oriented as was evidently the earlier Hellenistic oracle and the Persian sources of this. Collins also suggests the likelihood of some connection with the concept of the Great Year (a theme to be considered below).[64]

Twelve Periods

The original text of 4 Ezra 14:11-2 evidently divided history into 12 periods, 9½ of which have passed and 2½ of which remain.[65] The roughly contemporary Apocalypse of Baruch has two divisions of 12. In chapter 27 the endtime tribulation is divided into 12 parts. A recent interpretation begins the first period with Pontius Pilate's procuratorship and puts the eleventh period at the time of the writing of the book in the 90's A. D. The twelvth period was still future.[66] If this is correct, the scheme of 12 embraced only the "endtime." But the Vision of the Waters (53-74) takes in the whole of history from Adam to the Messianic age. The Apocalypse of Abraham 29 (c. 80-100 A. D.) speaks of 12 years which seem to encompass human history, but there are difficulties. Chapter 28 speaks of an hour's equalling 100 years. It has been suggested that chapter 29 should read "hour" instead of "year"; this would make the 12 periods equal less than human history.[67]

Periodization and Exact Calculation

Although periodization is not the same as exact chronographical calculation, both are definitely related and at times cannot be separated from one another. Chronography can be as stylized and artificial as periodization. Whether one preceded the other in the developing historical consciousness is a question which seems impossible to answer. But, in any case, chronography seems to be found as early in our extant sources as periodization. For example, the Sumerian king list which has been traced back to the 21st century B. C. gives specific lengths of reign to its antediluvian kings. The kings themselves are legendary and the fantastic lengths of reign are undoubtedly stylized on the Mesopotamian sexagesimal system. Nevertheless, this may represent chronography (actual dates) combined with periodization (the stereotyped figures of ten

---

[64]Ibid., 375-6.

[65]See note 36 above for commentaries on 4 Ezra.

[66]P. Bogaert, *L'apocalypse syriaque de Baruch* (SC 144-5; 2 vols.; Paris: Editions du Cerf, 1969) 1.291-3.

[67]G. H. Box, *The Apocalypse of Abraham* (London: SPCK, 1918) 76-8. There is a large Christian interpolation in chapter 29, but the passage in question does not appear to be a part of it.

kings).[68] Similarly, the OT genealogies combine chronographical data with periodized genealogies.[69]

That periodical listings can often lead to attempts at more exact chronology is clear. One thinks of Hellanicus of Lesbos who attempted to turn the Greek genealogies into chronology by reckoning three generations to the century.[70] The figure 480 years in 1 Kings 6:1 has been thought to be a stylized figure from 12 generations of 40 years each.[71] The use of the jubilee year is a case in which periodization and chronography meet. The writers who believed fervently in the efficacy of the jubilee would not find it difficult to think history was also divided into discrete whole jubilee periods. Thus, for the author of the Book of Jubilees, the Exodus came at the "jubilee of jubilees." The Assumption of Moses also seems to have made use of the "jubilee of jubilees" even though this jubilee cycle was different from that in the Book of Jubilees (50 years instead of 49).[72]

Naturally, no blanket statement can be made to the effect that periodization always or even often presupposes some sort of more exact chronographical scheme. On the contrary, periodization was probably chosen by some individual writers for the simple reason that no exact schematization with fixed numbers of years could be used. Thus, the Apocalypse of Weeks in 1 Enoch and the Vision of Waters in 2 Baruch seem to use periodization because this alone would fit their division of history whereas exact cycles of years would not. Periodization allowed them to see a divine plan in history

---

[68] For the Sumerian king list, see T. Jacobsen, *The Sumerian King List* (Oriental Institute Assyriological Studies 11; Chicago: University of Chicago, 1939). However, the antediluvian list of kings was evidently a later addition to the list (Jacobsen 55-68) though still at least as early as the early 2nd millennium B. C. Cf. also J. J. Finkelstein, "The Antediluvian Kings: A University of California Tablet," *JCS* 17 (1963) 39-51. It is still a moot point as to whether the 10 kings of Berossus or the 8 kings of the Sumerian king list is more original; the evidence at the present seems to favor the originality of 8 (Finkelstein 50).

[69] The figures of 10 generations from Adam to Noah and of 10 from the Flood to Abraham certainly suggest stylization.

[70] Lesky, *History* (note 51 above) 330. The question of Hellanicus' actual contribution is a moot point. On this and the question of historical genealogy in general, see D. W. Prakken, *Studies in Greek Genealogical Chronology* (Lancaster, PA: Lancaster, 1943).

[71] E. g., J. Bright, *A History of Israel* (2nd edition; Philadelphia: Westminster, 1972) 121.

[72] On the whole subject, see E. Wiesenberg, "The Jubilee of Jubilees," *RevQ* 3 (1961-2) 3-40.

even though chronography gave them no help.[73] Yet one must
always reckon with the possibility--unless there is proof to
the contrary--that a periodical scheme may actually hide an
exact chronographical scheme which the writer has not made
explicit or which the vicissitudes of history have obscured
through the preservation of the text in question.

A further consideration is that chronography may
apply to only one of a number of events. Various writings
give a sequence of events preceding the eschaton, e. g., the
Messianic woes, or the events in the apocalypse of the Gospels
or in the Book of Revelation. The author may not have a
chronographical calculation for each separate event but may
have one for the final culmination, e. g., the completion of
the 70 weeks of Dan 9:24-7 or the completion of 6000 years of
human history (Rev 20). In such cases chronography and
periodization may overlap at only one point but are still no
less tightly joined together.

Another concept which seems to have influenced Jewish writers is more problematic, perhaps because it has not
been so thoroughly studied. This is the idea of the Great
Year. The concept itself is not monochromatic but takes on
different forms in different sources. According to Seneca
(*Nat. quaes.* 3.29.1) this was even to be found in Berossus who
wrote of a "winter" (culminating in a deluge) and a "summer"
(culminating in universal conflagration) in each Great Year.
Whether Berossus actually wrote of such is still uncertain,
but the idea does seem to be Near Eastern in origin. The Great
Year was also accorded various lengths, again making an inter-
connection between periodization and chronography. The Great
Year does not appear to be explicit in any of the intertestamental Jewish writings. Nevertheless, it may lie behind some
of them. For example, a universal conflagration underlies a
number of the Sibylline Oracles; this conflagrations may
itself show influence or perhaps even a more wholesale
borrowing from the Great Year.[74]

---

[73]Cf. J. Licht, "Time and Eschatology in Apocalyptic
Literature and in Qumran," *JJS* 16 (1965) 177-82.

[74]Especially important is B. L. van der Waerden,
"Das Grosse Jahr und die ewige Wiederkehr," *Hermes* 80 (1952)
129-55. See also R. van den Broek, *The Myth of the Phoenix*
(Leiden: Brill, 1972), who discusses the question in the
context of the appearances of the phoenix in his chapter 5
(especially pp. 72-6, 89-112). For a recent argument that
Berossus did not hold the view expressed in Seneca, see W. G.
Lambert, "Berossus and Babylonian Eschatology," *Iraq* 38 (1976)
171-3. For a discussion of the Great Year and universal conflagration, especially as they relate to the Sibylline Oracles,
see J. J. Collins, *The Sibylline Oracles of Egyptian Judaism*
(SBLDS 13; Missoula, MT: Scholars, 1974) 101-6.

Comparison with Greek Chronicles
and Jewish Religious Writings

It is hardly any surprise that Jewish writers in
Greek often adopt Hellenistic modes and exhibit Hellenistic
values. Nor does acknowledgment of this fact in any way deny
that they also exhibit unique Jewish characteristics in contrast to pagan writers in Greek. The duty of the investigator
is to see how the two intellectual traditions have been synthe-
sized and to outline the characteristics of the resultant
product, in this case Hellenistic Jewish chronography. The
early Jewish writings in Hebrew or Aramaic are important because they often show the continued development or interpretation of the tradition with the minimum of Greek influence.
Even translation into Greek of original Semitic writings frequently represents an adjustment to Hellenistic models and
values.[75] But a writing like the Book of Jubilees evidently
shows how the OT tradition is developed by one with calendrical
and chronographical concerns apart from the direct influence
of Hellenistic historical writings. A consideration of both
Greek chronography and Semitic religious writing is important
for a correct assessment.

As already commented on, it is not entirely clear
how encompassing Wacholder intends his three-stage development
in Jewish chronography to be. His internal headings read,
"First Stage--Reconciling Biblical Dates," "Second Stage--
Fusion of Biblical and Greek Myth," "Third Stage--Fusion of
Bible with World Chronicle." There is no discussion which
gives an integrated theory of actual development, however, so
that any of the comments in the next few paragraphs may, in
fact, have nothing to do with Wacholder's actual point of view.
It seems to me that the development of Jewish chronography
has two major aspects: one is the internal momentum of the
Old Testament tradition itself; the other is the direct
influence of the common Hellenistic culture.

The OT tradition would of itself be continued in
certain directions without any outside influence. Like other
Near Eastern traditions, but in contrast with the Greek, the
OT tradition already had the makings of a chronographical
system in that actual dates, or figures which implied dates,
were a part of the tradition itself. Whereas Greek writers
such as Hellanicus had to try to work from bare genealogical
lists, the native historians of the Near East had ages of reign
or lifespan included along with their lists of rulers,
patriarchs, etc. It was only a matter of time before some
enterprising exegete took it upon himself to continue the

---

[75]Perhaps no better example of this can be found
than Ben Sira 51 in which the original was expressed in very
erotic language but was greatly transformed in the Greek
translation. See J. A. Sanders, *The Psalms Scroll of Qumran
Cave 11* (DJD 4; Oxford: Clarendon, 1965); *The Dead Sea Psalms
Scroll* (Ithaca: Cornell, 1967) 112-17.

process which had already begun. It required no Hellenistic
impetus to begin noticing contradictions and difficulties within the chronological data of the tradition itself and to
attempt to resolve these. Similarly, it was only natural to
begin asking when undated events took place in relation to
other events. Thus, Wacholder's "First Stage" (reconciling
biblical dates) would not have been a special Hellenistic
characteristic of Jewish chronography; similarly with assigning
dates to previously undated events. One cannot, of course,
rule out the possibility of Greek influence having something
to do with this stage of the development but such an explanation is unnecessary and unprovable.

        The OT historical and other writings were not ignor-
ant of events in the larger world. The existence and
activities of other peoples and empires are often referred to.
But this in no way compares with the Greek attempt to give the
history of nations other than one's own. The concept of
universal history was a definite Greek intellectual contribution, and undoubtedly supplied the catalyst for Jewish writers
to relate their history and tradition to that of Greece and
the broader world. Wacholder gives his next two stages as
"Second Stage--Fusion of Biblical and Greek Myth" and "Third
Stage--Fusion of Bible with World Chronicle." As he illustrates one can find examples of each in different Jewish
writings. However, it is a question whether the two can be
segregated as separate stages or whether they are only two
different aspects of one process which a Greek would not have
regarded as divisible.

        Jewish writers sometimes exhibit an astonishingly
free hand in reinterpreting the biblical tradition (e. g.,
Artapanus), but none of them seem to de-mythify their tradition in the same way that various Greek writers did.[76] This
is not to say that Greek historians were often willing to reject the mythical and legendary period out of hand. On the
contrary, it was generally regarded as historical in some way
even if criticized or slighted. With the progression of time
and the rise of universal history, Hellenistic historians
seemed more willing to incorporate the mythical/legendary
period into their schemes of world history. Thus, when the
Jewish or other Oriental writers such as Berossus and Manetho
wrote up their mythical past as if it were on the same level
as more recent history, theirs was only a difference in degree
--and not in kind--from the Greek historians. In dealing with

_____

        [76]One of the major elements of de-mythifying was to
assume that the gods were simply deified kings. This concept
is usually credited to Euhemerus (hence "euhemerism"), though
O. Murray claims Hecataeus of Abdera was actually the origina-
tor in "Hecataeus of Abdera and Pharaonic Kingship," *JEA* 56
(1970) 141-71, especially 151. On euhemerism, see also T. S.
Brown, "Euhemerus and the Historians," *HTR* 39 (1946) 259-74.
On the incorporation of Greek legend into universal history,
see Drews, "Assyria" (note 39 above) 131-7.

the Greek mythical period the Jewish writers naturally de-
mythified it by means of euhemeristic principles. Nevertheless, they treated it as an obscure, mythified but still
historical period much as the Greeks did. The only difference
is that they identified early figures with biblical ones and
otherwise attempted to show the antiquity and priority of
their own ancestors. This seems to indicate that the fusion
of the biblical tradition with Greek myth and the entry of
biblical history into Hellenistic universal history were all
part of the same process rather than separate steps.

When we turn to periodized schemes such as the world
week or the prophecy of the 70 weeks, we have left the Greek
for the purely Jewish again. While oracles were certainly not
unknown in the Greek milieu, these do not, to the best of my
knowledge, appreciably affect the pagan writing of history.
It is not yet clear whether the world-week concept has influenced the Jewish historians. Unless the idea is much older
than the 1st century, only Josephus and Justus would come into
purview in any case, but the question needs further investigation. On the other hand, the 70-weeks prophecy has plainly
affected Josephus' account at several places. By the time
Josephus sat down to write the *War* and especially the *Antiquities*, he opposed the Zealot and other radical movements and
the apocalyptic interpretations used to justify them. He lets
us know with some disdain how the people were exploited by
false prophets to continue the futile war against Rome. Certainly Josephus was a member of a stratum of Jewish society
which was less likely to be influenced by such apocalyptic
speculations. Yet it seems that we cannot presently rule out
a closer identification of Josephus' own opinions with such
speculations in his earlier life, especially before the war
turned against the Jews.[77] If Josephus was at one time more
sympathetic to views of this sort, his writings may exhibit
influences from these quarters which have not yet been noted
by scholars.

A Further Program

This essay has been an admittedly preliminary and
sometimes groping attempt to come to grips with a large and
complex subject. The whole question deserves a full-scale
study; present plans are that this paper is only the first
stage to full-scale treatment of the subject. Wacholder spoke
of "chronological hermeneutics" which developed as an adjunct
of interpretation already going on.[78] The use of chronography
as a midrashic or hermeneutical device certainly needs careful
investigation. Some of the questions still to be answered or
to be answered in greater detail are the following:

---

[77]Fischer, *Eschatologie* (note 28 above) 180-3, has
an interesting discussion of the question.

[78]Wacholder, *Eupolemus* 128.

1. What were the individual chronographical systems devised by different writers; how did they relate to one another in individual data; and in what way were they alike and different as conceptual systems?

2. To what extent did earlier writings (e. g., Demetrius) influence later (e. g., *Seder Olam Rabbah*) when no clear connection is immediately apparent?

3. What are the major characteristics in which Jewish historians resembled and differed from their Hellenistic colleagues?

4. To what degree have Persian ideas (especially in eschatology and periodization) influenced Jewish historiography in contrast to Greek historiography?

5. To what extent do early Christian chronographers preserve the schemes of Jewish chronographers whose writings have otherwise perished?

The task of answering these questions has only begun, but it is hoped that this essay has in some small measure moved toward the final goal.

EUSEBIUS, JOSEPHUS AND THE FATE OF THE JEWS
Robert M. Grant, University of Chicago

At the beginning of the Church History Eusebius
explicitly promised to discuss "the consequences which
came upon the whole nation of the Jews for the plot
against our Savior." He apparently derived the notion
of Jewish plots, along with the word epiboule, from the
Acts of the Apostles.[1] Others had spoken of plots;
indeed, the Church History itself is full of them.
Eusebius mentions plots against his hero Origen, and
Origen mentions them himself.[2] The idea of consequences
falling upon "the whole nation of the Jews," however,
clearly involves an interpretation of the fall of
Jerusalem in the year 70, and in the course of the
Church History it becomes clear that Eusebius connects
this event with the crucifixion of Jesus.

Other attempts had been made to explain the fall
of the city, notably by the Hellenistic Jewish general
and historian Josephus. He ascribed it primarily to
sedition and the rise of tyrants as rulers in Jerusalem.[3]
Christian writers had frequently discussed the topic but
had not connected the fall with the crucifixion until
early in the third century, when Tertullian developed
the theme in his treatise Adversus Marcionem.[4] We
should certainly not suppose that Eusebius got the idea
from any Latin writer. Instead, he indubitably derived
it from the Alexandrian-Caesarean theologian Origen,
and specifically from works produced in Origen's later
years at Caesarea.

Eusebius relied not only on Origen's theological
point or points but also on his interpretations of first-
century Christian and Jewish historical details. We
intend to examine these details and then turn to conclusions.

It was helpful to correlate the gospel accounts
of the crucifixion to Jesus with statements made by
non-Christian chronologists. Early Christian apologists
were able to find two such writers apart from the more
important Hellenistic Jewish authors Philo and Josephus.
These two were a Euhemerist antiquarian, of uncertain
date, named Thallus,[5] and a freedman of Hadrian named
Phlegon.[6] Thallus deserves little attention. Jacoby's
first Testimonium, from the Armenian version of the
Chronicle of Eusebius, states that Thallus dealt with
events from the capture of Troy to the 167th Olympiad
(112-109 B.C.). This is almost certainly wrong, not
only because Thallus is said to have discussed an
eclipse in the 4th year of the 202nd Olympiad "in the
third book of his Histories" but also because, according to Theophilus of Antioch he held that Belos, king
of the Assyrians, lived 322 years before the Trojan
war.[7] Our primary concern is with the fragment on the

70

eclipse. It comes from the Christian chronographer
Julius Africanus, who wrote of the darkness at the time
of the crucifixion that "Thallus calls this darkness a
solar eclipse -- unreasonably, it seems to me."[8] The
unreasonableness was of course related to the time of
the crucifixion, at Passover, when with a full moon a
solar eclipse is impossible. It remains uncertain
whether Thallus actually mentioned the "darkness" or
not. Perhaps he simply mentioned the solar eclipse
of November 24, 29.[9] The references to solar eclipse
Bithynian earthquake, and the collapse of buildings in
Nicaea[10]- cited by Eusebius without reference to
author -- may come from him.

Phlegon should be taken more seriously.[11] It looks
as though he actually discussed Jesus, though not very
accurately. According to Origen, in the 13th or 14th
book of his _Chronicle_ Phlegon "even grants to Christ
foreknowledge of certain future events, although he was
muddled and said that some things which really happened
to Peter happened to Jesus; and he testified that it
turned out in accordance with what Jesus had said." As
for the precise reference Origen betrays his own vagueness by adding "I think" to the book numbers.[12] It is
hard to tell just what he had in mind, except that in
the _Commentary_ _on_ _Matthew_ Origen relies on Phlegon for
the fact that the destruction of Jerusalem and the
temple took place in about the 40th year from the 15th
year of Tiberius Caesar.[13] Surely Phlegon would not
have mentioned that year of Tiberius had he not been
concerned with the Christian gospel. Again in Phlegon's
13th or 14th book, "I think," Origen knew that there
were accounts of the eclipse "in the time of Tiberius
Caesar, during whose reign Jesus appears to have been
crucified," and of "the great earthquakes that
happened at that time."[14] The _Commentary_ _on_ _Matthew_
again adds an important detail. "Phlegon . . . wrote
that this happened, but he did not indicate that it
happened at full moon."[15]

What looks like an explicit quotation is to be
found in the _Chronicle_ of Eusebius, where we read that
in the 13th book Phlegon writes thus:[16]

> And in the fourth year of the 202nd
> Olympiad there was a great eclipse of
> the sun, surpassing all that came be-
> fore it. At the sixth hour the day
> was turned into such complete darkness
> that the stars were seen in the sky:
> earthquakes in Bithynia overturned
> many buildings in the city of Nicaea.

The essence of the quotation recurs in Philoponus'
treatise _De_ _opificio_ _mundi_.[17] There is no reason to
question its authenticity. If the year was actually OL.

202, 4 there was an eclipse of the moon on April 3,
33, and this may be what Phlegon has in mind. There
is also little reason to suppose that Phlegon had the
events related to Jesus in mind when he was writing
such words. A passage now to be found in the remains
of Africanus' Chronicle suggests that Phlegon actually
dealt with a miraculous eclipse at the time of the
crucifixion, but this is open to a good deal of suspicion. The fragment reads that "Phlegon says that
under Tiberius Caesar there was a total eclipse of the
sun when the moon was full, from the sixth hour to the
ninth. Clearly this is the same" as the one hinted at
in the gospels.[18]   First, Africanus has already dealt
with the so-called eclipse described by Thallus and
has stated that he rejects the running together of
this with the gospels. Second, since he has dealt
with Thallus there was no reason for him to deal with
the analogous account in Phlegon and then accept it.
The passage is to be viewed as a late interpolation
by someone with more piety than intelligence.[19]   It is
not the normal third- or fourth-century view.

Writers about predictions and eclipses might
contribute something toward confirming the Christian
pictures of historical events. Obviously they did
not contribute much. For greater support it was
necessary to turn to the writings of Hellenistic
Jewish authors like Philo and Josephus, especially
since their writings were being preserved chiefly by
Christians rather than Jews, and specifically in support of apologetic theology. Since they lived and
wrote in the first Christian century it could be
expected that they would lend support if not credibility
to the Christian accounts.

The account of Jesus now found in Josephus'
Antiquities (XVIII 63-64) presents many difficulties,
not the least being the fact that in its present form
it is essentially Christian. "He was the Christ . . .
For he appeared to them, alive again, on the third day,
since the divine prophets foretold these and countless
other marvels concerning him." If Josephus said anything about Jesus, it cannot have been so complimentary,
as his reference to "the brother of the so-called
Christ" (Ant. XX 200) shows. In addition, Origen
explicitly testifies that Josephus did not "accept"
or "believe in" Jesus as Christ.[20]   The passage, at
least in its present form, cannot have stood in Origen's
manuscript of Josephus, the one available in the school
library at Caesarea. C. Martin has suggested that the
Christian statements to which we have referred come from
marginal notes in the manuscript, used by Origen or
even made by him.[21]   Such a suggestion has the merit of
agreeing with Origen's comments and explaining how it
was that Eusebius of Caesarea made use of the whole
passage.[22]   We may add that the passage was certainly

absent from the text of Josephus which Photius carefully
excerpted at Constantinople in the ninth century. Photius
diligently noted the deaths of John the Precursor and
James the Lord's brother, but simply said of Herod Antipas.
that "in his time the salvific Passion took place."[23] The
question of evidence was important to Photius. In
writing on the Chronicle of Justus of Tiberias he took
pains to point out that Justus wrote nothing about
Christ.[24]

     The account of John the Baptist was more certainly
present in the text of Josephus' Antiquities (XVIII 116-
19). The tetrarch Herod feared sedition or revolt because
of John's preaching, even though he had urged nothing but
virtue and piety, and therefore executed him. The
moral Josephus draws is one which his Christian readers
found attractive. "To some of the Jews the [later]
destruction of Herod's army seemed to be divine vengeance,
and certainly a just vengeance, for his treatment of John."
Again, "the destruction visited upon Herod's army was a
vindication of John, since God saw fit to inflict such a
blow on Herod." Origen, and especially Eusebius, shared
this kind of view.

     Origen referred to the passage but interpreted it
in his own special way.[25] Josephus had written that
piety had to precede John's baptism. It was to be
employed "not for the pardon of various sins but for the
purification of the body when the soul had already been
cleansed by righteousness." Such a description is not
entirely different from what could be found in early
Christian baptism, which obviously involved at least the
intention of righteousness. But there are different
emphases in the two cases. Origen made John's baptism
thoroughly Christian, claiming that he was simply
relying on Josephus. "A man who lived not long after
John and Jesus recorded that John was a baptist who
baptized for the remission of sins. For Josephus in
the eighteenth book of the Jewish antiquities bears
witness that John was a baptist who baptized for the
remission of sins." The expression "for the remission
of sins" is thoroughly Christian and Josephus did not
use it.

     Eusebius cites the passage about John the Baptist
as "confirming the testimony recorded in the gospel
writings about him" but more sensibly refrains from
discussing the kind of baptism provided by John."[26]
In the Demonstratio he is concerned with John as fulfilling
the prophecy of "a voice crying in the desert" (Isaiah 40)
and speaks of him as proclaiming "the cleansing of the
soul."[27] These words prove that Eusebius knew the whole
passage from Josephus, though in quoting it here he brought
it to a close just before the clause, "not for the pardon
of various sins but for the purification of the body when

the soul had already been cleansed by righteousness.
Eusebius obviously suppressed this as contradicting the
gospel accounts.

It is sometimes supposed that Origen made use of
Josephus' description of the false prophet Theudas
(Antiquities XX 97, followed by a reference to the rebel
leader Judas in 102). Such a supposition is quite unnecessary. In his Commentary on John Origen referred to
Theudas as coming before Judas but he did so not on
account of any correct or incorrect reading of Josephus.
He was following Acts 5:36-37 and, indeed, quoting part
of verse 37.[28]

More important is what later Christian writers do
with Josephus' account of James the Lord's brother
(Antiquities XX 197-203). The earliest witness to the
Josephan account might be supposed to be Hegesippus, as
cited by Eusebius in the Church History (II 23, 16-17).
In this section of Hegesippus' work, as in Josephus,
James is described as being stoned. But the account of
Hegesippus is so confused, portraying James as thrown
down from the wing of the temple, stoned, and struck
on the head with a launderer's club, that E. Schwartz
thought the mention of stoning had been interpolated --
though in any case from Josephus.[29] In the Nag Hammadi
Second Apocalypse James is thrown down and then stoned
in a peculiar way.[30] Probably one should conclude that
neither Hegesippus nor the author of this apocalypse
was acquainted with Josephus' story of the death of
James. And certainly it was unknown at Alexandria.
According to the Hypothyposes of Clement, James the Just
"was thrown down from the wing of the temple and beaten
to death with a launderer's club."[31] It is precisely
the stoning mentioned by Josephus that is omitted.
Clement did not know Josephus' account. Similarly
Origen is ignorant of it, at least in the form in
which it is known to others. He makes no reference
to a "political" narrative like the one Josephus gives.
Instead, he refers twice to the theological consequences of
James's death in such a way as to suggest that his interpretation has somehow replaced the original text.[32] The
first example occurs in the Commentary on Matthew.

> Josephus . . . desirous of setting
> forth the reason for which the people
> experienced such suffering that even
> the temple was destroyed, stated that
> these things happened to them in ac-
> cordance with the wrath of God because
> of what they ventured to do to James
> the brother of Jesus the so-called
> Christ. What is marvelous is that though
> Josephus did not accept our Jesus as
> Christ, he none the less ascribed such

> righteousness to James: he says that
> the people supposed that they suffered
> these things on account of James.

Origen rightly states that Josephus was concerned with the
causes for the destruction of Jerusalem. The theme comes
up repeatedly, especially in the Jewish War but also in
the Jewish Antiquities. But there is one cause for
the catastrophe which Josephus never mentions, and that
is the execution of James under the high priest Ananus.
Indeed, in the Jewish War Josephus argued that the sack of
Jerusalem took its beginning from the murder of Ananus
by revolutionary forces. "The overthrow of the wall and
the downfall of the Jewish state dated from the day on
which the Jews beheld their high priest, the captain of
their salvation, slain in the middle of the city."[33]
The oddness of this is all the greater because, as my
father noted, the expression "captain of salvation"
recalls what is said of Jesus in Hebrews 2:10, while
"slain in the middle of the city" is how Melito of
Sardis describes Jesus in his Paschal Homily.[34] What
Josephus does in the Jewish War is ascribe cosmic
significance to the death of the high priest Ananus.
On the other hand, by the time he comes to describe him
in the Antiquities and his own autobiography he is more
unfavorably impressed by Ananus' acceptance of bribes
to expel Josephus himself from Galilee,[35] and therefore
he is glad to describe his judicial murder of James,
"brother of the so-called Christ," in an account which
Origen could have used had he known it. What Origen seems
to know, however, is an account in which the death of
James actually led to the fall of Jerusalem, just as in
Hegesippus' Christian narrative we have first the death
of James and then the statement that "and at once Vespasian
began to besiege them."[36] What he has in common with the
real Josephus is no more than the name of James's brother
"the so-called Christ," and James's death.

> Origen takes up this subject again in Contra
Celsum I 47, where he reiterates the thought that Josephus,
though a non-believer, was seeking for the reason for the
fall of Jerusalem and the destruction of the temple.

> He should have said that the plot
> against Jesus was the cause of
> these disasters for the people,
> since they killed the predicted
> Christ; but as if unwillingly
> coming not far from the truth he
> said that these things occurred to
> the Jews to avenge James the Just,
> who was the brother of Jesus the
> so-called Christ.

Origen sums up his argument a little farther on.

> If then he says that the events
> related to the devastation of
> Jerusalem took place for the Jews
> because of James, is it not more
> reasonable to say that they took
> place because of Jesus the Christ?

It is clear that Origen has a text of Josephus that has
already been altered away from Josephus' own reading of
the events in the direction of a Christian theodicy
rather than a Jewish one. Origen also twice states that
James was famous for his righteousness or justice; this
note, ascribed to Josephus, comes from the Christian
tradition. But Origen does not go quite so far as
to quote Josephus directly on the subject of the death
of James. Similarly Eusebius, writing his early
Chronicle, contents himself with stating that "James
the Lord's brother, whom all called the Just, was killed
by stoning by the Jews."[31] The notion of James as "the
Just" is Christian, but the death by stoning is from
Josephus, as is the date in Nero's seventh year (A.D.
60-61 or 61-62). This must of course be approximately
correct for Albinus' arrival after the death of James.,
for according to Josephus, Bell. VI 300 and 305,
Albinus was governor four years before the war, i.e. in
62.

When Eusebius wrote the Chronicle, we can see, he
did not know or was not impressed by the account of Hegesippus, according to which James was rather more than stoned
and in addition was put to death immediately before the
siege of Jerusalem by Vespasian, probably in 69. He
knew some Christian story on the subject but his primary
source was the real Josephus.

In producing the Church History, however, he took
Origen's comments much more seriously. Thus after quoting
Hegesippus' story of the death of James and insisting
(wrongly) that it agrees with Clement's, he goes on to say
that "James was so famous for his righteousness that intelligent Jews supposed that this [his death] was the
cause of the siege of Jerusalem immediately after his
martyrdom; it happened because of nothing else but the
crime they had committed against him."[38] Who are the
intelligent Jews? None other than Josephus himself, as
described by Origen in the Commentary on Matthew: "He
says that the people too thought that they suffered these
things on account of James." The word "cause" (aitia),
used in regard to Josephus' search, also comes from Origen's
accounts. The word "immediately," however, was added
by Eusebius himself when he tried to connect his Origenist
Josephus with the fanciful account given by Hegesippus.
It was Hegesippus, not Josephus, who supposed that the
siege of Jerusalem began immediately after the death
of James.

Eusebius was not content with a periphrastic statement about Josephus. He wanted to appeal to Josephus himself as his authority. He therefore did so. "As a matter of fact Josephus did not hesitate to testify to this in writing, when he speaks in the following terms: 'Now these things happened to the Jews to avenge James the Just, who was a brother of Jesus the so-called Christ, since the Jews killed him though he was the most righteous of men.'"[39] This is exactly what Origen had claimed Josephus said; this time the language comes from the treatise Contra Celsum, adjusted from indirect to direct discourse. Unlike Origen, however, Eusebius looked up the passage about James in Josephus' Antiquities and found it in the twentieth book. It was too valuable a passage to omit from the Church History, even though it did not contain the passage Origen had mentioned. Eusebius therefore proceeded to quote it.[40]

By this time he was somewhat confused, since (no matter what he says about them) his sources did not agree on crucial matters. Hegesippus called James's opponents "scribes and Pharisees," while Josephus called the hostile high priest a Sadducee and claimed that "strict observers of the law" (Pharisees) opposed him. Hegesippus set the siege of Jerusalem just after James's death, while according to the chronology of Josephus it took place six or seven years later.

Apparently Eusebius at first maintained the view of Josephus, already followed in the Chronicle. He dates Paul's appeal to Caesar and Festus' rule in Judaea early in the reign of Nero, certainly not later than 62. For this reason he could quote a lengthy passage from the Jewish War in which Josephus definitely placed the rule of Albinus, procurator just after James's death, "four years before the war."[41] When he began making use of Hegesippus it was necessary to do a good deal of tinkering. He made the extraordinary claim that Hegesippus belonged to the first "succession" from the apostles and added that he gave the most accurate account of James's death. Next he added the word "immediately" to his first Origenist Josephus notice. He probably deleted the part of the story of Jesus son of Ananias in which the Roman governor was identified as Albinus.[43] And in writing Book III, still using Hegesippus, he referred to "the martyrdom of James and the capture of Jerusalem that took place immediately afterward."[44] All these passages illustrate the confusion resulting from contradictory sources.

In any case, by the time we reach the present state of the Church History the authentic text of Josephus is still present (as it was not for Origen) but it has been devalued in favor of the Origenist Josephus and Hegesippus.

Apart from episodes related to Jesus, John, and James, it was important for Christian authors to find Hellenistic Jewish support for the narratives related to the beginnings of Jewish suffering -- the suffering so well deserved on account of the crucifixion. In dealing with this subject we shall vary our usual procedure and deal first with the full-blown legendary picture to be found in Eusebius' writings, then with the way in which this picture was developed. Actually we should speak of two legendary pictures, for the one in the Chronicle is different from the one in the Demonstratio. In the Chronicle Eusebius first discusses his pagan authorities for earthquake and eclipse, then turns to Josephus as his authority for a startling event "around these times on the day of Pentecost."[45] Priests experienced an earthquake and heard a voice saying, "Let us go forth from this place." Josephus also told how "in the same year" at night Pilate put images of Caesar in the temple.[46] "And this was the first cause of sedition and disturbances for the Jews." Presumably Eusebius was aware that Origen had discussed both these passages from Josephus. Like Josephus himself, Origen[47] had given no date for the voices in the temple. This was Eusebius' contribution to this story. On the other hand, Origen had stated that in the time of Pontius Pilate there was an attempt to set up a statue of Caesar[48] in the temple; another took place under Gaius. Here Origen makes a contribution. He mixes up the episode of the military standards in Jerusalem under Pilate with that of the imperial statue in the temple under Gaius. Unfortunately he led Eusebius astray, though the expression about the event as the first cause of sedition and disturbances seems to come from Josephus' own comment on "very great disturbance."

The second legendary picture is to be found in the Demonstratio. First Eusebius quotes the Pentecost story, noting that according to Josephus it took place after the passion of our Savior. Then he paraphrases the account of the standards, with Josephus calling them "images of Caesar" and claiming that they were brought by night into the temple. Finally he comments on the "very great disturbance" thus provoked, adding mention of trouble and sedition. Finally he claims that Philo corroborates this narratives when he says that imperial standards (Josephus' word, not Philo's) were set up in the temple at night.[49] Actually Philo mentions neither the temple nor night. We must be dealing with an Origenist picture of Philo or, more probably, Josephus.

One would like to imagine that Eusebius tinkered with his Church History after he had written passages like these. In any case, his discussion in the History is much more restrained. He has other axes to grind. He uses the Pentecost passage just as Josephus had used it,

in the midst of a selection on omens before the fall of
Jerusalem and even before the revolt.[50] The episode of
the standards is still taken as punishment for crimes
against the Savior, but the standards do not go into
the temple.[51] To be sure, we are still told that according to Philo Pilate "attempted something contrary to
Jewish law in regard to the temple then still standing
in Jerusalem,"[52] but we are not told what the something
was. Maybe Eusebius has checked some of his references.

We have now gone through most of the quotations
from earlier authors which Eusebius found meaningful as
he was creating his picture of the crucifixion and the
events related to it. Now we must move onward to the
theological-historical inferences he drew, or claimed
to have drawn, from the sequence of events in the first
century. As we examine this question we shall see --
it might as well be stated at once -- that it was Origen,
and specifically the Origen who wrote at Caesarea, who
influenced him in some of his wildest generalizations
about the fate of the Jews in the first century. Our
primary text will be the Church History, where his
thoughts seem to be rather fully developed.

The basic points are set forth in two sections of
the History. First come II 5, 6--10, 10, where we learn
about the dire consequences of attacking either the Savior
or the apostles. In this section it is true that the
final destruction of Jerusalem is presented as an
important penalty, but most of the time the effects are
immediate. The Jews like Pilate suffer "shortly after-
wards" (II 5, 6; 6,5; 7); there is no long delay. Their
penalties begin "from the times of Pilate and the crimes
against the Savior" (II 6, 3). To be sure, they will
lead up to "finally, the siege under Vespasian" (II 6,8).
But after Herod Agrippa's attempt against the apostles
the avenging minister of divine Justice will overtake
him at once (II 10, 1). It makes no difference that both
in Acts and in Josephus the penalty is paid for deifica-
tion. Second comes the more interesting passage, in which
Eusebius explains the meaning of the fall of Jerusalem in
relation to the crucifixion. This is to be found in III
5, 2--8, 11. Most of the section consists of accurate
quotations from Josephus, and we need not concern ourselves
with them. Our purpose is to consider the historical-
theological context in which Eusebius sets these materials.
Basically, his setting consists of two parts: H.E. III 5,
2--7, and III 7, 7-9. We are primarily concerned with the
fact that these two sections contain theological explanations of the timing of the fall of Jerusalem that are both
inconsistent and not due to Eusebius himself. The first
passage (III 5, 2-7) explains that the Jews not only committed a crime against the Savior but also plotted against
his apostles -- for example, Stephen, James son of Zebedee,
and James of Jerusalem. The other apostles then went out
on missionary journeys. Before the war, in addition, the

people of the church in Jerusalem left the city in accordance with a divine oracle and migrated to Transjordanian Pella. The purpose was "that when holy men had completely abandoned the royal metropolis of the Jews and the whole land of Judaea, the Justice of God might then visit upon them all their crimes against the Christ and his apostles, by making that generation of wicked persons completely vanish from among men."

The flight to Pella may be interesting historically.[53] It appears[54] that Jewish-Christian Ebionites flourished in the vicinity. But as far as Eusebius' literary work is concerned, it matters only to clear Jerusalem for punishment. This generation already deserved drastic punishment, according to Josephus in a passage which Eusebius cited.[55] More than that, its vanishing is probably related to the general theme of vanishing as a fulfilment of Daniel 9:26, developed by Eusebius in III 5, 3-4 and in the Demonstratio (VIII 2, 124). But the idea that holy men protected Jerusalem until all this took place was already expressed by Origen in a rather ambiguous passage. "As long as the word [i.e., the Logos] was with the Jews, not depriving them of the kingdom of God, so long the temple stood and the affairs of the Jews were protected."[56] In a homily on Jeremiah written only a few years earlier, Origen clearly stated that "the Logos of God abandoned the assembly of the Jews."[57] In addition, though he uses the third person imperative in another homily, he is really describing past events when he says, "Let the angels who always gave aid to Jerusalem . . . abandon Jerusalem; her sins have become great, they have killed Jesus, they have laid hands upon Christ; as long as the sins were still minor, we could still make petition and exhort concerning them, we could spare Jerusalem, but who will spare after this crime?"[58] Presumably Eusebius historicizes the theological ideas of Origen by referring to the departure of the holy men. This is his primary concern: to summarize from Josephus "how many" penalties of one sort or another came upon the Jews, to point out that (nearly) three million Jews must have attended Passover at Jerusalem, and to follow him in noting the coincidental date of the destruction of the temple. Where Josephus compared the date with that of the first destruction of the temple,[59] Eusebius compares it with that of the passion of Christ. He then goes on to give excerpts from Josephus about the punishment given by God for the crime against the Christ of God.[60]

A historian tends to historicize, especially if he has theological guidance. Origen had taught him that the "seventy weeks until the coming of Christ the governor" predicted in Daniel 9:24 had already taken place. They were no longer in the future,[61] Eusebius shared this view and denounced a writer of Origen's time who thought they were still future.[62] Thus it is not surprising that underneath his comments on the fall

of Jerusalem is an emphasis on the fulfilment of Daniel's
predictions (Dan. 9:25-27). We hear of the mysterious
"disappearance" or "vanishing" of "that generation" and
of the temple itself (Dan. 9:26). And we learn that "the
abomination of desolation announced by the prophets was
set up in that famous temple formerly God's" (Dan. 9:27).
Comparison with the Eclogae propheticae and the
Demonstratio shows how important Eusebius found the
theme. His eschatology is historicized, not futuristic.[63]

The second passage again owes much to Origen,
as well as to Josephus. It speaks of "the philanthropy
of the all-good providence" which respected the protection
given by apostles living in Jerusalem, especially James,
and exhibited patience in case the Jews repented. Oddly
enough, Josephus says something like this in regard to
the emperor Titus. "Throughout the war he had compassion
on the populace, walled in by the insurrectionists, and
many times he put off the capture of the city and by
means of the siege gave the guilty ones time for repentance."[64] Of course "philanthropy" and "providence"
are characteristic of God and emperors alike. Origen,
on the other hand, insisted that God's longsuffering had
come to an end after the crucifixion.[65]

> If you examine the date of the passion,
> that of the fall of Jerusalem and of
> the destruction of the city, and in
> what way God abandoned this people
> because they had killed Christ, you
> will see that God did not use long-
> suffering with this people! Or if you
> prefer, listen: from the 15th year of
> Tiberius Caesar to the destruction of
> the temple there were only 42 years. A
> little time for repentance had to be
> allowed, especially because of those who
> were to be converted from the people by
> the signs and wonders to be achieved by
> the apostles.

These forty-two years, presumably from Phlegon as
suggested earlier, turn into "forty whole years" when
Eusebius paraphrases the passage. He too is concerned
with God's longsuffering but he wants to insist upon
how long it lasted. And his signs and wonders come
from Josephus, not from memories of the book of Acts.[66]

Finally, of course, we should speak of the
ambiguous oracle found in the sacred writings, that "at
that time one from their country would rule the earth."
Josephus says that many Jews in spite of wisdom went
astray in interpreting it. He himself was able to explain
that it referred to Vespasian.[67] Origen does not refer
to this passage in his extant writings,[68] and therefore we

cannot be sure how he would have taken it. Probably
however, he would have argued with Eusebius that
Vespasian ruled only the Roman empire, while Christ,
as stated in Old Testament predictions, ruled over the
ends of the earth.[89]   As usual, Eusebius gives us a
reinterpreted version of Josephus, in this instance not
certainly, but possibly, relying on Origen.

It is thus clear that whenever Eusebius is making
statements about the theological-historical importance
of the Jewish people in the first century, he relies
on ideas already set forth first by Josephus and then
by Origen. Of the two, Josephus was the more reliable.
It is a pity that so many of Origen's influential comments had little foundation or none at all.[70]

For dealing with events in Jewish history after
70 Eusebius suffers from several kinds of disabilities.
The moralizing of Josephus has come to an end; so has the
moralizing of Origen; and for the later events Eusebius'
sources are inadequate, distasteful, or both.

The first of them was Hegesippus, who told something about Jewish and Christian history at least up to
the reign of Trajan. Eusebius clearly indicates Hegesippus
as his source for the notion that "after the capture of
Jerusalem Vespasian ordered a search made for all who
were of the family of David, so that no one from the
royal tribe might be left among the Jews; for this reason
a very great persecution was again inflicted on the Jews."[71]
Perhaps Hegesippus relied on Josephus for this notion.
It is clear that mopping-operations continued well after
the fall of Jerusalem, and not just at Masada. Vespasian
suspected that new revolts might arise. In addition, he
investigated "the most reputable Jews both in Alexandria
and in Rome," acquitting them only "on the intercession
of Titus," and having their accuser burned alive.[72]   A
writer dealing with Jewish Christianity might well regard
these events as a persecution of the Jews. According to
Eusebius, Domitian, unlike Vespasian, persecuted Christians,
but the passage he cites from Hegesippus does not prove
the point. "Domitian ordered the execution of those who
were of the family of David," and for this reason the
grandsons of Jude were arrested, then released by the
emperor.[73]   Exactly the same situation recurred under
Trajan. Explicit quotations from Hegesippus show that
the grandsons of Jude were accused again "on the same
charge" (III 32, 6 -- wrongly described as faith in
Christ in a summary, 32, 5) or in a parallel but more
worked-over quotation, "of being descended from David and
a Christian" (III 32, 3, wrongly summarized as "for
being a Christian", 32, 2). Eusebius' judicious
combination of quotations and summaries has made it
hard to see that according to Hegesippus Christians
suffered as Jews under Domitian and Trajan.

On the other hand, in dealing with the revolts
under Trajan and Hadrian, both in the _Chronicle_ and in
the _Church History_, Eusebius clearly has rather reliable
sources.[74] The Trajanic campaigns make some sense, and
the end of the revolt under Hadrian is correctly
described. But since Eusebius has no theological
guide like Origen he has to do his own interpreting, as
we should expect relying on Josephus once more. "The
calamities of the Jews were at their height, and
disaster followed upon disaster." A revolutionary
"movement" arose. There was "an evil spirit of sedition."
Words related to _stasis_ appear four times in this brief
section about events under Trajan (IV 2). For affairs
under Hadrian Eusebius uses terms like "rebellion"
(_apostasia_), revolution, and "folly" (_aponoia_). The
The Jewish leader Bar Cochba was an assassin and a robber
(IV 6, 1-3). But Eusebius treats separately his demand
that Christians should deny that Jesus was the Christ.
This point, taken from Justin Martyr, is not integrated
theologically with his other materials (IV 8, 4). And
while Eusebius notes that finally "the city was emptied
of the nation of the Jews and its old inhabitants utterly
destroyed, and colonized by an alien race," he is
content to add that it was called Aelia in honor of
Hadrian (IV 6, 4). Evidently Eusebius' source at this
point, Aristo of Pella, did not engage in reflection on
the end of Jerusalem. And without the guidance provided
by Josephus or an Origen, Eusebius himself was unable to
do so. This may be why his narratives concerning the
revolts under Trajan and Harian are both more factual
and less rhetorical-theological than what he had to
offer in regard to the first revolt. He will not reach
his earlier level of rhetoric again until he comes to
deal with Constantine's opponents Galerius, Maximin, and
Licinius. Then he will pull out all the stops and offer
a grand crescendo on the theme of the fate of the enemies
of God.

BIBLIOGRAPHY

1. Acts 9:24, 20:3, 19; 23:30.

2. Eusebius, H. E. VI 3, 5; Origen, Ioh. comm. VI 2, p.
108, 8-9 Preuschen.

3. Bell. I 10; cf. II 454-57; 539; III 351-54; IV 104;
137; 147-57; 318-25; etc.

4. Adv. Marc. III 23, 4-5 (Adv. Iud. 13, 27-28). One
could mention Melito of Sardis, Pasch. hom. 99, but
because of the author's rhetorical polemic (on which
cf. K. W. Noakes, "Melito of Sardis and the Jews,"
Texte und Untersuchungen 116, 1975, 244-49) the
reference is not clear. See also O. Perler, Méliton
de Sardes Sur la Pâque (Paris, 1966), 198-99.

5. F. Jacoby, Die Fragmente der griechischen Historiker,
no. 256. The collection is not quite properly
arranged because it neglects the use of one author
by another.

6. Ibid., no. 257.

7. Theophilus (F 2-3 Jacoby) is the source of Jacoby's
T 3 and F 4.

8. FGrHist 256 F 1.

9. If so, it would be pointless to treat him as the
source of Tertullian. Apol. 5, 1-2, and Eusebius,
H. E. II 2, 5; cf. C. Cecchelli, "Un tentato
riconoscimento imperiale del Cristo," Scritt: in
onore di A. Calderini e R. Paribeni I (Milan, 1956),
351-62.

10. Chron. lat., p. 174 Helm; Greek in Syncellus, CSHB I
614, 10-11.

11. Cf. P. de Labriolla, La réaction païenne (Paris,
1934), 204-20.

12. Origen, C. Cels. II 14.

13. Matt. ser. 40; actually 42 years later, Jer. hom.
XIV 13 (cited below).

14. C. Cels. II 33 (cf. 59).

15. Matt. ser. 134.

16. Chron. lat., pp. 174-75 Helm.

84

17. FGrHist 257 F 16 (c).

18. Africanus, frag. 50 Routh (Reliquiae sacrae, ed. 2,
    II, 298, 6-8), from Syncellus (CSHB I 610, 12-14).

19. Routh, op. cit., 478; Labriolle, op. cit., 210.

20. Matt. comm. X 17; C. Cels, I 47.

21. "Le 'testimonium flavianum': vers une solution
    definitive?" Revue Belge de philologie et d'histoire
    20 (1941), 416; cf. 461-62.

22. H. E. I 11, 7-8; Dem. ev. III 3, 105-6; Theoph. V 44.
    See D. S. Wallace-Hadrill, "Eusebius of Caesarea and
    the Testimonium Flavianum," JEH 25 (1974), 353-62.

23. Cf. A. C. Bouquet, "The References to Josephus in
    the Bibliotheca of Photius," Journal of Theological
    Studies 36 (1935), 289-93. These passages in Photius
    occur in Cod. 238 (PG 103, 1188B-C and 1192B).

24. Cod. 33 (PG 103, 66B).

25. C. Cels. I 47.

26. H. E. I 11, 4-6.

27. Dem. ev. IX 5, 15.

28. Ioh. comm. VI 9.

29. "Zu Eusebius Kirchengeschichte I. Das Martyrium
    Jakobus des Gerechten," Zeitschrift für die neutestment-
    liche Wissenschaft 4 (1903), 48-61; cf. W.-P. Funk,
    Die Zweite Apokalypse des Jakobus aus Nag-Hammadi-
    Codex V (Texte und Untersuchungen 119, 1976), 172-76.

30. Cf. A. Böhlig, "Zum Martyrium des Jakobus," Novum
    Testamentum 5 (1962), 207-13.

31. Eusebius, H. E. II 1, 5 (cf. 23, 3).

32. Matt. comm. X 17.

33. Bell. IV 318.

34. Pasch. hom. 523, 710, 712, 724-25 Perler.

35. Vit. 196.

36. Eusebius, H. E. II 23, 18.

37. Chron., pp. 182-83 Helm.

38. H. E. II 23, 19. For wise Jews as interpreters cf. Josephus, Bell. VI 313.

39. Ibid., 21-24.

40. Ibid., 22, 8-23, 1.

41. Ibid., III 8, 7 (Josephus, Bell. VI 300).

42. Ibid., II 23, 3.

43. After H. E. III 8, 9 the manuscripts ER add Josephus, Bell. VI 305-9 Original or interpolation?

44. H. E. III 11.

45. Chron. lat., p. 175 Helm; Josephus, Bell. VI 299 (cf. Eusebius, H. E. III 8, 6).

46. Bell. II 169 (no year mentioned, but apparently on Pilate's arrival in Judaea)

47. Lam. comm., frag. 109 Klostermann.

48. Matt. comm. XVII 25.

49. Dem. ev. VIII 2, 121-23.

50. H. E.   III 8, 6.

51. Ibid.,   II 6, 4.

52. Ibid.,   II 5, 7.

53. Cf. S. S. Sowers, "The Circumstances and Recollection of the Pella Flight," Theologische Zeitschrift 26 (1970), 305-20; M. Simon, "La migration à Pella: légende ou realite?" Recherches de science religieuse 60 (1972), 37-54.

54. Cf. Epiphanius, Haer. XXX 2, 7-8 (Ebion to Kokabe): Julius Africanus in Eusebius, H. E. I 7, 14; Eusebius, Onom., p. 172, 2-3 Klostermann.

55. Josephus, Bell. V 566 (H. E. III 6, 16); cf. V 442-45; VI 408.

56. Matt. comm. ser. 29.

57. Jer. hom. XIV 15.

58. Jer. hom. XIII 1.

59. Bell. VI 250; 268.

60. <u>H. E.</u> III 5, 7 (cf. 5, 6; 7, 1). The term is Lucan
(9:20; cf. 23:35) and Jewish (Origen, <u>C</u>. <u>Cels</u>. I
49).

61. Origen, De princ. IV 1, 5.

62. <u>H. E.</u> VI 7.

63. R. Wilken points out that in writing against the
Christians Porphyry too had treated Daniel's
predictions as fulfilled -- but under Antiochus
Epiphanes. Eusebius finds a different time for
fulfilment but agrees that it lies in the past.

64. Josephus, <u>Bell</u>. I 10.

65. Origen, <u>Jer</u>. <u>hom</u>. XIV 13. In the next section he
refers to "the plot of the people against our
Savior."

66. Even Eusebius' idea that the people could have
obtained "salvation" (<u>soteria</u>, III 7, 9) is anti-
cipated in Josephus' words (<u>Bell</u>. VI 310).

67. <u>Bell</u>. VI 312-13.

68. Cf. H. Schreckenberg, <u>Die Flavius-Josephus-Tradition
in Antike und Mittelalter</u> (Leiden, 1972), 73-76.

69. <u>H. E.</u> III 8, 10-11; Ps. 2:8; 18:5.

70. Note that R. Helm ("De Eusebii in Chronicorum libro
auctoribus," <u>Eranos</u> 22 [1924], 34) suggested after
Schürer that Eusebius may have used Josephus via
Africanus. Origen seems a more likely candidate.
See also E. Fascher, "Jerusalem Untergang in der
urchristlichen und altkirchlichen Überlieferung"
<u>Theologische Literaturzeitung</u> 89 (1964), 81-98.

71. <u>H. E.</u> III 12.

72. Josephus, <u>Bell</u>. VII 421; 447-50; <u>Vit</u>. 424-25.

73. <u>H. E.</u> III 19-20.

74. Cf. A. Fuks, "The Jewish Revolt in Egypt (A.D. 115-
117) in the light of the papyri," <u>Aegyptus</u> 33
(1953), 131-58; H. Mantel, "The Causes of the Bar
Kokba Revolt," <u>Jewish Quarterly Review</u> 58 (1967/8),
224-42, 274-96 (esp. 277-79). R. L. Wilken suggests
that perhaps Eusebius got his information from Jews
at Caesarea.

WHAT IS PROOF? -- RHETORICAL VERIFICATION
IN PHILO, JOSEPHUS, AND QUINTILIAN

David M. Hay

Coe College

Conceptions of religious truth have varied from one
age to another, but the concern of genuinely religious
persons to maintain and defend the validity of their
convictions was probably as strong nineteen centuries ago
as it is today.   Hellenistic Jews like Philo of Alexandria
and Josephus appear simply to assume that Judaism can be
expressed effectively for missionary purposes and defended
cogently against hostile critics and persecutors.

In this paper I propose to explore the general method
(or literary structure) of two documents that seem to have
firm apologetic purposes, the In Flaccum of Philo and the
Contra Apionem of Josephus.   Then I will analyze and
compare the specific types of proof that each presents to
defend Jews and Judaism and excoriate their opponents.
Since both works appear to have been written largely for non-
Jewish readers, it will be useful to compare the literary
structures and arguments of the two writings with the
standards of hellenistic rhetoric of the period; and this
will be done chiefly with references to the Institutio
oratoria of Quintilian.[1]

Such a limited investigation will not begin to indicate all that might be of interest respecting these authors'
notions of religious verification.   Yet there can be little
doubt that each author, in his respective treatise, is
arguing earnestly against real critics.   The two documents
are relatively brief and self-contained, and we know or can
reasonably infer a good deal about the circumstances under
which each was written.

A. Literary Structures

H. D. Betz has recently shown how fruitful it is to
study some of the Pauline epistles as apologies following
the law-court conventions of hellenistic rhetoric.[2]   If
Paul could follow such conventions, there is little reason
to doubt that Philo and Josephus could do so as well. Both
IF and CA exhibit forensic qualities and turns of phrase,
though neither as it stands can have served as a courtroom
speech.

The basic divisions of a speech recognized in the
hellenistic handbooks on oratory are as follows: (1) introduction (exordium), (2) exposition of background and
factual details (narratio), (3) proof (probatio), and
(4) conclusion (peroratio).[3]   Another important element,
which Quintilian classifies as a part of the probatio,
is the propositio, the statement of what is to be proved.[4]

A.1. In Flaccum

Although IF has long been recognized as marked by
rhetorical features,[5] the form of the work is something
of a puzzle.   A passage of some length appears to have
been lost from the beginning of the work, primarily since
the opening reference to Sejanus seems to presuppose a
statement of some length about his mistreatment of the Jews.[6]
As we have the text, it appears to be an argument in the
form of a historical narrative, without separate exordium,
probatio, or peroratio.   IF reads like a mixture of
narratio and probatio, a combination not at all unprecedented
in hellenistic rhetoric.[7]

The key question is what this treatise seeks to prove.
There is no mechanical propositio at the beginning of the
treatise (as we have it), but near the beginning Philo
imagines someone breaking in to ask, "My dear sir, after
deciding to accuse a man you have stated no charge but
come out with a long string of praises.   Are you out of your
senses and gone quite mad?"   Philo responds to this
fictional inquiry by saying that his praises are only meant
to set Flaccus's villainy "in a clearer light" (IF 6-7).
The whole of IF 1-103 concentrates on demonstrating the
crimes of the governor committed against the Jews.   From
paragraph 104 to the end of the treatise, the subject is the
series of punishments Flaccus suffered, ending with his death.
The basic thesis guiding this second half of the work is
variously stated as the punishment of Flaccus at the hands
of justice (dikē) or divine providence (104, 125) or
the punishment of Flaccus by divine justice because of his
mistreatment of the Jews (116, 170-75, 179, 189-91).

Since Flaccus was dead when Philo wrote the treatise,
it is scarcely possible that Philo's chief purpose was to
prove the late prefect's guilt.   Likewise it is hard to
believe that the work was chiefly written as a glorification
of God's justice since it gives every sign of having been
addressed to Gentiles.[8]   Rather, a careful reading of
the work and consideration of the historical conditions
surrounding it suggests the correctness of Goodenough's
conclusion that the dominant purpose of the document is
to serve as a "bold warning that any prefect will bring
himself to the gutter if he deals unfavorably with God's
chosen people."[9]   The canons of hellenistic rhetoric
allowed for the threatening of judges in certain circumstances,
and it is not at all difficult to detect a tremendous threat
in the final lines of the treatise.[10]

Assuming the correctness of Goodenough's view of
the guiding purpose of IF, one can readily imagine that
Philo would not care to state that purpose explicitly
anywhere: the Roman magistrates for whom it is intended
could hardly be expected to respond kindly to a direct
threat.   Further, we may imagine that Philo chose a
rhetorical strategy that would allow his ultimate purpose
to emerge only gradually.   A Gentile reader might be
so offended that he would not read the second page of a
treatise that began with a harsh threatening of his life.
But a Gentile reader might well be willing to hear about
the crimes of a former governor (especially if he were the

prefect who succeeded Flaccus!), and he might even be open
to an argument that Flaccus's fall was the work of divine
justice.   Philo, building on such willingness and openness,
deftly leads his reader toward a strong but never-directly-
articulated conclusion that such pogroms as Flaccus allowed
must never be permitted to happen again.[11]

Was Philo capable of so subtle an employment of
rhetoric?   He does remark at one point that "I am not
a silly person who cannot see what the sequence of an
argument demands" (IF 6).   Despite his great appreciation
of Plato, Philo does not one-sidedly reject the value of
rhetorical training but on the contrary says that a good man
will be often helpless in public life unless he has acquired
rhetorical powers sufficient to match or overcome the
rhetorical skills wielded by many unscrupulous persons.[12]
Philo includes rhetoric among the desirable "encyclical
studies" and various passages in his writings indicate
deep familiarity with rhetorical forms.[13]   The very fact
that Philo was chosen to lead the Jewish embassy to Rome
implies that he must have been judged very competent to
argue a case by Gentile standards.

Thus IF is carefully designed as an argument in
narrative form.   It directly and fully argues on behalf
of two explicit theses, that Flaccus was guilty of criminal
mistreatment of the Alexandrian Jews and that his loss of
office and life was a divine punishment for that mistreatment.
The treatise also cleverly and indirectly argues for a
third thesis, which includes the first two: Flaccus's end
proves the folly of any persecution of the Jews!

A.2. Contra Apionem

The one major element of a traditional hellenistic
speech that is lacking in CA is the narratio, but this is
not surprising.   It seems obvious that Josephus thinks
his apology does not need to include an account of his
past life or details about the backgrounds of his opponents.
Quintilian remarks that a narratio is sometimes quite
dispensable (IO 4.2.4-8).

The exordium (1.1-5) is in line with Quintilian's
recommendations that this part of a presentation be brief,
clearly define the intention of the speaker, indicate that
he comes forward from high reasons of duty while his
opponents act from base motives, and avoid strong
emotional appeals (IO 4.1.1-34).   The peroratio
(2.287-96) agrees with Quintilian's views that the
conclusion should recapitulate the main points of the
speech and offer a strong emotional effect (IO 6.1.1-29).

The probatio is divided into two main groups of
arguments, the first (1.6-320) refuting charges that
the Jews are not an ancient people, the second being a
reply to various other criticisms of the Jews and their
Law (2.1-286).   It is also possible, however, to divide
the probatio into a refutation of specific accusations

(1.6-2.144) and a positive description of Jews and their Law (2.145-286). Quintilian says that refutation of charges followed by positive statement is the proper sequence for a defense argument (5.13.53).

Throughout the two-volume work Josephus has scattered indications to the reader of what he is trying to prove (e.g., 1.59, 70, 106, 128, 213; 2.1-8). The contrast between the statements of purpose in the exordium and the peroratio suggest that the CA is a fusion of two originally separate projects, which Josephus decided to bring together to provide a more comprehensive defense. Even so, the statements of purpose in this treatise are far more straightforward and frequent than those in Philo's IF. Unlike that work, the CA appears to have no concealed purposes: it is designed to give direct evidence to silence the critics who have spoken against Josephus's Antiquities and Judaism (1.2-3).

B. Specific Evidence and Arguments

1. In Flaccum

Philo's rhetorical strategy in IF may be clarified if we keep in mind a distinction between types of proof which goes back at least to Aristotle, a distinction between "inartificial proofs" (objective evidence in the form of documents, witnesses, decisions of previous courts, etc.) and "artificial proofs" (arguments developed by lawyers on the basis of the objective evidence).[14]

What was the objective evidence that Philo assumes anyone would recognize? First of all there are the major actions of Flaccus and the Alexandrian pagans taken against the Jews:

(1) Flaccus began a policy of neglecting Jewish petitions (24);

(2) on the occasion of Agrippa's visit Flaccus criticized him privately and allowed him to be vilified by an Alexandrian mob publically (33,40);

(3) Flaccus permitted an Alexandrian mob to install imperial images in the synagogues (42-43);

(4) he published a proclamation restricting the civic rights of Alexandrian Jews (53-54);

(5) he tolerated a pogrom that included assaults on Jewish property, creation of Jewish unemployment, the driving of Jews into a ghetto, and mob torture and murder of individual Jews (55-72);

(6) Flaccus ordered the public scourging of members of the Jewish senate in a particularly humiliating manner (73-77);

(7) he ordered or permitted the torture and execution of Jewish men and women in the theatre (84-85, 96);

(8) he failed to pass along to Caligula an official
message of congratulations from the Alexandrian Jewish
community (97-101).

Likewise the main facts of Flaccus's sufferings were
public knowledge:

(1) his sudden and unexpected arrest (104-15);

(2) his journey to Italy in winter (125);

(3) his trial in Italy based on accusations by Isidorus
and Lampo, two of his worst enemies (125-47);

(4) his loss of wealth and property (148-50);

(5) his banishment to Andros (151);

(6) his execution by Gaius's order (180-85).

On the basis of these facts Philo weaves a net of
argument designed to prove Flaccus's guilt as persecutor of
the Jews and God's punishment of him for that reason. As
regards Flaccus's guilt, Philo emphasizes that the governor
was at first highly competent in his office and throughout
his persecution of the Jews was fully conscious that that
persecution was unjustifiable and dangerous.   He argues,
evidently from the general tendency of Flaccus's decisions,
that the governor aimed at the liquidation of the Jews (116).
Philo represents the setting of of images of Gaius in the
Alexandrian synagogues as crucial to the whole pogrom and
insists that it violated Jewish worship customs previously
recognized and approved by Roman authorities.   In general
Philo implies that the Jews customarily proved their
loyalty to Rome (46, 47, 56), while the Alexandrian pagans
were seditious and Flaccus acted contrary to Roman interests
(43-52, 81).   Among the horrors of the persecution,
Philo repeatedly singles out the mistreatment of corpses,
something that may have been particularly abhorrent to
Roman officials.[15]

Philo frequently affirms or implies the total innocence
of the Jews, not admitting any fault on their side that
might have contributed to the sequence of events leading to
persecution.[16] He briefly notes that Flaccus withdrew rights
of the Jews, but says nothing about Jewish efforts to gain
legal parity with the Greek citizens of Alexandria.[17] He
also is silent about other potentially embarrassing issues
such as the reasons for Agrippa's display,[18] any Jewish
resistance to the setting up of standards in the meeting
houses,[19] or any provoking action of the Jewish senate at
the time of its meeting with Flaccus.[20]

To convince his readers that Flaccus suffered because
God chose to punish him for his assaults on the Jews, Philo
calls attention to a number of "proofs."   The suddenness
and unprecedented timing of the arrest (before the end of
Flaccus's term in office) point to divine action.[21] Philo
further perceives a clear proof (enargēs pistis) that

Flaccus suffered because of divine retribution for his
pogrom in the fact that he was arrested during the Feast
of Booths (116). The ex-governor's suffering during
his winter trip to Italy because of the buffeting of the
elements is for Philo another sign of providence: that
was just treatment for a person "who had filled the
elements of the universe with his impious deeds" (the
allusion seems to be to the world-wide consequences of
his persecution of Alexandrian Jews -- 125, 44-48). His
accusation by Lampo and Isidorus was so extremely painful
and dishonoring that again one can see more-than-human
justice at work (146). The climax of the argument is
set on Flaccus's own lips: Philo reports that in the
midst of his suffering

> It is said that once about midnight he became possessed
> as in a Corybantic frenzy.... "King of gods and men,"
> he cried, "so then Thou dost not disregard the nation
> of the Jews, nor do they misreport Thy Providence, but
> all who say that they do not find in Thee a Champion
> and Defender, go astray from the true creed. I am a
> clear proof (saphes pistis) of this, for all the acts
> which I madly committed against the Jews I have
> suffered myself. I allowed them to be robbed of their
> possessions.... For that I had taken from me my
> heritage...and other possessions.... I cast on them
> the slur that they were foreigners without civic
> rights...and, therefore, I have lost my rights and
> have been driven into exile.... Some I marched into the
> theatre and ordered them to be maltreated before the
> eyes of their bitterest enemies unjustly, and, therefore,
> justly was I maltreated in my miserable soul...with the
> utmost contumely.... (169-73)

Finally the execution of Flaccus is described by Philo as
resembling the carving of "a sacrificial victim," with
the miserable man receiving a number of wounds exactly
equal to the number of Jews who died during his pogrom.
With this thorough working out of a lex talionis penalty,
Philo concludes that Flaccus

> thereby became an indubitable proof (apseudestatē pistis)
> that the help which God can give was not withdrawn
> from the nation of the Jews. (191)

What would a pagan reader think of this series of "proofs"?
Would this account of a miraculously horrible execution
convince him of Philo's point of view? The question of
historicity would inevitably arise regarding several key
speeches in the treatise. The core of the case for the
Jews is summed up in an apologetic speech that Philo says
his fellow countrymen might have uttered (49-50). The
meaning of Flaccus's punishment is set forth most
lucidly in a series of statements Philo ascribes to him:
he begins by asking why he suffers (157-59), slowly grows
in understanding (163-65) until he finally confesses in
solitude the full reason for his misery (169-75, 178-79).

It seems likely that Philo would expect a sophisticated pagan to discern in most of these speeches not literal history but the serious dramatic fictions of an author bent on revealing the inner meaning of events.[22] If he was indeed writing primarily for such a reader, Philo must have been aware how hard it would be for such a person to recognize divine justice active through the brutality of Gaius (180-85) and seeking redress for the sufferings of the Jews (which surely was not the basis of the accusations lodged against Flaccus by Lampo and Isidorus!). Philo must have felt he had to employ every possible rhetorical device.

In general IF is marked by a series of dramatically vivid, often lurid, scenes which -- as Quintilian recommended -- would make the readers feel themselves eyewitnesses of the events.[23] The scenes are artfully drawn to excite emotions like awe, disgust, pity, and wonder in ways supportive of Philo's argumentation.

Finally we should note that, in developing his case against Flaccus, Philo offers a complex and nuanced analysis of his motives and moods: depressions (9-16), loss of autonomy (18,20), domination by men of ill-will (25, 30-31), anxiety for popularity (20, 41, 82). Above all Flaccus's actions against the Jews are plausibly explained as an effort to gain the support of the Alexandrian Greek population (22-23). All this conforms to Quintillian's recommendation that a horrible crime be rendered as credible as possible, particularly through believable delineation of character and motivation. (IO 4.2.52).

B.2. Contra Apionem

In the view of most modern readers, and probably in the view of most ancient ones as well, Josephus in CA has a much easier case to defend than did Philo in the second half of his IF. Essentially Josephus has to argue against denials of the antiquity of the Jews and against moral aspersions cast on the Law of Moses. His arguments fall into three categories:

(1) arguments about good and bad historiography;

(2) arguments from historical events, usual or unique;

(3) arguments based on the content of the Mosaic Law.

Josephus attaches the highest importance to good historical investigation. He gladly appeals to historians of distinction (2.238), including ones whom Greeks judge to be the most trustworthy (1.4). At the same time he maintains that, particularly with regard to the question of the antiquity of the Jews, the most reliable historical sources are not Greek but Near

Eastern: Egyptian, Chaldean, Phoenician and (of course)
Jewish (1.28-43).

What are Josephus's criteria for historical veracity?
One vital standard is eyewitness evidence, which is the
basis of the superiority of his own writing about the
Jewish war with Rome (1.47-56) and the reason why in
principle Chaldeans are more likely to be right than
Greeks on the question of who founded Babylon (1.142-44).

A second criterion is a strong tradition of accurate
historical record-keeping, such as exists among the
Egyptians, Babylonians, and Phoenicians (1.28, 106-112).
Jewish records excel all others in accuracy, however, both
because of the devoted human care motivated by loyalty
to God's commands and because Jewish prophets wrote by
divine inspiration (1.29-39).

Perhaps the fundamental criterion of historical
truth that Josephus expects his readers to appreciate
is the canon of agreement of witnesses. The Jewish
scriptures, he proudly declares, contain no contradictions
and are confirmed by Chaldean and Phonecian records
(1.37-40, 129-30, 145, 160). Josephus notes that his
history of the Jewish war was attested as accurate by
Vespasian, Titus, Agrippa, and other notables associated
with the events described (1.50-52).

Josephus calls attention to the special value of relevant testimony from hostile witnesses. He cites
writings of Egyptians and Phoenicians as providing
"evidence which is quite unimpeachable" since these peoples
"are notoriously our bitterest enemies" (1.70, 104, 106-27).

More than once Josephus points out the necessity of
doing one's homework fully as a historian in the sense of
consulting all the evidence, the implication being that
anti-Jewish writers had regularly failed to do so. He
repeatedly claims to have canvassed the relevant sources
fully himself (Greek and non-Greek sources alike -- 1.4,
70-72, 161, 163).

Another criterion of fair historical writing for
Josephus is that of reasonable inference. Thus he
concludes that Theophrastus was speaking of Jews when
he mentioned "Corban" (1.167) and that early Greek
literature fails to mention Jews because Jews were not
a maritime people (1.60-68).

Josephus refutes most of the historical claims of
his opponents by impugning the quality of their
historiography. He says that the critics of the Jews
are very commonly found to disagree among themselves
about the same events (1.4,22-26,293). They are
often guilty of manifest absurdities (e.g., 1.318-20;
2.17-18). Their motives for writing history have
often been shabby or unrelated to genuine concern for

factual accuracy (1.24-25).   Josephus accuses persons
who attack the Jews of malignity and intentional lying
(1.3; 2.295), but Apion is described as a writer of
particularly low character (2.3-7).   Further criteria
of bad historiography are reliance on conjecture (1.15,
22,46,293) or gossip (2.12-14) or dubious linguistic
data and etymologies (2.22-27).

Much of the argument in the second volume of CA,
however, is based on historical events rather than on
criticism of historians.   Apion maintained that

> a clear proof (tekmērion)...that our laws are unjust
> and our religious ceremonies erroneous is that we are
> not masters of an empire, but rather the slaves, first
> of one nation, then of another, and that calamity has
> more than once befallen our city.   (2.125)

Josephus does not question the assumption that political
independence has a bearing on religious truth; instead he
argues that (1) most nations have been enslaved at one
time or another, and (2) Jews have enjoyed extended
periods of independence (2.125-34).

Josephus refers to a number of historical events
that attest the greatness of the Jews or Judaism.
He produces a list of Alexandrian rulers from the Ptolemies
to the Caesars to prove that Jewish residents of Alexandria
have been highly esteemed by the rulers of that city
2.43-78).   Cleopatra, who is reported to have mistreated
the Jews of that city, proved her unworthiness to rule by
her miserable death (2.60; cf. IO 5.13.24).   Josephus
suggests that Cleopatra's suicide was proof of divine
wrath directed toward her wickedness.   At somewhat
greater length he describes the sufferings and demise of
Apion as an appropriate penalty for a person who neglected
his own country's laws and told lies about Jewish laws
(2.143-44).   Though Josephus does not explicitly declare
that Cleopatra and Apion died by God's hand as a punishment
for their attacks on the Jews, that is at least suggested.
Only once in the two-volume treatise does Josephus
directly mention a divine miracle, that of the refusal
of elephants to crush the Jews led by Onias (2.52-53).
In this passage Josephus speaks of "the deliverance so
manifestly vochsafed to them by God" and adds that the
miracle attested the righteousness of Onias.   Elsewhere
(2.290) he says that God bore witness to the merits of
Moses, but does not say how (cf. 2.218).   He urges that
time has borne witness to the greatness of the Mosaic
Law inasmuch as it has never required alteration (2.183,
290).

Josephus several times mentions typical or universal
actions of Jews as attesting the greatness of the Law.
It is well known among pagans, he observes, that all
Jews would rather die than commit the smallest infraction
of the Law (2.232-35, 218-19; cf. 1.42-45; 2.152-53).

To answer charges that Jews worship the head of an ass and
perform ritual murders of Gentiles, Josephus describes in
detail the customary rites practiced in the Jerusalem
temple (2.80-111). Replying to the accusation of
Jewish hatred of non-Jews, he remarks that no Greek
convert has ever mentioned a Jewish oath of hostility
toward Greeks in general (2.123-24); he also emphasizes
Jewish openness to proselytes (2.261) and general
humanitarianism (2.211-14, 273, 283, 293).

A final type of argument found in CA is that which
is based on the contents of the Mosaic Law. Josephus
dwells on the humanitarian regulations and even stresses
ones enjoining merciful treatment of animals (2.213-14,
237). He stresses the rigor of the Law, noting
that the most common penalty for infractions is death
(2.206, 208, 262); he also emphasizes that the reward
for keeping the Law (as all Jews do) is the immaterial
promise of life after death (2.218).[24]

The excellence of the Law is also for Josephus
revealed in its exalted concept of God (2.190-98) and
its regulations concerning marriage (2.199-203), family
(2.204-206), community (206-208), and aliens (2.209-10).
Merely by describing the contents of particular laws
Josephus plainly expects to gain Gentile admiration for
them. He also speaks of the conscience of the
Jew as attesting the value of living by the rules of
Moses (2.218). The Law has self-authenticating power;
its written demands correspond to a law in the human
heart.

To bring this section of our study to a close, we
may note some important types of apologetic argument
common to IF and CA: both tend to represent critics of
Jews and Judaism or persecutors in very black colors
(motivated by lust for glory -- IF 20, 41, 82; CA 1.23-25);
enemies of the Jews die by divine punishment (Flaccus,
Cleopatra, Apion); both works place only very limited
emphasis on outwardly miraculous events, probably
reflecting in part a dogma of hellenistic rhetoric that
miraculous evidence is ambiguous (IO 4.2.52; 5.7.35-36);[25]
both works emphasize Jewish traditional customs, tne
nigh-universal loyalty to them on the part of Jews, the
recognition and approval given these customs by pagan
and particularly Roman magistrates in days past (e.g.,
IF 50; CA 2.73); both declare that Jews will regularly
die rather than deny the Mosaic Law and both warn that
Jews will also fight anyone who threatens the Law
(IF 48; CA 1.42-43; 2.234-35, 272); both condemn persons
who attack the religious customs of other nations (IF 52;
CA 2.144, 269); both insist that Jews and the Jewish
Law are humane and not hostile toward Gentiles.[26]

Beyond substantive claims and bases of argument, we
may note a number of rhetorical devices utilized in both

treatises: rhetorical questions (IF 35-36, 94; CA 1.254-59, 313-17; 2.109, 115, 120, 184-85; 293-94), division of possibilities (IF 9, 33, 130; CA 1.314, 317; 2.88, 278; IO 5.10.65-67); direct address to readers (IF 6, 52, 62; CA 2.146, 296); mention of positive and negative historical parallels or precedents (IF 1, 50, 92-93, 105-106; CA 1.220-221; 2.171-72, 222-24, 227-31, 270; IO 5.11.1,6,12-13); appeals to general human experience (IF 58-61, 109, 114, 118, 146, 176, 186; CA 2.151-53, 176-77; IO 5.11.36,42); personal asserveration (IF 59, 78; CA 1.6, 47; 2.79, 102, 125, 143, 293; IO 5.12.12).   Some rhetorical devices present in CA but apparently absent from IF are: hypothetical arguments (CA 1.35,69; 2.68, 81, 267-69, 273; IO 5.10.95ff); introduction of sources as though their authors are being set in a witness-box for cross-examination (CA 1.74, 279, 288; 2.61); sarcasm and humor (CA 2.32, 112, 115, 125, 128; IO 6.3).

Conclusions

Despite great differences in structure and purpose (related to the criticisms they seek to refute), IF and CA display major similarities not only in fundamental religious ideas but also in types of apologetic argument.   This may reflect some knowledge on Josephus's part of the writings of Philo, but probably the similarities primarily stem from the circumstance that both writers drew on a long-standing tradition of hellenistic Jewish apologetic.[27]

In this study we have examined indications that Philo and Josephus followed some of the conventions of contemporary pagan rhetoric in designing the structures and particular arguments of their apologies.   This is not to say that their notions of truth and proof were completely shaped or determined by pagan rhetorical standards, but only that to a large degree each of these treatises is influenced by those standards.   Both works seem to have been written with mainly pagan readers in mind. Both seek to convince readers that Jews and Judaism merit respect; neither appeals overtly for conversion.   Neither work attempts a comprehensive description of Jews and their traditions.   Each treatise is a response to specific attacks from Gentiles, and each treatise attempts to deal with a limited number of questions.

To recognize the strong rhetorical cast of these works is not to deny that they deserve study for their historical, theological, and philosophical content; it only should put us on guard against imagining that they offer disinterested statements of truth.   At the same time, they offer invaluable clues as to the kinds of evidence and argument they thought might lead pagans in the direction of the truth.

NOTES

1. Hereafter the following abbreviations will be used: IF = In Flaccum; CA = Contra Apionem; IO = Institutio oratoria. Citation of texts and translations will be based on the Loeb Classical Library editions of the three works.

2. H. D. Betz, Der Apostel Paulus und die sokratische Tradition (Tübingen: J. C. B. Mohr [Paul Siebeck], 1972); "The Literary Composition and Function of Paul's Letter to the Galatians," New Testament Studies 21 (1975), 353-79.

3. IO 3.9.1. Cf. G. Kennedy, The Art of Persuasion in Greece (Princeton: Princeton University Press, 1963), 11.

4. IO 3.9.1-2. See Betz, "Literary Composition," 367f.

5. E.g., G. Kennedy, The Art of Rhetoric in the Roman World (Princeton: Princeton University Press, 1972), 452.

6. See H. Box, Philonis Alexandrini In Flaccum (London: Oxford University Press, 1939), xxxiii; A. Pelletier, In Flaccum (Les oeuvres de Philon d'Alexandrie 31; Paris: Editions du Cerf, 1967), 13-16.

7. Kennedy, Greece, 151n.; Rome, 143, 195.

8. E. Goodenough, The Politics of Philo Judaeus (New Haven: Yale University Press, 1938), 10. The interpretation of IF as an aretology is stressed especially by Pelletier, 16-19.

9. Goodenough, 10-11.

10. IO 4.1.21-22; cf. Demosthenes, De Corona 324.

11. See IO 4.5.5: the value of occasionally initially misleading judges regarding the direction of your argument.

12. Philo, De migratione Abrahami 70-85; cf. Kennedy, Greece, 13-23; IO 5.12.9

13. See É. Bréhier, Les idées philosophiques et religieuses de Philon d'Alexandrie (Paris: Libraire philosophique J. Vrin, 1950), 285f., 289.

14. IO 5.1.1-2.

15. The special law of Claudius against desecration of graves suggests a particular Roman sensitivity in this area (see, e.g., C. K. Barrett, The New Testament Background [New York: Harper & Row, 1961] 15].

16. For a well-reasoned reconstruction of the events and the background issues, see Box, xxxviii-lvi.

17. Philo implies that Flaccus sought to deny the Jews all civic rights (53-54; cf. 172), whereas the governor probably only decreed that the Jews would henceforth be restricted to privileges given them by the law, rather than by custom.   See Box, xxxviii, xliv.

18. E. Mary Smallwood, The Jews under Roman Rule from Pompey to Diocletian (Leiden: E. J. Brill, 1976), 238.

19. The reality of such resistance in some cases is indicated in the Legatio ad Gaium 132-35. See Box, lix-lxii.

20. The general rhetorical device is defense through attack (cf. IO 4.1.49-50).   Philo carefully conceals the crucial question of citizenship claims.   On this point, it would be naive to suppose that Philo has a naive view of the causes of the pogrom (cf. V. Tcherikover and A. Fuks, Corpus Papyrorum Judaicarum I (Cambridge: Harvard University Press, 1957), 66).

21. Philo seems to imply that the dishonor suffered by Flaccus balances that suffered by the Jews during the pogrom.

22. Cf. M. Dibelius, Studies in the Acts of the Apostles (ed. H. Greeven; London: SCM, 1956), 138-85. See IO 4.2.88-93 on the devising of oratorical fictions that cannot be refuted.

23. Cf. Pelletier, 20-21.   Cf. IO 4.2.123.

24. It has long been noted that the teachings Josephus mentions about kindness to animals, the primacy of the death penalty, and the orientation to immortality cannot readily be shown to derive from the Pentateuch.   S. Belkin explains these divergences from the Bible as the product of the impact of Alexandrian halakah plus the natural tendency of apologetic works to describe laws in idealistic terms (Belkin, The Alexandrian Halakah in Apologetic Literature of the First Century C.E. [Philadelphia: Jewish Publication Society (1936)]).   Cf. T. Reinach and L. Blum, Flavius Josèphe Contre Apion (Paris: Société d'edition 'Les belles lettres, 1930), xxxviii.

25. In Philo's Hypothetica 6.1,4,6-7 alternative explanations of biblical events are offered, some of them miraculous, and the reader is invited to choose whichever he prefers.   Both Philo and Josephus in other writings express complex attitudes toward miracles; they sometimes simply report them without any questioning of their historicity, at other times they entertain rationalistic interpretations.   I suggest that the absence of outwardly miraculous phenomena in IF and the almost total absence of such in CA is the result of deliberate rhetorical strategy: they are written for pagan audiences unlikely to convinced by appeal to miracle stories.   On the general

subject, see H. A. Wolfson, Philo (Cambridge: Harvard
University Press, 1947), I , 347-56; G. Delling, Studien
zum Neuen Testament und zum hellenistischen Judentum:
Gesammelte Aufsätze 1950-1968 (Göttingen: Vandenhoeck &
Ruprecht, 1970), 72-145; G. MacRae, "Miracle in The
Antiquities of Josephus," in C. F. D. Moule (ed.),
Miracles (London: A. R. Mowbray & Co., 1965), 127-47;
O. Betz, "Das Problem des Wunders bei Flavius Josephus
im Vergleich zum Wunderproblem bei den Rabbinen und im
Johannesevangelium," in O. Betz et al. (eds.), Josephus-
Studien (Festschrift O. Michel; Göttingen: Vandenhoeck &
Ruprecht, 1974), 23-44.

26. See, e.g., IF 48; CA 2.146.   Philo emphasizes
that when Flaccus was arrested the Alexandrian Jewish
community did not succumb to Schadenfreude (IF 121), though
both he and Josephus attribute that emotion to pagans
(IF 77, 147, 154; CA 2.4-5).   Philo himself has been
accused of Schadenfreude in the composition of IF, but
V. Nikiprowetzky offers a convincing rebuttal in
"Schadenfreude chez Philon d'Alexandrie? Note sur In
Flaccum 121 sq.," Revue des études juives - historia judaica
127 (1968), 7-19.

27. The polemical character of CA is well summarized
by Th. Reinach, who also contends that the work offers
in part the results of generations of anonymous
apologetical work in the synagogues of Alexandria
(Contre Apion, xx, xxxix).   The relation of the
discussion of the ethical portions of the Mosaic Law
in CA to a hellenistic Jewish apologetic tradition is
emphasized in Belkin, Alexandrian Halakah (he thinks Josephus
probably depended largely on Philo's Hypothetica) and E.
Kamlah, "Frömmigkeit und Tugend: Die Gesetzesapologie des
Josephus in c Ap 2,145-295," in O. Betz et al. (eds.),
Josephus-Studien (Festscrift O. Michel; Göttingen:
Vandenhoeck & Ruprecht, 1974), 220-32 (Kamlah recognizes
that CA shows some dependence on Diaspora apologetic,
but emphasizes Josephus's orientation toward Palestinian
Judaism).

ISAIAH 28, A REDACTION CRITICAL STUDY

David L. Petersen
University of Illinois

I. Introduction

In this age of ferment in biblical scholarship,
universally agreed upon propositions are rare. Those studying
prophetic texts would, however, agree almost to a person that
the primary unit of prophetic discourse was a relatively
short, usually poetic, oracle.[1] Form criticism has taught us
that much. Nevertheless, the biblical scholar, unlike the
Assyriologist focussing on the Mari letters, confronts
integrated collections of prophetic oracles--books.
Virtually all the prophetic literature in the Hebrew Bible
survives as products of collecting and editorial activity.
One important question which the biblical scholar may
therefore address to that literature is this: what sort of
formative process took place between the time that oracles
were spoken or written and the time that the prophetic books
achieved their final form?

The answering of such questions has generally been
termed redaction criticism, about which it is important to
make two points here. 1) Redaction criticism necessarily
entails virtually all other higher (and lower) critical
approaches to biblical study. A person interested in
answering a redaction critical question presupposes form
critical endeavors, a demonstration that the original oracles
or vision reports were relatively short and often independent
units. That same person must be sensitive to the traditio-
historical background of the oracles as well as to their
literary workings.[2] Rigorous philological work is, of course,
part of the package. In sum, to engage the question about how
a prophetic book was formed is to engage a panoply of
approaches to the text. Redaction criticism is not an island
unto itself.

2) There has been a tendency in Hebrew bible redaction
critical studies to assume that the process of formation was
a rather mechanical one in which one layer of material was
added to or spliced with another earlier or different layer,
often for no discernible reason. Surely this is the case
because of the earliest redaction critical issues which
biblical scholars faced. Source criticism first raised the
issue of separate traditions in the tetrateuch and suggested
that the tetrateuch was formed when one block of material
(e.g. "P") was added to another (e.g. "J"). The flood story
remains a classic example of that sort of redactional process.
This model has influenced significantly the study of prophetic
texts, even though the higher critical base for the redaction
critical investigation has shifted from source criticism
to form criticism. Hence redaction criticism of prophetic
materials has often been viewed simply as the juxtaposition

of oracles or as the addition of foreign material to earlier
("genuine") oracles.

Although the model inherited from tetrateuchal studies
is appropriate for some problems in the prophetic literature,
it does not address adequately the composition of the
prophetic collections. Whereas in the tetrateuchal literature,
one could reasonably assign texts to one of four basic
traditions, one is confronted in the prophetic collections
with a much greater variety of non-primary material (such
material has been labelled as eschatological, apocalyptic,
midrashic, deutero-prophetic, expansionistic, harmonizing,
historicizing, linking and up-dating.) Redaction criticism
of prophetic books confronts not more or less complete and
discrete narrative traditions or oral collections but rather
oracular material which has been organized in a variety of
ways and to which material has been added at different times
for a variety of reasons. Redaction criticism of prophetic
literature must, therefore, chart its own course.

After that very brief prolegomenon, I now propose to
address the issue of the formation of the prophetic book ,
by focusing on one book and one chapter of that book,
Isaiah 28. To the best of my knowledge, Cornill began the
modern study of the book of Isaiah's composition.[3] He
proposed that the book was ordered according to an intentional
chronological schema and, subordinately, according to a
principle of verbal, especially catchword, similarity. Since
Cornill, and since the impact of form criticism on the study
of prophetic literature, the discussion about the formation
of Isaiah has concentrated less on the ways in which small
sections of the book were composed and has concentrated more
on the place of small collections of oracles in the final book;
how these small collections were integrated into the final
product.[4] Although the place of the "collection" in the final
book is an important issue, a prior stage in the formation of
the book is always presupposed in such discussions, how were
the small collections created? This question has not received
the attention it deserves. It is my position that discussions
about the formation of Isaiah need to address this question
before moving to the issue of how the subcollections were
ordered.

Isaiah 28 has not been the subject of a detailed
redaction critical study. Nevertheless, numerous scholars
have commented upon the formation and unity of this chapter.
Representative positions include the following:

1. Ziegler argued that Isa 28:1-29 comprised an original
literary unity (although he excised 28:5-6, 16-17a as later
additions). His conclusions rested primarily on the word
correspondences present in the text.[5]

2. Mowinckel understood the chapter to be an artificial
unity created by the redactor out of independent sayings
(28:1-4, 7-13, 14-22, 23-29) and to which 28:5-6 were later
added.[6]

3. Donner advanced a position not radically dissimilar
from Mowinckel through he emphasized the original independence
of the constitutent oracles (28:1-4, 7-13, 14-17, and probably,
20-22). 28:5-6 are understood to be a much later addition.[7]

4. Fohrer, in a programmatic essay on the formation
of Isaiah 1-39, theorized that 28:7-32:14 was one subcollec-
tion. To this collection had been added a promise, 28:5-6, and
an oracle from the collection of oracles against the nation,
28:1-4. In describing the formation of 28:7-32:14 Fohrer
writes:

> The compiler has arranged the oracles principally
> according to the similarity of content, less often by
> catchwords. The section 28:1-4, taken from collection
> F [the oracles against the nations], is connected to
> 28:7-13 by the motif of drunkenness. As the priests and
> prophets scoff at Isaiah in this text, 28:14-22 follows
> with the catchword "scoffer." 28:23-29 stands isolated,
> unless one accepts that it has been transferred to
> this position to serve Isaiah as a defense against his
> scoffers."[8]

5. Childs wrote: "Chapter 28 is a collection of oracles
which were delivered at varying times to different audiences.
Nevertheless, there are many indications of redactional
activity which would join the oracles thematically. Just
as the proud drunkards of Ephraim disregarded their warning
and were destroyed, so will the scoffers in Judah fall. It
still remains a difficult and much debated problem to
understand how the parable in vv 23-29 fits into this
disputational framework."[9]

6. Kaiser, in his commentary, argued for the presence
of two primary Isaianic oracles: Isa 28:7b-12, 14-18. To
these have been added two levels of eschatological redaction:
earlier--28:1-4, 7a, 13, 19-22; and later--28:5-6. The
origins of the concluding poem, 28:23-29, are difficult to
assess; however, it is probably redactional.[10]

7. Dietrich proposed that 28:1-22 is an integrated
collection which has a basic leitmotif, against frivolity
towards Yahweh and his prophets. Isa 28:1-18 probably existed
as an earlier collection, to which 19-22, fragmentary
predictions, were then added.[11]

8. Barth challenges directly Donner's thesis that the
units which make up 28:7b-22 were originally independent.
Barth is inclined to view 28:7b-22 as a literary unit since
there are no easily reconstructable speech units. As for
the other parts of the chapter, he contends vv 1-4 are
Isaianic; vv 5-6 are post-exilic additions; and vv 23-29
are a didactic poem which did not stem from the hand of Isaiah
since the picture of Yahweh's action presented in the didactic
poem is so at odds with other descriptions of Yahweh's action
in Isaiah. Barth then argues that Isa 28:23-29 belongs to the
Assyrian redaction of the book, a systematic revision of the

book which dates to the late seventh century B.C.E.[12]

Common to virtually all this literature is the attempt
to specify authorship, to separate Isaianic from non-
Isaianic material. However, little is offered by way of
explaining how the various levels of the text work together,
or why one element or another was added to the earlier
material. (Fohrer, and Barth do, however, broach these
issues.) In this paper I will attempt to determine the
process by means of which Isaiah 28 was formed. To study
this process, I have found it necessary to undertake a brief
examination of each unit in the chapter. Within this context,
I shall formulate an argument about the ways in which this
booklet developed, an argument which will be presented
systematically in the conclusions.

In an earlier paper written for this group studying the
formation of prophetic books, March wrote, "How is the work
of the redactor(s) to be recognized, analyzed, interpreted?
In the earliest stages of collection arrangement seems to
involve chronological principles or the similarity in theme
or terminology. But very early on (and some will argue from
the outset) a different, more intentional, process takes
over--according to redaction criticism--which can be
studied."[13] It is this formative process, which we label as
redaction, that I hope to clarify in Isaiah 28.

II. Isaiah 28

A. Isa 28:1-4 A Crown in the Present

.1 "Woe, majestic crown,
        Drunkards of Ephraim,
    Withering flower,
        Their glorious beauty
            which is on the head of the fertile valley[14]
            of those struck down by wine.
.2 Behold, Yahweh has someone strong and mighty[15]
    like a hail storm,
        a stormy wind of destruction,
    like a storm of mighty and rushing water,
        he casts down to earth with strength.
.3 The majestic crown
        of the drunkards of Ephraim
    shall be trampled underfoot.
.4 Withering flower,
        Their glorious beauty
    which is upon the head of the fertile valley
        shall be like an early fig before summer
            which, whenever a person sees it;
                he devours it as soon as it is in his hand."

Introducing the post-Isaianic Apocalypse material,
Isa 28:1-4 comprises a woe oracle directed against Ephraim.
Like a typical woe oracle, it is made up of two primary parts:
an indictment section introduced by hôy which is followed by a
sentence or judgment section (vv 2-4). Further, the syntax,

hôy followed by a subject without intervening preposition, is typologically an early style of woe oracle.[16]

However, despite the clarity of this unit as a woe oracle, its interpretation remains difficult since the language is so highly symbolic. Any examination of that oracle therefore requires some study of this symbolism. In v 1, the crown apparently signifies Samaria, an image consistent with the poetry of Isa 7:9 in which Samaria is depicted as the head of Ephraim. Interestingly, in neither Isa 7:9 nor in Isa 28:1 is the head-crown image itself a negative symbol. gē'ût is not used to mean inappropriate pride or majesty; gā'ōn conveys that meaning. Rather, once the object of the woe has been registered, then the second phrase, "drunkards of Ephraim," introduces the derogatory tone. The crown is further defined negatively as a withering flower. In the second bicolon, the negative element is first and the positive, or at least neutral, element is last. Hence the argument of the first poetic subunit includes a chiasm-- majestic:drunk::withering:glorious. In the final bicolon, the symbolism of drunkenness reappears. By the end of the first verse, the picture is that of a teetering crown, as stable as a withered flower.

Verse two introduces a second set of images, those of an unidentified individual who is described using storm language. The thunderstorm with its lightning, fire, rain, thunder and trembling landscape is a typical symbol system used to depict Yahweh's theophany. However the symbolism in Isa 28:2 is not that system. In Isaiah 1-39, the water storm (rain, hail, flood; but without accompanying fire and lightning) is used to describe an historical threat, the Neo-Assyrians, so Isa 8:7. This liquid imagery is especially appropriate in Isa 28:7-13 since 1) the drunkenness introduced earlier is the result of liquid and 2) water is that which might be expected to revivify a fading flower. Despite this continuity in imagery, the syntax of the final clause in Isa 28:2 presents a problem. One looks in vain for an object of hinnîah. However, since Isa 28:1-2 share liquid imagery, the crown/flower which is high and unstable is a likely candidate for casting down action. Both symbolism and syntax therefore serve to unite Isa 28:1-2.

Whereas Isa 28:1-2 present the logic of the woe oracle in nuce, Isa 28:3-4, an expanded judgment section, explore the imagery and language already introduced in the first verse. In v 3b, the language of v 1a is quoted and in v 4ab, the language of v 1bc is quoted. In vv 3-4 the language which had earlier signified the object of the hôy now functions within the judgment context.

In Isa 28:3, the movement begun in vv 1-2 continues to its logical conclusion. In verse one we learn about a teetering crown. In verse two we hear that it will be cast down. And then in verse three, the crown will be trampled underfoot. What was on the head will be brought low and smashed with feet. The final verse, Isa 28:4, moves in a

quite different manner. Instead of continuing the imagery
of Isa 28:1-3, it introduces an entirely new set of symbols,
agricultural and culinary, and in so doing provides a
striking conclusion to the oracle. The language of fertility
from verse one is quoted and then developed in a simile. This
simile is particularly apt since it conjures a positive image,
the first ripe fig and its delectability. But its very
succulence leads to immediate consumption, a negative image.
In this sudden turn from positive to negative, the fate of
the ripe fig signals a similar view of the end of Samaria;
this state will, at the height of its effulgence, suffer sudden
destruction. It is on this rising and then falling note
that the oracle ends. The final simile drives home the
earlier and more detailed reversal- crown on head to thing
trampled underfoot.

That the oracle is a tightly constructed unit is difficult
to gainsay. The play on hand (yād in v 2, kap in v 4),
liquid imagery--water overcoming wine, food and drink ingestion
imagery, botanical imagery: withered flower, fertile fig--
all attest to a well-wrought poem.[17]

By way of drawing on these form critical and literary
comments, I will argue first that this oracle was composed
by someone using notions drawn from the Syro-Ephraimitic
material (Isaiah 6-9). 1) Isa 7:9 provides the imagery of
Samaria as a head. 2) Isa 8:7 introduces the image of
Assyria as powerful water. I argue Isa 8:7 is the source for
Isa 28:2, and not the reverse, because Isa 8:7 reflects a
specific situation--the adequacy of the Shiloah waters and
the consequent reversing, by Isaiah, of the water imagery so
that Assyria will come and destroy not only Ephraim, but also
Judah (in Isa 28:1-4, the waters will destroy only Ephraim).
3) In Isa 8:7, as in Isa 28:2, we learn about a person in
Yahweh's service, the king of Assyria. In sum, many of the
images in 28:1-4 are drawn from the Syro-Ephraimitic booklet.
However, the form of this oracle, the woe form, is a vehicle
which is foreign to the Syro-Ephraimitic material. One may
therefore suggest that this oracle is a poem which formulates
earlier traditions but in a form in which those traditions
did not regularly occur. Why?

Someone had made a decision that the major markers of the
Isaianic collection Isa 28-32(33) would be woe oracles, so
Isa 28:1; 29;1; 29;15; 30:1; 31:1; 33:1. Hence it was
appropriate, even necessary, to introduce chapter 28 with a
woe oracle.[18] Furthermore, there was apparently a certain
biographical component at work. Since Isaiah's earliest
activity focused on Ephraim, it made sense to introduce this
major collection with an oracle which reflected that period.
However, because the traditions and imagery which were
appropriate to that period were not preserved in woe oracle
form, someone (Isaiah or an editor/author) fashioned a
carefully-crafted poem to introduce both Isa 28 and the
larger collection, Isaiah 28-32(33).[19]

B.   Isa 28:5-6 A Crown for the Future

.5 "On that day,
        Yahweh will be a beautiful crown
            and a chaplet of glory
            for the remnant of his people.
.6   and a spirit of justice for the
            one who sits in judgment,
           and strength for those who turn back
            battle at the gate."

Despite the presence of language in v 5 which has appeared
in Isa 28:1-4, the transitional marker, bayyôm hahû', as well
as the marked shift in perspective sets Isa 28:5-6 off from
its context. The key argument here is that Isa 28:5-6
interrupt two units (Isa 28:1-4, 7-13) which share one motif,
that of drunkenness. Isa 28:5-6 is intrusive. Nevertheless
it is obvious that Isa 28:5-6 is somehow related to
Isa 28:1-4. Vocabulary from Isa 28:1-4 is taken up in
Isa 28:5: 'ăteret, şebî, tip'ārāh. And these words are used
quite differently than they are in the earlier woe oracle.
Whereas this language referred to a crown to be destroyed,
an object of woe in Isa 28:1-4, this language in Isa 28:5
now describes that which Yahweh will become bayyôm hahû'.

The image of the beautiful crown introduced in 28:1 has
been interpreted in 28:5. Why? To help answer this question,
it is necessary to recognize that there is another Isaianic
text introduced by bayyôm hahû' (Isa 4:2-4) in which the words
şebî and 'ăteret are used.[20] In Isa 4:2, "Yahweh's branch
will become beautiful (şebî) and glorious and the fruit of
the land shall be pride and glory (tip'eret) for the survivors
of Israel (and Judah-IQIsᵃ)". It is my thesis that the
author of Isa 28:5-6 knew, and probably wrote, 4:2-4 and
that he interpreted 38:1-4 on the basis of the sentiment
expressed 4:2-4. Both 28:1-4 and 4:2 share vocabulary and
a symbol--succulent fruit. Since there was an editor/author
interested in explicating "that day", that person revised the
image of the crown in Isa 28:1-4 by using the positive tone of
the adjectives and fruit image in Isa 4:2-4. Isa 4:2-4, and
the sentiment it represents, warrants the interpretation
which we find in Isa 28:5-6.

Isa 28:6 continues the picture of what Yahweh will be
"on that day." Yahweh will enable the judicial and the
military systems to function properly. Though human
instrumentalities are mentioned (the one sitting in judgment,
those fighting at the gate), the success of these ventures
will depend upon Yahweh's empowering spirit and strength.
This belief about Yahweh is no random addition to Isa 28:5.
The enabling power of Yahweh, the ruaḥ, (and more particularly
ruaḥ mišpāṭ) is referred to not only in Isa 28:6 but also in
Isa 4:4. That fact suggests Isa 4:2-4 as a whole, rather than
simply Isa 4:2, has influenced the formation of 28:5-6.

In sum, Isaiah 28:5-6 is an interpretation of the crown imagery present in Isa 28:1. This interpretation has been guided by the language and perspective in Isa 4:2-4 and may well represent the same authorial hand as does that latter text.

C. Isa 28:7-13 Knowledge and Nonsense

.7 "And these also stagger with wine
    and go astray with strong drink.
  Priest and prophet stagger with strong drink,
    they are engulfed by wine,
    they go astray with strong drink.
  They stagger in vision;
    they reel in making decisions.[21]
.8 For all tables are covered with vomit,
    no place is without excrement.
.9 To whom will he teach knowledge,
    or to whom will he explain the message?
  Those just weaned from milk?
    Those just taken from the breast?
.10 It would then be:
    ṣaw lāṣāw ṣaw lāṣāw[22]
    qaw lāqāw qaw lāqāw
    Here a little, there a little.
.11 Indeed, with those of derisive language
    with an alien tongue
    he will speak to this people,
.12 to whom he has (earlier) spoken:
    'This is rest.
      Give rest to the weary!
    This is repose.'
  But they were unwilling to respond.[23]
.13 Then the word of Yahweh will become for them:
    ṣaw lāṣāw ṣaw lāṣāw
    qaw lāqāw qaw lāqāw
    Here a little, there a little;
      so that they may go and stumble backwards,
      be broken, snared and captured."

That Isa 28:7-13 does not sit easily with Isa 28:5-6 has been long observed. However, once one recognizes the intrusive character of 28:5-6, the linkage between 28:1-4 and 28:7-13 becomes apparent. Not only is one motif—drunkenness—(28:1 šikkōrê and 28:7 šēkār) shared, but there is also a catchword connection (28:4 yiblāʿennāh and 28:7 niblᵉʿû).

The terminal boundary of Isa 28:7-13 needs little justification. The formulaic introduction in Isa 28:14 indicates clearly that Isa 28:13 is the final verse of the preceding oracle. Isa 28:7 is, however, an unusual beginning, so unusual that I will argue 7ab is a redactional creation which integrates the list of roles (prophet, priest) with previously mentioned drunkards, those of Ephraim. Since all of the words in 28:7ab (with the exception of wᵉgam ʾēlleh) appear in 28:7c-f, one may infer that an editor has formulated a connector out of the fabric of the ensuing oracle. For this reason, whatever standard introductory formula may have preceded 28:7-13 has now been irretrievably lost.

In this judgement oracle, the indictment is reasonably straightforward; priest and prophet are unable to enact their roles because of drunkenness. And there is an extended sentence, vv 11-13 (see below). Problematic is the disputational material, vv 9-10. The interpretation here turns on the referent of the verbal subject; who is the "he" of v 9? Most commentators have argued that "he" is Isaiah since it is he that is apparently condemning the religious establishment--priest and prophet--for drunken behavior. They respond by challenging his right to speak about them as a group needing instruction; presumably they have knowledge and understanding. Such an approach makes v 9a intelligible, but vv 9b-10 then become cloudy. Why would the authorities allude to themselves as those just weaned, or why would they charge Isaiah's critique as being either so much nonsense or learning the alphabet?[24]

There is another way of understanding Isa 28:9a which allows vv 9a-10 to make sense as well, and that is to understand the "he" of v 9a to be Yahweh. That is to say, one should read the text as follows: Isaiah has issued an indictment of the religious establishment in vv 7-8, they are a drunken and incompetent lot. Isaiah then poses a rhetorical question: "To whom will Yahweh teach knowledge and to whom will Yahweh explain his message?" Then comes an answer which, by dint of its being so unlikely, is obviously to be rejected. Yahweh will not instruct those who have just been weaned--those whose intellectual faculties are undeveloped. For to them, Yahweh's instruction would be so much gibberish, speech with as little meaning as a recitation of the alphabet.

The inability of the infants to understand Yahweh's knowledge--for them it would be nonsense--raises the possibility of Yahweh speaking strangely to non-infants, a possibility explored in Isa 28:11-13, the sentence component of this judgment oracle. Here Isaiah asserts that Yahweh will speak strangely to his people, that he will choose someone with an alien tongue in order to address his people. And he will do this because this people has rejected his earlier speech when that was intelligible ("This is rest. Give rest to the weary! This is repose.") To this reasonable and comforting language, the people did not respond.[25] Therefore, as punishment, the people will now experience Yahweh as an infant would experience someone giving a learned lecture. Yahweh will speak with an alien tongue. Yahweh's speech will now be "ṣaw lāṣāw..." instead of "This is rest."[26]

Put in form critical terms, the indictment derives from the inability of the priests and prophets to hear Yahweh's words of weal intelligently. The sentence states that Yahweh will, in turn, give them alien, unintelligible words.

One final issue requires discussion, the result clause in Isa 28:13. After the nonsense language, we are told, by means of a clause introduced by lᵉma'an, that Yahweh's speech will have a very specific impact on his people. It is my contention that the sequence of verbs in this result clause is an attempt to spell out the significance of the earlier nonsense, an attempt to make intelligible out of that which was intended to be unintelligible. Interestingly, just as was the case with the interpretation present in Isa 28:5-6, the interpreter has in Isa 28:13 drawn upon language from elsewhere in the book of Isaiah, from Isa 8:15. Of the five verbs in Isa 28:13ef only one is not present in the sequence of verbs in Isa 8:15, a sequence of verbs which describes Yahweh's action against Israel (8:15--wᵉkāšᵉlû, wᵉnāpᵉlû, wᵉnišbārû, wᵉnoqᵉšû, wᵉnilkādû; 28:13--yēlᵉku, wᵉkāšᵉlû, wᵉnišbāru, wᵉnoqᵉšû, wᵉnilkādu).

In sum, this judgment oracle depicting the reason for Yahweh's shift from intelligible to unintelligible speech has grown in two ways. First Isa 28:7a was formulated as a transitional link between Isa 28:7b-13a and 28:1-4. Second, Isa 28:13ef was added in order to specify what the alien speech would mean for Israel. This latter addition was influenced by language found elsewhere in the book, language in Isa 8:13.

D. Isa 28:14-22 An Alien Covenant and its Impact

.14 "Therefore, hear the word of Yahweh
        O Scoffers,[27]
        Rulers of this people[28]
        who are in Jerusalem.
.15 For you have said:
        'We have made a covenant with death;
        we have made a pact with Sheol.[29]
    When an overpowering scourge passes through,[30]
        it will not come to us
            because we have made a lie our refuge,
            we have hidden ourselves in falsehood.'
.16 Therefore, thus says the Lord Yahweh,
        'Behold, I founded Zion as a (foundation) stone,[31]
        as hard rock,[32]
        a valuable cornerstone of the foundation[33]
        Whoever trusts in it, need not worry.'
.17 I will now make justice a measuring line
        and righteousness into a level.
    Hail will sweep away the refuge of lies,
        and waters will overpower the hiding place.
.18 Then your covenant with death will be removed,
        and your pact with Sheol will not stand.
    When an overpowering scourge passes through,
        it will mean destruction for you.
.19 Whenever it passes through, it will take you,
        for it will pass through morning after morning
            day and night.

> And it will be sheer terror
>> to understand the message.
> .20 For the bed is too short on which to stretch oneself
>> out and the covering is too narrow in which to
>> wrap oneself up.
> .21 For as on Mount Perazim
>> Yahweh will rise up.
> He will be stirred up
>> as in the valley of Gibeon
> to do his work,
>> strange is his work,
> to do his labor,
>> strange is his labor.
> .22 So now, do not scoff,
>> lest your bonds be strong;[34]
> for I have heard of a decisive annihilation
>> from God, Yahweh of Hosts, against all the earth.

This unit is surely the most complex of the chapter. That it includes the basic elements of a judgment oracle has been argued, by among others, Childs and Melugin.[35] However, there are difficulties: 1) what the people are quoted as saying in v 15 makes no sense, and 2) an oracle of promise, vv 16-17, does not belong in a judgment oracle. As for 1), the indictment of the judgment oracle is expressed simply as a quotation of some Jerusalemites. They admit to having contracted a treaty with death and having trusted in lies. That such action is worthy of indictment needs no justification. However, that the people themselves should admit to such action is without parallel. Surely this quotation is an example of the literary technique in which words are put in someone's mouth to stress a certain point. In so doing, the poet/prophet has depicted the people as doing something strange, virtually unintelligible. The indictable offense is not just wrong, what the people have done makes little sense.

2) Moving to the judgment section, or at least the formula which would typically introduce the judgment section, we find an oracle which has traditionally been translated as if it were an oracle of future weal. As is clear from the translation and notes presented here, the proposal of Huber, which I follow, presents vv 16b-17 in an entirely new light. Rather than a promise of weal, this oracle comprises a statement by Yahweh about what he has done in the past-- founded Zion as his stable rock.

Admittedly, it is unusual to begin the threat component of a judgment oracle with a statement of past action. However, the logic and imagery are unassailably cogent. Yahweh has built Zion, and in so doing, acted beneficently in the past. The people have apparently ignored the significance of that action and have made a treaty which is strange in the extreme. Therefore, Yahweh will make justice and righteousness into tools of destruction rather than construction. The judgment continues in vv 18-19 (I take 17b to be intrusive, see below). V 18 picks up the confident assertion of the people and turns the tables by using this language to depict the coming judgment. V 19 continues the sentence by: 1) focusing on the "passing through" of the overpowering scourge, and 2) striking a theme which occurs elsewhere in this collection, the alien character of Yahweh's future action. Isa 28:19b provides an apt conclusion to the oracle since it ties the nonsensical treaty which the people have contracted to a "terrible to understand" punishment. Strange sin deserves alien punishment.

To this kernel oracle (Isa 28:14-17a, 18-19), two additions were made. First, v 17b, as many have recognized seems out of place.[36] I argue that a traditionist composed this bicolon using the language of Isa 28:2 to emphasize that vv 16-17 should be interpreted negatively, and not as an oracle of weal. Further, this addition is a felicitous interpretation not only because it links Isa 28:14-19 with Isa 28:1-4 and thereby serves to unify the collection, but also because it is consistent with the water imagery present in Isa 28:15, 18.

A second and more extensive commentary has been provided in vv 20-22, and it is these verses which have caused more problems for interpreters of Isaiah 28 than have any others. Dietrich understands vv 19-22 to be a "series of fragmentary prophecies which, though they do not themselves cohere, are bound together with vv 1-18."[37] That v 22a is related as a sort of inclusio to v 14, many, including Dietrich, have contended. That v 21b is related to the theme of Yahweh's unintelligible action (vv 11, 19) has also been recognized. However, no one has satisfactorily explained the function of vv 20, 21a or 22b in the context of this larger unit.

I will argue that vv 20-22 are a collection of three separate pieces, each of which provides a commentary on the earlier oracle.[38] V 20 has been construed form critically by many as a proverb.[39] This interpretation makes little sense if one takes seriously the form of the standard proverb. If a particular generic context, that of wisdom, does not illumine this bicolon, what does it mean? One may say two things. The picture formulated by v 20 is that of inadequate provisions for night and sleep. A bed too short and a blanket too small leave one uncomfortable, cold, and unable to sleep. Second, night, or more precisely, "by night," ballāyᵉlāh. has been mentioned in the previous verse. In Isa 28:19, the author notes that the šôṭ will be present both day and night. V 20 then suggests that Judah is as unprepared to confront the šôṭ at night as is one prepared to sleep during the night when the bed is short and the cover is scanty. V 20 therefore intensifies the sense of disaster which the šôṭ will create at night.

Aside from the introductory particle kî which both vv 20 and 21 share, these two verses are in no way related. And there is no obvious way in which v 21a is related to that which has preceded it in Isaiah 28. To be sure, v 21b strikes the theme of the unintelligibility of Yahweh's action with

Israel. However, that thematic connection does not serve to integrate v 21a with its larger context.

It has been a commonplace for commentators to observe that Perazim and Gibeon refer to Yahweh's military activity. And they then assert that reference to such action creates a threat that Yahweh will rise up against his own people. The obvious question then becomes, why did the author/editor choose Perazim and Gibeon as references to Yahweh's military activity, particularly if this activity is to be understood as a threat against Judah? This question is especially difficult since neither battle narrative was a famous example of Yahweh's holy war. At Ba'al-perazim, David is recorded as having engaged and defeated the Philistines. That this was not the decisive battle against the Philistines may be inferred from 2 Sam 5:22, a text which records that the Philistines immediately engaged David at Rephaim. The battle at Ba'al-perazim was not one of Yahweh's great and final victories. Similarly, in Josh 10:9-14, an historian records Joshua's defense of the Gibeonites against an attack by Amorite kings. As with the battle at Ba'al-perazim, this battle was not a final victory since conflict with the Amorites continues to the end Joshua 10.

I will, however, argue that these two references are a natural pair, remarkably well-chosen for the commentator's purposes. One may contend that the events at Ba'al-perazim and at Gibeon share some basic features: 1) Both Perazim and Gibeon signify victories, though not absolute ones. 2) In both narratives, Yahweh is explicitly described as an active agent. 3) The most important similarity, and most probably the reason why an editor/author chose these texts to explicate Isa 28:14-19, is that Yahweh is understood as having destroyed the enemy like or with particular natural elements: hail (Gibeon) and breaking out like water (Ba'al-perazim). [Josh 10:11, "And Yahweh threw down great stones from heaven upon them as far as Azekah, and they died; there were more who died because of the hailstones than the men of Israel killed with the sword." 2 Sam 5:20, "The Lord has broken through my enemies before me like a bursting flood."] These two elements, hail and water, are present two places in Isaiah 28--in v 2 where they are included in a list which describes the strength of Yahweh's agent, and in v 17b a bicolon which mentions only hail and water as the means by which the covenant death will be overpowered. V 21 is probably of the same basic stratum as v 17b, and is a comment designed to recall to the readers of this booklet that Yahweh had earlier used or been like hail and water and that such activity had defeated his enemies. Since v 21 is an integral syntactic unit, one must understand v 21b, yet another reference to the theme of unintelligibility, to stress that what was earlier an act on behalf of Israel will now be strange and foreign to Israel. The positive to negative movement implied in this verse parallels the movement in both primary oracles--that from an earlier oracle of weal to future alien action.

V 22, with its use of the verbal root lyz, functions as
an inclusio with vv 14, which also uses the root lyz, and in
so doing serves to integrate the commentary with the primary
oracles. This verse, like another traditionist's
formulation, Isa 28:17b, is created using language present
elsewhere in the book.

Isa 28:22bc kî kālāh wᵉneḥĕrāṣāh šāmaʿtî
             mēʾēt ʾădōnâ yhwh ṣᵉbāʾôt ʿal kol hāʾāreṣ

Isa 10:23   kî kālāh wᵉneḥĕrāṣāh
             ʾădōnâ yhwh ṣᵉbāʾôt ʿōśeh bᵉqereb kol hāʾāreṣ

Both prose texts, reflect a similar sentiment, that Yahweh's
military activity will result in cosmic destruction. In
Isa 28:22 this language emphasizes that Yahweh, and not an
accident or foreign power, is behind the coming Judahite
destruction. This verse underlines the "I" of Isa 28:17 and
underscores the massive scope of Yahweh's action.

By way of summary, Isa 28:14-22 is made up of a primary
judgment oracle, vv 14-17a, 18-19, into which has been
inserted a description of the punishment, a description
formulated from the material of Isa 28:2. Appended to the
primary oracle are three unrelated interpretations, one of
which explores the scourge by night, another of which
emphasizes the alien character of Yahweh's activity,
especially as that activity is understand to entail hail
and water, and a final one which creates an inclusio with
v 14, which shares the language of Isa 10:23, and which
emphasizes Yahweh as the source of the cosmic destruction.

E. Isa 28:23-29 Yahweh's Intelligible World

  .23 Listen, hear my voice!
        Pay attention, hear my word!
  .24 Does the plowman plow continually?[40]
        Does he unceasingly open and harrow his ground?
  .25 Does he not, when has smoothed its surface,
        scatter black cummin, sow cumin
        and put in wheat and barley[41]
          and spelt for its border?
  .26 He instructs him appropriately;
        his God teaches him.
  .27 Indeed, dark cumin is not threshed with a threshing
          tool
        nor is a cart wheel rolled over cumin.
      Rather, dark cumin is beaten out with a stick
        and cumin with a rod.
  .28 Bread grain is beaten,
        but not to dust;[42]
      he just threshes it.
      The wheels of his cart may rumble along,
        but his horses do not crush it.
  .29 This also comes from Yahweh of Hosts;
        he is marvelous in counsel
        he increases prosperity greatly.

Fortunately, the structure of this final poem is not obscure. Introduced by a call to attention, it comprises two major sections, each of which is concluded by a comment relating the activity described to Yahweh's wisdom.[43] Few would gainsay the prominence of wisdom elements in this poem. Whether the poem itself is a wisdom form, a parable, as Whedbee argues, strikes me as unlikely. A parable, as does Isa 5:1-7, regularly entails a narrative and a comparison. Isa 28:23-29 has neither of these elements. Hence rather than to designate the poem as a parable, I would prefer to label it simply as a poem which is informed by literary techniques prominent in wisdom literature.

More convincing is Whedbee's argument that the poem includes disputation.[44] And the point of the disputation is quite simple: as the process of planting and harvesting cumin suggests, Yahweh's universe is a productive and intelligible place in which to live. One need not seek an historical background for the poem and then hypothesize how this poem fits that background in order to discern the basic point of the disputation.[45] The poem as an artfully constructed unit, makes its point clearly.

Further the poem has a distinct function, a "larger" meaning within the context of this small collection. The two primary oracles, 28:7-13, 14-19, both emphasize two facts: 1) that Israelites are acting stupidly, and 2) that Yahweh's activity toward Israel will be strange, even unintelligible. To propound that claim forcefully is to raise serious questions about the general intelligibility of the universe. By the end of Isa 28:22, even Yahweh's earlier activity on Israel's behalf has been described as strange and alien. Surely the natural question at this point is: can one still speak about a world which is intelligible, about a cosmos in which a wise God rules? Isa 28:23-29, in its present place, answers this question affirmatively. Quoting Whedbee,"...the description of the orderly phases of the farmer's activities is given in order to demonstrate the thesis that Yahweh, like the farmer, acts wisely even though he does different things at different times."[46] And it is not only Yahweh who can act sensibly. The human, who is also symbolized by the farmer, can similarly learn a rational way of life. Put within the context of the other oracles in Isaiah 28, just because some people (prophet, priest, ruler) act crazily, and just because Yahweh is acting in ways which Israel will not understand does not mean that Yahweh has become an alien or unintelligible god, or that all people are necessarily irrational. Rather, by observing normal farming practices one can learn at least two things: that Yahweh himself is wise, and that people who avail themselves of his wisdom can learn to live intelligently. Yahweh is the proper source of human wisdom.

III. Conclusions

It is now possible to reconstruct the way in which Isaiah 28 was formed. The process began with two "seed" oracles, Isa 28:7b-13a and 28:14-17a, 18-19. These oracles share four basic elements:

1) Both indicted leading social roles: the first condemned priests and prophets whereas the second polemicized rulers.

2) Earlier words of weal from Yahweh are quoted in both oracles.

3) In both oracles, the earlier words of Yahweh were understood as having been rejected by the people of Judah.

4) Both oracles stressed the alien, unintelligible character of Yahweh's forthcoming response to his people.

Isaiah 28:7b-13a and 28:14-17a, 18-19 share a paradigmatic similarity. Although not identical form critically, they have fundamental structural and thematic ties. Someone observed these similarities and juxtaposed them.

Further, the order in which the oracles were juxtaposed is significant, and this for two reasons. 1) In Isa 28:7b-13a, we learn that Yahweh will say something that is unintelligible. More than that is not stated in the primary oracle. However, when vv 14-19 follow vv 7b-13a, we learn that this strange speech will result in action which is equally alien. In the present order of the oracles, there is an appropriate progression from speech to action. 2) Just as what is alien moves from general speech to more specific action, so those addressed move from the general to the specific. In vv 7b-13a, we are confronted with prophets and priests of no specific place. In vv 14-19, however, the oracle addresses rulers of a particular place, Jerusalem. For these two reasons, the specific ordering of these oracles is significant. This juxtaposition and specific ordering is the primary redactional move upon which the remainder of the chapter depends.

Ensuing redactional developments are difficult to chart chronologically. Nevertheless, what happened and the reasons for what happened are reasonably clear.

1) Both seed oracles elicited commentary which has been appended to the end of each oracle.

a) Isa 28:7b-13a, which predict unintelligible speech, provoked a result clause, v 13b. This clause attempts to make intelligible what was unintelligible--that those indicted would be overcome. The commentator used the language of Isa 8:15 to construct this result clause.

b) Isa 28:20-22 have been added to the second seed oracle. Vv 20-21 explicate respectively the terror by night (Isa 28:19) and the peculiar character of Yahweh's action

with rain and hail. V 22, again using language found
elsewhere in the book (Isa 8:15), creates an inclusio with
v 14 and thereby integrates the entire commentary into a
new and larger whole.

2) Other oracles were added thereby creating a more
sizeable collection.

a) Isa 28:1-4, an exceptionally well-wrought poem,
provides not only a chronological preface to Isaiah's
activity with Israel (and in so doing represents a biographic
impulse in the redaction), but also strikes a note which
continues in vv 7-13, that of drunkenness. Isa 28:7a appears
to be a transitional element formulated to facilitate the
move from vv 1-4 to v 7b.

Both Isa 28:1-4 and vv 7-13 include indictments of
drunkenness and corresponding sentences. The oracles are,
however, different in one crucial way. Isa 28:1-4 refer
explicitly to Ephraim whereas 7-13 refer to no particular
place. The indictment is open, and allows for the potential
inclusion of Judah, a potential which is actualized in
vv 14-22, an oracle directed explicitly against Jerusalem.
The three oracles (vv 1-4, 7-13, 14-22) work together to
create a transition, from an indictment and sentence against
Israel to an indictment and sentence against Judah.

Finally, Isa 28:1-4 was probably appended at the time in
which the larger collection, Isaiah 28-32(33), was being
formed. Its character as woe oracle is integral to the
structure of the larger collection.

b) Since the block of material, Isa 28:1-4, 7-22,
created such a powerful picture of unintelligible human and
divine activity, someone formulated a response to that
picture by appending a poem heavily influenced by wisdom
language. This final poem is not only an appropriate
response to the two issues which it confronts—the
possibility for intelligible divine and human activity—but
it continues imagery used at the beginning of the collection.
Agricultural imagery begins the collection (Isa 28:1   wine,
v 4 fig) and concludes it (Isa 28:24-25   planting, vv 27-28
harvesting).

3) As a function of the new and larger collection,
commentary upon the primary oracles has been introduced from
the accretionary material. Isa 28:17b has been formulated
using the destruction language (rain and hail) of Isa 28:2.

4) Interrupting the sequence Isa 28:1-4, 7-13 is an
oracle radically reinterpreting the symbols used in Isa 28:1.
These two verses, vv 5-6, are different in both style and
sentiment from the surrounding material. Furthermore, they
share features with Isa 4:2-4, features which allow one to
infer that both passages belong to a similar stratum in the
book (what some would call an early apocalyptic strand).

At the risk of oversimplification, I offer the following graphic depiction of the process by means of which Isaiah 28 was formed.

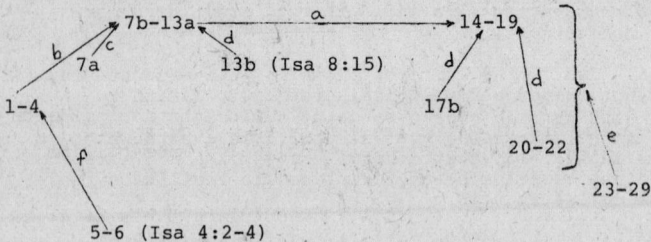

Type of relationship:

    a--sequence

    b--preface

    c--transition

    d--explication

    e--response

    f--reinterpretation

This study has revealed one very interesting tendency in the formative process. There appears to be an impulse to formulate redactional matter out of language found elsewhere in the book: 28:22 from 8:15; 28:5-6 from 4:2-4; 28:17b from 28:2. One may be justified in speaking of inner-Isaianic exegesis.

If the formation of one chapter in a prophetic book may serve as a microcosmic example for the formation of the prophetic book, or at least one stage in that process; then this examination of Isaiah 28 suggests the process of formation is complex indeed. Two metaphors seem appropriate to describe this process. On the one hand, the geological metaphor is apt. Following especially Barth, we may identify different strata in the book, though the degree to which a date may be assigned to these strata is now minimal. On the other hand, a more organic metaphor is also necessary since there seem to be seed oracles which, when preserved, naturally elicit juxtaposition and interpretation. To focus exclusively on stratigraphy is to risk missing the reason why commentary was inserted or linkages were formulated. To focus exclusively on the organic perspective is to risk not perceiving the growth as one in which various elements are outcroppings of one stratum.

This study suggests that the book of Isaiah is composed
of collections which have resulted from a complex process
of growth. Further study of the formation of Isaiah must
recognize the existence of such booklets, the process of
their formation, and their place in the final collection.

NOTES

1. Cf. the caveat of W. Holladay, The Architecture of
Jeremiah 1-20 (Lewisburg, PA: Bucknell Univ. Press, 1975)
30ff.

2. One may, of course, ask questions only about the final
literary form of the text. This I take to be the task of
rhetorical or literary criticism. The redaction critical
question, which focuses on the process of the text's
formation, is simply a different issue. I therefore disagree
with N. Petersen's contention that redaction criticism must
become literary criticism, Literary Criticism for New
Testament Critics (Philadelphia: Fortress, 1978) 18-19.

3. H. Cornill, "Die Komposition des Buches Jesaja," ZAW 4
(1884) 83-105.

4. So especially B. Duhm, Das Buch Jesaia (Göttingen:
Vandenhoeck & Ruprecht, 1968); O. Proksch, Jesaja I (KAT, 9)
(Leipzig: A. Deichert, 1930); L. Liebreich, "The Compilation
of the Book of Isaiah," JQR 46 (1955/56) 259-277, 47
(1956/57) 114-138; J. Eaton, "The Origin of the Book of
Isaiah," VT 9 (1959) 138-157; G. Fohrer, "The Origin,
Composition and Tradition of Isaiah I-XXXIX," Annual of the
Leeds Univ. Oriental Society 3 (1961-62) 3-38.

5. J. Ziegler, "Zum literarischen Aufbau verschiedener
Stücke im Buche des Propheten Isaias," BZ 21 (1933) 131-149,
237-254.

6. S. Mowinckel, "Die Komposition des Jesajabuches Kap.
1-39," AcOr 11 (1933) 267-292.

7. H. Donner, Israel unter den Völkern. Die Stellung der
klassischen Propheten des 8. Jahrhunderts v. Chr. zur
Aussenpolitik der Könige von Israel und Juda. (VT Supp 11)
(Leiden: Brill, 1964) 76, 149-150.

8. G. Fohrer, "The Origin, Composition and Tradition of
Isaiah I-XXXIX" 19.

9. B. Childs, Isaiah and the Assyrian Crisis (SBT 2nd Series
#3) (London: SCM, 1967) 29.

10. O. Kaiser, Isaiah 13-39 (OT Library) (Philadelphia:
Westminster, 1974) 234-235, 262.

11. W. Dietrich, Jesaja und die Politik (Beiträge zur EvTh 74) (Munich: Chr. Kaiser, 1976) 151-152.

12. H. Barth, Die Jesaja-Worte in der Josiazeit. Israel und Assur als Thema einer produktiven Neuinterpretation der Jesajaüberlieferung (WMANT 48) (Neukirchen-Vluyn: Neukirchener Verlag, 1977) 11, 26, 211.

13. W. March, "Redaction Criticism and the Formation of Prophetic Books," SBL 1977 Seminar Papers, ed. P. Achtemeier. (Missoula, MT.: Scholars Press, 1977) 88.

14. The plural, šᵉmānîm, is probably a plural of amplication; see GK 124e.

15. The syntax is awkward. There is something to be said for the proposal of BHS (ḥōzeq wᵉ'ōmeṣ), followed by W. Irwin, Isaiah 28-33. Translation with Philological Notes (Biblica et Orientalia 30) (Rome: Biblical Institute Press, 1977) 8.

16. See R. Clifford, "The Use of HOY in the Prophets," CBQ 28 (1966) 458-464. On the form critical study of the poem, see R. Melugin, "The Conventional and the Creative in Isaiah's Judgment Oracles," CBQ 36 (1974) 305-306.

17. Contra Kaiser, Isaiah 13-39 238.

18. Cf. Duhm, Das Buch Jesaia 194.

19. Contra Kaiser's (Isaiah 19-39 238) attempts to link this oracle with Hellenistic period anti-Samaritan sentiments.

20. Duhm (Das Buch Jesaia 196) and Proksch (Jesaja I 351) note the similarity between Isa 28:5 and Isa 4:2, but they do not attempt to explain the reason for the similarity in language.

21. Irwin (Isaiah 28-33 18-19) parses rō'eh from r'h "to drink one's fill and pᵉlîliyyāh from Arab pll=bll "soak, moisten"; and thereby Isa 28:7, "They reel with drink, they brim over with booze." Although this proposal is possible, I prefer the traditional analysis since the activities described correspond so well with the respective roles to which they are linked: prophecy--seeing; priesthood--decisions.

22. See especially, W. Hallo, "Isaiah 28:9-13 and the Ugaritic Abecedaries," JBL 77 (1958) 324-338.

23. Reading 'ābû with IQIsaᵃ instead of MT 'ābû'.

24. Childs senses the difficulty of an easy identification, Isaiah and the Assyrian Crisis 29-31.

25. See Isa 30:15-16 on this same issue, the people rejecting earlier intelligible speech.

26. See Isa 6:9-10 for reflection on the prophet's role in conveying alien speech.

27. The word is used with greatest frequency in the wisdom literature.

28. Cf. Kaiser (Isaiah 13-39 248) "proverb-makers" and Irwin (Isaiah 28-33 25) "reigning wits."

29. ḥōzeh makes no sense. I follow LXX.

30. See H. Gese, "Die strömende Geissel des Hadad und Jesaja 28, 15 und 18," Archäologie und Altes Testament (Galling Fest.) ed. A. Kuschke & E. Kutsch (Tubingen: J.C.B. Mohr, 1970) 127-134.

31. So F. Huber, Jahwe, Juda und die anderen Volker beim Propheten Jesaja (BZAW 137) (Berlin: de Gruyter, 1975) 91, 98, who reads MT yissad as a participle with past tense meaning (see Gen 37:17; 41:7 and GK 116o). See also Irwin, Isaiah 28-33 30-31 for a past tense translation. Further, read beṣiyyon as b-essentiae, so Huber, 91 and Irwin, 31.

32. I understand ʼeben bōhan to refer to the Egyptian bekhen stone, vgl. L. Köhler, "Zwei Fachwörter der Bausprache in Jesaja 28:16," ThZ 3 (1947) 390-393. The term apparently refers to one of several hard rocks (a fine-grained crystalline quartzose rock, a gneiss, or perhaps a basalt), so A. Lucas, Ancient Egyptian Materials and Industries (London: E. Arnold, 1948) 478-479. See similarly Huber, Jahwe, Juda und die anderen Volker 91; and Irwin, Isaiah 28-33 31.

33. Vgl. Huber (Jahwe, Juda und die anderen Volker 92) who notes the use of yiqra in IQS VIII, 7f to mean "valuable." In the Isaiah text, this sense fits well as a reference to a valuable foundation deposit.

34. On the significance of "bonds", see Irwin, who argues that the term may refer to the bonds of death, Isaiah 28-33 37. One should not therefore immediately seek an historical allusion here.

35. See Childs, Isaiah and the Assyrian Crisis 29-31; Melugin, "The Creative and the Conventional" 308-310.

36. So Childs, Isaiah and the Assyrian Crisis 31; cf. Melugin, "The Creative and the Conventional" 308-309.

37. Dietrich, Jesaja und die Politik 152. I contend that v 20 is an integral part of the judgment oracle.

38. Childs too contends that vv 20-22 are commentary on the preceding oracle, Isaiah and the Assyrian Crisis 31. However, he argues that vv 20-22 comprise one oracle. Melugin has more recently proposed that vv 20 (21)-22 "are dependent upon the preceding verses," and that they "take the edge off of the climax" of the earlier oracle, "The Creative and the Conventional" 310. How they "take the edge off" is not clear to me.

39. So Dietrich, Jesaja und die Politik 152.

40. Omit lizrōa' metri causa, so Ehrlich Randglossen, V. 4, 102. Cf. Irwin, Isaiah 28-33 38.

41. Omitting sôrāh and nismān as dittographic expansions, so Ehrlich, Randglossen V. 4, 102.

42. Irwin (Isaiah 28-33, 42) parses 'ādûš as an aphel causative and adduces IQIsa^a hdš as corroborating evidence. I read dôš following Syr.

43. See J. W. Whedbee on the structure of this poem, Isaiah and Wisdom (Nashville: Abingdon, 1971) 53-55. Cf. B. Childs on Isa 28:29 as an example of the so-called summary-appraisal form, Isaiah and the Assyrian Crisis 129-130.

44. Whedbee, Isaiah and Wisdom 59-62.

45. I do not find Whedbee's attempt to place this poem in or around the year 701 B.C.E. particularly convincing, Isaiah and Wisdom 64.

46. Whedbee, Isaiah and Wisdom 64-65.

ISAIAH 28-32: A LITERARY APPROACH

J. Cheryl Exum
Boston College

I. Introduction

It is generally agreed that Is 28-32 is a collection,
and a rather complex one at that, of independent oracles
from different situations, joined on the basis of catchword and theme.[1] In approaching Is 28-32 from a literary
perspective, my major concern is not just to show catchword and thematic connections, but to study the effect
produced when the material under scrutiny is read as a
literary whole. I am interested less in the editorial
principles behind the present arrangement of the oracles,
and more in the meaning the prophetic words take on in
light of their present context. In places I think this
meaning is different from the understanding one gains by
treating the individual oracles independently. Their context gives them new meaning.[2] Interpretation of the text
as it now stands, then, is the subject of this study. Our
attention will center on consideration of such literary
matters as the interrelations of certain key themes and
motifs, the use of tropes and how they work, the kinds of
rhetorical devices employed and the result they produce;
in short, on exploration of the relation of form and meaning.

An issue often raised with regard to this kind of
analysis of biblical texts is whether or not the observed
literary structures and devices are intended by the ancient
authors and editors. To pursue this kind of questioning
would be, in my opinion, to run the risk of falling into
the intentional fallacy.[3] E.D. Hirsch, Jr. makes a valuable observation with regard to conscious and unconscious
literary meanings; namely, that when meaning is compli-
cated, an author (or, we might say, editor) cannot possibly
at a given moment be paying attention to all its complexi-
ties.[4] The question whether or not certain literary features are deliberate or spontaneous receives a similar evaluation by Cleanth Brooks.

> The truth of the matter is that we know very
> little of the various poets' methods of compo-
> sition, and that what may seem to us the pro-
> duct of deliberate choice may well have been
> as "spontaneous" as anything else in the poem
> . . . . We shall probably speculate to better
> advantage--if speculate we must--on the possible
> significant interrelations of image with image
> rather than on the possible amount of pen-biting
> which the interrelations may have cost the
> author.[5]

While the above citation refers to written literature, and
we are dealing in Is 28-32 with material which most likely
grew up in oral tradition; and while both critics are concerned with modern literature, I find their observations
applicable to the literary study of Is 28-32 presented below.[6]

Whereas it is not the individual oracle or the growth
of the tradition which concerns me here, my analysis presupposes form critical and tradition critical investigation,
and will, at points, make use of insights gained through
these approaches. Nevertheless, I have sought to avoid
dealing specifically with redaction critical matters, as
these are treated in the companion study by David Petersen.
Since Petersen limits his study to Is 28, I shall also focus on this chapter. After subjecting ch. 28 to literary
scrutiny, I shall make some general remarks about its larger
context, chs. 28-32.

II. Isaiah 28

Is 28 begins with an oracle against the Northern Kingdom, Ephraim, and then moves to address the Kingdom of
Judah. Most commentators agree that only vv. 1-4 apply to
Ephraim, and that with v. 7 the indictment of Judah begins.[7]
We may accept the arguments for this assessment while at
the same time observing that from a literary perspective,
it is striking that not until v. 14 does the name Jerusalem
appear. One result of this delay is a certain ambiguity
with regard to the addressees of vv. 7-13. Vv. 7f. speak
of priest and prophet, and in vv. 9-13 "this people" comes
under judgment; but which priests, which prophets, and which
people are meant? From v. 7 on, suspicion may grow that
the situation applies to the Southern Kingdom, but only
with v. 14 is this applicability made explicit. Now that
Jerusalem's leaders are directly called to task, they should
be able to recognize themselves in the descriptions of vv.
7-13. Moreover, a strong similarity between vv. 14ff. and
vv. 1-4 in terms of both form and content serves to show
the Jerusalemites that their situation is not so different
from that of their northern neighbors.

Another consequence of the delay of direct reference
to Jerusalem is that the addresses to Ephraim and Jerusalem
in vv. 1 and 14 mark a kind of natural division of the
chapter into two major parts, vv. 1-13, vv. 14-29. Let me
say at the outset that I make this structural observation
tentatively. Nevertheless, I am struck by the number of
parallels which exist between the two parts. In particular,
the oracles against Ephraim (vv. 1-4) and Jerusalem (vv. 14-
19) display a remarkable correspondence, which justifies our
seeing the former as a lesson and a warning to the subjects
of the latter.

V. 1 addresses the proud crown of Ephraim, a metaphor
which suggests Ephraim's leaders. V. 14 speaks to the
rulers of Jerusalem. In each oracle, a similar pattern is
followed: 1) rich metaphoric language depicts the condi-
tion which calls forth Yhwh's wrath, v. 1, vv. 14f., 2)
Yhwh's response, introduced by הנה , is described with
new imagery and new terminology, vv. 2; 16-17a (17a where
Yhwh's שמתי' echoes the Jerusalemites' שמנו presents the only exception), 3) the oracle returns to the
images with which it began to describe the punishment:
vv. 3f. repeat the metaphors of v. 1; vv. 17b-18 use the
image of vv. 14-15.

For both Ephraim and Judah, Yhwh's instrument of
punishment is the same. Against Ephraim Yhwh sends one
strong and mighty, like a downpour of hail (ברד) and of
mighty overflowing waters (מים כבירים שטפים),
v. 2. Although the Jerusalem leaders imagine through their
alliances to have avoided the overflowing scourge
(שוט שיטף), v. 15, Yhwh informs them that, to the
contrary, hail (ברד) will sweep away their refuge of
falsehood and waters will overflow (מים ישטפו)
their hiding place, vv. 17f. Destruction pushes beyond
the storm imagery. The proud crown of Ephraim will be
trampled (תרמסנה) under foot, v. 3, and the destruction of the Jerusalemites will be like a trampling
(למרמס), v. 18.

In vv. 5f. mention is made of a remnant, and justice
(משפט) is associated with it. I am doubtful whether
vv. 16-17a holds out much hope for a remnant,[8] but if so,
its presence and its association with justice (משפט)
present another point of contact between the two parts
of the chapter. In any event, the prophet continues, so
that as the chapter now stands, salvation is not the final
word in either of the two parts. Vv. 1-13 conclude with
an example of unsuccessful instruction. The prophet asks
whom will Yhwh teach (יורה) knowledge, v. 9, but because the people are unwilling to hear (שמוע), v. 12,
a lesson will be taught which will destroy them. Vv. 14-
29 also conclude with instruction; in this case it is left
open for the people to decide whether or not they will
hear (שמעו), v. 23. In contrast to the confusion
created by the instruction given in vv. 9-13, this final
lesson in vv. 23-29 makes its point with clarity. Yhwh
teaches (יורנו) the farmer, v. 26, and no one would
dispute the benefits of this instruction. Should not the
farmer serve as a model for the Jerusalemites to follow?

Instruction is an essential theme in ch. 28. We shall
explore below the development of three motifs in which it
finds expression: teaching, hearing, and understanding the
message. Suffice it here to say that, like the motif of
teaching (vv. 9, 26), the motif of understanding the

message occurs once in each section of ch. 28 (vv. 9, 19).
The motif of hearing receives greater elaboration in the
chapter, giving expression to the basic concept that to
understand the message (שׁמעצה) one must be willing to
hear (שׁמע) it. We may assume that the message includes
the idea of rest and trust in Yhwh, for this is the gist
of the message as it appears in each section, vv. 12 and 16.
In the first part of the chapter, the message is outrightly
rejected; in the second, it is significant that no explicit
statement about its rejection appears.

Destruction comes about, vv. 9-13, because the people
reject instruction. A decree of destruction, v. 22, precedes the instruction of vv. 23-29. The order indicates
that perhaps there is yet time to hear and thus avoid the
catastrophe. In each instance, destruction is directly
associated with the strange and alien action of Yhwh. In
vv. 11-13, the issue is Yhwh's strange, incomprehensible
language; in v. 21, Yhwh's strange and alien work. To
those unwilling to be instructed, Yhwh's actions will, indeed, be incomprehensible.

The similarities noted above between vv. 1-13 and
14-29 do not indicate some sort of static or artificial
division of the material within the chapter. On the contrary, one part flows into the next; and it is this movement within the chapter which calls for exploration. Since
I do not find in ch. 28 some kind of clear-cut strophic
arrangement, the division of this material in the discussion which follows is used purely for convenience. Some
of these sections may well have once been individual poems
(oracles), but they are now associated in such a way as to
give the whole chapter a remarkable unity.

Isaiah 28:1-6

1) Woe to the proud crown,
        drunkards of Ephraim,
     And to the fading flower,
        its glorious beauty,
     which is upon the head of the fertile valley,
        those smitten with wine.
2) Behold, the Lord has one strong and mighty
        like a torrent of hail, a storm of destruction,
     like a torrent of mighty waters overflowing
        he casts down to the earth with (his) hand.
3) Underfoot will be trampled the proud crown,
        drunkards of Ephraim;
4) and the fading flower, its glorious beauty,
        which is upon the head of the fertile valley,
     will be like a first-ripe fig before summer,
        which, when the one who sees, sees it,
     as soon as it is in his hand, he swallows it up.

5)' In that day, Yhwh of hosts will be (like) a crown of beauty
and (like) a diadem of glory to the remnant of his people,
6)   and (like) a spirit of justice to the one sitting in judgment,
and (like) strength to those turning back the battle at
the gate.

Is 28:1-6 represents the densest figurative language in
all of chs. 28-32. These few verses describe judgment upon
Ephraim (vv. 1-4) and promise for a remnant (vv. 5f.) using
no less than seven similes, which themselves appear among elaborate metaphoric descriptions. Metaphor and simile alternate
in the poem. It begins in v. 1 with a metaphor describing
certain Ephraimites, who by virtue of their drunkenness (itself perhaps symbolic) have brought upon themselves Yhwh's
wrath. It moves, v. 2, to two similes which describe Yhwh's
instrument of punishment in terms of a mighty storm, which,
one might expect, will sweep away the unworthy Ephraimites.
Contrary to this expectation, v. 3 presents a metaphor in
which Ephraim's punishment is described as a trampling. V. 4
continues the description of punishment with an extended
simile in which the swiftness and completeness of the destruction are conveyed by comparison to an early fig, eaten as
soon as it is seen. In vv. 5f. the imagery climaxes in four
similes describing Yhwh in various roles as provider of
strength and security for a remnant.

Even a casual reader will note that metaphor in these
verses is not only dense, it is mixed as well, a fact which
has led some interpreters to consider it less than successful.[9] For example, we move from the description of Yhwh's
instrument of punishment as a storm (v. 2) to the image of
a trampled crown (v. 3), though a storm does not trample.
Moreover, comparison of a fading flower to an early fig,
v. 4, strains the imagery. Density of metaphor makes interpretation of the poem difficult, while mixed metaphor
defies explanation. Fortunately, our goal is not to explain the imagery here, but rather to comment upon how it
works: how is it used and what effects does it produce?

The terms tenor and vehicle will be useful in this
analysis to refer respectively to the subject to which the
metaphor is applied and to the metaphoric description itself.[10] Let us consider first the tenors. There are three
tenors in the poem, corresponding to three important figures in the background of the oracle. The first is marked
by a certain vagueness; exactly who or what is meant by
the phrase "proud crown, drunkards of Ephraim"? The word
"crown" brings to mind Ephraim's leaders, and the image of
the head of the fertile valley suggests Samaria (cf. 7:9).
The imagery is fluid, for one can also think of Samaria
as the crown on the head of the fertile valley, and the
drunkards as the citizens of Samaria. The Ephraimites

about whom the oracle is uttered are described as a proud
crown, but through a series of ironic, sometimes obscure,
images, they are shown to be no crown at all.

Whereas the first tenor is somewhat vague, the next
tenor is implicit. Yhwh's instrument of punishment is
never identified in the poem. We are probably correct in
understanding the tenor to be Assyria, if, as most commentators think, this oracle comes from the period between
the Syro-Ephraimitic war and the fall of the Northern Kingdom.[11] Assyria is described in a similar manner in Is 8:
6-8. Only the third tenor is explicit. Yhwh is presented
as the true crown of the people, in contrast to the transitory crown of the leaders of Ephraim.

The differences with regard to specificity of tenor
reveal the concerns of the poem. The most important tenor
is explicit; the least, implicit. The clear identification
of Yhwh as crown, diadem, spirit of justice, and strength,
as well as the fact that these four similes climax the poem,
serves to underscore a fundamental theological tenet of
Isaiah, that deliverance or salvation comes only through
Yhwh. By not mentioning Assyria by name, the prophet denies
Assyria ground for boasting. Elsewhere Isaiah comments
upon Assyria's folly in regarding itself as responsible
for the conquest of Israel.

> Shall the axe vaunt itself
>   over the one who hews with it,
> or the saw magnify itself
>   against the one who wields it? (10:15)

The Assyrians are simply an instrument of Yhwh, and as far
as the poet of 28:1-6 is concerned, specific identification
of Yhwh's instrument is irrelevant. As for the Ephraimites,
the metaphor "proud crown, drunkards of Ephraim" points to
the leaders in Samaria, while at the same time permitting
through its indefiniteness extension of the indictment to
all Ephraimites.

As we turn our attention to the vehicles of the metaphors in vv. 1-6, we shall consider at the same time other
literary and rhetorical features of the poem. The first
two stichoi introduce the intricate imagery which characterizes the poem.

> Woe to the proud crown
>   drunkards of Ephraim
> and the fading flower
>   its glorious beauty . . . .

We move from imagery of majesty to imagery of drunkenness,
to imagery of agriculture and frailty, back to imagery of
majesty. Thus the imagery of majesty surrounds the other

descriptions of the Ephraimites just as a crown surrounds
their head; yet the descriptions which are surrounded be-
lie the claim to honor. Already the crown fits ill. The
first stichos of the poem ushers us into the world of
ironic metaphor.[12] The term "drunkards" may be taken in
a literal sense, or it may be figurative for their confusion and faulty perception of Yhwh's will and their inability to grasp the realities of their political situation (cf. 29:9f.). A double meaning is likely.[13] It is
surely ironic that the drunkards of Ephraim are referred
to as its source of pride. But proud crown, too, in this
context appears ironic, in which case the Ephraimites suffer not only from drunkenness but also from hubris.

V. 1c shifts from the themes of pride and drunkenness
to agricultural imagery, which v. 1d then connects through
paronomasia to the imagery of pride. Ephraim's glorious
beauty (צבי) is a fading flower (צץ). The participle indicates that Ephraim's degeneration ("fading") is
ongoing, and not yet complete. Another word play is presented by the term תפארתו , which contains the consonants of the word אפרים in a different order. The
transitory and fragile nature of Ephraim's glory is exposed through the image of a fading flower. So much for
glory. In v. 1e, the agricultural imagery is expanded
with the image of the fertile valley. The "head" of the
fertile valley would be the most luxuriant part, but (as
I read the imagery) what we have at the head of the fertile valley is not, for example, a fruitful field (cf. 29:
17; 32:15), but rather a fading flower! Agricultural and
drunkenness imagery merge in v. 1f. The phrase "those
smitten with wine" (יין), recalls the drunkards
(שכרי) of Ephraim, while יין at the same time suggests the fruitfulness of the vine. "Smitten (הלומי)
with wine," moreover, implies that the drunken Ephraimites are the victims of the very thing they pursue.

A third instance of paronomasia in v. 1, גאות
and גיא , sets up a contrast between the high and the
low.[14] It draws attention to Ephraim's pride and anti-
cipates the humbling of the proud crown which we meet in
the following verses. This kind of contrast between attitude and physical height or depth receives fuller development in 2:6-22, where pride is associated with
things possessing physical height (mountains, hills,
towers, walls) and humility with low places (caves, holes,
caverns).[15]

V. 2 introduces new imagery. The series of related
images (torrent, hail, destructive storm, mighty waters
which overflow) constitutes the vehicle. As we noted a-
bove, the tenor is implicit, and we have here only a
description of it with the adjectives "strong" and
"mighty." The most important thing about this strong
and mighty force is that it belongs to, and thus is under
the control of, Yhwh. The verse appears to be chiastic:

> a Behold, one strong and mighty (belongs)
>   to the Lord
> b like a torrent of hail, a storm of de-
>   struction
> b' like a torrent of mighty waters over-
>   flowing
> a' he casts down to the earth with his hand

The subject of a and a' is Yhwh's destructive force and its
action, while b and b' present this force as a storm through
the use of two similes beginning with כְּזֶרֶם . V. 2d (a')
is, however, ambiguous. Whereas some interpreters seek to
identify the subject of this verse as either the strong one
or Yhwh,[16] and the object as either the flower, crown, or
Samaria, I would resist trying to pin down the metaphoric
language. It is precisely the ambiguity of the language
which allows a variety and complexity of image. Whereas
a fading flower might benefit from a gentle shower, a
mighty storm would surely beat it quickly to the ground (the
image of a mighty downpour against a single, wilting flower
is almost ludicrous). A mighty storm could also knock a
crown from the head to the ground. The imagery becomes
anthropomorphic. The proud crown is cast down from the
head (רֹאשׁ) to the ground with the hand (בְּיָד). Once
on the ground, it can be trampled with the feet
(בְּרַגְלַיִם), v. 3.

Thus far Ephraim has been threatened with storm and
trampling; in v. 4 the imagery shifts again. The poem returns to agricultural imagery and, at the same time, ex-
changes the idea of drinking (which describes the sin of
the Ephraimites) for the idea of eating (which describes
their punishment). The fate of the fading flower of
Ephraim's glory will be like that of an early summer fig.
Although at first sight, the image of an early fig before
summer suggests renewal, this is not the case. The simile
of the fig is deftly extended with a description which conveys vividly the suddenness which will mark Ephraim's destruction. No sooner is this delicacy seen by someone
than it is in his hand and then his mouth. With the palm
of the hand (בְּכַפּוֹ), we have the fourth reference to a
part of the body in the poem. The description of Ephraim's
punishment begins with its flower/crown cast down with the
hand and ends with its flower/fig gobbled up from the hand.

Vv. 5f. are commonly recognized as a message of hope
appended at a later time to the oracle of destruction
against Ephraim.[17] With considerable skill, a later editor has added these verses so that they build with vv. 1-
4 a unified poem. Only after establishing a link with
the preceding by picking up three key words (עֲטֶרֶת ,
צְבִי , and תִּפְאָרָה) does the poet move to something
new in v. 6. Moreover, these verses exhibit the same reliance on metaphorical language and delight in word play
as the rest of the poem.[18] "In that day" in this context
applies to the day of destruction for the proud crown of
Ephraim. That this day has not yet arrived is clear from

the imperfect tense, as well as from vv. 7ff. which plunge
us back into the real world. Four similes introduced by
ל expound what Yhwh will be in that day to three categories of people.

like (ל) a crown of beauty	
and like (ל) a diadem of glory	to (ל) the remnant of his people
and like (ל) a spirit of justice	to (ל) the one sitting in judgment
and like (ל) strength	to (supplying ל) those turning back the battle at the gate

To the remnant Yhwh will be like a crown of beauty and a diadem of glory. The repetition of עטרת from v. 1 draws
out the contrast between illusory crown (the leaders of
Ephraim) and true crown (Yhwh). Why the combination
עטרת צבי and not עטרת גאות to describe Yhwh?
I shall offer a tentative suggestion. Perhaps because it
is possible to see גאות in v. 1 as a pejorative term for
pride, the poet has taken the three other terms of v. 1
which unequivocally suggest honor, עטרת , צבי , and
תפארה , and applied them to Yhwh. And now comes the
crowning word play! Yhwh is going to be a crown, but not,
as the Ephraimites in v. 1, a crown for the head (ראש),
but rather a crown for a remnant (שאר). This word play,
based on reversal of consonants, calls attention to a dramatic change in the situation. The beginning of the poem
presents a picture of all of proud Ephraim, with Samaria
at its head, but, in the end, what will be left is only a
remnant.

     Having established continuity with the imagery of the
rest of the poem, the editor now moves beyond it. Yhwh
will be a spirit of justice (משפט) to the one sitting
in judgment (משפט) and strength to those turning back
the battle at the gate. V. 6a points to internal, v. 6b to
external, security. This expansion of imagery sets the sin
of Ephraim in a new context. Vv. 1-4 present drunkenness
as the reason for Ephraim's destruction; an implicit reason
may be pride. Since Yhwh in v. 5 is described as a true
crown of glory in contrast to the unworthy crown of the
drunkards of Ephraim, we may conclude that what characterizes Yhwh in the role as crown is absent among those who
should provide responsible leadership for Ephraim. Establishing justice and providing military defense are precisely the areas in which Ephraim's leaders failed, and the
last verse of this poem permits Is 28:1-6 to underscore
this point.

Isaiah 28:7-8

7) These also reel with wine
        and stagger with beer,
      priest and prophet reel with beer,
        they are engulfed by wine;

            they stagger from beer,
        they reel with the vision,
            they stumble in giving a decision;
8) for all tables are full of vomit,
        no place is without filth.

There is no denying the abruptness of the transition
between vv. 6 and 7. The contrast between the picture of
peace and security of vv. 5f. and the charge of inebriety
against priest and prophet is jarring. The abrupt transition serves to set 28:1-6 apart from what follows. The ramifications of this separation we shall explore below. An
abrupt transition can also signal a move to something new.
It seems we have left the Ephraimite leaders. But where
are we? Perhaps the prophet has turned to the Southern
Kingdom, but can we be sure? Notice that the subject is
delayed: "these also reel with wine and stagger with beer."
Who? The answer comes in the second stichos: priest and
prophet. Which ones? These verses do not give an answer.

Vv. 7f. present a situation not totally new. The renewal of the charge of drunkenness establishes a link between the Ephraimites of vv. 1-4 and the priests and prophets. Both groups represent persons from whom one would
expect responsible action. Given the rejection of the
Ephraimites, one might ask, who will constitute the remnant of vv. 5f.? To whom would one look for special guidance? Priest and prophet. Yet priest and prophet are no
better than Ephraimite, and may be even worse. The key
word יין appears once in vv. 1-4 and twice in vv. 7f.;
the root שכר , twice in vv. 1-4 and three times in vv.
7f. Is greater insobriety implied by the frequency with
which these terms reappear (five times as against three)?
Clearly the issue of drunkenness receives more attention
in vv. 7f. But drunkenness is not the only offense attributed to these two groups. Just as the leaders of Ephraim
fail in their responsibility of maintaining justice and
military security (vv. 5f.), so also priest and prophet
fail in fulfilling the functions of their office: for the
prophet, having a vision; for the priest, rendering a decision.[19] A further catchword connection exists between
vv. 1-4 and 7f. In the former, something is seen
(יראה הראה) and swallowed up (יבלענה), v.
4. In the latter, priest and prophet are swallowed up
(נבלעו) by wine and thus cannot see (בראה) properly: "they reel with the vision," v. 7.

A distinguishing feature of these two verses is their
creative use of repetition. The words יין and שכר
(for alcoholic drink) and שגו and תעו (for the effect of drinking) are repeated in various combinations,
back and forth, in an almost willy-nilly fashion which
suggests the staggering of the drunkards. The repetition also creates affect by arousing the expectation of a
certain consequent, only to present a different one.[20]
For example, v. 7 begins to set up a pattern:

> with wine they reel
> and with beer they stagger
> they reel with beer . . . .

The objects "wine" and "beer" come first in the first two
lines for emphasis. To complete the pattern, one would expect "they stagger with wine." But the text gives us something else: "they are swallowed up by wine." Instead of
continuing to emphasize how drunk they are, the poet shows
us that the thing which they consume, in reality, consumes
them. V. 7e returns to the earlier imagery, "they stagger
from beer," and v. 7f continues, "they reel . . . ." But
suddenly, it is no longer wine or beer with which they
reel, but rather something quite different--the vision.
Since שׁגו may also mean "they err" (cf. RSV) the result is a double meaning eminently suited to the situation.
The ambiguity allows us to imagine either that their drunkenness prevents them from carrying out their functions
properly or that they are as intoxicated with their own visions as they are with strong drink. Similar imagery and
double meaning complete the picture: they also stumble in
giving a decision, פקו פליליה (note the alliteration, as well as the rhyme, פקו with שׁגו and תעו).
V. 8 puts the finishing touch to the tableau with a graphic
illustration of their wretched situation.

Isaiah 28:9-13

9) Whom will he teach knowledge
    and whom will he cause to understand the message?
    Those weaned from milk,
    those taken from the breast?
10) For it would be ṣaw lāṣaw ṣaw lāṣaw

    qaw lāqāw qaw lāqāw,
    a little here, a little there.
11) For with stammerings of speech
    and with another tongue
    he will speak to this people,
12) to whom he has said:
    "This is the rest, give rest to the weary;
    and this is the repose," but they were not willing to
       hear.[21]
13) So the word of Yhwh will be to them,
    ṣaw lāṣaw ṣaw lāṣaw

    qaw lāqāw qaw lāqāw,
    a little here, a little there;
    In order that they may go, and stumble backward,
    and be broken, and snared, and taken.

V. 9a raises a question of major concern in Is 28. It
forms an inclusion with the parable of the farmer in vv. 23-
29, where instruction is also the topic. The crucial word
"teach" (יורה) occurs in Is 28 only here and in v. 26.
The root שׁמע appears here and in the introduction to the
parable, v. 23; between vv. 9-23 it appears three times
(vv. 12, 14, 19), taking on additional significance with

each repetition. That v. 9 is a question rather than a statement leaves open, for the moment, the issue whether or not instruction is possible.

A number of scholars posit that vv. 9-13 reflect a dispute between Isaiah and the priests and prophets of vv. 7f. It has been suggested, for example, that the priests object that Isaiah is treating them like school children; or they are making fun of Isaiah's speech or his message; or they point to a lesson going on nearby as an analogy to Isaiah's methods of instruction.[22] To varying degrees, such interpretations attribute some of the words in vv. 9-13 to the priests and prophets. In the absence of any indication in the text that Isaiah is referring either directly or indirectly to the words of his opponents (e.g. it is clear when he quotes in v. 15), assigning parts and providing reconstructions of a dispute seems too precarious. Let us simply take the oracle as it stands.[23]

The "he" of v. 9 is not identified. Some commentators who take these verses as part of a disputation think the priests and prophets are speaking of Isaiah. I take the "he" to refer to Yhwh, a reading which finds support in the context of vv. 11 and 13. If the close association of v. 9 and vv. 23-29 is accepted, further support for Yhwh as teacher appears in v. 26. According to vv. 1-6, the leaders of Ephraim are drunk; in vv. 7f., the priests and prophets. Who then remains, that Yhwh might teach them the message? Perhaps infants just weaned from milk, who have not yet had the occasion to succumb to wine or beer as the Ephraimites, priests, and prophets have. The suggestion is, of course, absurd, and is meant to draw out the irony of the situation, for if Yhwh were to teach children, what would the message be? Ṣaw lāṣaw ṣaw lāṣaw qaw lāqaw qaw lāqaw ('v. 10). Baby talk--not, to be sure, the babble of drunkards, but babble just the same. Or is that the meaning of this cryptic verse?

These strange words test the ingenuity of commentators. It seems to me, following as they do the description of the crapulous priests and prophets, that some such interpretation as above makes sense. Since the terms "teach" and "explain the message" may be thought of as referring to the functions of priest and prophet respectively,[24] v. 9 reflects ironically upon the incompetence of these two groups. Driver makes the intriguing suggestion that the words צ and ק in v. 10 are chosen to echo אמצ and קיא of v. 8, and thus to suggest the drunken cries and shouts of the revelers.[25] If this be the case, the befuddled speech of the priests and prophets is being compared to the nonsense talk of infants, with the implication that the priests and prophets are about as effective in serving Yhwh as infants would be.

V. 11 introduces a new frame of reference for the words of v. 10. Like v. 10 it begins with the deictic particle כִּי , which here picks up the idea of unintelligible speech and associates it with foreigners.[26] Yhwh will speak to this people in a foreign tongue, and according to v. 13, the message will be : ṣaw lāṣāw ṣaw lāṣāw qaw lāqāw qaw lāqāw, a little here, a little there. Van Selms' attempt to give the words meaning by seeking an Akkadian prototype works nicely for v. 13, but presents difficulties in v. 10.[27] In fact, a single meaning or translation for the words in these two verses is difficult to obtain. We are obviously dealing with irony and with words which are meant to take on different meanings. If the words are taken to represent unintelligible speech, the point seems to be that in the past (v. 12), Yhwh offered a clear message to the people, but they were unwilling to hear. Now, therefore, Yhwh will speak gibberish to them. I find v. 13 ambiguous. It may mean that Yhwh will speak unintelligibly through a foreign language (in which case the message would be only too clear!). Or it may express an idea similar to 6:10, that the divine word would be incomprehensible to them in order to prevent their returning to Yhwh and being delivered.

Another possible meaning of the words in vv. 10 and 13 is that they refer to letters of the alphabet.[28] In that case the point would be that just as Yhwh begins at the most elementary level to teach children, so also Yhwh is going to give the people a lesson, the meaning of which is as simple as a, b, c--but the language of the lesson will be a foreign one. According to this interpretation the words of vv. 10 and 13a represent the basic significants of meaning, letters, whereas according to the interpretation discussed above, they are meaningless. For the present reader that is a striking example of double meaning. But the outcome is the same in either case: beneficial instruction (v. 12) has been rejected, and now the people will be given a lesson in destruction.

We should look briefly at the instruction which the people rejected. In vv. 11-13 it is not the priests and prophets who are being reproached, but rather the people. Moreover, we have moved from the harmony conveyed by the phrase "his people" in v. 5 to the rejection implied by "this people," v. 11. The question of v. 9, whom Yhwh will cause to understand the message (שְׁמוּעָה), becomes more poignant when we learn that the people are not willing to hear (שְׁמוֹעַ). It seems we now have a negative answer to the question: no one. Vv. 11-13 contain a message within a message. Irwin draws attention to the concentric structure of v. 12 in which speaking ("to whom he has said") corresponds to listening ("they would not hear"); "this is the rest" matches "this is the repose;" and "give rest to the weary" stands at the center.[29] If v. 12 is chiastic, the emphasis would appear to fall on social responsibility. Obtaining rest (הַמְּנוּחָה) depends upon giving rest (הָנִיחוּ).[30] Since the

people refuse this instruction, Yhwh determines a different lesson, the purpose of which (לְמַעַן) is to destroy
rather than to protect. Repetition in v. 13ef emphasizes
the completeness of destruction: "that they may go, and
stumble backward, and be broken, and snared, and taken."
These words convey a different kind of stumbling from that
brought about by wine and beer (vv. 7f.)--a stumbling
caused by the word of Yhwh.

Isaiah 28:14-22

14) Therefore hear the word of Yhwh, you scoffers,
    rulers of this people who are in Jerusalem:

A   15) Because you have said,
         "We have made a covenant with death,
            with Sheol we have an agreement;[31]
         the overflowing scourge, when it passes through,
            will not come to us;

B   for we have made a lie our refuge
         and in falsehood we have hidden ourselves."

C   16) Therefore thus says the Lord Yhwh:
         "Behold, I am founding in Zion a stone,
            a tested stone,
            a precious cornerstone,
            a foundation founded;
         the one who stands firm will not hasten.

B'   17) And I will make justice the line
            and righteousness the plummet;
         and hail will sweep away the refuge of lies;
            and the hiding place waters will overflow.

A'   18) Cancelled will be your covenant with death
            and your agreement with Sheol will not stand;
         the overflowing scourge, when it passes through,
            by it you will be trampled.
     19) As often as it passes through it will take you;
            for morning by morning it will pass through,
            by day and by night.
         And it will be sheer terror
            to understand the message."

     20) For the bed is too short to stretch oneself out,
            and the covering too narrow to wrap oneself up.
     21) For like Mount Perazim Yhwh will rise up
            and like the valley of Gibeon he will shake,
         to do his deed, strange is his deed
            and to work his work, alien is his work!
     22) And now do not scoff,
            lest your bonds be strengthened;
         for a decree of destruction I have heard
            from the Lord Yhwh of hosts against the whole
               land.

These verses form an inclusion based on the address
to "scoffers" in vv. 14 and 22. Two oracles of Yhwh introduced by לכן form a chiasmus. The first, vv. 14f.,
reveals what the rulers have said, אמרתם (v. 15); the
second, vv. 16-19, reports what Yhwh says, כה אמר
אדני יהוה (v. 16). That the structure of
these verses is chiastic is clear, although there is disagreement among interpreters on precise division of the
material.[32] I take vv. 14-19 as the core of the message
and vv. 20-22 as an elaboration upon it. According to the
division indicated in the translation above, A and B refer to the rulers' words and their arrangements for security; while C, B', and A' refer to Yhwh's words and arrangements to show the ineffectiveness of that security. Yhwh's
foundation of true security appears in the center, C. Its
position focuses attention upon it, and, as the structure
indicates, this action has no counterpart in human endeavors.
In B' and A' Yhwh demolishes the false supports established
by the Jerusalem rulers. These two sections are longer
than the corresponding sections A and B, and the expansion
gives increased attention to the destruction which results
from trust in self-made shelter rather than in Yhwh. Within this large chiasmus, chiastic structures appear in divisions A, B, B', and A'.

The call to hear in v. 14 contains a delightfully
ironic pun. In parallelism with "rulers of this people
who are in Jerusalem," 14b, one would expect "men of Zion"
in 14a. This suggests that לצון is a play on ציון .
But the fact that 14a uses a term from the language of wisdom raises the possibility of understanding משל in 14b
in wisdom terms also, "proverb-makers of this people." The
pun rests on suggested double meaning: men of Zion--rulers;
scoffers--proverb-makers. The rulers of "this people" are
called to hear (שמעו) the word (דבר) of Yhwh. The
command presents a striking contrast to vv. 11f., where
Yhwh will speak (ידבר) to this people incomprehensibly
because they were not willing to hear (שמוע).

The words of the Jerusalem scoffers in v. 15 are
chiastic.

```
            a                    b
  we have made a covenant     with death
        b'                a'
  with Sheol        we have an agreement
```

They claim on this basis that the שיט שוט שוטף (note
the alliteration) which overcame their neighbors the
Ephraimites (מים כבירים שטפים, v. 2) will not come "to us."
Their reasoning is also chiastic, with the verbs appear-
ing at beginning and end and the objects, their places of
refuge, in the middle.

```
         a                      b
   for we have made      a lie our refuge
         b'                    a'
   and in falsehood      we have hidden ourselves
```

In v. 12 Yhwh offered the people a resting place and a repose, but they refused; in v. 15 the leaders of the people claim to have established a refuge of their own. But what is meant by a refuge in falsehood, and what kind of covenant is a covenant with death? It seems to me that we are again in the realm of metaphor, with a tenor which is implicit. The fact that they say they have made a lie their refuge and have hidden themselves in falsehood indicates that this is not a direct quote. Good has called this citation an example of irony by way of attribution; that is, the prophet assigns words to the Jerusalem leaders which, in their mouths, become ironic.

> The prophet parodies the communiqué from Judah's state department about a mutual assistance pact with Egypt, which might have said: "We have made a covenant [treaty] with Egypt, with Pharaoh we made an agreement. Assyria's invasion therefore will not trouble us, for we have protection with Egypt and security with Pharaoh." By substituting words, the prophet ironically criticizes the treaty-making . . . .[33]

Although we cannot be certain that Egypt and Assyria are meant, that identification seems likely in view of the historical situation. We noted above the striking similarities in the choice of metaphor (hail, overflowing waters, trampling) to describe the punishments of Ephraim and Judah, vv. 2f., 17f. These similarities suggest an identity of tenor. Although in both cases the tenor is implicit, Assyria fits both situations and thus seems a likely candidate for the שׁוֹט שׁוֹטֵף . V. 15 may also contain mythological allusions, in which case the metaphor represents a skillful merging of religious and political considerations.[34]

With v. 16 begins the description of Yhwh's response to the leaders of the people who are in Jerusalem. Yhwh's first action is a positive one, the building up of a sure foundation for Zion (C, v. 16); the subsequent action, however, is destructive, the tearing down of the Judahites' false refuge (B' and A', vv.17-19). The meaning of v. 16 is debated. Whether Yhwh has founded (reading the perfect) or is founding (reading a participle) the stone, whether the stone is Zion or is in Zion; whether the stone is tested or is itself an instrument of testing; the meaning of the phrase הַמַּאֲמִין לֹא יָחִישׁ and its relationship to the stone--all these are problematic issues. From my translation it can be seen that I take the founding to be in process and the stone to be in Zion, though I am prepared to be convinced by arguments to the contrary.

Although the precise meaning of the verse is uncertain, the intention of the imagery is, I think, clear.
Lindblom has pointed out that the foundation stone is the
metaphorical counterpart to the covenant with death.[35]
The contrast is between a foundation which will stand firm
and a refuge which will be swept away by storm waters and
hail. Yhwh has laid a sure foundation, and the one who
trusts in it will be like it, standing firm. Such a one
will neither rely upon foreign alliances nor fear the onslaught which may come. The verse does not appear to be
a guarantee of future salvation, as in vv. 5f., but rather
to offer the possibility of escaping disaster to the one
who trusts in Yhwh. The fact that in the following verses
we hear of destruction and not deliverance indicates that
the prophet holds out little hope of convincing the leaders
to change their policy.

The firmness of Yhwh's foundation stone is emphasized
through repetition. The piling up of phrases in v. 16 is
itself a building process. The juxtaposition of אבן and
אבן , מוסד and מוסד , the repetition of initial
and final consonants, and the preponderance of _alephs_ and
nuns render v. 16 particularly assonant.

בציון אבן אבן בחן
פנת יקרת מוסד מוסד
המאמין לא יחיש

If one follows Irwin in rendering יקרת as "weighty,"
the firmness and security of Yhwh's stone is emphasized all
the more.[36] The description אבן בחן conveys the
double meaning, "tested stone" and "granite stone."[37]
Again the accent falls on the surety of Yhwh's foundation.

In v. 17 (B') the metaphor moves from the founding of
the stone to the divine measuring instruments of justice
and righteousness. "Justice" recalls the justice Yhwh
brings to the remnant of the people in v. 6; and "line" is
a word play on קו in v. 10. In B (v. 15) the Judahites
established (שמנו) lies as their refuge; in B' Yhwh
establishes (שמתי) justice as the measuring line.
Against justice, the Judahites' edifice does not measure up.
We saw that the leaders' statement about their refuge is
chiastic. The devastation of this refuge is recounted in
an even more intricate chiasmus of verb-subject-object/ob-
ject-subject-verb.

a'	b'	c'	c	b	a
ישטפו	וסתר מים	מחסה כזב	כרד	ויעה	

Similarly, whereas in A (v. 15) the leaders spoke of their
covenant with death and agreement with Sheol in chiastic

140

order, so too in A' (vv. 18f.) Yhwh cancels it with a
chiasm.

```
         a                          b
   cancelled will be      your covenant with death
         b'                         a'
and your agreement with Sheol      will not stand
```

The leaders had boasted, "The overflowing scourge, when
it passes through, will not come to us." But Yhwh retorts,
"The overflowing scourge, when it passes through, by it you
will be trampled." The outcome will be precisely the opposite of that they had devised; and, to make the picture
more ironic, they will meet the same fate which befell
Ephraim, v. 3. A' underscores its point through expansion,
v. 19: "as often as it passes through" (i.e., there will be
more than one onslaught), it will take them. How often will
it pass through?

```
        morning by morning it will pass through
        by day and by night
```

The result of this constant attack will be that "it will be
sheer terror to understand the message."

Melugin considers the message referred to here as Yhwh's
promise of security to those who trust, vv. 16-17a. Understanding the message will be terrible because, ironically, one
understands its promise that the faithful will stand firm
while one is being swept away.[38] We may also take this promise of security for the faithful as the substance of the message elsewhere in the chapter--in the question of v. 9, and
in the variant of the message of attentive trust in Yhwh in
v. 12. The corollary of the promise, however, is destruction
for those who will not stand firm--for those who refuse to
hear the message or who try to arrange their own security.
Vv. 20-22 develop this aspect of the message.

Destruction unfolds in vv. 20-22 with two explications
introduced by כִּי . V. 20 sounds like a proverb, which is
fitting in an address to "proverb-makers" (v. 14). It
points to the inadequacy of the Judahites' arrangements for
security through an illustration based upon length and
width: the bed is too short, the covering is too narrow.
V. 21 shows why the arrangements are inadequate: Yhwh will
fight against the people, like Mount Perazim and like the
valley of Gibeon. The inadequacy of the Judahites' prepara-
tions, exposed through the imagery of length and width, is
contrasted to the scope of Yhwh's action, indicated through
that of height and depth.[39] The simile in v. 21 presents
a paradox. Earlier Yhwh had fought for Israel at Perazim
and Gibeon (2 Sam 5:17-25; Jo 10:9-14); now Yhwh fights
against them. In 2 Samuel 5, Perazim receives its name
on the basis of a statement made by David, comparing Yhwh's
"breaking through" his enemies to a bursting flood. In
Joshua 10, Yhwh sends hail against the enemies of Israel.

The allusions to flood and hail in the Perazim and Gibeon
comparison complement the storm imagery in vv. 14-19.[40]
The action of Yhwh in v. 21cd receives attention through
the threefold repetition of the roots עשה and עבד ;
the paradoxical nature of this action is highlighted by
the fact that the only words not repeated are the synonyms
"strange" and "foreign."

לעשות מעשהו זר מעשהו

ולעבד עבדתו נכריה עבדתו

The alienness of Yhwh's action recalls Yhwh's alien speech
in vv. 9-13.

V. 22, like v. 14, contains a direct address to the
scoffers. Here they are told not to scoff, lest their
bonds be strengthened. What bonds are meant? Irwin pro-
poses the bonds of their covenant with death.[41] Thus
the irony becomes deadly: dependence on a covenant with
death strengthens death's claim on them. Who will do the
strengthening (יחזק) of the bonds? In view of the
points of contact we have already observed between the
storm imagery here and that of vv. 2f., perhaps we should
think of the strong one (חזק) of v. 2.

In v. 22cd the prophet speaks of his own-experience,
"for a decree of destruction I have heard (שמעתי)."
This is the fifth appearance of the root שמע in Is 28.
The root gives expression to the dominant theme of instruction in the chapter, and its associations in different
contexts produce important variations on that theme. It
first occurred in v. 9, "Whom will he cause to understand
the message" (שמועה)? The question seemed to stem
from the fact that the priests and prophets (vv. 7f.) as
well as the Ephraimites (vv. 1-4) were too drunk to be
taught. As a question, v. 9 held open the possibility
that a positive answer might follow. However, the root
then occurred in an accusation of the people, "they were
not willing to hear" (שמוע), and it seemed we had a
negative answer to the question. Immediately following
the statement that the people would not hear came a command to hear (שמעו) addressed to the leaders of the
people. שמע then became a part of the punishment
which the leaders could expect to encounter in the future: it will be a terrible thing to understand the message (שמועה). In v. 22 we discover one person out
of all these--Ephraimites, priests, prophets, people,
Jerusalemite leaders--who has heard (שמעתי), the
prophet Isaiah. We saw in vv. 14-19 that the message
is double-edged, security for those who trust in Yhwh,
and destruction for those who seek safeguards apart
from Yhwh. In v. 22 the prophet hears only the latter.

Isaiah 28:23-29

23) Give ear and hear my voice,
    listen and hear my speech.
24) Is it all the time that the plower plows for sowing,
    that he opens and harrows his soil?
25) Does he not, when he has leveled its surface,
    scatter dill and throw cummin,
    and set wheat in rows,
    and barley in plots,
    and spelt at its border?[42]

26) He instructs him properly,
    his God teaches him.

27) For dill is not threshed with a sledge,
    nor is a cart wheel rolled over cummin,
    but with a staff dill is beat out,
    and cummin with a rod.
28) Grain is crushed,
    but not unceasingly;
    one carefully threshes it.[43]
When he drives his cart wheel,
    his horses do not crush it.

29) This also comes from Yhwh of hosts,
    he makes wonderful counsel
    he magnifies wisdom.

Is 28:23-29 is a beautifully crafted poem of two stanzas (vv. 23-25; vv. 27-28) plus refrain (v. 26; v. 29), dealing with techniques of sowing and harvesting. It begins with a call to hear in the style of a wisdom teacher and presents its lesson in the form of a parable.[44] The first stanza deals with sowing; the second, with techniques of harvesting. The refrains indicate that knowledge in both areas comes from Yhwh. After calling for the audience's attention in stanza 1, the poet poses two rhetorical questions. Rhetorical questions are a forceful way of making a point. The first calls for a negative answer; the second, a positive one. The first deals with proper timing, and the second speaks of timing in connection with the sowing of dill, cummin, and various grains. V. 25b is a chiasmus, which my translation above does not reveal.

a	b	b'	a'
he scatters dill		and cummin he throws	

The refrain, v. 26, gives the reason for the farmer's correct procedures: his God teaches him.

·The second stanza focuses upon techniques of harvesting. Like the first stanza, it moves from negative observation to positive. It begins with dill and cummin, indicating how the harvesting should not be done (with sledge and cart wheel) and then how it is done (with a staff). The proper procedure is presented as an inclusio.

with a staff dill is beat out, and cummin **with
a rod**

In a similar fashion, v. 28 deals with grain. The crushing
should **not** be done unceasingly; it **should** be done carefully.
Two terms used in the description of how dill and cummin
should not be harvested, v. 27ab, are applied to grain in
v. 28. "Dill is not threshed (יוּדַשׁ) with a sledge,"
however, grain is carefully threshed (אדושׁ
יְדִישׁוּ). The wheel of a cart (עֲגֻלָה) is not rolled
over cummin, nor does a cart wheel (עֶגְלַת וֹ) crush
grain. Both stanzas contain the notion of proper timing.
Whereas the first stanza begins with it (the plower does
not plow all the time), the second ends with it (grain is
not endlessly crushed). Each time emphasis is on an action
which ought to take place, but, at the proper time, one
should cease and (we must infer this for the second stanza) turn to the next phase.

The refrain of v. 29 shows that "this also" is from
Yhwh. "This also" may refer to stanza 2; that is, the
farmer is not only instructed in sowing but also in harvesting. The point is that Yhwh's instruction is thorough.
Yhwh does not teach half a lesson and withhold the necessary counterpart. At the same time, "this also" may refer
to the whole lesson of vv. 23-29.[45] Childs suggests that
v. 29 is an example of what he calls the summary-appraisal
form. It "relates organically to the parable, but stands
apart as an independent reflection on the wisdom of God."[46]
Thus v. 29 may be seen to have three referents, which move
from the narrow to the broad: 1) the preceding stanza, 2)
the entire poem, and 3) the wisdom of Yhwh in general.

Having examined the structure of the parable of the
farmer, we shall now inquire about its relationship to
its present context. The parable begins with a call to
hear (וְשִׁמְעוּ , 2 times), the final occurrences of the
root שׁמע in the chapter. It is also the second use of
the root as an imperative, although in this case the audience is not specified. As in the case of the Jerusalem
leaders, v. 14, the call to hear in v. 23 follows a message of destruction (vv. 13, 22). There it also led to
a message of destruction; here the possibility of hearing is left open, and nothing is said about either doom
or deliverance. If the people hear the message of the
parable, might they thereby avoid decimation?

I find no compelling reasons to take vv. 23-29 as a
parable or allegory of God's activity in history.[47]
Whedbee's contention that the parable is a defense of
Yhwh's wisdom is convincing,[48] though I find the confirmation of Yhwh's wisdom more important for the larger context of chs. 28-32 than for the immediate context of
ch. 28. The emphasis in the parable is not only on
Yhwh's wisdom but also on Yhwh's **teaching**. Fohrer's attempt to connect vv. 23-29 with the preceding, by suggesting that Isaiah is defending himself against the

charge that his message is inconsistent, does not seem
to me to find enough support from the text. However,
Fohrer's observation that the farmer is a divinely taught
person is important.[49] As I noted above, the parable in
vv. 23-29 shares with v. 9 an interest in teaching
(יׄרׄה) and in hearing (שׁמע). I submit that we have
in vv. 23-29 an implied answer to the question about
teaching in v. 9. Whom will he teach; whom will he cause
to understand the message? The answer is, in effect:
those who have ears, let them hear (ושׁמעו , v. 23).
In v. 22, we encountered the first statement to the effect that someone has heard the message, the prophet. In
v. 26 we learn for the first time of someone who is taught,
the farmer. And what is the result? The farmer knows the
proper time and the proper means. The implication is that
if the people will follow the farmer's example and hear
(v. 23), God may teach them also.

Is 28 concludes with the issue of instruction unre-
solved. The chapter moves from confusion (confusion caused
by drunkenness, incomprehensible language, Yhwh's strange
and alien action) to clarity (the clarity of the final lesson in vv. 23-29). Along the way there are allusions to
a clear message (v. 12, v. 16), the rejection of which leads
to awesome results. Yhwh creates confusion through alien
speech (vv. 11-13) and alien work (v. 21). Only by hearing
the message and being taught can clarity be obtained. From
vv. 23-29 the benefits of instruction are evident.

There is one point early in the chapter (vv. 5f.)
where a clear promise of salvation appears. I mentioned a-
bove that the abrupt transition between v. 6 and v. 7 sets
vv. 1-6 apart from what follows. We also saw above that
similarities in form and content between vv. 1-4 and vv.
14ff. warrant comparison between Ephraim and Jerusalem. The
Judahites have a lesson to learn from the example of the
Ephraimites: if they are no better, they will meet the same
fate. But the lesson extends beyond v. 4. Ephraim will be
humbled by storm and trampling, yet there will be a remnant.
Who will constitute the remnant? Judah is threatened with
similar treatment. Who will hear the message (v. 23) and
make the decision to stand firm (v. 16)? Or, to repeat: who
will constitute the remnant?

The chapter begins with intricate metaphoric language
and ends with a parable, metaphoric language par excellence.
It uses agricultural imagery to describe judgment, vv. 1-4,
and in vv. 23-29, it returns to agricultural imagery to make
its final point. In the process, Is 28 shifts its focus from
Ephraim to Judah. While the parable of the farmer in vv. 23-
29 follows upon the message to the leaders of Jerusalem, it
is not aimed specifically at them. Addressing neither Ephraim,
with whom the chapter begins, nor Jerusalem, with whom it ends,
the parable is an invitation to all.

III. The Larger Context, Is 28-32

Following the apocalypse of chs. 24-27, Is 28 is
easily distinguishable as the beginning of a collection.
Where the collection ends, however, is open to debate.
Duhm considers 28-32(33) to constitute a collection;[50]
Cornill, 28-32(33);[51] Kaiser, 28-32;[52] Fohrer, 28-32;[53]
and Liebreich, 28-35.[54] I shall confine my remarks to the
material organized as a series of five woe oracles addressed
to Israel in chs. 28-32, although I recognize points of contact with ch. 33, which also begins with הֹוִי.[55] The introduction of the collection with הֹוִי (28:1) is balanced
by its conclusion with אַשְׁרֵי (32:20; a second אַשְׁרֵי saying appears in 30:18).[56] These verses draw a contrast between two groups and represent a movement from judgment to
promise.

Since, as scholars agree, the subject of 28:7-32:20 is
Jerusalem/Judah, why does an oracle against Ephraim introduce the collection? Many years ago Cornill recognized its
transitional function: "Cap. 28 bildet eine sehr angemes-
sene Ueberleitung von den Reden gegen die Völker [Cap. 13-
27] zu der eng zusammengehörigen Gruppe 29-33; indem es
anfängt mit Samarien steht es gewissermassen noch mit Einem
Fusse in den 'Völkern,' während es im weiteren Verlaufe mit
Jerusalem zu dem ausschliesslichen Gegenstand von Cap. 29-33
übergeht."[57] Not only does ch. 28 serve as a transition, its
first six verses also provide a paradigm for the movement
within the collection 28-32(33). The abrupt transition which
sets 28:1-6 apart from vv. 7ff. calls attention to the introductory function of the judgment against Ephraim with its
promise of a remnant. Though judgment and promise alternate
in 28-32, the essential development both within the collection and of the collection as a whole is from judgment to
promise.

Space does not allow discussion of catchword connections within these chapters or any kind of careful attention
to common themes and motifs.[58] Let us focus therefore on
the dominant theme of ch. 28, confusion versus clarity, with
its attendant motifs of teaching and hearing, instruction
and counsel. Not surprisingly, this theme plays an important role in chs. 29-32. As one might expect, a movement
from confusion to clarity accompanies the essential movement
from judgment to promise. Drunkenness as an aspect of confusion appears only once more in the collection, 29:9, where
it is used figuratively. The theme of incomprehensibility
is developed in the following verses (10-14), with Yhwh
acting, as in ch. 28, to create confusion. Instruction and
understanding will, however, take place "in that day," vv.
18-21, and the description of the security which results
is reminiscent of the promise for "that day" in 28:6. Even
those who murmur and err in spirit will accept instruction,
v. 24. The refusal to hear and the rejection of a clear
message, both prominent in ch. 28, are taken up again in
30:9-11 and 15-16. As before, this refusal leads to destruction. In 30:20f., however, the situation is reversed, and
the people will discover their teacher (מוֹרֶיךָ) and will

hear (תִשְׁמַעְנָה). Here we have a positive answer to the
question about teaching (יוֹרֶה) and understanding the message (שְׁמוּעָה) in 28:9. Finally, Yhwh's incomprehensible
speech and confusing deeds of ch. 28 give way to their oppo-
sites in the human realm in 32:1-8, where even the tongue of
stammerers will speak distinctly, and noble and wicked deeds
will be easily distinguished.

For the people, the way out of confusion is to accept
instruction. But if Yhwh acts incomprehensibly, how can one
be sure Yhwh's counsel is wise?[59] The collection explores
the tension between human and divine counsel and shows a concern to defend the latter. The importance of the theme of
counsel is confirmed by its structural prominence in Is 28-
32. The five blocks of material introduced by הוֹי either
begin or end with an expression of this theme (29:15-24 does
both). The affirmation in ch. 28 that Yhwh makes wonderful
(הִפְלִיא) counsel (עֵצָה) is echoed in 29:14, "I will
again do wonders (לְהַפְלִיא) with this people, wondrous
and marvelous (הַפְלֵא וָפֶלֶא)." But the wondrous action
here is a variation on the incomprehensibility theme of
ch. 28: Yhwh will hide wisdom and understanding (v. 14b).
The woe oracle which begins 29:15-24 picks up the motif of
hiding with an address to those who hide counsel (עֵצָה).
Here the issue is human counsel, which the people think they
can conceal from Yhwh. To think they could deceive their
creator is absurd; do they suppose Yhwh has no understanding
(v. 16)? A message of promise follows immediately. In contrast to 29:14, where human wisdom is confounded, 29:24 relates that human understanding will not only be possible,
but that it also will be given to those erring in spirit and
those who murmur.

With 30:1 Yhwh's wisdom begins to receive less emphasis.
This woe-section does not, like the previous ones, end with
a focus on instruction. It does however, like 29:15 before
it, begin with the idea of human counsel (עֵצָה). Its concern is to show the folly of following a plan (turning to
Egypt for aid) which is not Yhwh's. Ch. 31 pursues the
theme of turning to Egypt without consulting Yhwh. "Yet he
is wise and brings disaster," v. 2. This final reference to
Yhwh's wisdom makes the point forcefully: Yhwh's enmity toward them may seem incomprehensible to Yhwh's people, but it
does not mean that Yhwh acts unwisely. Disaster derives, as
we saw in ch. 28, from their refusal to hear--from their pur-
suit of their own course rather than Yhwh's. The last reference to human counsel appears in 32:1-8. For the first time,
it is not in conflict with divine counsel. These verses
speak of an ideal time when what people plan (יָעַץ) will
be clearly recognizable for what it is--noble or foolish.

To summarize: like 28:1-6, 28-32 moves from judgment
to promise. Like ch. 28, the collection in 28-32 displays
an essential development from confusion to clarity. And,
like 28:23-29, the collection is concerned to demonstrate
the wisdom of Yhwh, and it places this demonstration at crucial junctures. Numerous other points of contact among

chs. 28-32 could be explored. Detailed literary analysis
of Is 29-32 along the lines of the present investigation of
Is 28 remains for future study, and one hopes such study
will contribute to our appreciation of the literary quality
of prophetic collections and to our understanding of aesthetic concerns which guided the arrangement of this material.

NOTES

[1]On the arrangement of these chapters, see esp. G.
Fohrer, "The Origin, Composition and Tradition of Isaiah I-
XXXIX," Annual of Leeds University Oriental Society 3
(1961-62) 19-20; and his discussion in Das Buch Jesaja, 2.
Band (2. Aufl.; Zürich: Zwingli, 1967); cf. H. Barth, Die
Jesaja-Worte in der Josiazeit, WMANT 48 (Neukirchen, 1977)
284-85, 279-80; L.J. Liebreich, "The Compilation of the Book
of Isaiah," JQR 46 (1956) 268-69; 47 (1956) 121-22. For particular sensitivity to literary style in portions of these
chapters, see J. Ziegler, "Zum literarischen Aufbau verschiedener Stücke im Buche des Propheten Isaias," BZ 21 (1933) 131-
49, 237-54.

[2]Cf. J. H. Eaton, "The Origin of the Book of Isaiah,"
VT 9 (1959) 150.

[3]See W. K. Wimsatt, Jr. and Monroe C. Beardsley, "The
Intentional Fallacy," in The Verbal Icon: Studies in the
Meaning of Poetry (Kentucky: University Press, 1954) 2-18.

[4]Validity in Interpretation (New Haven: Yale University,
1967) 22.

[5]The Well Wrought Urn (New York: Harcourt, Brace & World,
1975) 23-24.

[6]Cf. the pertinent remarks in D. Robertson, The Old
Testament and the Literary Critic (Philadelphia: Fortress,
1977) 2-15.

[7]E.g., B. Duhm, Das Buch Jesaia (Göttingen: Vandenhoeck
& Ruprecht, 1892) 173; O. Procksch, Jesaia I, KAT 9 (Leipzig:
Deichert, 1930) 353; R. B. Y. Scott, "Introduction and Exege-
sis to Isaiah, Chs. 1-39," IB 5, 313-15; W. Eichrodt, Der
Herr der Geschichte: Jesaja 13-23 und 28-39 (Stuttgart: Cal-
wer, 1967) 122-23; Fohrer, Jesaja, 43; H. Wildberger, Jesaja,
BKAT X/Lieferung 13-15 (Neukirchen, 1978) 1044.

[8]See the discussions in B. Childs, Isaiah and the
Assyrian Crisis, SBT 2d Series, no. 3 (London: SCM, 1967) 65-
67, and R.F.Melugin, "The Conventional and the Creative in
Isaiah's Judgment Oracles," CBQ 36 (1974) 307-10.

[9]E.g., O. Kaiser, Isaiah 13-39 (Philadelphia: Westminster, 1974) 238-40; E.M. Good, Irony in the Old Testament (Philadelphia: Westminster, 1965) 143.

[10]The terminology was introduced by I. A. Richards and is widely accepted; see Philosophy of Rhetoric (Oxford: University Press, 1965) chs. 5 and 6.

[11]Fohrer, Jesaja, 44; H. Donner, Israel unter den Völkern, VTS 11 (Leiden: Brill, 1964) 77; Wildberger, Jesaja, 1046.

[12]For discussion of ironic technique in Isaiah, see Good, Irony, 116-30.

[13]Kaiser, Isaiah 13-39, 239; N. K. Gottwald, All the Kingdoms of the Earth (New York: Harper & Row, 1964) 160.

[14]Good, Irony, 143.

[15]See the discussion of these verses in Good, Irony, 139-42.

[16]Wildberger, Jesaja, 1048, identifies the strong and mighty one as Assyria, but sees Yhwh as subject of v. 2d. Oddly, he claims the feet are not Yhwh's but Assyria's. One might read ḥōzeq w^e'ōmes in v. 2a (cf. BHS), so that Yhwh becomes the subject of v. 2. W.H. Irwin, Isaiah 28-33: Translation with Philological Notes, Biblica et Orientalia 30 (Rome: Biblical Institute, 1977) 8-9, takes the l of l'dny as emphatic and reads the final colon of v. 2 with v. 3. The result is attractive: each of the first three verses of ch. 28 has a tripartite structure and each begins with an initial h word (and v. 4 has waw plus a h word).

[17]E.g., Duhm, Jesaia, 172; Fohrer, Jesaja, 48; Donner, Israel unter den Völkern, 76; Wildberger, Jesaja, 1050-51.

[18]Contra Good, Irony, 159.

[19]Duhm, Jesaia, 173; cf. Wildberger, Jesaja, 1058. For a different reading, based on the idea that "'vision' and 'judgment' are out of place in parallelism with 'strong drink' and 'wine,'" see G. R. Driver, "'Another Little Drink'--Isaiah 28:1-22," in Words and Meanings (Fs D. Winton Thomas), ed. P. R. Ackroyd and B. Lindars (Cambridge: University Press, 1968) 52-53.

[20]For this particular way of discussing the possibilities of a poem, see E. M. Good, "The Unfilled Sea: Style and Meaning in Ecclesiastes 1:2-11," in Israelite Wisdom (Fs S. Terrien), ed. J. G. Gammie, et al. (Missoula: Scholars Press, 1978), esp. pp. 60-63.

[21]Reading 'ābû with many mss and IQIs[a].

[22]See the commentators; and cf. the interpretations in Good, Irony, 128-29; and G. Pfeifer, "Entwöhnung und Entwöhnungsfest im Alten Testament: der Schlüssel zu Jesaja 28:7-13?," ZAW 84 (1972) 341-47.

[23]Although many commentators take vv. 7-13 as a unit, I am not convinced that form critically vv. 9-13 belong with vv. 7f. There are no repetitions of terms and no mention of priest and prophet in vv. 9-13, rather "this people" is the subject of the accusation. The connection is supported by the context, which suggests understanding v. 10 in light of drunken babble. If the interpretation discussed below is accepted--that v. 10 refers to alphabetic instruction--the connection with vv. 7f. is even more problematic in my opinion.

[24]Duhm, Jesaia, 174; Kaiser, Isaiah 13-39, 244-45; Wildberger, Jesaja, 1059.

[25]"'Another Little Drink,'" 55.

[26]On the significance of $k\hat{i}$ as a connective and pointer to what follows, see J. Muilenburg, "The Linguistic and Rhetorical Usages of the Particle כ׳ in the Old Testament," HUCA 32 (1961) 135-60.

[27]A. van Selms, "Isaiah 28:9-13: An Attempt to Give a New Interpretation," ZAW 85 (1973) 332-39.

[28]Esp. W. W. Hallo, "Isaiah 28:9-13 and the Ugaritic Abecedaries," JBL 77 (1958) 337-38.

[29]Isaiah 28-33, 23-24.

[30]S. H. Blank, Prophetic Faith in Isaiah (New York: Harper & Brothers, 1958) 24; Gottwald, All the Kingdoms, 162.

[31]Following LXX, Vg, and most commentators; on the variations between v. 15 and v. 18, see Irwin, Isaiah 28-33, 26-27.

[32]On the structure, see esp. N. W. Lund, "The Presence of Chiasmus in the Old Testament," _AJSL_ 46 (1930) 112-13. My arrangement differs from Lund's in that he reads v. 17ab together with v. 16 and sees in these verses a further development: C = 16bcde, D = 16f, C' = 17ab. He ends the chiasmus at v. 18. While I find Lund's arrangement attractive, I prefer to read 17ab in B' because of the appearance of šamtî, which echoes šamnû in B.

[33]_Irony_, 119-20; the citation is from p. 120.

[34]So Gottwald, _All the Kingdoms_, 161; on the mythological imagery, cf. Irwin, _Isaiah 28-33_, 28-29.

[35]J. Lindblom, "Der Eckstein in Jes. 28, 16," _Interpretationes ad Vetus Testamentum pertinentes S. Mowinckel_ (Oslo: Fabritius & Sonner, 1955) 126-27.

[36]_Isaiah 28-33_, 31.

[37]See L. Koehler, "Zwei Fachwörter der Bausprache in Jesaja 28, 16," _TZ_ 3 (1947) 390-93.

[38]"The Conventional and the Creative," 309.

[39]Irwin, _Isaiah 28-33_, 36.

[40]The point about flood imagery is made by Irwin, _Isaiah 28-33_, 35-36.

[41]_Isaiah 28-33_, 37.

[42]The translation is conjectural. Cf. S. C. Thexton, "A Note on Isaiah XXVIII 25 and 28," _VT_ 2 (1952) 81-82.

[43]Reading, with Good, _Irony_, 126, dôš.

[44]See J. W. Whedbee, _Isaiah and Wisdom_ (Nashville: Abingdon, 1971) 57-67 et _passim_.

[45]So, e.g., R. B. Y. Scott, "The Literary Structure of Isaiah's Oracles," in _Studies in Old Testament Prophecy_ (Fs T. H. Robinson), ed. H. H. Rowley (Edinburgh: T. & T. Clark, 1950) 183.

[46]_Isaiah and the Assyrian Crisis_, 130.

[47]See Whedbee's criticism of this view, _Isaiah and Wisdom_, 57-62.

[48]Isaiah and Wisdom, 61-63.

[49]Jesaja, 2. Band, 69-70.

[50]Jesaia, xii.

[51]C. H. Cornill, "Die Composition des Buches Jesaja," ZAW 4 (1884) 100.

[52]Isaiah 13-39, 234-36.

[53]"Origin, Composition and Tradition," 18-20.

[54]Liebreich, "Compilation of the Book of Isaiah," JQR 46, 268-69.

[55]For points of contact, see Leibreich, "Compilation of the Book of Isaiah," JQR 46, 268-69; Childs, Isaiah and the Assyrian Crisis, 115-17; cf. the classic treatment of this chapter by H. Gunkel, "Jesaia 33, eine prophetische Liturgie," ZAW N.F. 1 (1924) 177-208.

[56]The framing with hôy and 'ašrê is of particular interest if these formulas have the same original Sitz im Leben; see E. Gerstenberger, "The Woe-Oracles of the Prophets," JBL 81 (1962) 258-61; Whedbee, Isaiah and Wisdom, 87-90.

[57]"Die Composition des Buches Jesaja," 100.

[58]Though some groundwork has been laid, much remains to be done in these areas; on catchword connections, see esp. Liebreich, "Compilation of the Book of Isaiah," JQR 46, 268-69; 47, 121-22, 132-33; Fohrer has given special attention to thematic arrangement, see n. 1 above.

[59]I owe the substance of this idea to D. Petersen, who develops it in his redaction critical study of Is 28; Whedbee also argues the point, see Isaiah and Wisdom, esp. pp. 61-67.

METAPHYSICAL IMPLICATIONS OF KELBER'S APPROACH

TO ORALITY AND TEXTUALITY

A Response to Werner Kelber's, "Mark and the Oral Tradition"

Theodore J. Weeden, Sr.

St. Bernard's Seminary

Werner Kelber's paper, "Mark and the Oral Tradition," has raised a telling challenge to the adequacy of Bultmann's reconstruction of the evolution of the pre-Markan oral tradition and the textuality of the Markan Gospel. But more than that, in both his challenge to Bultmann and in his own reconstruction of the process which led from orality to textuality, Kelber has surfaced critical metaphysical issues which call into question the metaphysical grounding of the traditional historical-critical approach to the synoptic tradition.

Kelber contends that Bultmann's reconstruction is flawed in the following ways:

(1)   Bultmann too simply and narrowly explained the evolution of oral tradition to gospel text as the necessary function of intrinsic causation. As though dictated by some genetic code, the oral tradition, as Bultmann depicted it, grew inevitably from simple oral units to complex aggregate patterns of orality until by sheer gravitational force the Markan text became a natural consequence (1.2-1.3).

(2)   Bultmann oversimplified the case when he argued that the dominant shaping force of the Markan text as well as the pre-Markan oral material was the collective consciousness of the early community. Neither in the coalescing of bits of oral tradition nor in the composition of the Gospel did Bultmann allow for the influence of individual versatility or creative originality. He categorized the Gospel, as well as the oral traditions before it as Kleinliteratur. For Bultmann, the evangelist's reactiveness did not extend beyond editing his community's received traditions under the rubric of a Hellenistic redeemer myth and the messianic secret (1.1-1.4, 1.7).

(3)   Bultmann mistakenly assumed that the laws which govern orality are essentially the same laws as those which govern textuality (1.6-1.11).

(4)   Bultmann erred in his interpretation of the evolutionary pattern of the formal development of orality. He posited that the formal development of orality evolved progressively from pure and distinct oral forms to increasingly expanded and hybrid modifications and extensions of those forms. By virtue of this presupposition, Bultmann also erroneously concluded that one could trace, via a socio-historical route, the relative age of different variations of any given oral story or saying. Thereby he assumed one could identify the trajectory a story/saying followed from its origin

to its final stage.

(5) Bultmann was prone to oversimplify the sociological and theological character of the early Christian community which generated the oral tradition. The Bultmannian profile of that community tended to cast the community as essentially homogeneous and possessing a singleness of mind. This tendency has been further accentuated by historians of early Christianity to the point that the community of the oral tradition is customarily characterized as a "tightly formed community of people living at one spot in virtual social isolation" (7.3).

Kelber challenges these Bultmannian arguments for the following reasons:

(1) Studies of orality point to the fact that oral material does not evolve according to the law of intrinsic causation. Pre-Markan orality, like other orality, is a "pulsating phenomenon, expanding and contracting, waxing and waning, progressing and regressing...: the oral synoptic traditions represent proliferating tracks going into different directions, some intersecting, some running together and apart again, some fading and resurging, but altogether not an inevitable forward march controlled by the law of intrinsic causality" (7.4). Furthermore, gospel textuality represents neither the final culmination nor the exhaustion of pre-synoptic orality. While Markan textuality participates in pre-synoptic orality, that oral stream both precedes and, without essential interruption, flows beyond the eddies of gospel textuality (10.0).

(2) Quite apart from whatever forces are operative in the development of the oral tradition, the Markan Gospel, as redaction criticism and the new criticism have demonstrated, is a distinctively individualistic creation. Its author is a theologian who carefully molds and shapes his received material and then blends it with his own created material into a holistic narrative reflecting his own peculiar theological purpose (2.1).

(3) The laws governing orality are significantly different from those governing textuality. Orality is driven by two laws, the law of social identification and the law of social rejection or preventive censorship (6.0-7.2). The laws of textuality are those which are characteristic of the creativity of an author.

(4) The waxing and waning fluidity and the multidirectional thrust of pre-synoptic orality makes it evident that the drive from simplicity to complexity is only one of many force-factors pulsating through the organic matrix of orality. Consequently, Bultmann and other form critics to the contrary, "not only is it not possible to recover the pure or original form amidst the ebbing and flowing or oralities, but the very concept of an "ursprüngliche Form" contradicts the facts of oral life" (7.5).

(5) Recognition of the complexity and diversity of the oral tradition and recognition of the role and function of various itinerant, spirit-led prophets in producing and disseminating the oral tradition renders untenable the model of the pre-synoptic Christian community as a community which belonged to a single place and possessed a

single mind (7.3).

The Metaphysical Ramifications of Kelber's Challenge of Bultmann

Kelber's criticism of Bultmann's reconstruction of the socio-historical character of synoptic orality and its relationship to the textuality of the Gospel of Mark are for the most part quite persuasive. But the scope of his challenge to Bultmann and its devastating effect is far more comprehensive than even Kelber may realize. For the ramifications of Kelber's criticism of Bultmann's classic position, set forth half a century ago in <u>Die Geschichte der synoptischen Tradition</u>, strike at the very roots of the Bultmannian historical-critical methodology -- to say nothing of the historical-critical methodology in general.

Kelber's critique of Bultmann's history of the synoptic tradition exposes an inherent problem in his historical-critical methodology. His epistemology and its underlying metaphysical foundation are flawed. The genius of Bultmann's hermeneutical approach, both as historian and hermeneut, lay in his ability to make effective use of Kantian epistemology in concert with Heideggerian ontology.

Drawing upon one dimension of Kantian epistemology, Bultmann as a historian pursued the view that history is known by clearly and distinctly isolating events, chronologically aligning them in their relative order and discovering from such an arrangement the meaning events share in their causally-linked continuum. Axiomatic to this orientation, as Kelber has noted, is the position that chronological history, <u>Historie</u>, is driven by the law of intrinsic causation.[1] Guided by such an epistemological perspective in seeking to grasp the character and meaning of the history of the synoptic tradition, Bultmann naturally followed the logic set forth by the directives of his epistemology. He isolated and identified the various oral forms of early Christian kerygmatic transmission. He made judgments as to their indigenous history-of-religions setting. He aligned the formal development of the tradition according to the relative order of evolutionary growth; and then he reconstructed the historiographic meaning of the total oral development as it causally grew from simple forms, mixed, expanded and aggregate forms of orality to its issue in the textual form, gospel.

Drawing upon the other side of Kantian epistemology and linking it with Heideggerian ontology, Bultmann, as a hermeneut of the faith, epistemologically explained how one gains or encounters knowledge about an entirely different kind of history, authentic history (<u>Geschichte</u>). Disclosure of such history for Bultmann provokes an encounter with the authentic meaning of one's historicness. Such knowledge, existentially disclosed, illumines the inner events of human experience. By willingly and decisively responding to such knowledge, one, Bultmann asserted, can affect the course of <u>Historie</u>. But this affect on <u>Historie</u> is beyond empirical observation and can be perceived only by the eye of faith.[2]

At the level of historical-critical inquiry, the epistemology which informs Bultmann's methodology derives its cogency by its grounding in a metaphysical view of reality traditional to Western philosophical thought, a metaphysical view that is, as James Robinson puts it, "static, substantival, essence/accidence-oriented."[3] In such a view of reality events are located along a fixed time-space continuum which inexorably unfolds on a metaphysical stage whose setting or backdrop is

basically static. This dual perspective accounts for why it is
that in his reconstruction of early Christian orality Bultmann
characterized the oral tradition as evolutionary, but tended to
depict its Christian environment (_Sitz im Leben_) as monolithic,
possessing a singleness of mind.

It is precisely the adequacy of this metaphysical paradigm
which has traditionally guided the historical-critical method
that Kelber's criticisms of Bultmann have called into question.
The paradigm is inadequate because it no longer satisfactorily
accounts for features of orality and textuality to which Kelber
has drawn our attention. We have a paradigmatic crisis.

Whenever the emergence of new data challenges the organizing paradigm of one's investigatory methodology, the immediate tendency is to preserve the paradigm even if it means
sacrificing the data. One tries to force the new data to fit
the paradigm, ignore or dismiss the data or at best make minor
adjustments in the paradigm to accommodate the new data. There
is a strong resistance against giving up on a working paradigm
which has proved its fruitfulness.[4] This is particularly true
in the sphere of biblical criticism when it comes to the question of the metaphysical basis for the historical-critical
methodology. The so-called scientific method has so dominated
the practice of historical-critical inquiry that biblical
critics have assumed that it self-legitimizes itself. Fearing
that the introduction of metaphysical considerations might
cloud the empirical objectivity of the historical-critical
methodology, biblical critics have either ignored or forgotten
that the credibility and cogency of the methodology rests
solely upon the validity of its inherent metaphysical paradigm.
In the arena of biblical study, that metaphysical paradigm is
now being challenged from a number of quarters. Walter Wink,
for example, represents a point of view that argues that the
linking of the historical-critical study to the metaphysical
paradigm of technological science has led to functional
atheism and to bankruptcy of the historical-critical method.
It has failed to produce what "its practitioners considered
its purpose to be: so to interpret the Scriptures that the past
becomes alive and illumines our present with new possibilities
for personal and social transformation."[5]

From another quarter comes the challenge of structuralism,
which as an ideology dismisses history, and consequently historical-critical inquiry, as providing any source for or
guidance in uncovering the nature of reality. Some structuralists deny any realistic ontology, empirical or existential.[6] The mind alone is conceived as the seat of reality.
The mind creates reality, like a game, according to the dic-
tates of its imagination.

From yet another quarter, from within the Bultmannian
camp itself, has emerged the recognition that, as Robinson puts
it, we are faced with a crisis of historical-critical and
history-of-religions categories to which the traditional static,
substantival metaphysics is incapable of adequately responding.
Only by abandoning this outmoded metaphysical foundation of the
historical-critical methodology and replacing it with "a dynamic, historic, existence/process-oriented new metaphysics" can
the crisis be met.[7] Kelber is not the only voice being raised
in the metaphysical wilderness. The need for a new metaphysical paradigm for biblical studies which takes seriously the
historical, cosmological and theological character of Judeo-
Christian religion is an urgent priority today. What would the
profile of such a paradigm be like?

The Whiteheadian Process Paradigm

James Robinson has announced the need for a "dynamic, historical, existence/process-oriented" metaphysics to resolve the "crisis of categories." Kelber in his profile of the processes which were the drivers for the development of orality and textuality describes features of these processes which suggest that something like this new metaphysical paradigm for which Robinson calls may already be operative in Kelber's methodology without his conscious recognition of its influence. When he characterizes the pre-Markan oral history as "a pulsating phenomenon, expanding and contracting, waxing and waning, progressing and regressing," and when he argues that the early Christian environment from which this orality emerged was not monolithic or static but variegated and in continual change, Kelber implicitly abandoned the traditional historical-critical metaphysical paradigm for a process oriented one. What is faintly apparent in Kelber's approach, I wish to make more pronounced. By sketching what a possible process paradigm might look like, the provocative character and validity of some of Kelber's insights can be reinforced, while others can be shown to have fuller and more suggestive fruitfulness, once they are freed from the residue of the old metaphysical paradigm which still holds sway in some of Kelber's perception.

A process paradigm that I have found helpful for the New Testament hermeneutical enterprise is one derived from the thought of Alfred North Whitehead.[8] Briefly, Whitehead viewed reality as a holistic, organic, dynamic and creative process in which everything that is is interrelated in an ever-emerging process of becoming. It is also the nature of reality that every entity, no matter how simple or how complex, is indebted to its inherited past in its own coming into being. But such indebtedness is not total nor is it fully deterministic. An entity's coming into being is also the function of its own creative impulse. Thus in every occasion of the creative advance the many become one and are increased by one. And in every occasion of the creative advance there is an element of novelty, however small, in the midst of the flow of organic continuity.

Since all entities from the smallest puff to the most complex forms of life share directly in the experience of this interrelatedness of reality, our primary awareness is the sense of participating in the organic pulsation of life. Our primal and most direct knowledge, contrary to Hume and Kant, is, as Beardslee puts it, "indistinct, loaded with feeling, and imprecise, while our clear perceptions are indirect projections upon reality."[9] Our direct but indistinct knowledge is linked with our clear but fallible perceptions through the agency of symbolic reference. Language, orality and textuality, is a major but not the only symbolic system which mediates reality via this phenomenon of symbolic reference. "For Whitehead, it is an arbitrary system. A statement in language is, by itself, thoroughly indeterminate. But, given a context, a history, a trajectory, it can become an instrument of contact with reality, however fallible."[10] Underlying the language system as well as other symbolic systems of reference pulsates an area of symbolic reference in which creative imagination entertains concrete possibilities for an experienced reality. This, what lies behind the evocation of language,

oral and textual, is a response to felt or experienced
propositions which are embodied, though perhaps not fully,
in the linguistic expression. Similarly, when a text or
oral saying evokes a response in the hearer or reader,
what is being felt or experienced are propositions elicited by the linguistic phenomenon. Whitehead argued that
the primary function of a proposition is to elicit interest and not to provoke judgments as to truth or falsehood.
The acceptance or rejection of a felt proposition on the
basis of its truthfulness or falseness is of secondary
importance. An either-or, yes-no decision in response
to a felt proposition is neither automatically called for
nor necessarily required. While such yes-no decisions are
often an appropriate response, there are times when some
propositions are preserved in the course of being incorporated into a larger conceptual context merely for the
purpose of providing aid to the maintenance of contrast.
Or there are times when propositions are retained in the
interest of finding compatible, novel associations for
them in a synthesizing of data into a unity of the greatest possible whole.[11]

The Process Paradigm and Kelber's Profile of Mark
and the Oral Tradition

Elements of Kelber's reconstruction of the development of the oral tradition and its relationship to textuality of Mark resonate harmoniously with the Whiteheadian
metaphysical paradigm. Already we have noted the process
perspective of Kelber's description of the organic, pulsating fluidity of orality. We noted also his view of
the early Christian community which gave birth to this
orality as a community both variegated in its composition and growing in processive development. There are
other compatible and mutually supportive links between
the process paradigm and Kelber's insights on both orality
and textuality. There are also in Kelber's profile of
the relationship of pre-Markan textuality problematic areas
which a process point of view can address in such a way
as to bring about both resolution of the problems and
further advancement of Kelber's insights. Our attention
turns to illustrations of these contributions of the
process paradigm.

First, with respect to the textuality of Mark, the
process paradigm coheres well with Kelber's redaction-
critical view of the relationship of the evangelist to
the creation of his gospel. The Gospel is an autosemantic entity which its author-theologian has created by
weaving together diverse parts of his inherited material,
along with his own creative writing, into an artistic
whole reflecting his own theological purpose (2.1).

The process paradigm also supports Kelber in his
contention that the creation of Markan textuality signals
a novel departure from the use of the oral medium to
transmit Jesus traditions in the early community. Yet
his emphasis on this novel departure leads Kelber into
the error of overstating the discontinuity between oral and
textual processes. While Bultmann erred in arguing that
there is an intrinsic causation inevitably driving orality
to textuality, the sharp distinction Kelber draws between
oral drives and textual drives and their respective purposes is overdone   at least from a process perspective

and, as I shall show, from the perspective of New
Testament evidence. It is precisely at the point of
depicting the nature of this distinction that Kelber's
argument slips into ambiguity and logical conflict.

The logic of Kelber's argument with respect to the
distinction between orality and textuality appears pulled
in two directions. On the one hand, according to one line
of his reasoning, Kelber contends that Markan textuality
is a distinctively different phenomenon from pre-Markan
orality. Kelber considers it a methodological error to
equate oral history with written history (3.1). "A
perceptual chasm separates the oral, associative thinking (of orality) from Mark's causal thinking as it is
expressed in his gospel's sequential pattern" (6.3).
Orality distinguishes itself from textuality by "its
intimate and creative association with social life" (7.51).
By writing, Mark has distanced himself from social life
(9.2). The laws driving orality are different from those
driving textuality. "Mark's composition is thus more in
conflict than in continuity with his oral past" (9.3).

As a consequence of the categorical difference between orality and textuality, so Kelber argues, one
cannot use form criticism to interpret Mark. Redaction
criticism and form criticism are by virtue of their
peculiar methodological objectives two different and
distinct methodologies that must be kept separate and
applied only to their intended sphere of study. They are
"discontinuous phenomena.... The perception of redaction criticism as a natural extension of form criticism,
undertaking on a larger scale the kind of operations form
criticism undertakes on a miniature scale, is at best a
half-truth" (2.12). The view of the Gospel developed by
form criticism is entirely different from redaction
criticism. Form criticism when used to interpret Mark
actually misrepresents the nature of the Gospel. Therefore redaction criticism recently, under the influence of
the New Criticism, has abandoned the practise of sepa-
rating redaction from tradition in seeking clues to the
interpretation of Mark (2.1).

In contrast to this line of argument, Kelber states
on the other hand that Mark is indebted to the oral traditions before him. The evangelist has incorporated oral
patterns into his text, and they survive on "a new conceptual level" (8.1). Though under the control now of a
literary mentality rather than their former oral mentality,
they are, nevertheless, treated "as witnesses to be inter-
rogated" (9.3). In fact, so respected is the orality by
Mark that he appropriates some of their oral drives. The
presence in the Gospel of oral forms "in cluster-like
density betrays Markan indebtedness to the oral habit of
hoarding like experiences." Likewise "the simple linking
together of sentences by kai parataxis, the habitual use
of euthys, the preference for direct speech, the pre-
dominance of the historical present, the lack of an artis-
tically reflected prose, and incomplete characterization
of the Jesus figure, the gospel's exposition as a series
of events, and little enthusiasm for the abstract--these
and many other features indicate Markan allegiance to the
vitality of the spoken word" (8.0). Moreover, "Markan
sensitivity to failing discipleship, the failure that is
to hear and appropriate what is being said, dramatizes

the second law of oral tradition, the rule of social rejection or preventive censorship " (7.0).

In this vector of Kelber's argumentation he employs
form-critical methodology in order to point up Markan
redactional techniques. For example, he draws attention
to what he refers to as "Mark's well documented insertion
technique" by showing how Mark has interpolated the oral
form, apophthegm, into oral form, miracle story, in Mk 2:1-12.
And finally, with respect to this slant in Kelber's argument,
he argues that the textuality of Mark was in fact provoked
by what really amounts to an intimate association with the
social life of his community, though perhaps in counter
dependence, namely his reaction to what he considered to
be an abuse of orality (10.0-11.6).

Finally, with respect to Kelber's argumentation, he
commits a methodological error in his comparison of orality
and textuality. When he speaks of the Markan textuality he
speaks of it as having a single direction, "a single-minded
textual performance" (9.5), whereas when he speaks of
orality he characterized it as multidirectional and multi-
faceted. There is a logical fallacy in this comparison, a
fallacy analogous to the fallacy common to the comparing
of apples and oranges. He treats Markan textuality as a
coherent entity. But while referring to orality as an
entity, he really treats it as a collection of many diverse
entities. He speaks of it in terms of the whole but the
comparison he draws with Mark is really with orality's parts.
If he were treating it as a whole, then orality as a whole
which integrates all its parts would have to be seen from
the process perspective as also single directional, having
a single-minded performance. If the many become one and
are increased by one for the text of Mark, then the many
become one and are increased by one for orality. One
could argue that textuality is multidirectional also if
one chose to speak in terms of component parts of the text
or if one chose to examine different texts under the category of gospel textuality, e.g. the textuality of Matthew,
Mark, Luke and John.

The pull of Kelber's argument in different directions
and the error in his comparison of textuality with orality
can be accounted for as a result of the influence of the
old metaphysical paradigm which appears to inform his
understanding of form criticism and redaction criticism
and their interrelationship. In the Kantian-Heideggerian
philosophical trajectory novelty or creative freedom and
causal continuity do not interdependently co-exist in
concert with each other. Discontinuity is sharply juxtaposed to continuity in this orientation. Existential
historicness stands in radical tension with chronological
history. Consequently novelty and continuity are
conceived as separate and countervailing phenomena.
Since form criticism is basically a methodology for
identifying causal relationships (Bultmann) or organic,
pulsating relationships (Kelber), not much consideration
has been given in form critical analysis to the possibility that the unfolding occasions of oral proclamation
or transmission may, like the text of Mark, have their own
autosemantic quality, authorial individuality, and novel
creativity. Furthermore, since Mark according to the redaction criticism, particularly redaction criticism informed
by the New Criticism, must be seen as an independent, autosemantic entity of creative artistry, then the inherent
indebtedness of the Gospel to its inherited past for shaping
its coming into being has tended to be bracketed out in
recent critical treatments.

What the old metaphysic would not permit, a process paradigm does. For a process view of orality affirms Kelber's view of its organic fluidity, but it also argues that in each occasion of proclamation or transmission there is also the novelty of the self-created experience. Kelber hints in this direction when he notes that the oral tradition did not come into being as the work of some monolithic community with a collective mind-set but through the individual ministry of itinerant charismatic prophets. Kelber, however, does not develop the implications of this insight. The process paradigm argues for both the creative autosemantic character of each textual phenomenon and for the creative character, however minimal, of each oral phenomenon.

From the process point of view form criticism and redaction criticism are neither discontinous methodologies nor methodologies which clash over conflicts of interest or purpose. Rather they are perceived as not only compatible but complementary methodologies, with each enriching and informing the understanding of the other as each is applied to its specific task. This methodological cooperation is made possible in the process paradigm because the paradigm form critically respects and values highly the self-creating, individualistic and novel impulses which occasion oral evocation, proclamation or transmission, and because it redaction critically respects and values highly the rich dependency upon the inherited oral patterns to which a text as autosemantic entity is indebted. When the Markan text is studied via such methodological cooperation, it is discovered to be a much more complex and provocative entity than is recognized when the Gospel is examined with the methodological position that form and redaction criticisms are discontinuous or competing phenomena. One of the most valuable returns from such a process approach is the recognition that the Markan text may contain a diverse inheritance of many traditions, each reflecting various stages of development and each reflecting different kairotic moments when autosemantic life was realized. Using the Markan text to trace back and recover the echoes of such moments in the early Christian experience is, of course, fraught with great hermeneutical problems. But the recognition of the possible existence of such former kairotic moments makes the hermeneutical challenge alluring.

Early in our discussion it was stated that Kelber's sharp categorical distinction between orality and textuality stands in some tension with the process paradigm and certain New Testament evidence. Having explored the matter with respect to the process perspective we turn to the consideration of New Testament evidence.

Kelber's position that textuality is a totally different linguistic phenomenon, not only with respect to the medium of communication but also with respect to its relationship to social life and performance function, conflicts to some degree with Paul's perception. Though there is a decided difference between the genre of epistolary communication and direct oral address, Paul does not seem to acknowledge any essential difference in the

expected performance function of the two mediums. One
gains the distinct impression that in his written communication Paul addresses his congregation and expects a resultant response from them in about the same way as he
would address and expect a response through speech (e.g.
I Cor.5:1-5). Though the Pauline written word may not
have exactly the same existential immediacy as his
spoken word, some of his opponents apparently found the
linguistic performance of his written communication was
more powerful than his oral proclamation (II Cor.10:9-11).
And certainly in much of his correspondence there is the
ring of orality's "intimate and creative association with
social life" (e.g. I & II Cor.; Gal.). It is generally
true, as Kelber asserts, "the spoken word is the living
word which carries a sense of immediacy and presence which
the written word cannot convey with like intensity" (5.1).
But when the letters of Paul were read as oral performance
by his surrogate in the listening congregation, there is
no reason to believe that the oral performance of the letters produced much less an existential encounter than if
Paul had delivered the same message orally before the
congregation.

Space does not permit the pursuance of what could be
a very fruitful discussion of the issue of orality vis-
à-vis textuality with respect to the author of Revelation.
Suffice it to note that the author's conscious use--and
frequent reminder to the reader of his use--of the text-
medium for the proclamation of the oracles of the Lord
does not seem to have meant for him that the oracles were
delivered with any less existential intensity than if he
had chosen the oral medium of communication. It is also
fair to say that he looked upon his inscribed words as
living words which in their existential encounter would
communicate a "sense of immediacy and presence." He
hardly envisioned them as frozen words; and while we do not
know how the first century readers received these words,
there is abundant evidence in the twentieth century that
Christian sectarian groups have existentially experienced
the text of Revelation as living words, having an intimate and creative association with the life experience of
their groups. In Revelation we encounter oral and textual
features in creative mixture.

Finally, the Gospel of Mark itself witnesses against
Kelber making too strong a categorical distinction between
the character and purpose of orality and textuality as
they were used among early Christians. I find Kelber
rather persuasive when he argues that the textuality of
Mark was born out of a polemical reaction to the abuse and
misrepresentation of the oral tradition by charismatic
prophets in his community. It may well have been that the
misuse of orality by these prophets and the resultant
excesses which led to a loss of confidence in its efficacy caused Mark to turn to the medium of textuality to
blunt the oral excesses, counteract the disastrous mis-
interpretation of the kerygma and restore confidence in
Christian proclamation (11.0-11.5).

But Mark's choice of textuality in preference to
orality does not mean that he meant to make his narrative

any less an intimate and creative association with social
life or any less an experience of existential encounter.
In fact the evangelist's choice of euaggelion as a term
that captures the totality of this linguistic impact (1:1)
suggests that he intends the narrative to function the way
orality functions in performance. For euaggelion for Mark
is not a text-type nor even an oral-form type. It rather
is a word which he uses to capture the essence of the oral
proclamation of the kerygma (1:15; 13:10). His use of
euaggelion is not unlike Paul's use of it (e.g.Gal. 1:6-12).
As Kelber, along with Boring, has insightfully shown, Mark
rejected his opponents' use of logoi and their attempt to
effect the real presence of Christ through their logoi
(11.1-11.11). In opposition to these false Christs and
false prophets Mark makes Jesus real but not materially
present for his community through the control of his text-
proclamation, euaggelion (11.31-11.32). Jesus is known and
experienced in but not apart from the euaggelion (8:35;
10:29; 13:10), and is only so experienced until the time
when he will be fully and materially experienced at the
parousia (13:27).[12]

If as Kelber claims, the evangelist hides behind his
words, and in this way appears to have "detribalized" himself (9.2) and distanced himself from the intimacy of
social life, it is only an appearance demanded by the
nature of the polemic he is waging against his opponents
who present themselves as "the authoritative carriers of
oral tradition" (11.0). Mark could not confront them
personally, as Paul might have done, because his opponents
claimed the authority of the disciples. Against such an
authoritative tradition Mark was personally impotent.
Consequently, he presents himself and his case through
the figure of Jesus.[13] Appearance to the contrary, Mark
has neither detribalized himself nor distanced himself
by his choice of the textual medium over the oral medium.
He is very much a part of and intimately involved in the
crisis of his community via the performance function of
his euaggelion.

Matthew and Luke may have moved self-consciously
toward the choice of a written text-type (cf. Matthew's
biblos, 1:1; and Luke's akribōs kathexes...grapsai, 1:3)
as they approached their own compositional tasks. But
Mark's attempt to produce a controlled effect of the
linguistic performance normally achieved through orality
led him to create by accident (or by necessity) a novel
genre, an oral text, which we have since labeled "gospel."
For this reason I find Theissen's depiction of Mark as
written orality   an appropriate characterization of the
Markan phenomenon (see 8.1).

As a postscript to this discussion, it should be noted
that a process paradigm argues for perceiving textuality
as well as orality, as participating in the organic and
dynamic process or, better, as the linguistic presentation of that process. It is tempting because of the
medium-control of each kairotic occasion of a given
textual trajectory to treat those occasions in suspended
time, artificially dislocated from the organic processes

that swept them into being and sweep them on into ever
emerging new kairotic occasions. Such artificial dislocation (Whitehead's fallacy of simple location) leads us
erroneously to ascribe permanence to textuality in contrast to orality. To do so is to ignore the nature of
process even with respect to what appears to be the permanence of writing. For markings on a page are only an
illusion of permanence. Each time the text (the linguistic phenomenon) is encountered new propositions are
experienced by virtue of the fact that each occasion
constitutes an entirely new environment coming into being.
In this sense no text is permanent. It emerges in each
encounter as a new text, even if that newness is only
minimal.

I bring my response to Kelber's provocative and semi-
nal paper, "Mark and the Oral Tradition," to a close with
two final observations about the way in which a process
paradigm impacts his contributions. First, Kelber, drawing upon the work of Theissen, contends that the transmission and preservation of oral sayings through the
course of the organic flow of early Christian orality
were dependent upon the sayings satisfying the law of
social identification (i.e. social relevance and social
acceptance) and the law of social rejection or preventive censorship. According to these laws, "the continu-
ation of oral tradition depended upon the existential
intensity with which the message articulated and consoli-
dated the experiences of those who conveyed and heard
the words" (6.0). If a saying or tradition were "entirely alien to the audience, or a matter of indiffer-
ence , or socially unacceptable," it was either altered
to meet the prevailing social situation or it became
eliminated (7.).

It may well have been that the fate of oral material
was determined by such processes of selection and rejection, but such either-or judgments may not have always
determined whether a saying or tradition either survived
or passed into oblivion. The Whiteheadian theory of
propositions leads us to recognize that transmission
and preservation of orality in the early church might
not always have hung on whether the transmitters and
receivers of oral traditions made immediate existential
identification with the oral message and their own Sitz
im Leben. As we noted earlier, the primary function of
a proposition is to elicit interest and not to provoke
existential judgments as to truth or falsehood. Compelling interest elicited by a proposition may in fact call
for the suspension and/or delay in judgment. Consequently some sayings may have survived in the course of the
orality-process not because they were judged existentially
relevant by a given community but because they persisted
in eliciting interest. Even a saying or story that "con-
tradicted" a community's or individual's experience might
have been preserved because of its aesthetic contrast,
though it may have been made "safe" for preservation by
being drawn into a larger unity of associative sayings
where its message could be tolerated or its dissonance
muted. This input provided by the process paradigm makes

the very attractive logic of being able to link sayings
and stories respectively with transmitters via the law
of social identification less certain--though still very
attractive.

Second, although Kelber strongly dismisses any possibility of recovering an original oral form or even
positing that there was such a phenomenon because of the
very complex and convoluted character of the organic process of orality (7.5), a process paradigm would not totally
share such pessimism. Since the process evolution of
reality tends to evolve from relative simplicity to ever-
greater complexity in creative advance, with allowance for
manifestations of entropy, and since every occasion contains within it some memory of its past through the appropriation of its past in its moment of self-creation, then
recovering oral routes of sayings, traditions and clusters
of the same is not impossible. For the many do become one,
are increased and, in some measure, preserved by the one.
To be sure, the task of reconstructing oral routes is
fraught with exceeding difficulty and requires due consideration to, among other factors, the fluid nature of oral
forms, the role content plays in the shaping of forms, and
the complex environmental relationships that any given oral
tradition embraces in each kairotic occasion that makes up
the route of its trajectory.

Notes

1. History and Eschatology (New York:Harper & Row, 1955)
    pp. 116ff., 130, 139f.

2. Eschatology, pp. 43f., 116f., 130-135, 140-146, 150;
    Jesus Christ and Mythology (New York:Charles Scribner's
    Sons, 1958), p.63; "The Problem of Hermeneutic," Essay's
    trans. J.C.G. Grieg (London:SCM Press, 1955), p.254.

3. James M. Robinson and Helmut Koester, Trajectories
    through Early Christianity (Philadelphia:Fortress Press,
    1971), p.9 and cf. 8-11.

4. See T.S. Kuhn, The Structure of Scientific Revolutions
    (Chicago:University of Chicago Press, 1970) and W. Wink,
    The Bible in Human Transformation (Philadelphia:
    Fortress Press, 1973),pp. 16-18.

5. Human Transformation, p.2.

6. Cf. J.D. Crossan, "A Metamodel for Polyvalent Narration,"
    Semeia, 9, pp. 107-112, and also Kovacs'discussion of the
    philosophical foundation of structuralism: "Philosophical
    Foundations for Structuralism," Semeia, 10, pp. 85-106.

7. Trajectories, p. 9.

166

8. See particularly A.N. Whitehead, _Process and Reality_
   (New York: Harper and Row, 1960), and _Modes of Thought_
   (New York: Free Press, 1968), and W. Beardslee,
   "Whitehead and Hermeneutic," _JAAR_, XLVII (1979), 31-37.

9. "Whitehead and Hermeneutic," p. 32.

10. "Whitehead and Hermeneutic," p. 33.

11. Beardslee, "Whitehead and Hermeneutic," pp.33f.

12. Cf. T.J. Weeden, _Mark--Traditions in Conflict_
    (Philadelphia: Fortress Press, 1971), pp.82-90.

13. Weeden, _Mark_, pp. 59-168.

JULIAN'S REBUILDING OF THE TEMPLE:
    A SOCIOLOGICAL STUDY OF RELIGIOUS COMPETITION

Charles Robert Phillips, III
Lehigh University

This paper will begin by analyzing fourth century accounts
of Julian's project in order to demonstrate the ways in which
those accounts decisively influenced the later tradition. Secondly, the largely Christian accounts of the events in early
363 will be related to the Christian hermeneutic of the destruction of the Temple in 70. Finally, through building on these
perspectives, it will be possible to demonstrate why what otherwise might have been a minor historical event captured the
interest of so many authors.   .

The sources fall into three chronological strata. The
first group lies in the fourth century and comprises Ambrose,
Ammianus Marcellinus (the one pagan account), Gregory Nazianzus
and John Chrysostom. The second category belongs to the fifth
century: Philostorgius, Rufinus, Socrates, Sozomen and Theo-
doret. The final group I classify as "late" (ninth through
fourteenth centuries) and include in it Cedrenus, Glycas, John
of Rhodes, Nicephorus, Theophanes and Zonaras. A Syriac tradition runs roughly parallel with the pseudo-Cyril letter,
Ephraem and Michael the Syrian.

A detailed examination of the fourth century group will
show how it has strongly influenced all later accounts. I
divide it into two subgroups; one comprises Ambrose (*Ep.* 40.1),
Ammianus Marcellinus (23.1.2-3) and John Chrysostom, while the
other has Gregory Nazianzus. All the authors of the first sub-
group are unanimous that some sort of unearthly fire halted the
construction. There exist good reasons why they present a relatively simple account as opposed to Gregory's fabulistic report.

There can be no doubt that Ammianus represents the most
trustworthy source for Julian. This close acquaintance of
Julian's accompanied him on the ill-fated Persian expedition
and would certainly have been privy to reports from Alypius,
whom Julian had placed in charge of construction. Although
Ammianus began composing his history from 378 onwards, his intimacy with the emperor gives his account primacy. Chrysostom
lived at Antioch, Julian's residence while the project was conceived: he would thus, although writing later (380), have been
in a position to hear the same sort of reports which reached
Ammianus. Finally, Ambrose held an important position at the
Italian court; he, too, would have heard official reports. It
is impossible to demonstrate closer interrelations; rather, it
seems clear that all three ultimately reflect Alypius' report.

Some scholars have considered Gregory the most reliable
source; they base their arguments on the c. 363 date of composition for his *Orations Against Julian*. This is untenable.
Gregory had both political and geographical distance at the time
from the circles of the other three; consequently, he would have
been in no position to hear privileged accounts. Moreover,
these were the times of Gregory's stay in the desert and forced
ordination; hardly the circumstances conducive to level report-

ing. It seems more likely that a popular tradition grew up
around the event and that this was the only account available
to Gregory. This popular tradition runs on through the other
strata of authorities and also forms the basis for the Syriac
accounts. Before examining the tradition's later developments,
we must consider further the implications of the primacy of
Ambrose, Ammianus and Chrysostom.

The philosophical implications of a possible genuine divine
intervention are irrelevant to this paper; rather, the working
hypothesis will be that some sort of fire did occur, caused
either by an earthquake or, possibly, an accident. How could
such a relatively common occurrence as a fire achieve such an
elevated status in these authors? Again, why does the relatively sober Ammianus speak of *metuendi globi flammarum* and *elemento
repellenti* (23.1.3)? He readily rationalizes a fire (22.13.3)
or describes a disaster at Nicomedia in 358 (17.7.1-14) without
reference to the divine. But, on the other hand, given what he
considers sufficient evidence, the supernatural can play a role;
a believer in portents himself (21.1.7-14; 31.1.1), he characterizes Julian as fanatic in this regard: *praesagiorum sciscitati-
oni nimium deditus* (25.4.17). We must consider that at the
start of XXIII Ammianus has been building up an aura of doom
for Julian's Persian campaign. Thus, whatever the precise
nature of Alypius' account, Ammianus must have decided at some
point that the Temple failure represented still one more sign
that the expedition was doomed. The tone is deliberately enhanced through a Vergilian allusion: *metuendi globi flammarum*
recalls the *globos flammarum* of *Aeneid* 3.544. Unless one reads
the account in such ways, one must indeed question why Ammianus
regards the fire as sufficient to halt the enterprise. We can
only guess at the real reasons; Julian himself (295C) makes it
clear that the project has halted. Perhaps the emperor intended
to resume it on his return from Persia. Certainly the fire, in
Ammianus' omen-laden atmosphere, achieves a far larger meaning
retrospectively than it ever did at the time; Julian's silence
on it is decisive. Thus the events have a contribution to make
to Ammianus' evaluation of Julian as an emperor who usually pays
too much attention to omens but now, at the precise time when he
ought to heed them, ignores them (cf. 24.6.17). The construction ceased but the expedition continued and that, to Ammianus,
represented part of Julian's problem.

Since Ambrose writes during the time of Ammianus' literary
activity (*Ep.* 40 dates to late 388), it seems clear that his
important position at court would have enabled him, via either
Ammianus or Alypius, to learn the essentials of the events,
which he records in much the same way as Ammianus: *divino igne*.
Again, Chrysostom's residence at Antioch would have enabled him
to hear the same traditions at the time of composing his
Orations Against the Jews; it will later become clear why he did
not elaborate. Thus all three authors, in one way or another,
reflect Alypius.

Scholars ancient and modern have attempted to rationalize
the fire to an earthquake. One may well have occurred; they are
not rare in the area and a small quake might well have escaped
popular notice. Certainly Libanius attests a quake earlier in
the year (*Oration* 1.134; cf. Ammianus 22.13.5) while the Ethiopic

chronicle attests one for the middle of May. Avi-Yonah has argued that this latter quake cause the fire and hence the cessation of the project. Unfortunately for his case, as Bowersock has pointed out, the chronicle says nothing about the Temple project being halted by the quake. Chronologically, too, the use of the chronicle will not work. Ammianus makes it clear that the fire took place prior to Julian's departure from Antioch in March 363. Again, Julian's own account (op. cit.) written prior to the departure makes it clear that work had already stopped.

Gregory, for reasons indicated previously, marks the start of the fabulistic tradition. Here the fire represents not only something vaguely divine but, more specifically, God's value-judgment on the Jews. Thus in the various accounts we find celestial crosses, crosses on clothing or, as in Philostorgius (followed by Nicephorus) a chamber with a Bible open to John 1.1. It is evident that the fifth century was far more concerned to develop an anti-Judaic hermeneutic for the events than the violent Chrysostom. But Chrysostom was an orator of considerable skill; moreover, he was addressing a group which seems to have had pronounced Judaic leanings. Thus he would have no need to elaborate portents, since the failure of Julian's project could readily be placed (5.11) in the already flourishing Christian hermeneutic about the destruction of the Temple. But by the fifth century the stereotypes have become fixed and all of the authors, in a way, seem to be manipulating formulae, albeit for their own purposes. The same judgment applies to my third grouping. The entire Syriac tradition shows a like development --here Brock's arguments for the interrelation of Gregory, Ephraem and pseudo-Cyril seem cogent. Again, we must ask why the event of Julian's failure with the Temple possessed such significance for an anti-Judaic tradition already thriving.

To sum up the results thus far. A fire, which caused no special alarm at the time, received a twofold elaboration. One version made it a divine fire boding doom for Julian; this account builds on Alypius' own report. The other version took the fire as a basis for anti-Judaic polemic and added to it to further the growth of such polemic. One need not speak of conscious fabrications; oral traditions are prone to elaborate. The combination of anti-Judaism and popular gossip explain much. Thus Bishop Warburton's rationalizations of the clothing crosses with reference to phosphorus or Professor Jones' report of meteorological events paralleling a cross in the sky are not needed.

It is clear from the frequency of anti-Judaic interpretations that there existed an audience for this sort of thing. Indeed, the ancient mind, of whatever religious persuasion, was especially prone to interpret natural phenomena as divine signs. For example, natural disasters in Asia Minor were often rationalized as originating from neglect of the gods (Cyprian Ep. 75. 10; Origen, Contra Celsum 8.45) while at least one third century persecution of Christians directly followed an earthquake (Origen Comment. in Matth, 39); Tertullian's general remark in Apology 40.2 is famous. Of course, the relationship of natural disaster to divine ire has a long heritage in the Mediterranean regions. Here it is striking that while Ammianus puts a divine stamp on the fire, he makes no further interpretation; amassing omens is enough. Yet Ammianus was in a good position to know Julian's precise plans for stamping out Christianity. One of the methods relied on a systematic disproof of scriptural traditions, both through the polemic *Contra Galileos* and, obviously, the Temple project. This latter would prove the falsity of one of Christ's prophecies (Mark 13.2, Matthew 24.2, Luke 21.6). It is irrelevant that Julian's treatise does not say as much; only fragments are preserved in a Christian source and the emperor's recorded feelings on the Temple may well lie in a lost segment. Certainly, Julian knew the Bible far too well to be ignorant of the Temple's significance. Ammianus is silent on all this; one may conclude that the historian saw the project mainly as causing an omen more significant for Julian's demise than for his religious world-destruction.

The tradition's elaborations show specific Christian events; these, at the rebuilding of a Jewish edifice, make Divinity's theological presuppositions clear. Chrysostom had stated (5.11) that God had decided that Julian could not rebuild the Temple. Furthermore, Chrysostom places this as one more attempt to rebuild what was destroyed in 70 for what he considered all the right reasons. Elsewhere he asserts that this destruction and the continued desolation of the site represents God's punishment of the Jews for the killing of Christ. Thus, to appreciate fully the Christian hermeneutic, we must turn briefly to interpretations of 70.

Chrysostom represents a relatively later part of a tradition that originates at least in the early second century with Justin Martyr (*Dial.* 16, 1 *Apol.* 47) and Origen (*Contra Celsum* 1.47, 2.8, 4:22). There is reason to suspect that such interpretations start earlier still with Mark's Little Apocalypse, since it seems influenced both by the events of 70 and Caligula's attempted idolatry of 39. Thus there exists evidence to show that at least soon after 70 a hermeneutic on the destruction began. Such interpretations rapidly expand along with other anti-Judaic Christological interpretations to regard the destruction as proof both of the accuracy of Christ's proof and God's punishment of the Jews. This punishment marked the dissolution of the old covenant with Israel in favor of the new relationship with the Gentiles. Thus the miracles in the traditions about Julian's project would serve as further verification of the already established fact that God is a Christian.

Such interpretations had an important role in early Christian world-maintenance. Recent work has shown that Christianity, in its post-millenial phase, had an important cognitive dissonance to deal with in the non-event of the kingdom. Put simply, it had to maintain the faith of the converts. One method would be to prove the competing belief systems erroneous. Here lies the growth of a tradition that the early Christians alone had accurately read the Old Testament prophecies and thus recognized Christ as the promised Messiah. Jewish ignorance on this score had meant not only the killing of Christ, but also had demonstrated that they had forfeited any right to interpret their own scripture. The continued desolation of the Temple, then, constituted not only verification of Christ's prophecies, but also demonstrated how God was punishing multiple

Jewish errors with a kind of ongoing vendetta. Any rebuilding attempts could thus be regarded as still further evidence of error, since the Jews evidently, to the Christian mind, did not understand the Christian hermeneutic that the true Temple is now spiritual (1 Cor. 3.16-17, John 2.19-21). Thus Christian world-maintenance would rely on ongoing proof that Judaism was a proven source of error.

But by the latter fourth century Christianity was the official religion of the Roman Empire--why should Christians remain so concerned to continue anti-Judaic traditions? A general answer would be that persecutions possess a kind of perverse appeal which long outlives any putative causes. More specifically, Judaism of the times seems to have offered very powerful competition to Christianity. This is a time of demi-Christians. An era in which Christian orthodoxy struggles to define itself in response to various movements which one area or the other considered heretical. A time in which even non-heretical communities could mix Christian and Jewish and pagan belief systems. Pagan formulae regularly appear in Christian epitaphs. Christians utilize martyrs' relics with an almost pagan talisman-like atmosphere, a situation at which Augustine often fulminates. Libanius' letters give evidence of close Christian and pagan interactions, while both groups seem to have been nearing a like kind of monotheism (*Pan. Lat.* 4.7.3, 12.26.1; Augustine, *Ep.* 16. 90, 103, 234). Magic was on the rise, a situation which caused considerable official concern (Ammianus 19.12.3-18, 28.1.1-57; *Theodosian Code* 9.16, 11.36.1-7, 16.34). As for the Jews, Christians were willing to annex traditions such as the Seven Maccabean Brothers which, to save face, the Church finally had to claim. Again, they believed in healing miracles from Jews, a Talmud tradition that has implicit Old Testament roots. Thus there existed a strong movement of minds to Judaism, again a cause for official concern (*Theodosian Code* 16.8; Council of Laodicea, canons 29, 37, 38; Council of Antioch, canon 1).

More importantly, Judaism was often rife with messianic hopes. Bar Kochba's revolt seems predicated on frustrated Jewish hopes on this score (*Epistle of Barnabas*). They thought Hadrian would rebuild their own city of Jerusalem and with it the Temple; instead he gave them Aelia Capitolina. Bar Kochba is himself recorded as having a messianic self-image; coinage of the time both makes this clear and shows the role of the Temple in the revolt. While the fourth century Judaic traditions are largely silent on Julian's plans, there still exists enough evidence to see that there was an appeal to some segments of Judaism. Messianic promises could make a strong appeal to Christians disappointed by the now official Christian tradition that the Kingdom was not physical, but spiritual. There thus existed the possibility of a kind of millenial supermarket. Here we should note the tradition that the Antichrist would rebuild the Temple as a prelude to the End. In theory, this view could have regarded Julian's project as marking the advent of the Antichrist and hence the long-anticipated Apocalypse. That Christianity did not seize this obvious millenial opportunity shows how far the concept of spiritual kingdom dominated theology. Put differently, when confronted with a choice of kingdom or anti-Jewish community, it opted for the latter.

Jewish messianic predictions thus represented a far greater threat to Christianity's world-maintenance than the possible appearance of the Antichrist in connection with the Temple. In an era of increasing taxation and vicious extraction of revenue from humble folk, a *colonus* might well hunger for the change of a Kingdom. Paganism could not offer this. Christianity once had but no longer offered fast physical relief; its spiritualizing interpretations would remain unsatisfying for the theologically unsophisticated. Thus Judaism, already competing with Christianity elsewhere, would be able to offer what the earliest Christians had considered central. It is here that we may see the intensity of Christian concern for the continued desolation of the Temple as God's ongoing proof that their hermeneutic was correct. As Peter Berger remarked in a very different connection, "Ideas do not succeed in history by virtue of their truth, but of their relationship to specific social processes." Thus the Temple must remain ruined, not only to show the continued worthlessness of another religion, but also to maintain Christianity in the face of a competitive Judaism.

THE EPISTLE OF JAMES
AS A JEWISH-CHRISTIAN DOCUMENT

DAVID L. BARTLETT
The University of Chicago, Chicago, IL 60637

In the first part of this paper I argue that two motifs in the Epistle of James show sufficient affinity with Jewish exegesis to suggest that James arises out of a Jewish-Christian milieu. Obviously in such arguments we deal with probabilities and tendencies. In both style and content the Epistle also shows "Hellenistic" features, and the attempt to demarcate sharply the lines between Hellenistic and Jewish backgrounds for early Christian material has largely and wisely been abandoned. However, there is sufficient evidence to suggest that James' treatment of Abraham (and Rahab) in the faith-works discussion and his use of the terms δίψυχος,δίψυχοι can best be understood in relationship to Jewish (and Jewish-Christian) material.

In the second part of the paper I want briefly to describe a few of the features of that Christianity which the Epistle of James represents, so that the seminar can discern whether there are continuities between this kind of Christianity and other literature and communities we might call "Jewish-Christian."

I. Jewish-Christian Motifs in the Epistle of James:
   A. Abraham, Faith and Works.
   Three major claims emerge from our study of Abraham as an example in the faith-works discussion in James 2:18-26. 1) The basic understanding of Abraham and his faith in James is consonant with much Jewish exegesis. 2) The terms of the discussion in James, however--with the contrast between faith and works --are almost certainly drawn from Paul or from the Paulinists. Jewish exegesis is used in the service of an intra-Christian debate. 3) Abraham (and Rahab) function in James as they do in some Jewish material, as examples of proselytes, and the issue for James (as for Paul) is: what is the appropriate faith for a proselyte: in this case, for a Christian who is not Jewish?

1. Our research has largely confirmed Dibelius' claim that the background for James' understanding of Abraham and his faith is to be found in Jewish exegesis.[1]

The importance of Abraham as a prototype of the faithful person is evidenced in a number of texts. In some texts, as in James, Abraham's status as an exemplar of faith is derived from Genesis 15:6.

Philo makes much use of Genesis 15:6. In Leg. All. III, 228 he contrasts Abraham's trust in God, evidenced in Gen. 15:6, with "our dim reasonings and insecure conjectures." In Mut. Nom. 177 he cites Gen. 15:6 (over against Gen. 17:7) to show that Abraham really did believe God's promise. In an extended discussion in Quis. Rer. 94 Philo writes of Abraham:

And it is well said "his faith was counted to him
for justice" (Gen.xv.6) for nothing is so just or
righteous as to put in God alone a trust which is
pure and unalloyed.

In at least two places, the Mekilta cites Abraham's faith
as attested in Genesis 15:6.

And so also you find that our father Abraham
inherited both this world and the world beyond only
as a reward for the faith with which he believed,
as it is said: "And he believed the Lord," etc.
(Gen. 15:6). beShallah 7 [2]

"The faith with which their father Abraham believed
in me is deserving that I should divide the sea for
them." For it is said: "And he believed in the Lord."
(Gen. 15:6). beShallah 4 [3]

Other references to Abraham's righteousness or faithfulness which may include allusions to Gen. 15:6 include Jubilees
23:10, 24:11(?), b. Tal Meg. 11a.

Even more pertinent to the claim that James shows the influence of Jewish exegesis in his treatment of Abraham are those
passages in Jewish material where the claim of Genesis 15:6 is
explicitly related to the binding of Isaac in Genesis 22 (as
in James 2:21-23).

Apparently the clearest example is I Maccabees 2:52: "Was
not Abraham found faithful in temptation, and it was reckoned
unto him for righteousness." However, it is not absolutely
clear that the temptation here mentioned is the temptation of
the binding of Isaac. Apparently the tradition included
stories of the ten tests of Abraham, of which the binding was
only one. See for example Pirke Aboth 5:4: "Ten trials our
father Abraham was tried with, and he bore them all, to make
known how great was the love of Abraham our father." [4] (Cf.
Jub. 19:8) So, too, Sirach 44:20 may refer to the binding of
Isaac, but might refer to other trials; and the reference to
Gen. 15:6 here is at best implicit.

(Abraham) kept the commandment of the Most High
And entered into a covenant with Him:
In his flesh he engraved him an ordinance,
And in trial he was found faithful.
(21) Therefore with an oath He promised him
'To bless the nations in his seed.'

In Jubilees 18:16, God speaks in response to Abraham's
binding of Isaac in terms that at least commend Abraham's
faithfulness (whether or not they include an allusion to
Gen. 15:6):

"Because thou hast obeyed my voice, and I have shown
to all that thou art faithful unto me in all that I
have said unto thee: Go in peace."

A clearer link between Genesis 22 and Genesis 15:6 is in
Philo, Deus Immutab. 4, where Philo writes specifically of
Abraham's binding of Isaac's feet:

"...he was taught to see how changeable and inconstant
was creation, through his knowledge of the unwavering
steadfastness which belongs to the existent (τὴν
γένεσιν) for in this we are told he put his
trust."

Here, while the binding of Isaac is not exactly the outworking
of Abraham's faithfulness, it does affirm and illumine that
faithfulness.

So, too, though Josephus uses "piety" (θρησκεία)
rather than "faith," he sees the binding of Isaac as a part of
Abraham's trusting relationship to God. (Cf. Antiquities I,
223 and 233-4.)

Therefore in a variety of Jewish material, Abraham's
faithfulness is closely related to the trials he underwent,
and in some instances--certainly Philo and probably Maccabees
and Sirach--Genesis 15:6 is explained in the light of the test
of Genesis 22. In this exegesis, then, James stands very much
within the line of Jewish interpretation of the Abraham story.

Where James does not sound like the Jewish interpreters is
in the distinction he makes between faith and works. As Dibelius suggests [5] the Jewish material does not distinguish
Abraham's faith from a manifestation of that faith called
"works;" rather Abraham's faith or faithfulness is itself the
work which is evident in the ten tests and the binding of
Isaac. The terms which James uses to make his point are different from the Jewish terms, though the point he makes--that
Genesis 15:6 is to be read in the light of Gen. 22 and Abraham's other tests--is thoroughly consonant with Jewish
exegesis.

The reason that James needs to make his point in terms
uncongenial to Jewish exegesis is almost certainly that the
terms of the debate have been set by Paul or the paulinists.

What then shall we say about Abraham, our forefather according to the flesh? For if Abraham
was justified by works, he has something to boast
about, but not before God. For what does the
scripture say? "Abraham believed God, and it was
reckoned to him as righteousness." Romans 4:1 ff.

Let me ask you only this: Did you receive the
Spirit by works of the law or by hearing with
faith? Are you so foolish? Having begun with
the Spirit are you now ending with the flesh?
Thus Abraham 'believed God, and it was reckoned
to him as righteousness.' Galatians 3:2,6

It may be that James turns to Genesis 15:6 to make his
point because that is the great proof text of Paul and the
paulinists. At any rate it seems reasonably clear that James
frames his argument about the relationship of Genesis 15:6 to
Genesis 22 in terms drawn from Paul or paulinist material.

There is, however, at least one place in the Jewish material itself where a distinction between faith and works is
apparently drawn, though not with regard to Abraham. That is

in IV Ezra. Regarding the last days, IV Ezra says:

> And everyone shall (then) be saved, and shall be
> able to escape on account of his works or his faith
> by which he has believed, such shall survive from
> the perils aforesaid and shall see salvation in my
> land. (IV Ezra 9:7, Charles ed.)

It is less clear that a distinction is being drawn between
faith and works in IV Ezra 13:23 which says of survivors at the
last day that they are "even such as have works and faith toward (the Most High and) the Mighty One." (Charles ed.)

What we apparently have in James, therefore, is a Christian whose understanding of the relationship between Abraham's
faith and the tests he underwent (as in Genesis 22) is almost
entirely Jewish. However, the author defends his "Jewish"
exegesis in terms drawn from the intra-Christian discussion,
terms related to faith and works. In this sense the tendencies of the argument may be said to be Jewish-Christian.

There is another feature of James' use of the Abraham
material which shows continuities with Jewish exegesis and
which may also show an awareness if not of Paul's understanding
of "faith," at least of the context in which Paul's discussion
about faith and works arises.

One striking feature of the Abraham example is that it is
expanded by the reference to the works of Rahab. Abraham and
Rahab are also mentioned in discussions of faith in Hebrews
11:17ff, 31 and in I Clem. X, 6ff; XII, 1ff. In the Hebrews
citation, Rahab is commended for her "friendly welcome to the
spies," and in I Clem. both Abraham and Rahab are examples of
"faith and hospitality." Roy B. Ward has suggested that an
implicit allusion to Abraham's hospitality may also lie behind
the   juxtaposition of these two figures in James. [6]

However a study of Jewish material suggests another
explanation. Both Rahab and Abraham are cited in Jewish exegesis as examples of proselytes to the true faith.

In Numbers Rabbah VIII, 9, a discussion of God's relationship to proselytes, we find the following discussion of
Rahab:

> In the same manner we find in connection with Rahab,
> the harlot, that because she brought the spies into
> her house and rescued them, the Holy One, blessed be
> He, accounted it unto her as though she had performed
> the act for Him, and he gave her her reward...What
> reward did she receive? Some of her daughters were
> married into the priesthood and bore sons who stood
> and performed service upon the altar and entered the
> Sanctuary, where, uttering the ineffable Name of God,
> they would bless Israel...Thus we have learned that
> the text speaks of none but the true proselytes; hence
> it says, 'And see thy children's children. Peace be
> upon Israel.' [7]

In the Talmud b. Zebahim 116b, at the age of fifty, Rahab

became a proselyte, and begged forgiveness for her former ways "as a reward for the cord, window, and flax." According to Strack-Billerbeck, Pesiq 9 (167b) reads:

> R. Alexandrai (um 270) hat gesagt: Gott richtet die Völker durch ihre eigenen Rechtschaffenen, durch Rahab, durch Jethro, durch Ruth. 8

Other literature suggests that Abraham was sometimes understood as the prototypical proselyte.

In the Mekilta, III, 140 we read:

> Abraham called himself a stranger (ger) as it is said, "I am a stranger and a sojourner with you." (Gen. 23:4)...

> Beloved are the strangers (gerim). It was for their sake that our father Abraham was not circumcised until he was ninety-nine years old. Had he been circumcised at twenty or at thirty years of age, only those under the age of thirty could have become proselytes to Judaism. Therefore God bore with Abraham until he reached ninety-nine years of age, so as not to close the door to future proselytes (gerim). 9

In the Talmud, Haggigah 3a (which is the same as Sukka 49b), we read:

> 'Prince's daughter' means the daughter of Abraham our father who is called prince, as it is said: The princes of the peoples are gathered together, the people of the God of Abraham. 'The God of Abraham', and not the God of Isaac and Jacob? (It must mean), therefore, the God of Abraham, who was the first of the proselytes. 10

Moreover, there are various places in the literature where Abraham's faith, like that of the proselyte, is understood as primarily monotheism, in contrast with the polytheism of his forebears:

Jubilees 12:1ff. recounts Abram's conversation with his father, Terah:

> And it came to pass in the sixth week, in the seventh year thereof, that Abram said to Terah his father, saying, 'Father!' And he said, 'Behold, here am I, my son.' And he said,
> 'What help and profit have we from those idols which thou dost worship,
> And before which thou dost bow thyself?
> For there is no spirit in them,
> For they are dumb forms, and a misleading of the heart.
> Worship them not.
>
> Worship the God of heaven,
> Who causes the rain and the dew to descend upon

the earth
        And does everything upon the earth.
        And has created everything by His word,
        And all life is before His face.

Similarly, Jubilees 11:16 recounts:

        ...and (Abraham) was two weeks of years old,
        and he separated himself from his father, that
        he might not worship idols with him. And he
        began to pray to the creator of all things that
        He might save him from the errors of the chil-
        dren of men... 11

Josephus, in the Antiquities I, 155 says of Abraham: "He was
the first boldly to declare that God, the creator of the universe, is one..."

        Philo in Praem. Poen. 27 says of Abraham that he was:

        The leader in adopting the godly creed, who
        first passed over from vanity to truth, came to
        his consummation of virtue, gained through
        instruction, and he received for his reward
        belief in God. (τὴν πρὸς θεὸν πίστιν)

        Abraham and Rahab, therefore, are joined in James as
examples of faith because in Jewish tradition they are both
prototypical proselytes, coming to faith in God from outside
(or before) the law. Abraham especially is the example of the
person who comes to monotheism from idolatry, thereby affirming
the first article of faith for the true proselyte.

        It is therefore thoroughly appropriate to the context in
Jewish exegesis that when James wishes to explicate that faith
which requires works for its fulfillment, he says: σὺ πιστυεις
ὅτι εἰς θεος ἐστιν.   (Jas. 2:19) That may be a
misunderstanding of Paul's version of "faith," but it is
precisely appropriate to a discussion of Abraham and Rahab as
exemplary proselytes. The "faith" to which they were won was
monotheistic faith; James argues that such faith, without
works, is unsufficient.

        All this suggests, further, that Dibelius and Hahn may be
right in saying that James misunderstands Paul's doctrine of
justification by faith. (These scholars claim that James
therefore did not know Paul directly; though there is ample
evidence from Pauline correspondence that those who heard his
gospel often did not understand it.)11 However, James understands the context of Paul's affirmation quite correctly. The
question for Paul, as for James, is: "What is required of
those who, like Abraham, are proselytes to true faith?" James
and Paul read the same texts differently, but they apply the
texts to the same problem: "How shall those outside of Israel
be saved?" 12

        The material on Abraham therefore suggests that James was
written in a Jewish-Christian context. The question for James,
as for Paul, was how shall new proselytes comes to faith? What
is to be required of them? On the basis of considerable Jewish

tradition and exegesis James argues that Abraham was not justified by his monotheistic faith alone but by the works which
accompanied that faith, just as Rahab, another proselyte, was
justified by her faith accompanied by works. The terms of the
argument, however, are taken from Paul and not from Jewish
exegesis. The context of the argument appears to be Jewish (in
its background) and Christian (in its foreground).

B. The "double-minded" in James:

In two places, James refers to a double-minded person(s).
1:8 occurs in a discussion of steadfastness in prayer:
Εἰ δέ τις ὑμῶν λείπεται σοφίας,,,αἰτείτω δὲ ἐν πίστει,
μηδὲν διακρινόμενος, ὁ γὰρ διακρινόμενος ἔοικεν
κλύδωνι θαλάσσης ἀνεμιζομένῳ καὶ ῥιπιζομένῳ·
μὴ γὰρ οἰέσθω ὁ ἄνθρωπος ἐκεῖνος ὅτι, λήμψεται τι
παρὰ τοῦ κυρίου, ἀνὴρ δίψυχος, ἀκατάστατος ἐν
πάσαις ταῖς ὁδοῖς αὐτοῦ.

4:8 occurs in a call for repentance, urging sinners to turn
from the devil toward God.
ὑποτάγητε οὖν τῷ θεῷ· ἀντίστητε δὲ τῷ διαβόλῳ,
καὶ φεύξεται ἀφ' ὑμῶν· ἐγγίσατε τῷ θεῷ καὶ ἐγγιεῖ
ὑμῖν, καθαρίσατε χεῖρας, ἁμαρτωλοί, καὶ ἁγνίσατε
καρδίας, δίψυχοι. ταλαιπωρήσατε καὶ πενθήσατε
καὶ κλαύσατε...

The closest parallels I have found to these two bits of
parenetic material are both in the Shepherd of Hermas (along
with considerable other material on double-mindedness). 13

Mandate IX, 5 ff. sounds much like James 1:5-8:

But if you doubt in your heart, you shall receive
none of your petitions. For those who have doubts
toward God, these are the doubleminded (οἱ δίψυχοι   )
and they shall not in any wise obtain any of their
petitions. But they who are perfect in faith ask
for all things, 'trusting in the Lord' and they
receive them, because they ask without doubting,
and are double-minded in nothing. For every double-
minded man, unless he repent, shall with difficulty
be saved. Therefore purify your heart from double-
mindedness (καθάρισον οὖν τὴν καρδίαν
σου ἀπὸ τῆς διψυχίας   ),
but put on faith, because it is mighty, and believe
God, that you shall obtain all your requests which
you make.

Sim. VIII, xi, 3. recalls the relationship between repentance and double-mindedness evident in James 4:8:

And he answered me and said: "As many," said he,
"as repent with all their hearts and purify themselves from the wickednesses which have been mentioned before, and no longer add anything to their
sins, shall receive healing from the Lord for their
former sins, if they are not double-minded." (cp.
Sim. VI, i, 2-3)

Many scholars maintain that the Shepherd of Hermas itself emerges from a Jewish-Christian milieu. [14] At any rate, there is no evidence for the use of the term διψυχος   or διχυχια   in Hellenistic literature, [15] while the use of the term in both Hermas and James can perhaps best be explained on the basis of Jewish material and exegesis.

For one thing, double-mindedness in Hermas (and perhaps in James) is clearly contrasted to the biblical notion of whole-heartedness. In Sim. VIII, xi, 3 we read: "As many...as repent with all their hearts,...shall receive healing from the Lord for their former sins, if they are not double-minded." In Mand. VI, i, 5 and Mand. IX,i f. there are contrasts between double-mindedness and "turning to the Lord with all your heart." Here the primary reference is probably Jeremiah 24:7 (cp. Joel 2:12):

$$\text{ה ב ל} \quad \text{ל כ ב} \quad \text{' ל א} \quad \text{ו ש ' ' כ}$$

(ὅτι επιστραφήσονται επ'εμε εξ ὅλης της καρδίας αὐτῶν)

It is not surprising that the whole heart should be contrasted among Greek-writing Jews (and Jewish Christians) with the double-psyche. In many passages from Deuteronomy, (e.g. 30:10, cp. Hermas, Sim. VI, i, 2-3) the phrase "with all your heart" is expanded and paralleled by "with all your psyche." Furthermore, in the Septuagint the MT ב ל or   ב ב ל is translated twenty-five times by ψυχη   . [16] Most strikingly, in 2 Chron. 15:15 and 31:21 the Hebrew ב ל ב כ ל is translated by the Greek εξ ὅλης της ψυχης . Here at least, whole-heartedness and whole-'mindedness' are seen as synonymous. In Isaiah 44:19, the Hebrew ב ל is translated once by καρδία   and once by ψυχη. indicating again that the two terms were used interchangeably by Greek-speaking Jews.

We can, therefore, perhaps find the background for the notion of double-mindedness in Jewish material dealing with double-heartedness.

In apocryphal and pseudepigraphal material Sirach 1:28 reads:

μὴ απειθήσης φόβω κυρίου
και μὴ προσέλθης' αὐτῶ εν καρδία δισσῆ.

So also, I Enoch 91:4 (Charles ed.) suggests that double-heartedness consists in being torn between righteousness and unrighteousness:

Love uprightness and walk therein, and draw not nigh to unrighteousness with a double heart, and associate not with those of a double heart.

In the Qumran material, O.J.F. Seitz cites I QH 4:14:

(The servants of Beliar) devise plans of wickedness, and they enquire of thee with a double heart, (ב ל ב   ב ל ב) and do not stand firm in the truth. [17]

Seitz persuasively argues that the "divided heart" is in contrast to the whole-heartedness enjoined by Jeremiah in another
warning against false prophets in Jer. 29:8-9, 12-13: "Let
not the (false) prophets among you and soothsayers deceive you
...You shall pray to me, and I will hearken to you; you shall
seek me, and find me, when you seek me with all your heart." 18
Perhaps related is the claim of I QS IV, 23-24: "Until now the
spirits of truth and falsehood struggle in the hearts of men
and they walk in both wisdom and folly." (Vermes trans.)

In the <u>rabbis</u>, there are also suggestions of a distinction
between whole-heartedness and the double heart. Mishnah Berakoth 9:5 plays on the double ב of לבב in Deut. 6:5 and associates the two ב's with the two yesarim:

> Man is bound to bless (God) for the evil even
> as he blesses God for the good, for it is written,
> 'And thou shalt love the Lord thy God with all
> thy heart and with all thy soul and with all thy
> might. With all thy heart (לבב) with both
> thine impulses--thy good impulse and thine evil
> impulse.

Sifre Deut. Wa'ethanan 32, as quoted in Montefiore, begins
with a similar interpretation of the לבב and then goes on to
add: "'with all thy heart' let not your heart be divided--
i.e. not wholly one--as regards your love for God." 19

O.J.F.Seitz notes Tanhuma V, Tavo, par. 1: "When you
make your prayer before God, you shall not have two hearts,
one before God and the other directed toward some other
object." 20

In <u>early Christian literature</u> references to double-mindedness occur in Barnabas 19:5, and closely associated, Didache
4:4. Interestingly Barnabas uses the term "double-heartedness"
in 20:1. In none of these instances is the meaning of the term
terribly clear, though in Barn. 19:5, Did. 4:4 double-mindedness is apparently related to doubt. Both of these writings,
of course, are associated with Jewish Christianity.

A quotation from an unknown source occurs in I Clem. XX
xxiii, 3 and II Clem. xi, 2. In the Second Clement passage the
quotation reads "Miserable are the double-minded who doubt in
their <u>heart</u>." I Clem. says "doubt in their <u>psyche</u>." O.J.F.
Seitz argues convincingly that the connection between double-
mindedness and the doubting heart is original in II Clem., and
that I Clem. has introduced <u>psyche</u> for reasons of literary
consistency. 21 The source of the quotation is unknown, and so
this material is otherwise less helpful to us than Hermas.

In the Jewish material and in Hermas, therefore, double-
mindedness (διψυχία) is contrasted to whole-heartedness.
There is a close correlation, almost synonymity, between heart
and soul, so that double-heartedness many mean double-souled-
ness (διψυχία) as well. Hermas (and some of the other material) refers to double-mindedness (double-heartedness) in a
number of contexts, but two prominent contexts are prayer
(Mand. IX), and repentance (often).

Turning now to James, we can see that the two passages
on double-mindedness fit remarkably well into this cluster of
ideas. James 1, like Mand. IX 5 ff. contrasts faith and
double-mindedness in a context of prayer.

Even more striking in its closeness to Jewish and Jewish-
Christian material is James 4:1-8.

i) The call to repentance to the double-minded (Jas. 4:7
-8) recalls passages in Hermas (e.g. Sim.VIII, xi, 3; Sim. VI,
i, 2-3) which call the double-minded to repent with their
whole heart.

ii) Similarly we note that in James the double-minded
are called upon to "purify your hearts"(αγνισατε καρδιας) (4:8).
This suggests the parallel we saw between heart and soul in
the deuteronomic material, and the interchangeability of the
terms in the Septuagint translations. It also suggests the
contrast between double-mindedness and whole-heartedness which
is present in Hermas (and closely paralleled by the double-
heart of Misnah Berakoth and Sifre Deut.). For an almost
direct parallel to James cf. Hermas Mand. IX 7:
καθάρισον οὖν τὴν καρδίαν σου ἀπο τῆς διψυχίας.

iii) As the Qumran and rabbinic materials suggest that
double-heartedness may result from conflicting spirits or
inclinations, so James 4:1 speaks of conflict in the double-
minded person: "Is it not your passions that are at war with
your members?" Even more clearly double-mindedness is related
in James to the conflict between the Spirit God gives and those
spirits which are subject to the devil: "God yearns zealously
over the spirit which he has made to dwell in us...Submit
yourselves therefore to God. Resist the devil, and he will
flee from you. Draw near to God, and he will draw near to
you." (James 4:5-8)

Compare Hermas, Mand. V i, 2-4.

For the Lord dwells in long-suffering, and the
devil dwells in ill-temper. If therefore both
spirits dwell in the same place it is unprofitable
and evil for that man in whom they dwell.

Our study suggests, therefore that
in James is not simply a catchword used randomly in parenetic
material. It comes out of a fairly defined milieu of Jewish
and Jewish-Christian material. Seen against this background
James' use of the term is both consistent and clear.

II. Part Two: The Shape of James' Christianity:

I have argued that two test cases, the use of Abraham as
an example of faith, and the use of the terms dipsychos,
dipsychia, indicate that James' concepts, terminology, and
concerns are in large measure shaped by Judaism and by issues
appropriate to Jewish Christianity.

In closing I want briefly to suggest some of the shape
of that kind of Christianity which is implied by the Epistle
of James.

Law: There is no indication that James' concern for law
(or for works) emerges out of a desire to require such practices as circumcision. The work for which Abraham is justified
is the binding of Isaac. The Law, which is binding in its
entirety, appears to consist primarily of the decalogue.
(2:10-11) This binding law is further summed up in the "royal
law" (νόμος βασιλικος) from the scripture (Lev. 19:18): "You
shall love your neighbor as yourself." (2:8) [22] It is apparently this central law which is open to various applications,
for example in the appeal against slander and judgment: "He
that speaks evil against a brother or judges the brother, speaks
evil against the law and judges the law." (4:11)

The law is closely associated with the "word" (λόγος)
which is the implanted gift of God (1:21). One is to "do the
word" just as one is to "obey the law" and perform the works of
righteousness. (1:22 ff) In 1:25 the "word" has become "the
perfect law, the law of liberty."

The word and the law are closely related to that wisdom
(σοφια) which also comes from above (3:15), (Cf. also 1:5)
and which bears good fruits. (3:17)

The Jewish Christianity which James represents, therefore,
is concerned with right keeping of the law. That law is identified most clearly with the decalogue and summed up in the
commandment of Leviticus 19:18. There is at least the implication that the law, like the word and like wisdom, is a gift from
God implanted in the believer. There is an implied connection
between the gift of law and the gift of wisdom.

Eschatology:

Not surprisingly, an ethic which stresses a royal law is
related to an eschatology which stresses God's future role as
judge.

There is no sense of Kingdom as already present but considerable stress on future judgment. The grounds for judgment
are resistance to trial (1:12), love of God as manifest in
impartiality toward the poor (2:5), and especially fulfillment
of the commandment to love the neighbor--love which is manifest
as mercy (2:12-13), or as charity (2:14 ff), or as refusal to
slander or judge the neighbor (4:11-12).

The injunction to believers is to be patient and wait for
the Lord's coming (5:7). The Lord who comes is again explicitly described as the Judge, and his appearance seems imminent:
ιδου ο κριτης προ των θυρων εστηκεν (5:9).

Both eschatology and theology are summed up in the claim:
"There is one lawgiver and judge, who is able to save and to
destroy." (4:12)

It is unclear whether the Lord who is coming is Jesus, or
whether we have here a more typically Jewish understanding of
the coming day of Yahweh.

The Poor:

There is obviously considerable discussion in James about rich and poor, their relationship to each other, and their standing in the coming judgment.

What is hard to adjudicate is whether the poor in James are the economically poor or whether the pious of James' community refer to themselves as "poor."

In some places there seems indication that economic poverty is the question, especially in the discussion of partiality in James 2:1-7 (and in James 5:1-6).

The "lowly brother" of James 1:9-11, however, sounds somewhat like the "poor" of Psalms of Solomon, a term for those who are loyal members of the believing community:

Just and kind is our Lord in His judgments forever, And Israel shall praise the name of the Lord in gladness, And the pious shall give thanks in the assembly of the people, And on the poor shall God have mercy in the gladness of Israel. (Psalms of Solomon 10:6 ff.) 23

Put in other words, the question is whether the understanding of the relationship between rich and poor in James is closer to Luke's version of the beatitude or Matthew's:

Blessed are you poor, for yours is the kingdom of heaven...but woe to you that are rich, for you have received your consolation. (Luke 6:24)

Blessed are the poor in spirit, for theirs is the kingdom of heaven. (Matthew 5:3)

Finally, the description of the rich and the judgment on them in James 4:13-17 sounds much like Jewish wisdom material in Sirach 11:8:

There is a man who is rich through his diligence and self-denial, and this is the reward allotted to him; when he says, 'I have found rest, and now I shall enjoy my goods,' he does not know how much time will pass, until he leaves them to others and dies. (cp. Luke 12:16-20)

This is obviously only a preliminary sketch of the Jewish-Christianity which James represents. The community identifies with the poor, probably with the economically poor, and also with the spiritually poor who know the vanity of riches. James stresses obedience to Torah, which like wisdom is a gift from God to the believer. Torah consists most clearly in the decalogue and is summed up in the commandment about the neighbor. The Day of Judgment is coming soon, when "The Lord" as law-giver and judge, will judge people on how faithfully they have obeyed that law which God has given them.

185

FOOTNOTES:

1. Cf. the excursus, "The Abraham Example," in M. Dibelius and H. Greeven, ed. James, tr. M.A. Williams (Philadelphia: Fortress, c. 1976) 168 ff. So, too, F. Hahn in "Genesis 15:6 im Neuen Testament," in H.W. Wolff, ed. Probleme biblischer Theologie, (Fest. G. von Rad) (Munich: Kaiser Verlag, 1971) 97. A number of our references to Jewish material on Abraham are cited also in the Dibelius excursus and in H.L. Strack and P. Billerbeck, Kommentar zum Neuen Testament aus Talmud und Midrasch (Munich: Beck'sche, 1926) III, 755 and 186-201.

2. J.Z. Lauterbach, ed. Mekilta de-Rabbi Ishmael (Philadelphia: Jewish Publication Society, 1949) I, 253.

3. Ibid., 220.

4. Abraham is cited as "our father" here, in Romans 4:1, and often elsewhere.

5. Dibelius, James, 179; Hahn, "Genesis 15:6," 97.

6. Roy B. Ward, "The Works of Abraham," HThR LXI/2 (1968) 283-290.

7. Freedman and Simon, ed. Numbers Rabbah (London: Soncino, 1939) I, 234-235.

8. Cf. also Mekilta 18, 1 (64b), Pesiq R9 (167b), and NumR 3(139a). All cited in Strack-Billerbeck, I, 121.

9. Lauterbach, ed. Mekilta III, 140. Cited in Strack-Billerbeck, Introduction III, 195.

10. Tr. I. Abrahams (Bennet publ., 1959) 8.   Cited in Strack-Billerbeck, Introduction III, 195. Cf. also Midrash Tanchuma תזריע 6 (32a) cited Ibid.

11. Dibelius, James, 79f.; Hahn, "Genesis 15:6," 97.

12. I Thess. 1:9 indicates that Paul understands the first article of the proselyte's faith in the same way as James.

13. The Hermas quotations are from Kirsopp Lake, ed. and tr. The Apostolic Fathers (Loeb Library, London and New York: Heinemann and MacMillan, 1913).

14. Cf. R.M. Grant, The Apostolic Fathers (New York: Nelson, 1964) 98 and G.F. Snyder, The Apostolic Fathers, VI. Hermas (Camden: Nelson, 1968) 16f., and the other references cited therein.

15. Cf. W.F. Arndt and F.W. Gingrich, A Greek-English Lexicon of the New Testament (Chicago and Cambridge: U. of Chicago, 1952) 199f; E. Schweizer in Friedrich (Kittel) ed. Theological Dictionary of the New Testament, tr. G.W. Bromiley, IX, 665. H.G. Liddell and R. Scott, A Greek English Lexicon (Oxford: Oxford University, 1968) 440. Concerning Philo Frag. II, 663 cf. note in Arndt and Gingrich, 200.

16. Cf. Jacob article in Friedrich, <u>Theological Diction-ary</u> IX, 617 for the list.

17. "Afterthoughts on the Term 'Dipsychos'" NTS IV (1957-8) 328.

18. Ibid., 330.

19. C.G. Montefiore and H. Loewe, <u>A Rabbinic Anthology</u> (London: MacMillan, 1938) 276.

20. O.J.F. Seitz, "Antecedents and Signification of the Term ΔΙΨΥΧΟΣ " JBL 66 (1947) 214.

21. O.J.F. Seitz, "Antecedents," 215; "Relationship of the Shepherd of Hermas to the Epistle of James" JBL 63 (1944) 134.

22. Here James sounds very much like Romans 13:9-10. In Matthew 5:43 the discussion of this commandment concludes the discussion of what Torah is binding on Christians.

23. Cf. Dibelius, <u>James</u>, 40.

Mark 10:32-52 -- A STRUCTURAL, LITERARY AND

THEOLOGICAL INTERPRETATION

Dan O. Via, Jr.
University of Virginia

The purpose of this paper is to gain a view of the structure and meaning of Mk. 10:32-52, partly by way of comparing a structuralist approach to approaches which are more historically oriented. Also some critical evaluation of structuralism will be offered.

INTRODUCTION

I have considered the segmentation of Mk. 10:32-52 given by five Marcan scholars, who employ the historical critical method. Two basic, and not very different, outlines emerge from this survey, and the picture would probably not be much different if many others were considered. The two are as follows:

(1)	10:32-34		(1)	10:32-34	
(2)	10:35-40		(2)	10:35-45	
(3)	10:41-45		(3)	10:46-52	
(4)	10:46-52				

(Taylor, Nineham, Kelber)   (Cranfield, Schweizer)

It will be observed that the two groups agree that 10:32-42 and 10:46-52 are definite sub-divisions. The most obvious difference is over whether 10:35-45 is one section or two, and actually Schweizer argues tacitly that it is composed of two parts.[1] Kelber[2] sees the limits of the two middle parts as being 10:35-41 and 10:42-45 (as does Schweizer's tacit position) rather than 10:35-40 and 10:41-45. I take Kelber to be more nearly correct as will appear later.

If our text is then viewed in light of two ways of grasping deep narrative structure, these outlines emerge. Each of them registers the segmentation produced in the surface structure (manifestation) by the deep structure:

(1)	10:32-34		(1)	10:32a	
(2)	10:35-41		(2)	10:32b-52ab	
(3)	10:42-45		(3)	10:52c	
(4)	10:46-52				

Clearly the four-fold outline is very like the one viewed above while the three-fold one is quite different.

I should now like to consider briefly the context of presuppositions and intentions which surrounds the articulation of these segmentations. Mark is for Vincent Taylor basically a source for knowledge of the historical Jesus, and emphasis is given to the reliability of Peter's testimony. The Gospel is intended to serve both historical and religious ends, to present the religion and theology of the historical Jesus. Mark wants to tell the good news, not present a scientific history, but his presentation is broadly factual and accurate. Taylor believes that Mark's sources are valuable and that he used them objectively.[3] It is congruent with this that Taylor sees Mark, not as a carefully planned literary composition, but as a popular writing conditioned by the state of the tradition. Mark's failure to break up his sources in order to produce a more satisfactory literary arrangement is actually an advantage to the historian.[4] The complement to "historical, not literary" is "communal, not individual." Mark is not so much a private undertaking as a product of the life of the church inspired by the Spirit.[5]

Taylor's outline of Mark as a whole is oriented largely to geographical categories, although the chronological is also apparent and the dramatic is not wholly absent: the story moves to the climax of the passion and resurrection. And Taylor speaks of the unity of the Marcan style.[6] But his general lack of literary concern is seen in the absence of a systematic effort to grasp the formal and conceptual unity of 10:32-52. And even when literary connections are glimpsed,[7] this insight is not exploited for interpretation.[8]

When we come to D. E. Nineham, Mark is again understood to have both a religious and historical character. But the history in the light of which it is to be understood is that of the church, not of Jesus. Mark worked primarily with disconnected materials and ordered them so as to meet the religious and practical needs of his community; therefore, his theology reflects a view of Jesus current c. A. D. 75.[9] Nineham's outline of Mark is oriented primarily to geography, but there are also chronological and theological elements in it. He is not unaware of the conceptual and narrative unity in 10:32-52, but he does not use literary categories to grasp this.[10] Nineham grants that Mark has created in form a connected historical narrative, but he claims in effect that individual incidents take their meaning from the Gospel's theological purpose (although he denies Mark has achieved theological unity) rather than from the narrative form.[11] Nineham seems to discount form and oppose form to theology because he associates form with biography or history. But if the apparently historical form were clearly seen as literary, then form could be recognized as the expression of theological meaning, as a matter of fact, as could historical form as well.

For Eduard Schweizer, also, Mark is more concerned to preach to his own situation than he is to write a biography of Jesus. The Evangelist's main concern is his theology, and his message is to be found chiefly in the way he has arranged and framed the individual units and collections he was working with.[12] Thus at least implicitly, Schweizer sees the significance of form for meaning. His outline of Mark as a whole is oriented more to theological than to geographical categories, and Schweizer recognizes the intention of Mark creating a unified whole in 10:32-52 by relating the four parts to each other;[13] however, he does not pursue a literary-critical approach to the text.

Finally, Werner Kelber also sees Mark's concerns as both religious and historical. Mark did not intend to reproduce exact facts about the historical Jesus but to interpret the religious significance of Jesus for his own historical situation-- the conflict between Galilean and Jerusalem Christianity shortly after A. D. 70.[14] Kelber's outline of Mark as a whole is primarily theological in character, although the chronological also appears. The main thing that distinguishes Kelber from the earlier redaction-critical approaches is that he self-consciously intends to interpret Mark as a single coherent story.[15] This is done in an illuminating way; however, the narrativity of the Gospel does not receive focal attention. For

example, he is sensitive to the interrelationships of the four
parts of 10:32-52, but the narrative movement is subordinated
to his concern with the theme of the disciples' lack of perception.[16]

Turning for a moment to the two structuralist products, the
fact that there are two (and could be more) is worth commenting
on. The choice of a particular deep structure (or two) in the
light of which to view a text rather than some other is an interpretive judgment. Moreover, the identification of particular
items in the surface of a story as manifestations of a deep
structural unit (say a function or an actant) is also an interpretive judgment. Structural interpretation, therefore, is as
involved in the inter-subjectivity of the hermeneutical circle
as other interpretive methods. It is, then, a mistake for
structuralists to claim to be more scientific than others, and,
by the same token, it is a mistake to criticize structuralists
for failing to produce results that everyone will agree on.

In concluding this section we may observe that presuppositions do not seem to have had a far-reaching effect on the identification of the sub-sections in 10:32-52, but they do influence attention to and evaluation of the connections and interrelationships. For example, Schweizer and Kelber see the
Bartimaeus story as shedding important light on the behavior and
fate of the disciples,[17] while Taylor sees almost no organic
connection between that story and the rest of the text and comes
close to denying any justification for its presence.[18]

A STRUCTURAL APPROACH

I should now like to discuss the structuralist categories
which I will use and which gave rise to the two outlines already noted. I mention first the test sequence of A. J. Greimas.
For this scholar there is a supra-sentential narrative syntax
whose structures (deep) are relational networks or systems of
abstract units which are semantically (relatively) empty. These
structures are deep in that they are abstracted from the partic-
ularities of narratives in general. At the same time they are
thought to account for the organization of surface structures
(particular texts), which result from the concrete semantic
specification or manifestation of the deep structures.[19] One
such structure which Greimas has defined is the test sequence,
which is composed of five functions (or motifemes): (1) Mandating, (2) Acceptance (or Rejection), (3) Confrontation, (4) Success or Domination, (5) Consequence, Attribution, or Communication. These five functions in the view of Greimas may be considered to comprise the irreducible diachronic element of a
narrative. On the other hand, he can say that the scheme is a
logical consecution.[20] This apparent tension leads us to observe
the distinction between fabula and plot. A fabula is a sequence
of motifemes or functions whose order is determined by motifeme
syntax (perhaps by "natural logic" or by generic or culturally
determined probability). The fabula is the deep structure of a
narrative, or of its plot. A plot is a sequence of motifs
(specific elements which in a given narrative, manifest functions or motifemes) whose order is determined by the text, that
is, by the choices made by the author from an indeterminate
number of possibilities.[21] Thus Greimas' test sequence is
fundamentally a fabula. If the plot motifs in a particular
story happen to have the order of the motifemes in Greimas' test
sequence as the structure of their chronology, that is simply a

matter of chance, or stylistic choice.

It should also be noticed that Greimas distinguishes three
kinds of tests: qualifying, main, and glorifying. All three
have the same five functions, but they are differentiated in
that the Consequence or Attribution function differs in each of
them in content with regard to the object communicated. In the
qualifying test power or a helper is attributed to the hero; in
the main test a good or value, liquidation of lack, is communicated to him; and in the glorifying test recognition, or a
message, is attributed to him.[22] Obviously, in order to distinguish the three tests, it was necessary to give the fifth
function a more specific semantic content than it has in the
test sequence per se. Therefore, the three-test pattern is less
abstract (less "deep") than the simple test sequence and should
be called, in our frame of reference, an "intermediate" structure.

Some use will also be made of Daniel Patte's adaptation of
the Greimas system. The broad deep structure of an ideal narrative would contain at least three sequences: an initial correlated sequence, a topical sequence, and a final correlated
sequence. The first relates a social rupture or a failure to
carry out a contract. The second deals with a new contract, the
carrying out of which would be the means for or a contribution
to the repairing of the initial breach. The third narrates the
reestablishment of the social order. Any character, thing or
place in a sequence may be more fully dealt with in a sub-
sequence.[23] The sequences in Mk. 10:32-52 seem to be sub-
topical sequences.

Sequences are composed of syntagms, syntagms of
statements, and statements of functions and actants.[24] An
actant is a sphere of action (helping or opposing, for example)
usually manifested in a character. A function is the abstract
constant which includes the concrete variables of the same kind
of action or doing, For example, mandating is the function
which includes (or is manifested by) the indeterminate number of
concrete commands, directives, suggestions, requests, etc., that
occur or may occur in the stories of the world. My interpretation will make some use of sequences but focuses primarily on
functions. Therefore, I present the functions as listed by
Patte:[25]

> arrival vs. departure
>   departure vs. return
> conjunction vs. disjunction
> mandating vs. acceptance (or refusal)
> confrontation
> domination vs. submission
> communication vs. reception
> attribution vs. deprivation

A couple of additional comments might be made about this
approach. When a character refuses a mandate, the sequence
aborts, and the following steps do not take place.[26] The story
thus must come to an end or begin again. As I will try to
demonstrate in the next section, the four sub-divisions in my
four-part outline are (1) mandate (10:32-34); (2) refusal
(10:35-41); (3) mandate (10:42-45); (4) acceptance (10:46-52).
The first sequence aborts because the mandate is refused, but
the story does not end because the mandate is re-issued to begin

a new sequence.

According to Patte movement (disjunction/conjunction) normally occurs after a character has accepted a contract, the movement being the first stage in the realization of the contract.[27] This means that the disjunction/conjunction comes more or less in the middle of the sequence. But Patte also states that a second movement may occur after the completion of a contract, and this introduces a new sequence.[28] This means that the movement is on the boundary between two sequences. But Patte also says that this second movement is the disjunctional statement of another sequence,[29] which would have to mean that it is in the middle of the sequence. Both in the light of natural logic and because functions are defined not only by content but also by their relationship to the whole of a sequence[30] a disjunction/conjunction cannot be both in the middle of a sequence and also on the edge of it. The inconsistency is largely solved by Robert Funk's observation that arrival/departure (or conjunction/disjunction) are sometimes basic functions and at other times only a part of the "narrative scaffolding," a distinction which should be regarded.[31] I judge that the notations of movement in Mk. 10:32, 35, 46 are more nearly a part of the scaffolding while Bartimaeus' leaving his seat and coming to Jesus (10:50) is a functional disjunction/conjunction.

My three-fold outline is generated by the notion that any narrative, as a process, has three moments or functions: (1) initial state as potentiality; (2) process actualized or simply process; (3) goal or result (final state). The initial (or final) state may be one disequilibrium: a surplus of good (satisfactory state) or a lack of good (deficient state). Or the initial state may be a balance of good and bad. Any one of these states is a potentiality for change and thus the source of process. A satisfactory state can be degraded; a deficient state can be ameliorated; and a balanced state can be unbalanced for either good or evil.[32] The functions in this scheme correspond in a general, but not exact, way to the sequences of the other scheme.

In concluding this section I should like to reflect for a moment on the relationship between structuralism and hermeneutics. A synthesis between them needs to be made, but in exactly what fashion can they be joined? Can they be combined in such a way that each has equal force? If it is true that structuralist thinking is not totally dominated by logical and objective thought but itself contains a hermeneutical core,[33] we must still assess this fact. What are the defining features of the two approaches?

Frederic Jameson [34] argues that Saussure's very distinction between causes external to a phenomenon and causes intrinsic represents a definition of the idea of system itself. Applied to a narrative text this would mean that its meaning is its relationship to the formal structures of narrativity and not its relation to patterns in the situation of the interpreter. Jonathan Culler[35] has stated that a structuralist poetics, rather than discovering or assigning meanings, strives to define the conditions of meaning. Culler[36] then represents Roland Barthes as maintaining that the task of structuralist poetics is to make explicit the underlying system which makes literary effects possible. Its object will not be the full meanings of

works but the empty meanings which support the variety of full
meanings. Daniel Patte in his translator's preface to Calloud's
Structural Analysis of Narrative observes that structure as a
relational network is semantically empty and is only manifested
when invested in variable semantic features. The analyst must
reduce (my italics) the variables in order to uncover the
structure.[37] Calloud[38] then states that analysis begins with
the text and ends when the system or immanent structure is
brought to light. There is a passage from the concrete text
to abstract units which can be elements of a system. At the
level of abstract structure everything is rigorously logical.
Now these are to be sure a very few brief illustrations, but
they reveal, in my judgment, what is essentially structuralist
in structuralism. It is defined by the analytical movement
away from the text toward those abstractions from the concrete
text which are the deep structures of structuralism.

In hermeneutics, on the other hand, the thrust is from the
text toward the reader/interpreter understanding himself in the
world through the interaction of the text and his own horizon.
Do not structuralism and hermeneutics, then, move from the text
in opposite directions? And it is not that this dual movement
is a dialectic within hermeneutics itself such that the meanings
uncovered by structural analysis can then be used to relate the
interpreter meaningfully to the world. It is not, because the
meanings discovered by structuralism are empty, abstract
patterns.

One may point out, of course, that structuralism is never,
or not usually, so narrowly practiced as I have suggested above;
there are other elements in it. But to the extent that this is
true are those other elements really structuralist? Do they
not reflect some hermeneutical or some other literary-critical
point of view? There may be non-structuralist elements in
structuralism, especially as practiced, but this still leaves
open the question how the structuralist and non-structuralist
elements are related to each other. Both may be present in a
given scholar but they may nevertheless be logically incom-
patible. That is, it does seem to me that what defines structuralism as such, distinguishes it from other approaches to
textual phenomena, cannot be combined with hermeneutics in an
equal partnership. One will have to give way to the other
because at the most fundamental level they are mutually exclusive. I value hermeneutics more highly than structuralism
and thus would favor making the latter bend. One could, for
example, use deep structures--motifeme or functional patterns,
actantial relations--simply as a means for organizing the surface phenomena which are to be treated hermeneutically. What
structuralism per se discovers--abstract patterns--may not be
directly useful to hermeneutics, but these patterns can be used
by aesthetic literary criticism to organize concrete surface
elements which in turn can be used by hermeneutics. It is in
this way that I have tried to use structuralist categories in
this paper. So employed, structuralist narrative units and relationships may be more heuristic than generative of meanings
which could not have been gained from the use of other methods.
However, a structuralist approach used with circumspection does
require the interpreter to be explicitly aware of narrative as
narrative. And the difference between such an approach and one
which is hardly literary-critical at all may be a difference in
degree so decisive as to be almost a difference in kind.

In at least one other way structuralist abstracting may be hermeneutically significant. By showing that Biblical narratives manifest the same deep structures that other narratives use, the hermeneutical gap is partially bridged. The universality of Biblical thinking is pointed up, the participation of Biblical revelation in general revelation. Attention to surface structure will reveal possible differences between the Biblical and other views of reality. Differences may also be indicated not just by how deep structures are manifested but by whether they are.

STRUCTURAL AND LITERARY INTERPRETATION

I will offer here a fuller presentation of the four-fold outline and then some interpretive comments about it.

Sequence of the twelve (10:32-41)
Mandate to the twelve to follow the Son of Man in the way of suffering (10:32-34)
Refusal (in the persons of the two and the ten) (10:35-41)=
    Sub-sequence of the two (10:35-40)
    Mandate of the two to Jesus to give them places of honor (10:35-37)
    Refusal by Jesus (10:38-40) +
        Sub-sequence of the ten (10:41)
        Confrontation (the ten are indignant at the two)

Second sequence of the twelve (10:42-52)
Mandate of Jesus to the twelve to serve and suffer (10:42-45)
Acceptance (10:46-52)=
    Sub-sequence of Bartimaeus
    Mandate (10:46-47a). Hearing of Jesus prompts Bartimaeus to action.
    Acceptance (10:47b). He responds to the prompting by seeking mercy from Jesus.
    Confrontation (10:48). The many oppose Bartimaeus' effort to get Jesus' attention.
    Domination (10:49). But he has overcome the opposition and secured Jesus' attention.
    Disjunction and Conjunction (10:50). Bartimaeus leaves his seat and comes to Jesus.
    Domination (reprise) (10:51-52ab). Bartimaeus receives his sight from Jesus.
    Attribution (10:52c). He follows Jesus in the way.

That the passion prediction (10:32-34) is an implied mandate is confirmed by the fact that in 10:42-45 the disciples are explicitly mandated to renounce authority and the seeking of first place in favor of servanthood and being last. And this mandate is grounded on the servanthood and self-giving of the Son of Man (10:45), whose suffering is predicted in 10:33-34.

James and John represent the twelve in their uncomprehending refusal of the mandate to suffer, for it is the disciples as a whole who fail to understand and who behave inappropriately after the passion prediction in Mk. 9 (see 9:32 ff.). As a matter of fact, for Mark almost anyone can represent anyone as resistive to suffering--the two (10:35-40), the ten (10:41), the twelve, Peter (8:32-33) and, by implication, the multitude (8:34).

The refusal of James and John is elaborated as an effort on their part to mandate Jesus to give them places of glory. Thus the sub-sequence of the two is introduced. Jesus refuses them and this sub-sequence aborts, but before returning to the twelve there is manifested a part of another sub-sequence, that of the ten.

The confrontation, in which the ten are indignant because of the ambitions of the two, presupposes that the ten had mandated the two to walk the way of suffering or had themselves walked it. But the ten had no right to make such a claim because they had earlier been involved in the discussion about who was the greatest (9:34), and in the end they, too, would fail Jesus (14:50). Thus the indignation of the ten manifests not only the function of confrontation but also the function which Propp called unfounded claims by a false hero.[39] This sub-sequence aborts because the claim implied in the indignation is pretentious and unjustified to begin with. The confrontation lacks the energy to continue or to generate additional actions because its moral basis is fraudulent. The sub-sequence of the two aborts, as we have seen, because Jesus refuses their mandate, and the sequence of the twelve aborts because the mandate of the two (representing the twelve) to Jesus is a refusal of Jesus' mandate to them to suffer.

Thus we are brought to a second sequence of the twelve. Jesus mandates them to follow him as Son of Man in the way of servanthood and suffering. As the preceding confrontation between the ten and the two was also an unfounded claim, so in relation to that latter function is this renewed mandate also an (implied) exposure of the false hero.[40] When Jesus tells the disciples that whoever would be great among them must be servant, he is suggesting that they have missed this paradoxical greatness and have rather chosen the greatness of the "gentiles"-- lording it over -- as indeed they had (9:34). The verb katakurieuo in the LXX usually is used of the rule of an alien and has the sense of using lordship for the disadvantage of the ruled and the advantage of the ruler.[41] The ten are exposed as no different from James and John.

That a second mandate has been issued to the twelve makes more pressing the question whether they will accept or refuse it. The acceptance/refusal function so far as it pertains to the disciples is postponed; in fact the disciples' acceptance is never manifested in the plot. In its place at this point we have the Bartimaeus story, which is an acceptance function expanded into a sub-sequence containing functions of its own.

The explicit change of place (10:46) in part signals a new sequence. The mandate to Bartimaeus is Jesus' coming (erchontai) to Jericho (10:46) which enables what Bartimaeus heard (10:47). These elements pick up Jesus' original coming (elthen) into Galilee (1:14) with the imperative to repent and believe in the gospel (1:15) and his coming (exelthon) into the towns to preach (1:38). Bartimaeus' acceptance of the mandate to believe is also his mandate to Jesus to be what he (Jesus) has been mandated by God to be (redeeming Son of God/Son of Man [1:11, 38; 2:17; 8:31; 10:45]), and Bartimaeus' domination of the opposition to his effort to regain his sight is also Jesus' acceptance of Bartimaeus' mandate to him to have mercy. We could penetrate the surface further by observing that Jesus' acceptance of Bartimaeus' mandate to have mercy is a mandate by

Jesus to the blind man to persist in faith and be healed. (We might note that structural analysis, by showing that a given segment of text actualizes more than one formal possibility, explains why a passage intuitively felt to be powerful actually is so.) What is finally attributed to Bartimaeus is following Jesus in the way. Hodos is a frequent word in Mark. It is often Jesus' way and, in our text it is clearly the way (10:32) which leads to suffering in Jerusalem (10:33). Bartimaeus at the beginning of his story can only sit beside the way and beg (10:46), but by the end he has overcome obstacles and is following Jesus in the way (10:52). This is not the attribution of a helper, nor is it recognition, but it is a good or value, what has been lacking -- the last that is first (10:44), the loss which is saving (8:35). Thus this is a main, and not a qualifying or glorifying, test.

What light does the Bartimaeus story shed on Mark's view of the disciples? Kelber sees Mark to be contrasting the disciples with Bartimaeus. The insiders who received instruction fail to see while the outsider who received no instruction sees and follows in the way. In Kelber's view the disciples abandon the way of discipleship totally, and because of the failure of the women at the tomb (16:1-8) their fate in separation from Jesus is sealed and they never return to Galilee. [42]

An argument can be made, however, on the basis of a number of elements in Mark that while the plot does not narrate the restoration of the disciples to faith and service Mark's narrative world, nevertheless, assumes it. [43] Norman Petersen [44] has developed such an argument, and I present a selection of his points. Mk. 9:9 suggests that the incomprehension of the disciples will end after the resurrection. This seems to be a necessary presupposition for Mark's view that the disciples will be related to Jesus (8:34-9:1) and will be his representatives till the parousia (13:5-8, 23, 31) and that they will be vehicles of the Holy Spirit (13:11). Mk. 14:28 and 16:7 anticipate the reunion of the resurrected Christ with his disciples. Since the predictions made in the course of the story tend to be fulfilled, the reader is encouraged to think that this one will be, too. The coming to pass of what Jesus intends does not depend on the reactions of the disciples -- or the women at the tomb.

I had made a similar argument in Kerygma and Comedy. In Mark the authoritative (1:22), forgiving (2:5), life-giving (1:41; 5:41-42) word of Jesus never passes away (13:31). Moreover, the resurrection and the word that brings life out of death (8:34-37) are alternate ways of expressing the function of victory: they belong to the same paradigm. Since the life-giving word as resurrection can be present at any time, the disciples are not beyond the hope of salvation for Mark.

Now what does the Bartimaeus story specifically in its context contribute to Mark's hope for the disciples? Bartimaeus' acceptance of the mandate to suffer occurs where we might have expected a response from the disciples; therefore, what occurs in the encounter between Jesus and the blind man is suggestive for what will ultimately be the response and destiny of the disciples. What should have occurred in their case (8:31-9:1; 9:30-37) does now occur with Bartimaeus. It still, then, may with the disciples, for the response of Bartimaeus (10:46-52) continues the sequence which begins again with the twelve

196

(10:42); it is the acceptance which the mandate (10:42-45) calls
for. The Bartimaeus story continues the sequence of the twelve,
which thus does not abort, even if it is not completed.

The request of James and John to have privileged positions
in Jesus' glory is equivalent to Peter's calling Jesus Messiah
(King) (8:29) and rejecting his suffering (8:31-32). But that
the two brothers will in the future confess Jesus' true identity
is suggested by his saying that they, too, will suffer (10:39).
Moreover, that the disciples will move from seeing themselves
as followers of a king -- or divine man -- to seeing themselves
as followers of the suffering Son of Man is intimated by the
fact that Bartimaeus seems to pass through a similar transformation. The very movement of the story suggests that Mark
tends to discredit[45] rather than affirm [46] the Son of David
title. If Mark himself inserted the Son of David motif,[47] it
must have been to criticize it. In the early acceptance of the
mandate to believe and into the confrontation with the crowd
Bartimaeus calls Jesus Son of David: he is blind. After he has
succeeded in getting Jesus' attention and has made the effort to
move toward Jesus, he changes his address from Son of David to
rabbouni, master, a term stronger than rabbi and one which implies a master-disciple relationship.[48] But this is still not
for Mark a fully adequate title, and it is only after Jesus has
restored his sight that Bartimaeus can follow in the way.

This brings me to a briefer consideration of the three-fold
structural outline. Mk. 10:32 may make a distinction between
disciples in the broader sense and disciples in the narrow
sense, the twelve. If that is the case, probably those who were
going up amazed are the larger group while those who followed
afraid are the twelve. That is supported by the fact that it
is the twelve who have followed in 10:28.[49] One of the things
that holds Mk. 10:32-52 together as a unified sequence is that
the beginning and ending contain the same significant Marcan
vocabulary. In 10:32a we have en te hodo .... hoi de
akolouthountes ephobounto. And in 10:52c we have kai
ekolouthei auto en te hodo. What is present in the beginning
but not in the ending is fear. Fear is a negative surplus --
or a lack. The initial function, then, is a situation of lack--
a lack of resolute following. And in the final function
(10:52c) -- the goal or result function -- the lack is liquidated.

Since a lack can always be liquidated, it is a possibility
for amelioration, and that possibility begins to be actualized
in the process which begins at 10:32b. Jesus' speaking to them
does actually begin the process of amelioration because in Mark
Jesus' word is effective (1:22; 1:41; 2:5, 11; 5:8, 13, 41-42;
7:34; 9:25-26). And the process begun by the word of suffering
and death is one of amelioration because for Mark life in the
fullest sense can come only through loss and death (8:34-37;
9:35; 10:43-45). Jesus, then, seeks to lead them into the way,
the process, of life through death. That evokes a process of
opposition when James and John seek places of glory and the ten
manifest an unjustified indignation, a process which reaches
no goal within the confines of our text. The process of
amelioration recommences with Jesus' word about paradoxical
greatness and continues in the response of Bartimaeus. This
process reaches its goal in Bartimaeus' following Jesus in the
way. This three-fold structure can be schematized as follows:

(1) Initial
    situation
    of lack
    10:32a

(2) Process:

    amelioration   amelioration   amelioration
    10:32b-34   10:42-47   10:48b-52ab

              opposition   opposition
              10:35-41   10:48a

(3) Goal --
    lack liquidated
    10:52c

THEOLOGICAL IMPLICATIONS

Let us approach a limited consideration of the theological
implications of our text by reviewing briefly the four-fold
structure. A mandate is (1) given and (2) refused. The mandate
is (3) given again and (4) accepted: There is a second chance.
This sequence in Mark's narrative moderates one of the aspects
of the "extravagant" as Paul Ricoeur has identified it in the
parables of Jesus. There is only one opportunity, which makes
everything hinge on one momentous decision, and if that decision
is not properly made, all is irretrievably lost (Mt. 5:25;
22:11-13; 25:1-12; Lk. 16:1-8).[50] There is no second chance.
Ricoeur[51] contrasts this paradoxical and hyperbolic vision with
our actual experience in which we expect another chance. Let
us look more closely at Mark in the light of this contrast.

One could say that Mark also should have presented the one-
opportunity vision in view of his eschatological theology.
Because the Son of Man who suffers, dies, and rises is the
eschatological Son of Man who has authority to forgive sins
(2:10) and dispense with the sabbath (2:28) and who will come
at the end as judge and savior (8:38; 13:26-27), his death and
resurrection is the eschatological event, as is his word about
it; therefore, the choice to walk or not to walk in his way is
a once-for-all decision. It would be just as possible to write
a gospel-length -- or novel-length -- narrative portraying one
opportunity which must be grasped or lost as to tell a parable-
length narrative with this vision. Mark does not do that, but
neither does he abandon the eschatological for the ordinary.
Rather the paradox portrayed by his narrative is that the once-
for-all opportunity/demand may recur repeatedly, or what can
only occur once -- the last chance -- occurs again.
This interpretation of Mark is not, of course, dependent
only on 10:32-52. The mandate is given twice in each of the
earlier passion predictions (8:31, 34-37; 9:31, 35). Jesus'
death and resurrection occur in various symbolic forms throughout the Gospel, and especially do transfiguration, resurrection,
and parousia belong to the same paradigm.[52] Not only is a
number of eschatological opportunities plotted, but they are
projected into the indeterminate future beyond the plot.

Schweizer,[53] in commenting on the Bartimaeus story, has observed that for Mark discipleship would be impossible without a divine miracle. Apart from the latter there is no opening of the eyes (10:52); following Jesus is not a human possibility but must be enabled by God (10:21-22, 26-27). As I have argued above, the disciples have in Mark repeatedly had revelation experiences. More specifically, James and John, who in this very context do not see, have had their eyes opened by what they saw at the Transfiguaration and the ensuing interpretation. The glorified Son of God (9:1-3, 7) is the suffering Son of Man (9:12-13). The revelation which they have received is no less God's real disclosure than is the opening of Bartimaeus' eyes and the resurrection before which they still stand. But they do not see. They typify the situation of the disciple in a history of revelation. They stand both before and after the resurrection. Revelation is both given and withheld -- yet to be given.

The multiplicity of eschatological revelations raises the question of the relationship of Mark's narrative form to his theological interpretation of Jesus, and I should like to deal with two recent treatments of this matter. According to J. D. Crossan, Mark created the gospel form in order to counter the authority of Jesus' relatives and disciples with the authority of Jesus himself and in order to propose the message of Jesus' absence in place of the belief that the resurrected Christ was present to intervene and save his own. The Marcan sequence is: (1) death of Jesus; (2) resurrection-as-departure; (3) absence from the community; (4) parousia-as-return. Mark trapped the other Evangelists in his form with a content they could not accept: the others present the resurrected lord as present.[54]

But Mark could have accomplished the purpose which Crossan attributes to him just with individual stories and sayings presenting the absence motif. He did not need the gospel genre for this purpose. What Mark and the other Gospels have in common is the tragi-comic plot developed in a realistic mode interlaced with the extraordinary. Absence has no unique or necessary relation to this but is just a theme which Mark inserted (if in fact it is a theme in Mark) which was omitted by the other Evangelists. Since it was readily omissible and could have been expressed in the first place apart from a whole Gospel, it can hardly have been the formal generative principle of Mark. If Mark, on the other hand, was generated by the kerygma activating the tragic-comic genre, any number of themes could have been inserted into the various performance texts of the genre.

In Norman Petersen's view the narrative form was necessitated by Mark's desire to undercut the authority which certain errorists claimed from some of the disciples by showing that the disciples themselves once held an erroneous view but later abandoned it.[55] But his intention does not necessitate a narrative form. It could simply have been stated propositionally that the view once held by the disciples and now maintained by the errorists has been proven wrong.

I return to the Markan affirmation that the last chance occurs more than once. Perhaps the interplay of narrative form and the theological sense of repeated eschatological opportunities is one reason why Mark wrote a narrative rather than simply affirmed Jesus' death and resurrection as a once-for-all event. And if one aspect of the meaning of the narrative is

that the death and resurrection of Jesus (salvation event) is
offered repeatedly in the course of time, then the narrative
has not been adequately accounted for if its chronology is
reduced without remainder to a set of logical relations among
abstract units.[56] Even if it were possible -- which it is not
completely -- to rearrange chronological connections as logical
ones, it may be an essential part of the meaning of particular
stories that things take time -- which appears to be the case
with Mark.

Wrede long ago argued forcefully that Mark presents Jesus
as both the revealed and concealed Messiah. According to Wrede
these two contrasting motifs generate a series of contradictions, but in Mark's mind they did not clash. Mark's objective
is to present Jesus as the Son of God; therefore, he must be
revealed and not completely concealed. But it was necessary to
portray Jesus as concealing his messiahship in order to reduce
the tension between the non-messianic tradition about Jesus and
the belief in his messiahship which arose after the resurrection.[57]

What Wrede calls contradiction I would call paradox: a
logical tension which is yet believed to be necessary to
account for reality as experienced. The phenomenon under discussion expresses itself in Mark as two related paradoxes.
Revelation when given is still concealed: the disciple stands
both before and after the resurrection. When revelation does
occur, human beings resist the existential entailments of what
they know intellectually. These two paradoxes intertwine in
that the full existential appropriation of what is known intellectually is prevented by the incompleteness of the revelation.

The revealed/concealed motif is illuminated by our text
and has a bearing on the problem of Mark's use of the narrative
form. That Jesus is revealed is seen in the facts that James
and John know he will enter into glory and Bartimaeus senses
in him a wonder-working power which he then demonstrates. His
true glory is concealed, however, in that it lies within and
on the other side of suffering and death (10:33-34). The con-
cealment is manifested in that James and John do not understand
what Jesus' particular kind of glory entails for them
(10:42-44), as is seen in their inappropriate request
(10:36-37). Yet the disciples can at least understand intellectually what Jesus says about his coming fate, and they must
have had some inkling of its implications for them. Otherwise
why would they be afraid (10:32)?

Let us consider that Mark's use of the narrative mode is
one factor that inclined him to give expression to the re-
vealed/concealed motif. Paul writing explicitly from a post-
resurrection position and not narrating the earthly ministry of
Jesus can generalize the latter as an unmoderated humiliation.
But a circumstantial narrative expressing a Christian interpretation of Jesus' ministry would need to present the revelation
which is concealed. Moreover, if Jesus is now the Son of God
and exalted Son of Man (14:61-62), and if there is continuity
in his existence, which Mark's narrative assumes, then Jesus
must always have had that dignity. Mark's belief about who
Jesus is and his sense of continuity required that Jesus be
portrayed as revealed (not too different from Wrede's position). His understanding of the interrelation between

revelation and faith required that Jesus' identity be concealed
(considerably different from Wrede's position). Because the
revelation is never fully given in history, faith must be a
seeing beneath the surface (3:28-30; 15:39). Although the "I
believe; help my unbelief" comes to explicit expression only
once in the Gospel (9:24), it is quite congruent with Mark's
overall view that faith is in need of being completed.

In concluding, I summarize my suggestion that Mark's view
of repeated eschatological opportunities found appropriate expression in narrative and narrative inclined him to portray
Jesus' true glory as both revealed and concealed. But the
vision of the recurring last chance does not necessitate
narrative, for this position can be stated propositionally, and
the vision of one and only one opportunity can be rendered
narratively. I think I am inclined to acquiesce in the view
that narrative does not say anything conceptually that cannot
be said otherwise. What narrative does accomplish that can not
be accomplished -- at least in the same degree -- otherwise is
to attract the attention and involvement by the informing of
content and to create the sense of living the portrayed possibilities for existence in the course of time.

NOTES

1. Eduard Schweizer, The Good News According to Mark, trans.
   D. Madvig (Richmond: John Knox Press, 1970), p. 217.

2. Werner H. Kelber, Mark's Story of Jesus (Philadelphia:
   Fortress Press, 1979), p. 56.

3. Vincent Taylor, The Gospel According to Saint Mark (London:
   Macmillan and Co., 1953), pp. 95, 105, 112, 123, 130-131,133,
   139-140, 147-148, 447.

4. Ibid., pp. 105, 112.

5. Ibid., P. 104.

6. Ibid., pp. 68, 106, 107-111.

7. As Ibid., p. 443.

8. Cranfield's approach to Mark is in essentials very
   similar to Taylor's. See C. E. B. Cranfield, The Gospel
   According to St. Mark (Cambridge: University Press, 1959),
   pp. 14-18, 334-346.

9. D. E. Nineham, Saint Mark (Harmondsworth and Baltimore:
   Penguin Books, 1976), pp. 16, 21, 27-29, 34, 50-51.

10. Ibid., pp. 278, 282.

11. Ibid., pp. 30, 36-37.

12. Schweizer, Mark, pp. 13, 14, 24.

13. Ibid., pp. 217-218.

14. Kelber, Mark's, pp. 11-12, 88-96.

15. Ibid., pp. 11-12.

16. Ibid., pp. 49-53, 56.

17. Schweizer, Mark, p. 225; Kelber, Mark's, p. 56.

18. Taylor, Mark, p. 100.

19. See Jean Calloud, Structural Analysis of Narrative, trans.
    D. Patte (Philadelphia: Fortress Press; Missoula:
    Scholars Press, 1976), pp. x-xii, 3-5.

20. A. J. Greimas, Sémantique structurale (Paris: Larousse,
    1966), pp. 196-197, 205.

21. See Lubomir Doležel, "From Motifemes to Motifs," Poetics
    4 (1972).

22. Greimas, Sémantique, pp. 197, 202-203, 206; Calloud,
    Structural, p. 28.

23. Daniel Patte, What Is Structural Exegesis? (Philadelphia:
    Fortress Press, 1976), pp. 38, 51.

202

24. _Ibid._, pp. 39-40.

25. _Ibid._, p. 41

26. _Ibid._, pp. 39, 42.

27. _Ibid._, p. 45.

28. _Ibid._

29. _Ibid._

30. See Alan Dundes, "From Etic to Emic Units in the Structural Study of Folktales," _Journal of American Folklore_ 75 (1962), 101-104

31. Robert W. Funk, "The Form of the New Testament Healing Miracle Story," _Semeia_ 12 (1978), 70.

32. This scheme is a synthetic adaptation of several related constructions. See Claude Bremond, "Morphology of the French Folktale," _Semiotica_ 2 (1970), 247-252; Tzvetan Todorov, _The Fantastic_, trans. R. Howard (Ithaca: Cornell University Press, 1973), pp. 163-166; Doležel, "Motifemes," p. 62; William O. Hendricks, "The Structural Study of Narration: Sample Analyses," _Poetics_ 3 (1972), 101, 105.

33. As suggested by Edgar V. McKnight, _Meaning in Texts_ (Philadelphia: Fortress Press, 1978), p. 267.

34. _The Prison - House of Language_ (Princeton: Princeton University Press, 1974), p. 8.

35. _Structuralist Poetics_ (Ithaca: Cornell University Press, 1975), p. viii.

36. _Ibid._, pp. 118-119.

37. _Structural_, p. xii.

38. _Ibid._, p. 3.

39. See V. Propp, _Morphology of the Folktale_, trans. L. Scott (Austin and London: University of Texas Press, 1968), p. 60.

40. Propp, _Morphology_, p. 62.

41. See Cranfield, _Mark_, p. 341

42. Kelber, _Mark's_ pp. 56, 75, 77, 84.

43. For the distinction between plot and world in Mark see Norman R. Petersen, _Literary Criticism for New Testament Critics_ (Philadelphia: Fortress Press, 1978), pp. 49-52.

44. _Ibid._, pp. 64-65, 70-71, 76-78.

45. See Paul J. Achtemeier, " 'And He Followed Him': Miracles and Discipleship in Mark 10:46-52," _Semeia_ 11 (1978), 127, 130-131.

46. See Vernon K. Robbins, "The Healing of Blind Bartimaeus (10:46-52) in the Marcan Theology," _Journal of Biblical Literature_ 92 (June, 1973), 234-236, 239-240.

47. As Robbins (_Ibid._, pp. 235-236) argues.

48. See Cranfield, _Mark_, p. 346, and Achtemeier, "Miracles," p. 124.

49. See Schweizer, _Mark_, p. 217. Cranfield (_Mark_, p. 335) has the opposite view of the identity of the two groups.

50. Paul Ricoeur, "The Specificity of Language, " _Semeia_ 4 (1975), 116-117.

51. _Ibid._, p. 116.

52. See Dan O. Via, Jr., _Kerygma and Comedy in the New Testament_ (Philadelphia: Fortress Press, 1975), pp. 117-118, 121, 123, 140, 142.

53. _Mark_, p. 217.

54. J. D. Crossan, "A Form for Absence: The Markan Creation of Gospel, " _Semeia_ 12 (1978), 44-45, 51-53.

55. Petersen, _Literary Criticism_, p. 80.

56. On the tension between the chronological and logical nature of narrative connections see Roland Barthes, "Introduction à l'analyse structurale des récits, " _Communications_ 8 (1966), 12; Greimas, _Sémantique_, pp. 196-197, 205, 207, 212; Ricoeur, "The Narrative Form," _Semeia_ 4 (1975), 48-50.

57. William Wrede, _The Messianic Secret_, trans. J. C. G. Greig (Greenwood, S. C.: The Attic Press, 1971), pp. 124-128, 213, 218, 220, 223, 227-229.

1 CORINTHIANS 6.9ff:

WAS HOMOSEXUALITY CONDONED IN THE CORINTHIAN CHURCH?

Peter Zaas

Durham, NC

9. Don't you know that the unrighteous will not inherit God's kingdom? Do not be misled: Neither pornoi[1] nor idolaters nor adulterers nor malakoi[1] nor arsenokoitai[1] 10. nor thieves nor greedy people nor drunkards nor slanderers nor robbers will inherit God's kingdom. 11. And some of you were these. But you have been washed, but you have been sanctified, but you have been justified in the name of your lord Jesus Christ and in the spirit of our God.

Few passages in the Pauline corpus have received as much newspaper space in recent years as 1 Cor. 6.9-10, and, to pay recognition to the context in which this publicity has most often occured, we might justifiably refer to the passage as the "Anita Bryant logion."[2] In rather sharp contrast to the citation of this text in the popular press, however, stands the relative lack of discussion of it in recent scholarly literature.[3] It is true that some commentaries duly treat the passage[4], as do some specialized studies of Pauline ethics[5], but no recent work combines an adequate critical treatment of the passage in its literary context with a discussion of it in the context of the life of the Corinthian church to which it is addressed. This essay attempts to bridge this gap, not merely because of the notoriety the text has gained in contemporary anti-homosexual polemic, but also because the passage raises some interesting questions in the realm of Pauline ethical thought, and provides a glimpse of Paul applying his moral teaching to specific problems he faced as a founder of churches.

The question posed by the title of this essay may seem naive by the standards of contemporary scholarship. Since the pioneering studies of Weizsäcker, Seeberg, and Klein[6] at the beginning of this century, and Vögtle and Carrington[7] a generation or so later, 1 Cor. 6.9f has most often been viewed in relation to a primitive Christian catechesis, fundamental moral instruction whose vices and virtues were borrowed from the popular morality of the day, from Stoicism, from Hellenistic (or occasionally Palestinian) Judaism, or from some combination of these. Deissmann demonstrated the occurrence in Latin of all the vices in 1 Cor. 6.9f, except idolatry and greediness, in a Roman game we might call "conversation checkers."[8] Vice-catalogues are sprinkled throughout popular philosophical writings, Hellenistic Jewish moral literature, and in such syncretistic sources as astrological charts[9]. The Qumran literature is replete with catalogues of both virtues and vices[10]. Given the prevalence of these vice-catalogues in antiquity, why try to apply the specific vices of our text to the concrete situation of a particular church?

Even if we relate 1 Cor. 6.9ff to some pre-Pauline catechesis, we can still observe Paul's application of this material to the specific situation in Corinth. 1 Corinthians is not itself a catechetical document, but a letter written in response

to a particular historical situation. Thus we can observe Paul
invoking a traditional catechetical unit, in fact reminding his
audience of a particular part of his previous catechetical
teaching[11]. In this way we can raise the question of the bearing of 6.9ff upon the situation presupposed by the letter. We
can ask (a) why Paul invokes the vice-catalogue at all at this
point in the letter, and (b) why he chooses the specific vices
in the catalogue. The vice-catalogues throughout the literature
contain a great variety of vices, so great a variety, indeed,
that we may consider Paul's selection of the vices in 6.9f a
free choice, so far as the catalogue form is concerned. Thus
question (a) is a literary question, but (b) is primarily an
historical one. By treating both of these questions in turn,
we can attempt to penetrate the surface of Paul's ethical
thought at this point.

In order to illuminate the literary context of 1 Cor. 6.9ff,
let us begin by comparing chapters 5 and 6, which are closely
analogous at several points. Each chapter deals with a specific
moral problem in Corinth of which Paul has become aware: Chapter 5 deals with an incestuous relationship; a man "has taken his
father's wife." (5.1) Chapter 6 concerns a Christian who has
taken another before a civil court. In each case Paul discusses
the particular sin under its genus. The incestuous relation he
describes as porneia (5.1 [2], 9, 10, 11), the Christians' use
of civil courts he describes as adikia (cognates appear at 6.1,
7, 8, 9.) In both cases he extends the general vice to include
a number of specific vices by using vice-catalogues. Thus, as
Paul explains, in his previous letter he had extended pornoi to
include greedy people, robbers, and idolaters (5.9f), and now
extends the term to comprise slanderers and drunkards as well
(5.11).

Paul's argument in 5.9ff hinges on the distinction between
Christian and non-Christian pornoi. He had already written to
the Corinthian community not to "mix together" with pornoi, but
by this he did not mean (ou pantos "not at all") the pornoi "of
this world," i.e., non-Christian pornoi, "because then you would
have had to go out of the world." (5.10) He now wants explicitly to extend his proscription to the extent of refusing to
eat (the cultic meal?) with "any so-called brother" who is a
pornos, or any of the other sinners in the catalogue in 5.11
(5.16). Paul concludes the section with a refusal to judge
"those outside," (5.12) and invokes the language of the Septuagint to urge the community to cast out the evil person from
their midst (5.13), perhaps with the word play poneros/pornos in
his mind.

The Corinthian church has not taken it upon itself to judge
those inside, however, and this failure is the next item on
Paul's agenda: A certain member of the community who has a
grievance against a fellow Christian dares to take him before
the adikoi "unrighteous" and not before the saints (6.1). Just
as he does in the case of porneia in chapter 5, Paul proceeds to
invoke the difference between Christians and non-Christians in
the moral sphere. He reprimands the church for accepting as
judges hoi exouthenēmenoi "the despised" in the church (6.4),
which must refer to the civil judges mentioned in v. 1, despite
the ambiguity in the sentence[12].

Paul's argument in chapter 6 turns on the central, generic vice adikia "injustice." The Christian brethren have taken their case not before the hagioi but before the adikoi (6.1), whom Paul also describes as the apistoi (6.6). Rather than thus jeopardize the distinction between Christians and non-Christians, the Christians should rather "permit themselves to be wronged," adikeisthe[13]. Instead, they "commit injustice," adikeite, to a brother. Thus by a rhetorical tour de force Paul has transferred the vice of adikia from non-Christian judges to Christian litigants. So as the adikoi who "will not inherit God's kingdom" (6.9) Paul addresses primarily the Christian unrighteous, although we may presume that unrighteous pagans won't inherit it, either.

Just as Paul extended the vice of porneia to include other major vices in chapter 5, so does he extend the vice of adikia to include the other members of the vice-catalogue in 6.9f. He concludes with the statement "and some of you were these," and the reference to baptism which completes verse 11.

We have thus established the function of the vice-catalogues in chapters 5 and 6, to extend the specific vices of porneia and adikia, which Paul knows to be at work in the Corinthian community, to include other major vices. Now let us turn to the lists themselves. Are the individual vices depicted, beside porneia and adikia, vices which were present in the Corinthian church, or are they present in the catalogue for traditional or for some other reasons?

We may note immediately that every vice of those enumerated in 5.11 is present in the catalogue of nine vices in 6.9ff[14]. This list includes all six vices in 5.11, and adds kleptai "robbers," and three sexual vices, moichai "adulterers," and malakoi and arsenokoitai, the two vices associated with homosexuality. Each of these vices appears only here in the Pauline vice-catalogues[15], although theft and adultery occur in the list of vices that come out of the heart in Matt. 15.19 and Mark 7.22, and arsenokoitai appears in the catalogue of vices at 1 Tim. 1.10.

The similarity of the two lists in chapters 5 and 6 is surely deliberate. No two other New Testament lists show the same degree of overlap, nor can any dissection theory of the Corinthian correspondence account for this degree of closeness[16]. Of the 94 vices enumerated in the table of all the vices from all the New Testament lists in Wibbing, Die Tugend- und Lästerkataloge im Neuen Testament[17], only 22 appear in at least three lists, or 23%. Of those 52 vices that appear in the Pauline lists, only ten, or 19%, appear in three lists or more. Even the two lists in the analogous pericope in Matt. 15 and Mark 7 show a smaller degree of overlap, 78% vs. 81%.

Thus Paul is quoting his own list of a chapter earlier in our text in 6.9f. His addition of three vices of a sexual nature, however, suggests that he has returned to his earlier theme of porneia, and the fact that of the ten vices in the catalogue, four, pornoi, moichoi, malakoi, and arsenokoitai, are overtly sexual, supports this suggestion. Let us examine these four vices, their interrelationships, and their connection with the remaining member of the pentad of vices in 6.9, idolatry, to

see if we can shed further light on Paul's application of his
moral teaching to the Corinthian situation.

The term pornos is fairly rare in the New Testament and
appears in Paul only in the two chapters under discussion here.
The context in chapter 5 indicates that Paul uses the term to
denote sexual sinners in general. The man guilty of taking his
father's wife, who commits porneia (5.1), is a pornos (5.9). We
may reasonably expect this general denotation to carry over into
the vice-catalogue at 6.9. The term carries this general sense
in the rest of the New Testament uses as well[18]. Pornoi is thus
a fitting term to head the list of sexual vices in 6.9. We
should bear in mind, however, the connotations the word carries.
Its original meaning in classical Greek is specifically a male
prostitute, but even then it can denote a catamite, a male
homosexual in the passive role[19], or a sodomite[20].

Upon turning to the literature of Hellenistic Judaism,
which often lies close to Paul's usage, we note a strong connection between the pornos and the idolater, the second vice in
our list. Philo expresses this connection philosophically. In
commenting upon Deut. 23.3, "No child of a prostitute (LXX ek
pornēs) will enter into the assembly of the Lord," in Leg. All.
3.8, Philo changes the text ek pornēs to pornoi, and defines pornoi as "those who have shunned the rule of the One," i.e., poly-
theists. Likewise in Migr. Ab. 69, the "child of a prostitute"
of Deuteronomy is a polytheist, because he does not know his
real father[21].

Philo's reasoning is an allegorical tour de force, although
it presumably emerges from a connection in his own mind between
idolatry and sexual vice. This connection is explicit, however,
in Wisd. 14.12, "considering idols is the beginning of porneia."
The connection occurs even closer to home: Paul himself associates the two in 1 Cor. 10.7f, where he juxtaposes the incident of the golden calf (Ex. 32.6) with the Hebrews' porneia
with the daughters of Moab (Num. 25.9). Incidentally, all of
Paul's uses of the verb porneuō appear in this letter, and always retain their basic meaning of "consort with prostitutes"[22].

Idolatry and sexual vice are so closely linked in Hellenistic Jewish and early Christian literary sources that Suidas,
under the influence of these sources, records eidōlolatrēs as
the definition of pornos, citing mainly Biblical examples[23].

Paul specifically associates adultery with gentiles in
1 Th. 4.5. If that difficult passage refers to "using one's
own wife in holiness and honor," then Paul is contrasting marital purity with "lustful suffering like the gentiles who do not
know God," (1 Th. 4.5) a phrase which in Gal. 4.8 Paul specifically links with idolatry. Idolatry and adultery go hand in hand
in Wisd. 14.24 and Test. Lev. 18.11, and especially in the Shepherd of Hermas M. 4.1.9, "whoever does such things as the gentiles commits adultery."

The two remaining sinners on our list, the malakos and the
and the arsenokoitēs, remain to be related to the complex of
vices surrounding porneia and idolatry. Of the two, arsenokoitēs is the easiest to define, at least by its etymology, "one
who lies with a man." But the word is late--no sure examples

before Paul are known[24], and most examples are from the moral literature of Hellenistic Judaism[25] and from the syncretistic astrological literature[26].

Malakos presents a more difficult problem of translation in our passage. The word normally means soft or gentle, and can be applied to persons' dispositions, as well as to inanimate objects; it refers to clothing twice in Matt. 11.8 = Lk 7.25. The term can take the sense of "catamite" by extension from the Latin mollis[27], but sure examples of this are rare, with the ambiguity of the term often difficult or impossible to reconcile. This ambiguity is overtly expressed in Dion. Hel., Antt. 7.64, where the historian explains the nickname of Aristodemus, a fourth century BC tyrant of Italian Cumae. He was called "Malakos" either because he "suffered things fitting for women" as a youth, or because he was "gentle in wrath." Cleanthes's calling a homosexual (kinaidos in the text) a malakos[28] is probably a pun based on the man's sexual proclivities as well as the weakness exhibited by his sneezing. Hibeh papyrus 54.11, which refers to a musician Zenobius as "the malakos" as likely refers to the music as the man[29]. In Stoic morals, softness and effeminacy are approximately equivalent, as in the anecdote about Cleanthes cited above. Thus in Epictetus, Diss. 2.16.45 the philosopher urges his students to cast out malakia among other human weaknesses. As long as this ambiguity is borne in mind, malakos in 1 Cor. 6.9 can possibly take the sense of "catamite," but only because of its association with the less ambiguous term arsenokoites[30].

Homosexuality is closely associated with the gentiles' idolatry in Jewish polemic. Paul's familiar connection of the two in Romans 1 relates closely to the same connection in Wisd. 14.26, T. Naph. 3.3-4, and Philo, Spec. Leg. 3.39, which associates transvestitism with idolatry as well as homosexuality.

Thus the five vices of 1 Cor. 6.9 are related. All are associated with idolatry in Jewish polemic; all are summarized by the leading term, pornoi. Idolatry itself must be considered a sexual vice, or at least a cause of sexual vice, in this passage.

We have seen that the vice-catalogue in 6.9, including the two homosexual vices, refers back to the incident of porneia in 5.1ff, although it also serves as a warning to Christian adikoi that they will not inherit God's kingdom. We are now able to return to our original question: To what extent do these vices represent actual vices which Paul complains are being condoned in the Corinthian church?

We have observed that Paul condemns porneia, the first of the vices in our list, in 5.1. He condemns idolatry per se in 10.7, and the eating of meat sacrificed to idols he condemns, with reservations, in chapter 8, and again in 10.19. We know that Paul is likely to associate idolatry with sexual vice; this connection is implicit in 10.7-8 and explicit in Rom. 1.23ff. But Paul's criticism of idolatry in 1 Corinthians does not deal directly with sexual immorality surrounding the pagan cult, but rather with the breakdown of church discipline that results from some Christians' eating sacrificial meats (8.7-13) and with the demonic aspect of the idolatrous worship (10.20ff).

Thus, while we may safely assert that Paul has inserted the vices _pornoi_ and _eidololatrai_ into his list because he is angry about specific instances of these vices being condoned in the Corinthian church, we are not on safe ground in asserting that he has inserted _moichai_, _malakoi_, and _arsenokoitai_ for the same reason. These latter three vices were all specifically associated with the complex of sexual vices, _porneia_, surrounding idolatry in Jewish anti-gentile polemic.

We must take into account, however, the phrase with which Paul closes his vice-catalogue, _kai tauta tines ēte_, "and some of you were these." Here is the closest evidence that Paul has selected those vices from his primary list that most closely apply to his Corinthian audience. While Paul's use of this phrase in no way proves that the Corinthian church condoned any one of the vices in 6.9f, it does indicate that Paul is addressing real or potential abuses of his ethical message, not citing primitive tradition by rote. The baptismal reference that follows points clearly to the radical nature of Paul's moral gospel; baptism into the body of Christ has permitted a new start to the most vicious sinner.

Some nominal Christians in Corinth have abused this new start, perhaps under the influence of Cynic-Stoic theorizing about the freedom of the wise man. Paul is particularly aware of abuses connected with the pagan cult, and to his mind, these are primarily sexual abuses, homosexuality included. There is no room for such abuse in Paul's Christianity.

We have thus observed Paul's application of his moral teaching to a specific problem in the Corinthian church. We have observed that Paul's abhorrence of the particular vices, including homosexuality, in our passage has as much to do with their religious aspect as with their intrinsic morality. Homosexual Christians, in Paul's view, are tainted by association with the pagan cult. How modern Christianity is to evaluate Paul's association of homosexuality with idolatry is probably a matter best left to individual churches and to individual Christians.

NOTES

[1]Because this paper deals in part with the precise sense of the terms _pornos_, _malakos_, and _arsenokoitēs_, we shall not translate them in our exposition. They are translated somewhat differently in the various English versions. RSV translates _pornoi_ as "immoral," and takes _malakoi_ and _arsenokoitai_ together as "sexual perverts." KJV renders the three terms "fornicators," "effeminate," and "abusers of themselves with mankind." Moffatt translated them as "immoral," "catamites," and "sodomites;" Goodspeed as "immoral," "sensual," and "given to unnatural vice."

[2]New York Times, February 21, 1978, p. 18.

[3]An exception is E. Dinkler, "Zum Problem der Ethik bei Paulus: Rechtsnahme und Rechtsverzicht (1 Kor 6,1-11)," ZThK 49 (1952), 167-200, which does not deal with the question posed by this paper. Except for John Gager's article on the eschatological language in 6.10, "Functional Diversity in Paul's Use of

End-Time Language," <u>JBL</u> 89 (1970), 325-337, the passage is not indexed in <u>New Testament Abstracts</u>. It is not indexed at all in <u>Elenchus Bibliographicus Biblicus</u> or <u>Internationale Zeitschriftenschau für Bibelwissenschaft und Grenzgebiete</u>.

[4]For a recent discussion of many of the significant issues, see H. Conzelmann, <u>1 Corinthians</u> (Hermeneia Commentary, Philadelphia: Fortress Press, 1975) in loc. and the "Excursus: The Catalogues of Vices and Virtues," Pp. 100-101.

[5]Most recently, the chapter on homosexuality in V. Furnish, <u>Moral Thought in Paul</u> (Nashville: Abingdon Press, 1979.)

[6]K. Weizsäcker, <u>The Apostolic Age</u>, trans. J. Millar. (London: Williams and Norgate, 1897.) A. Seeberg, <u>Der Katechismus der Urchristenheit</u> (Leipzig: G. Böhme, 1903.) G. Klein, <u>Der älteste Christliche Katechismus</u> (Berlin, 1909.)

[7]A. Vögtle, <u>Die Tugend- und Lästerkataloge im Neuen Testament</u> (Münster: Aschendorff, 1936.) P. Carrington, <u>The Primitive Christian Catechism</u> (Cambridge: University Press, 1940.)

[8]A. Deissmann, <u>Light from the Ancient East</u>, trans. L. Strachan. (New York: G. H. Doran, 1927.) P. 316, n. 6.

[9]See the pertinent chapters in Vögtle.

[10]See S. Wibbing, <u>Die Tugend- und Lästerkataloge im Neuen Testament und ihre Traditionsgeschichte unter besonderer Berücksichtung der Qumran-Texte</u>. (Berlin: A. Töpelmann, 1959.) Pp. 43-76.

[11]I am detailing this assertion in my PhD thesis, "Morals and Membership, A Study in Pauline Ethical Thought." (Diss: U. of Chicago, Dept. of New Testament and Early Christian Literature.)

[12]For the alternative punctuation and sense see J. B. Lightfoot, <u>Notes on Epistles of St. Paul</u>. (London: MacMillan and Co., 1895.) Pp. 211-12.

[13]Construing the verb as a "permissive middle," Blass-De-Brunner-Funk, <u>Grammar</u>, P. 165.

[14]<u>Adikoi</u> is not, strictly speaking, part of the catalogue.

[15]<u>Moichai</u> appears in Gal. 5.21 t.r.

[16]See references in Conzelmann, in loc.

[17]Pp. 87-8.

[18]Eph. 5.5; 1 Tim. 1.10; Heb. 12.16, 13.4; Ap. 21.8, 22.15.

[19]Aristophanes, <u>Plutus</u> 155; Xenophon, <u>Memorabilia</u> 1.6.13.

[20]Democritus, Ep. 4.11; Phalaris, Ep. 4, in R. Hercher, ed. <u>Epistolographi Graeci</u> (Amsterdam, A. M. Kahhert, 1965.) p. 409.

[21]Cf. <u>De Mut. Nom.</u> 205.

[22] 1 Cor. 6.18, 10.8 [2].

[23] G. Bernardy, Ed. (Holis, 1853.) 1. 369.

[24] T. Nägeli, Der Wortschatz des Apostels Paulus (Göttingen, 1905.) p. 46, cited in J. Moulton and G. Milligan, The Vocabulary of the Greek Testament (London: Hodder and Staughton, 1930.) p. 79.

[25] I.e., Or. Sib. 2.73.

[26] The term appears twice in a vice-catalogue associated with a particular astrological configuration in the Paris Astrological Codex, F. Cumont, ed., Catalogus Codicum Astrologorum Graecorum (Brussels, Lamertin, 1929.) 8.4.196. Malakoi appears later in the same list, apparently with its basic sense of "softness," or "effeminacy."

[27] H. Herter, art. "Effeminatus," RAC 2.620.

[28] Diog. L. 7.173.

[29] Contra Deissmann, LAE, p. 164, n. 4. The term is often associated with music; W. Kroll, art. "Kinaidos," Pauly-Wissowa, 11.1.460.

[30] It is so understood by Grotius in his commentary: "Id est, pathici." Annotationes in Epistolam I ad Corinthios, in H. Grotius, Opera Omnia Theologica (Amsterdam, 1679.) 2.2.784.

ST. PAUL'S TREATMENT OF MISOGYNY, GYNEPHOBIA, AND SEX SEGREGATION IN FIRST CORINTHIANS 11:2-6

Richard and Catherine Clark Kroeger
University of Minnesota

One of the major contributory factors of the widespread homophilia in Greek society appears to have been its hatred and fear of women. This misogyny was declared to rest upon the strongest of theological, philosophical, and intellectual arguments. If pederasty was a revered and spiritualized institution, then its corollary was the spiritual, moral, intellectual, and physical inferiority of women. Perhaps Pseudo-Lucian expressed it most succinctly at the termination of a discussion of the relative merits of homosexuality versus heterosexuality. There are several such literary debates still extant, and in two of them a Corinthian defends the love of women. Here Charicles of Corinth loses to an Athenian pederast by the judge's verdict:

> Therefore let marriage be for all, but let the
> love of boys remain alone the privilege of the
> wise, for a perfect virtue is absolutely unthink-
> able in women. But do not be angry, my dear
> Charicles, if the crown belongs to Athens and
> not to Corinth.[1]

If marriage was second-best, the problem lay with the inferiority of women, a concept deeply entrenched in Greek thought. While certain thinkers did indeed affirm the equality of women and the validity of heterosexual experience, they were pitted against Plato, Aristotle, Euripides, Aeschylus, and Hesiod, giants whose words left a lasting imprint on the attitudes and mores of the succeeding centuries. And if the ancients made a correlation between misogyny and pederasty, modern scholars have concurred:

> In the upper classes (where most of the litera-
> ture was written) male homosexuality was tied
> to civic education and the exclusion of women
> from public and educational life. The practice
> was associated with fear and disdain of women.[2]

Margaret Mead points out that the feeling of disparity produced predictable results:

> One-sex patterns also restrict the sex that
> practices them the longer they are practiced
> by one sex alone . . This may result in a
> secondary solution, such as the split in
> Greek society between the uneducated wife and
> the sophisticated mistress: it may push a
> large part of society toward celibacy or homo-
> sexuality, simply because a heterosexual rela-
> tionship involves unbearable complications.[3]

Elsewhere she observes that "one of the strong tendencies that

makes for homosexuality" is "the tendency to love the similar
rather than the antithetical person."[4] It would be difficult to
find another society which so elevated one sex and so subjugated
the other. Slater sees Greek homosexuality as "a defense
against hidden but incapacitating fears of the opposite sex."[5]
Paul appears to have sought an opportunity to address certain
attitudes toward women in his First Epistle to the Corinthians,
especially in 11:2-17. The immediate context was apparently a
question regarding head-covering and length of hair appropriate
for both sexes, but the Apostle seems to have seized upon the
occasion to address more basic aspects of sexuality. To a congregation newly converted from an ecstatic and uninhibited paganism, Paul propounds women as a gift from God and a treasure
for man.

It was essential for him to declare that the original purpose in the creation of woman was positive and beneficent.
Hesiod held that the gods devised women as a hateful trick upon
men[6] and "Zeus who thunders on high made women to be an evil to
mortal men, with a nature to do evil."[7] Euripides' Hippolytus
asks Zeus why he brought women as a "fraudulent evil" to see the
light of the sun.[8] One even finds the concept of maleficent intention in Hellenistic Judaism of the New Testament era.

> And I took from him a rib and created him a
> wife, that death should come to him by his wife.[9]

Well into the Roman era the creation of woman was regarded in
some quarters as a catastrophe. Pseudo-Lucian (second century
A.D.) quotes Menander with approval:

> Then are not painters right when they depict
> Promethus nailed to rocks? With brands of fire
> but naught else good can he be credited. But
> all the gods, me thinks, hate what he did in
> fashioning females, a cursed brood . . .[10]

Against this view of woman as the result of a maleficent action
on the part of the pagan gods, Paul counters with a recycling
of Genesis 2. Woman was created for a positive purpose, on
man's account. "Neither was the man created for the woman, but
the woman for the man" (v. 9). She was created as a minister of
blessing rather than as "something evil to man".[11] The concept
of woman's creation for the sake of man has often been regarded
as derogatory, but this is not necessarily so. $\Delta\iota\grave{\alpha}$ with the
accusative is used at several points in the Corinthian Epistles
to imply an aspect of ministry. Jesus became poor "for your
sakes" $\delta\iota$ ʼ $\dot{\upsilon}\mu\tilde{\alpha}\varsigma$ (II Cor. 8:9). Paul makes an application "for
your sakes" $\delta\iota$ ʼ $\dot{\upsilon}\mu\tilde{\alpha}\varsigma$ (I Cor. 4:6). The term occurs with the
idea of positive and spiritual benefit in I Cor. 4:10, 9:10, 23;
II Cor. 4:5, 11, 15. It need be no more derogatory when applied
to women than it is when applied to Jesus or to Paul. The emphasis is positive and affirming: Man, for whom it was not good
to be alone, is provided with the greatest of creation's blessings, a suitable partner, one whom he may receive with affection
and trust. Jointly they bear the image of God, and she is his
glory (v. 7).

· But if Paul presented the benefit of God's gift to mankind, he must contend with the Greek concept of woman as an
inferior order of creation. According to Hesiod man is sprung
from Zeus, while woman is molded of clay and imbued with: "a
shameless mind and a deceitful nature",[12] as well as the thoughts
and strategems of a bitch. Therefore she is created from
another substance and endowed with another nature. Semonides
carries matters much further, however: "In the beginning God
made woman's mind apart from man's."[13] One woman was made from
a sow and possessed the nature of the beast, filthy, fat, and
unwashed. Another was formed of a vixen and partakes of her
nature, another of earth and therefore is lacking in wits. "Such
a woman knoweth neither evil nor good; her only art is to eat."
Another is descended from a bitch and the next made from the sea,
unstable and raging. Others derived from the sneaky cat, the
supercilious mare, the ape, and the only good woman was descended from a bee.[14] Phocylides also likened women to beasts, and
the young husband of Xeonophon's _Oeconomicus_ appears to think of
his wife in animal terms:

> She was not yet fifteen years old when she came
> to me, and up to that time had lived in horse reins,
> seeing, hearing, and saying as little as possible.
> . . Well, Socrates as soon as I found her docile
> and sufficiently domesticated to carry on a con-
> versation, I questioned her.[15]

In the ensuing conversation she is told that she must take on
the responsibilities and household duties of a bee. The Hippolytus of Euripides asserted that women were unworthy of con-
versing with any but beasts.[16] Aristotle held that woman was
fundamentally and essentially inferior and that "the inequality
is permanent",[17] her deliberative faculty inadequate[18] and her
virtue always inferior to that of a man.[19] Perhaps one finds
an echo of this opinion in Sirach 42:14: "Better is the wickedness of a man than the goodnes of a woman." Such sentiments of
Hellenistic Judaism could not have totally escaped the Jewish
elements of the Corinthian congregation. Plato, although he
declared women to have a virtue equal to that of men, cannot be
said to have viewed them as equals. Men were the superiors of
women and children,[20] and their nature was formed from males
who in a former existence had been "cowards or led unrighteous
lives."[21] While an individual woman might excel in some way,
and capable ones might become guardians in his Republic, still
they could never really measure up to men, nor hold the office
of philosopher-king. Socrates asked,

> Can you mention any pursuit of mankind in which
> the male sex has not all these gifts and qualities
> in a higher degree than the female? . . . All the
> pursuits of men are the pursuits of women also,
> but in all of them a woman is inferior to a man.[22]

Certain of the later thinkers were far kinder in their apprais-
als of women, but those defending homophilia continued to emphasize the inferiority of the female sex. The pederasts of
Plutarch, Achilles Tatius, and Pseudo-Lucian viewed women as
vicious, deceitful, lazy, and vain. The character of a young
boy is more noble, unaffected, and soul-satsifying while "with

a woman everything is fake, both words and appearances."[23]

In such a context Paul's affirmation of woman as made from man becomes a statement of the common humanity of both men and women. Woman was formed from the very substance of man and shares the same qualities of heart and mind. Her origin was neither in clay nor in base animals nor inferior males, but from Adam while he yet represented all of mankind, both male and female. She was not an alien creature to be regarded with suspicion and distrust but an extension of his own body, to be received and cherished as true soul-mate. The concept, mentioned both in v. 2 and v. 12, is an important antidote for the physical revulsion which was often expressed toward women and their sexuality. Freud found an ancient symbol of the vagina in the terrifying Medusa's head which turned men to stone.[24] Slater, Simon, and others have explored the menacing aspects of the sexuality of the mature woman in the Greek World. The rear entry position seems to have been the preferred one in intercourse so that it was not necessary to view the feminine genitalia.[25] Especially the child-bearing functions of women were repudiated. Aschylus' Apollo pronounced the mother not truly the parent but merely an incubator of the child[26] and Hippolytus protested that to buy sons for gold at the temple would be better than the present arrangement.[27] Significantly, three of the Twelve Great Gods were said to have avoided the natural process of birth. Paul points out that women do indeed bring forth male children but that man is the primordial source. He can no more reject her sexuality than he can his own, for it was born of his own being.

Paul's argument is appreciably strengthened if κεφαλή is understood to denote head in the sense of "source" rather than of "chief." Woman then has her source in man, whose creation was wrought by Christ, who proceeded forth from God. Thus her origin is both human and divine. La Rue Van Hook notes that κεφαλή "although complimentary as used in Homer, in subsequent Greek poetic and prose literature is used as a term of affection or hatred."[28] Surely the purpose here is one of affection. One must keep in mind Paul's concept of one body having many members, where the head cannot discard the feet (I Cor. 12:21). Nor can the man discard the woman or despise her as inferior.

But the Greek profession of the inferiority of women was the basis for the philosophic rationale of the love of boys. The argument of Plato's Aristophanes begins with a myth of primordial beings who were male-male, female-male, or female-female. They were severed by an act of the gods in the fashion of Siamese twins, and all of humanity goes about seeking to be reunited with the other part of its original being. The finest men and boys are those who came from a purely male source. "When they reach manhood, they are lovers of youth, and are not naturally inclined to marry or beget children."[29] Pausanias also holds the exclusively male source to be the source of the noblest affections.

> The offspring of the heavenly Aphrodite is
> derived from a mother in whose birth the
> female has no part, - she is from the male

> only; this is that love which is of youths,
> and the goddess being older, there is nothing
> of wantonness in her. Those who are inspired
> turn to the male, and delight in him who is the
> more valiant and intelligent nature.[30]

These same Platonic arguments in favor of pederasty were revived for hundreds of years.[31] Professors of philosophy used Socratic arguments to seduce their students,[32] "so that divine philosophy and with it love of boys might come to maturity."[33] Such "genuine love has no connection whatsoever with the women's quarters. I deny that it is love that you have felt for women or girls."[34] A Hellinistic epigram declared that irrational beings copulate with women while the truly intelligent have found "something more" with boys.[35]

To a perplexed community in a sexually preoccupied city, Paul argued the interrelation and continuity of man and woman. The source of each lay within the other, and neither could come into being without the other. The God who is above and beyond sexuality has given them to one another, both made in the divine image. Man is God's glory (I Cor. 11:7) while woman is man's glory. Titus and the brothers are called "the glory of Christ" (II Cor. 8:23), and the Thessalonians are told, "You are our glory and joy" (I Thess. 2:20). All Christians, reflecting the glory of Christ are "continually being transformed into the same likeness, from glory to glory as by the Lord" (II Cor. 3:13). Feuillet points out that δόξα contains not the notion of reflection but rather of a manifestation of God's power or attributes; and in the case of men, that which brings them honor or glorifies them.[36] This was important in a society where it was a disgrace for a woman to be seen at the window,[37] and where the lover was honored by the achievements of his boy-favorite rather than by any qualities in his wife.

> Much that in Rome we hold to be correct is thought
> shocking in Greece. No Roman thinks it an embar-
> rassment to take his wife to a dinner party. At
> home the wife (mater familias) holds first place
> in the house and is the center of its social life.
> Things are very different in Greece, where the wife
> is never present at dinner, unless it is a family
> party, and spends all her time in a remote part of
> the house called the Women's Quarter, which is
> never entered by a man unless he is a very close
> relation.[38]

Part of the sex segregation which characterized the society, then, seems to have been based upon the "embarrassment" of having a woman of citizen status visible. Hence it is significant that at the point where women may pray or prophesy, they are called "the glory of the man". A husband might take pride rather than embarrassment from his wife's ministry. The concepts of woman as the glory of man and "neither the man without the woman nor the woman without the man" (v. 11) were important ones in combatting the sex segregation which the Greeks themselves saw as a contributory factor in homosexuality.[39]

It is apparent, however, that Paul wishes this "glory" to

be veiled. He is to return to the themes of glory and veiling
in II Cor. 3:7-18. In that passage we find an expression of a
second glory which is greater than the earlier one (v. 10). To
say that the woman is the glory of the glory as he does in I Cor.
11:7 may be an advancement rather than a demotion. And with the
tradition of glory, there is also a tradition of covering (vv.
13-18) in the Hebrew records (Exodus 13:21-22; 19:16-18; 24:16-
17; 34:29-35; 40:34-35; I Kings 8:10-13; Isaiah 4:5-6; Ezekiel
10:4; Psalm 18:11). The purpose of the veil, smoke or a cloud
covering is to conceal the glory as a protection for eyes not
ready to behold it. Undeniably there was a social necessity to
veil the heads of women in a city given over to prostitution,
but Paul makes a virtue of the necessity. Ramsay considered the
woman's veil to be a symbol of honor, independence, and mod-
esty.[40] He comments on I Cor. 11:10 which literally translates,
"A woman ought to have authority over her head."

> Most of the ancient and modern commentators say
> the 'authority' which the woman wears on her head
> is the authority to which she is subject - a pre-
> posterous idea which a Greek scholar would laugh
> at anywhere except in the N.T., where (as they
> seem to think), Greek words may mean anything
> that the commentators choose.[41]

Feuillet points out that $\dot{\epsilon}\xi o\upsilon\sigma\dot{\iota}\alpha$ never signifies submi-
sion to the power of another bur rather of power exercised by
the individual and indicates authority, autonomy, and liberty.
He cites seven usages where the word has the sense of liberty
in I Cor. 7:37; 8:9; 9:4,5,6,12,18.[42] A woman then might have
integrity in her own personhood and be a fit partner for the
rational and spiritually minded male.

The religious and social situation of Corinth was surely
a difficult one in which to establish norms, especially in a
congregation of newly converted heathen who met next door to the
Jewish synagogue(Acts 18:7). Roman men veiled their heads in
worship except before the Father of the Gods and before the deity
known as honor or "Glory"[43], a significant point in view of
Paul's rationale of glory for establishing hair lengths and head
dress appropriate for each sex. Greek men veiled during initia-
tion rites[44] and adopted women's clothing and jewelry and long
hair in some of the cults.[45] Long hair on lads, however, also
excited the admiration of pederastic poets[46], and it may have
been this which caused Paul to call the long hair of men a "dishonor" (v. 15) as the "dishonor" of v. 4 may apply to sex reversal. Women at the same time would be stayed from the unveiling,
clothing exchange, and shorn hair which characterized their worship in some of the less decorous pagan cults.[47] Underlying
these strictures is a fundamental respect for the integrity of
both sexes. But above and beyond this Paul must speak to an un-
spoken question: "Who am I as a sexual human being? and with
whom can I establish a significant relationship?" Zeus[48] Apollo,
Hercules, Eros, and even Aphrodite[49] might opt for the love of
boys; but Paul frames a positive endorsement of heterosexuality
and an integrated Christian community, one body in the Lord.
"All things are of God" (v. 12) who ordained that man and woman
should belong to each other, equal partners, bound together in
Christ Jesus.

FOOTNOTES

1. Pseudo-Lucian, Erotes, 51.

2. Bennett Simon, Mind and Madness in Ancient Greece: the Classical Roots of Modern Psychiatry, Cornell University Press, 1978, p. 250.

3. Margaret Mead, Male and Female: A Study of the Sexes in a Changing World, Morrow and Co., New York, 1949, p. 378.

4. Sex and Temperament in Three Primitive Societies, Morrow and Co., New York, 1935, p.318.

5. Philip E. Slater, The Glory of Hera, Greek Mythology and the Greek Family, Beacon Press, 1968, p. 12.

6. Theogony, 568-592; Works and Days 55-89.

7. Theogony, 600-601. Loeb Classical Library.

8. Euripides, Hippolytus, 616-620.

9. The Book of the Secrets of Enoch 30:18.

10. op. cit., 43.

11. Hesiod, Works and Days, 87.

12. ibid., 69.

13. Semonides, On Women, 7, LCL.

14. ibid.

15. Xenophon, Oeconomicus, vii, 5-10, LCL.

16. Euripides, op. cit., 640.

17. Aristotle, Politics, 1254 b, translated by Ross.

18. ibid., 1259. b.

19. ibid., 1260. a.

20. Plato, Laws, 917. a. translated by B. Jowett.

21. Plato, Timaeus, 91, translated by B. Jowett.

22. Plato Republic V 455. Jowett.

23. Achilles Tatius II, 38. LCL.

24. Slater, op. cit., p. 16.

25. Pseudo-Luc. 17. Strato, Musa Puerilis. K.J. Dover, Greek Homosexuality, Harvard University Press, 1978, p. 134.

26. Eumenides, 658-66.

27. Eur. Hipp. 621-626.

28. La Rue Van Hook, "On the Idiomatic Use of Kara, Kephale, and Caput," Hesperia Supplement, viii, pp. 413-414. He also quotes Knapp's commentary on Verg. Aen. IV, 613. Caput "as denoting a vital part of a man's physical nature, stands often for his whole being or existence, usually with an indication of strong feeling, affection or the opposite."

29. Plato, Symposium, 192. Jowett.

30. ibid., 180.

31. Lucian, Dialogues of Courtesans, X, 307.

32. Pseudo-Lucian, op. cit., 39.

33. ibid. 40.

34. Plutarch, Amores, 750 C, LCL.

35. Antholgia Palatina, XII, 245.

36. A. Feuillet,"La Dignite et Le Role de La Femme d'apres Quelques Textes Pauliniens: Comparaison aven l'Ancien Testament" New Testament Studies, vol. 21, Jan. 1975, No. 2, pp. 157-191.

37. Strabo viii, 378ff. For a more extreme example in Athens see Lycurgus, Against Leocrates, 40.

38. Cornelius Nepos, praef. 6 f, as quoted in J.P.V.D. Baldon, Roman Women, John Day Company, New York, 1963, p. 200.

39. Eupolis fr. 120.

40. W.M. Ramsay, The Cities of St. Paul, Their Influence on His Life and Thought, London, 1907, pp. 202-3

41. ibid.

42. Feuillet, op. cit., p. 160.

43. Plutarch, Roman Questions, X.

44. Jane Harrison, Prolegomena to the Study of Greek Religion, Arno Press, 1975, p. 521ff.

45. Philostratus, Life of Apollonius, IV, xxi. Plutarch, De Mul. Virt. 261 F. 1 245 F. Athenaeus XII, 525. Socrates veils his head before discussing the mysteries of pederstic love Plato, Phaedrus, 237.

46. Anth. Pal. xii, 192   Horace, Odes i,32,19. Petronius, Satyricon, 27,31,41. Aelian, Var. Hist., ix,4. Pherecrates frag. 189; CAF I, 201.

47. Scholion, *Iliad* II, 280.

48. Xenophon, *Symposium*, 29-30, LCL.

49. *Anth*. *Pal*. xii, 86. LCL.

THE PRONOUNCEMENT STORIES IN PLUTARCH'S
             MORALIA: A TYPOLOGICAL RE-EVALUATION

                        Richard A. Spencer

              Southeastern Baptist Theological Seminary

        In an earlier paper[1] a preliminary attempt was made to
catalogue the pronouncement stories in a selection of Plutarch's
Moralia using a typology of pronouncement stories proposed by
Professor Robert C. Tannehill.[2] Owing to the advances which
the Work Group on the Pronouncement Story has made in developing this typology and a much more thorough study of the Moralia
than the original investigation allowed, a re-evaluation of
Plutarch's pronouncement stories is in order. While the present
study involves a much more extensive examination of the materials, the conclusions regarding the form and substance of
Plutarch's pronouncement stories found on pages 5 and 8 of the
earlier paper are not herein negated. The primary advance of
this study beyond the former is in the attempt to apply
Professor Tannehill's typology in its most recently developed
form to Plutarch's stories without consideration for the proposal of alternative categories or systems of typology.

        Of the 85 "pronouncement stories" treated in the former
study, 45 seemed not to fit into any of Professor Tannehill's
categories. Reviewing all of those stories along with others
collected since that study in light of Professor Tannehill's
more recent treatments of his typology proved most fruitful, in
that almost all of Plutarch's pronouncement stories fit rather
comfortably into Tannehill's categories when they are considered formally. For the present study, 133 pronouncement stories
have been collected from Plutarch's Moralia found in the Loeb
Classical Library Series volumes 2, 7, 8, 9, 10, 11, 12, 13, 14,
and 15.[3] The primary objective of this paper is to employ the
typology proposed by Tannehill on these pronouncement stories.
After that exercise, a critical evaluation of the typology for
studying Plutarch's materials, a summary of findings, and
suggestions for further study will be given.

             Types of Pronouncement Stories in Plutarch's Moralia

        Tannehill has suggested that the pronouncement stories
may be divided into two groups: I. stories in which the primary character responds to an open question or request
(Inquiries, Tests, Quests); II. stories in which the primary
character reacts to an assumption or position on the part of a
secondary character or to some situation or occasion (Corrections, Commendations, Objections, Descriptions).[4] Recently,
he has added another type, Witty Responses, which, it seems to
me, may fit well into either of the two groups mentioned above
as each case allows. Therefore, the two-group division will
serve for the following presentation, with Witty Responses and
Hybrids treated lastly. Professor Paula J. Nassen's paper of
last year[5] was arranged in this manner. Since many of the
findings in this study closely parallel her findings in the
Lives of Diogenes Laertius, a similarity of approach in presentation may facilitate dialogue and comparative analysis.

I. Inquiries, Tests, Quests: Responses to an open question or
    request

                              223

A. <u>Inquiries</u>: Fifteen of the pronouncement stories seem to fit into this category. These examples exhibit the variety of style employed in Plutarch's Inquiries:

> As often as Plato found himself in the company of persons whose conduct was unseemly, he was wont to say to himself, 'Is it possible that I am like them?'
> 88E Loeb 2:17

> Plato was asked by the Cyrenaeans to compose a set of laws and leave it for them and to give them a well-ordered government; but he refused, saying that it was difficult to make laws for the Cyrenaeans because they were so prosperous.
> For nothing is so haughty
> harsh, and ungovernable
> by nature as a man
> when he possesses what he regards as prosperity.
> 779D Loeb 10:53

> Epameinondas, when asked what was the pleasantest thing that had happened to him, replied that it was winning the battle of Leuctra while his father and mother were still living.
> 786D Loeb 10:95

> Testimony to the point is what Epameinondas the Great said to the Thebans when in winter weather the Arcadians invited them to come into the city and be quartered in their houses. He forbade it, saying 'Now they admire you and gaze at you as you do your military exercises and wrestle, but if they see you sitting by the fire and sipping your bean porridge, they will think you are no better than they are.'
> 788A Loeb 10:103

> For this reason also King Cleomenes, when a recital made at a banquet was applauded and he was asked if it did not seem excellent, replied that the others must judge, for his mind was in the Peloponnesus.
> 961B Loeb 12:331

In a number of Inquiries the primary character's views on life or his values are portrayed. In these examples, the stimulus or setting is often simply a situation or occasion which elicits a free response from the primary character. Unlike the Synoptic examples, the Inquiry is not a request for an explanation of preceding teaching; but that is because of the difference in the types of literature involved, moral essays and gospel story.

B. <u>Tests</u>: Only two tests could be found in these <u>Moralia</u>. They are these:

> Somebody asked Iphicrates the general, as though undertaking to expose him, who he was, since he was 'neither a man-at-arms, nor archer, nor targeteer'; and he answered, 'I am the man who commands and makes use of all these.'
> 99E Loeb 2:87-89

> When (Thucydides) was asked by Archidamus King of the Spartans whether he or Pericles was the better wrestler, he replied, 'Nobody can tell; for whenever I throw him in wrestling, he says he was not thrown and wins by persuading the onlookers.'
> 802C Loeb 10:181

These "tests" are not so simply designated in context as the Synoptic examples ("they sent some of the Pharisees and Herodians 'to catch him in his words'"--Mk. 12:13; "One of them, an expert in the law, tested him . . ."--Mt. 22:35; "To test him, they asked him for a sign . . ."--Mk. 8:11). Plutarch prefers to have his heroes meet adverse or contradictory circumstances more by Corrections and Objections than by Tests. One reason for the paucity of these stories in the Moralia is the uniqueness of the competitive audience Jesus has in the Jewish religious establishment and the lack of such a rival group in Plutarch's framework.

C. Quests: Only two quests appear in the essays surveyed.

> Archelaüs, king of the Macedonians, when asked at dinner for a golden cup by one whose only notion of propriety was that it is proper to receive, ordered the servant to give it to Euripides, and looking the fellow in the face remarked: 'You are just the man to ask and not receive; he to receive even when he does not ask.' 531E Loeb 7:63

> And yet when Simonides asked for something that was not just, he (Themistocles) said to him: 'Neither is he a good poet who sings contrary to metre, nor is he an equitable ruler who grants favours contrary to law.' 807B Loeb 10:205

These examples have to be fit into the category of Quests with a bit of force, for the questioners are not positively or sympathetically portrayed as are the "questers" of the Synoptic pronouncement stories. Yet these are not Inquiries, because there is tension here, dramatic inter-action which is said to be lacking in Inquiries.

II. Corrections, Commendations, Objections, Descriptions: Reactions or responses to an assumption or position of a secondary character, or to some occasion

D. Corrections: The pronouncement story with a corrective seems to be Plutarch's favorite type. Forty-one stories fit nicely into this category. These examples show their multiformity:

> A young Spartan woman, in answer to an inquiry as to whether she had already made advances to her husband, said, 'No, but he has made them to me.' 140C Loeb 2:311

> When a young man of the court had married a beautiful woman of bad reputation, Olympias said, 'That fellow has no brains; else he would not have married on sight.' 141E Loeb 2:315-317

> Theano, in putting her cloak about her exposed her arm. Somebody exclaimed, 'A lovely arm.' 'But not for the public,' said she. 142C Loeb 2:321

> Meeting a young man of his acquaintance pacing slowly by the city wall, and learning that he was avoiding a friend who expected him to give false testimony in his behalf, Zeno said: 'Fool! This man, who is dealing unfairly and unjustly, has no fear or respect

for you; and you, to defend the right, dare not
stand up to him?'   534A Loeb 7:75

The Roman people, when Carbo promised something and
confirmed his promise with an oath and a curse, unan-
imously took a counter-oath that it did not trust
him. And at Lacedaemon, when a dissolute man named
Demosthenes made a desirable motion, the people rejected it, but the ephors chose by lot one of the
elders and told him to make that same motion, in
order that it might be made acceptable to the people,
thus pouring, as it were, from a dirty vessel into a
clean one.   801B-C Loeb 10:173-175

So it was, for example, with Leo of Byzantium; he
once came to address the Athenians when they were in
political discord, and when they laughed at him
because he was a little man, he said, 'What if you
should see my wife, who hardly comes up to my knee?'
Then when they laughed louder, 'And yet,' he said,
'little as we are, when we quarrel with each other,
the city of Byzantium is not big enough to hold us.'
                                        804B Loeb 10:189

And at Thermopylae, after the encirclement, wishing
to save two men of noble family, he [Leonidas] gave
one a dispatch to carry and sent him off, but the man
refused, saying angrily: 'I came with you to fight,
not to carry messages' and when he ordered the other
man to take a message to the Spartan authorities, he
answered: 'I shall do my duty better if I stay here,
and the news will be better if I stay here'; and he
picked up his shield and took his place in the ranks.
                                        866C Loeb 11:81

Every one of these stories is composed of a response to
a situation or occasion, or a comment which is given in indirect
discourse. In only four of the stories does the situation or
setting require a verbal response from the primary character.
At the same time, all of the responses except two are verbal (a
few in indirect discourse), thus emphasizing Plutarch's concern
for the well-timed word or appropriate word for the occasion.
Therefore, Plutarch's corrective apophthegms are voluntary
retorts by notable figures.

When compared with the Synoptic Corrections, the first
and most obvious difference is the high profile of the secondary
characters there--the situations are all given in direct statements or questions, except for Lk. 4:42-43. This means that the
tension or conflict between the primary and secondary characters
is much less pronounced in the Moralia than in the Synoptics,
and also that the way in which the correction is delivered and
the objective of the correction are different.

E. Commendations: Six stories fit into this category:

When Caesar gave orders that the statues in honour
of Pompey which had been thrown down, should be restored, Cicero said to him, 'You have restored
Pompey's statues, but you have made your own secure.'
                                        91A Loeb 2:31

Demetrius of Phalerum was quite right when, in reference to a saying of Euripides:

Wealth is inconstant, lasting but a day,
and also:
Small things may cause an overthrow; one day
Puts down the mighty and exalts the low,
He said that it was almost all admirably put, but
it would have been better if he had said not 'one
day,' but 'one second of time.' 104A-B Loeb 2:119

We can listen on the one hand to Polyneices, when, on
being asked
What is the loss of country? A great ill?
he replies
The greatest; and no words can do it justice.
599D Loeb 7:521

Alexander, who, seeing Diogenes at Corinth, admiring
him for his natural gifts, and being astonished by
his spirit and greatness, said, 'If I were not
Alexander, I should be Diogenes.'
782A Loeb 10:65-67

Python, when he was admired and honoured by the
Athenians for slaying Cotys, said, 'God did this,
borrowing from me the hand that did the deed.'
816E Loeb 10:253

This might be classified as a Correction, according to how one
determines the angle of Python in making reply.

Colotes himself, while hearing a lecture of Epicurus
on natural philosophy, suddenly cast himself down
before him and embraced his knees.
1117B Loeb 14:249

Only this last example has a non-verbal response. Only
in 599D does the setting require a response.

F. Objections: Only Corrections are used more frequently than Objections in the materials under consideration.
Twenty-seven stories belong to this category. Some examples
are these:

Leo of Byzantium, being reviled by a humpback for the
weakness of his eyes, said, 'You reproach me with
that which can happen to any man, while you bear on
your back the mark of God's wrath!' 88F Loeb 2:19

The Roman, on being admonished by his friends because
he had put away a virtuous, wealthy, and lovely wife,
reached out his shoe and said, 'Yes, this is beautiful to look at, and new, but nobody knows where it
pinches me.' 141A Loeb 2:315

It is reported that Alexinus the sophist was roundly
abusing Stilpon of Megara in the Promenade when one
of the audience said: 'But he was praising you the
other day.' 'Exactly,' said Alexinus, 'he is the
most honest and outspoken of men.' 536B Loeb 7:87

Lycurgus said at Athens when abused for buying off an
informer: 'What do you think of my character as a
citizen, when after all these years in office I am
caught giving money dishonestly, instead of taking
it?' 541F Loeb 7:131

And it is said that Sophocles, when defending himself
against the charge of dementia brought by his sons,
read aloud the entrance song of the chorus in the
Oedipus at Colonus, which begins:
> Of this region famed for horses
> Thou hast, stranger, reached the fairest
> Dwellings in the land,
> Bright Colonus, where the sweet-voiced
> Nightingale most loves to warble
> In the verdant groves;

and the song aroused such admiration that he was
escorted from the court as if from the theatre, with
the applause and shouts of those present.
785A Loeb 10:87

When Timotheus was hissed for being new-fangled and
was said to be committing sacrilege upon music,
Euripides told him to be of good courage, for in a
little while the theatres would be at his feet.
795D Loeb 10:141

Crassus the orator, when Domitius said to him, 'It
was you, was it not, who wept when a lamprey died
that you kept in a tank?' retorted with the question, 'It was you, was it not, who buried three
wives without shedding a tear?' 811A Loeb 10:223

In his Objections, Plutarch is more interested in the
recovery of standing of the primary character. For example,
he introduces 541F this way: "There is a certain graceful
effect in showing that the opposite of what one is charged with
would have been shameful and base." He is concerned to show
the reader how great men handled objections (and thereby to
instruct the reader in like recovery by use of the well-timed
word).

One way Plutarch effects the recovery of his heroes is to
take the objection and capitalize on it, as in 541F, so that the
hero speaks quite directly to the objection. Another way of
handling the objection is to raise an even more penetrating
objection, and so dismiss the initial objection (88F). In
almost all Objection recoveries a correction of some sort is
delivered.

G. Descriptions: Seventeen stories fit into this category. Some stories which bordered on the status of "short story"
fit in here. One area which seems to need clarification is the
relation (or distinction) between apophthegm, pronouncement
story, and short story. Plutarch's style is so strongly influenced by his delight in apophthegmatic rhetoric that borderline
cases of "pronouncement stories" are not infrequent in the
Moralia. It seems to me that in an apophthegm the saying bears
almost all the weight of the situation-response; in the pronouncement story (i.e. the Synoptic pronouncement story) the
saying requires the story much more in order for its meaning to
be delivered; when description of the setting or saying or both
becomes the dominant interest, the apophthegmatic material
borders on a short story.

Here are some of the various examples of Descriptions:

Aristodemus, king of the Messenians in the war against
the Spartans, when dogs howled like wolves, and
quitch-grass began to grow around his ancestral

hearth, and the seers were alarmed by these signs,
lost heart and hope by his forebodings, and slew
himself by his own hand.   168F Loeb 2:479

But Timesias of Clazomenae was in other respects a
good man in his service to the State, but by doing
everything himself he had aroused rancour and hatred;
but of this he was unaware until the following
incident took place:--Some boys were knocking a
knuckle-bone out of a hole, but the boy who had
struck at it said: 'I'd like to knock the brains
out of Timesias as truly as this has been knocked
out of the hole.' Timesias, hearing this and understanding that dislike of him had permeated all the
people, returned home and told his wife what had
happened; and directing her to pack up and follow
him, he went immediately away from his house and out
from the city.   812A-B Loeb 10:229

Thus Zeno, the disciple of Parmenides, after an unsuccessful attempt upon the life of the tyrant
Demylus, revealed when tried in the fire that the
teaching of Parmenides in his heart was like the
purest gold and equal to the proof, and demonstrated
by the evidence of deeds that what a great man fears
is shame, whereas pain is feared by children and weak
women and men with such women's souls, for he bit off
his tongue and spat it in the tyrant's face.
                                  1126D Loeb 14:307

In all seventeen stories, the settings or situations are
non-verbal (one is verbal and non-verbal), and in the responses
six are verbal, nine are non-verbal, and two are both verbal and
non-verbal. The high rate of non-verbal components indicates
that the Descriptions are given as narrated or "described"
stories with little premium on direct discourse and intensity
of relationships between primary and secondary characters.

III. Witty Responses, Hybrids

    H. Witty Responses: Although humor and salience may be
characteristic of some of the stories of another type, stories
belong here which have their primary interest in a witty or
"snappy" response. There are twenty-one of these, among them
these examples:

There is a jocose remark attributed to Epameinondas
in regard to a good man who fell ill and died about
the time of the battle of Leuctra: 'Good Heavens!
How did he find time to die when there was so much
going on?'   136D Loeb 2:287

On one occasion, asked by a Cynic for a drachma, he
(Antigonus) answered: 'Kings do not give so little';
and when the other countered, 'Then give me a
talent,' he replied, 'Or Cynics take so much.'
                                  531F Loeb 7:63

Once in Rhodes a teacher of literature, giving a
display in the theatre, asked to be given a line; a
man offered him
    Clear out double quick from the island, most
    wicked of all men alive!   737C Loeb 9:227

> Phocion also made a witty retort, when after Demades
> had screamed 'The Athenians will put you to death,'
> he replied 'Yes, if they are crazy; but you are the
> one whom they will execute, if they are sane.'
>
> 811A Loeb 10:223

Some of these stories are little more than "one-liners"
with a set-up. Others seem to place value in showing the ill-
use of an otherwise worthy word. Some are turns of phrase and
plays on words. Still others derive their sharpness from social
or customary values (such as having a pretty wife, 525E). The
center of gravity in all cases seems to be the saying or
response. It is there that the climax comes or the surprising
turn is introduced.

I. Hybrids: Only two hybrid stories appear in these
materials. They are these:

> Tiribazus, they say, when an attempt was made by the
> Persians to arrest him, drew his sword, being a man
> of great strength, and fought desperately. But when
> the men protested and cried out that they were arrest-
> ing him by the King's command, he instantly threw
> down his sword and held out his hands to be bound.
>
> 168E Loeb 2:477

> The statesman needs to . . . be obliged to say, as
> Iphicrates did when defeated through the eloquence
> of Aristophon's orators, 'My opponents' actor is
> better, but superior my play.'   801F Loeb 10:177

Both of these stories are correction-commendation hybrids.
There is a non-verbal stimulus in both stories (the men's
"protesting" and the orators' "eloquence" in these instances
amount to no more than "when x occurred.")

Critical Evaluation, Summary, and Suggestions

In evaluating this typological exercise, the principal
question to be addressed is whether the types proposed and
defined by Professor Tannehill are well-fit or ill-fit to these
materials. This is a subjective and perhaps circuitous query,
since the present investigation from its inception (that is,
even during the survey of the Moralia) has been colored by a
search for pronouncement stories of the types designated by
Tannehill. Not many stories were excluded, though, because
they did not fit the requirements for Tannehill's types. Most
often, they were rejected as incomplete pronouncement stories
(lacking a satisfactory stimulus/setting element, e.g. "For
example, the retort of Epameinondas to Callistratus, who
reproached the Thebans and the Argives because Oedipus killed
his father and Orestes killed his mother: 'When we had driven
out the doers of those deeds, you took them in.'" 810F) or as
apophthegmatic short stories. By this, I mean to say that so
long as one is considering the form of pronouncement stories,
Professor Tannehill's typology quite adequately covers the range
of examples found in the Moralia which are engaged here.

At the same time, the types are not so evenly represented
in Plutarch's Moralia as they are in the Synoptic Gospels. The
following illustration shows the distribution of these 133 pronouncement stories according to type and the percentages which
those examples represent of the whole set of stories. For the
purpose of an illustrative comparison (a "test," as it were),

the table will show the distribution of the pronouncement
stories in Diogenes Laertius's _Lives_ as Professor Nassen has
categorized them.

Plutarch (133 examples)		Diogenes (393 examples)	
Corrections	41--(31%)	158--(40%)	
Objections	27--(20%)	61--(16%)	
Witty Responses	21--(16%)	devised since this study	
Descriptions	17--(13%)	65--(17%)	
Inquiries	15--(11%)	90--(23%)	
Commendations	6--(4.5%)	7--(2%)	
Quests	2--(1.5%)	4--(1%)	
Hybrids	2--(1.5%)	4--(1%)	
Tests	2--(1.5%)	1--(0%)	

This table shows a definite preference for Corrections,
Objections, Witty Responses, Descriptions, and Inquiries, and
very little preference for Commendations, Quests, Hybrids, and
Tests. Considering the role and function of the primary and
secondary characters in these types of stories, such a distribution is not surprising. Plutarch intends to quote from the
lives and experiences of "great men" as examples of how his
readers might come to a better life. He uses heroes as extraordinary examples of human greatness and secondary characters
to represent the normal, customary perspectives of men. Corrections show the hero to be master of life's experiences, as he is
mature, independent, and uncommonly insightful. In Objections,
the hero shows the reader how a worthy person recovers from
abuse, criticism, and such experiences. The well-timed word,
indicative of the man of _paideia_, is best delivered by the
types of stories used by Plutarch most frequently.

Tests and Quests are not so serviceable for Plutarch in
his attempt to educate his readers by examples. In them, much
greater interest in and sympathy for the secondary character
is given than Plutarch allows. In the Quest, the focus of
attention is on the quester and his fate. For Plutarch, the
center of attention is almost always the primary character who
corrects, recovers from objections, and delivers the well-timed
retort. It may well be that Tests and Quests are not really a
part of Plutarch's repertoire of pronouncement stories, and that
they may be deleted from the typology as applied to his materials. Regarding Tests, it was mentioned above that the two
Tests found do not so clearly appear to "test" the primary
character as do the Synoptic examples, and the two examples
might be re-assigned to Objections or Inquiries. Regarding
Quests, it was noted that the two examples are somewhat forcibly
fit into that category.

While the Commendations and Hybrids are few in number,
those categories should be retained, with reservations. The
Commendations in Plutarch differ significantly from those in
the Synoptics in that in the _Moralia_ Commendations one great
figure commends another great figure: Cicero commends Caesar;
Demetrius commends Euripides; Plutarch commends Polyneices, the
primary character; Alexander commends Diogenes; Python commends
God; Colotes commends Epicurus. There is no humble widow giving
her mites nor helpless centurion asking for help being commended
here. In spite of this difference, the commendation function is
the central feature of these stories. Therefore, the category
is an appropriate one for Plutarch's stories. Hybrids are
expremely scarce also; but that type is by definition a com-
posite of other types, and the hybrids shown in this study
would be a sub-type of Corrections, which is Plutarch's favorite.

In answer to the question whether the types are well-fit or ill-fit to Plutarch's pronouncement stories, all the categories serve the Moralia apophthegms well except for Tests and Quests. There may be other ways in which the pronouncement stories of Plutarch may be arranged, for example, the sayings of a "Correction" and an "Inquiry" may make their point by arguing a fortiori and thus those two stories may be more alike than two randomly-selected "Corrections" or "Inquiries." The multiformity of the examples in the types proposed by Tannehill must not be overlooked. Nevertheless, this typology is quite helpful in getting a hold on the many diverse pronouncement stories in the Moralia.

Having delineated the types of pronouncement stories in a selection of Plutarch's Moralia and Plutarch's preference for certain types, we now are better prepared to proceed to a study of the values and opinions treated in these stories, and the ways in which affirmation and negation of those values and opinions are made. Further study might analyze the varieties of stylistic forms within the pronouncement story types (especially the Corrections, Objections, Witty Responses, Description, and Inquiries) with a view to their usefulness in affirming or rejecting the values/assumptions/opinions represented by the primary and secondary characters in the stories.

Notes

[1]"A Typology of Pronouncement Stories in a Selection of Plutarch's Moralia," distributed to the members of the Work Group on the Pronouncement Story at the AAR-SBL Annual Meeting in December, 1977.

[2]His paper entitled "A Typology of Synoptic Pronouncement Stories" was read at the AAR-SBL Annual Meeting in St. Louis in 1976. That typology has been developed by Professor Tannehill in several successive treatments of the pronouncement stories, especially in his article "Types and Functions of Synoptic Apophthegms" to appear in Aufstieg und Niedergang der römischen Welt, ed. by H. Temporini and W. Haase.

[3]As noted in the earlier paper, the following distribution of labor on the Moralia was agreed upon by Professor John E. Alsup and myself: Prof. Alsup--Loeb volumes 1, 3, 4, 5, 6; Prof. Spencer--Loeb volumes 2, 7, 8, 9, 13; both Alsup and Spencer--Loeb volumes 10, 11, 12, 14, and 15. It is this division of labor which has provided the sample of materials for this study.

[4]I prefer to refer to these stories as Inquiries rather than Inquiry stories (for example), because referring to them as Inquiry stories connotes more about the formal commonality among the representative examples of that type than can be shown. That which is basic to all "pronouncement stories" is their apophthegmatic quality, the "pronouncement." There is no uniform pattern for Inquiries (or any of the other types). The multiformity of examples within the pronouncement story types is mentioned in this paper and needs further study. Such a study is beyond the scope of the present exercise.

[5]Paula J. Nassen, "The Pronouncement Story in Diogenes Laertius' Lives and Opinions of Eminent Philosophers," in the Society of Biblical Literature 1978 Seminar Papers (Scholars Press, 1978), 2:11-19. Professor Nassen's work has been most helpful in the execution of the present study.

RELIGION AND SOCIOPOLITICAL STRUCTURE IN EARLY ISRAEL:
AN ETHNO-ARCHAEOLOGICAL APPROACH

Frank S. Frick
Albion College

With the progressive and increasingly convincing critique
of the amphictyonic and bedouin analogy models as heuristic devices for an understanding of the place of religious ideology
and practice in early Israel (ca. 1250-1000 B.C.), the need has
become more pressing for the development of new models.
De Geus (1976) and others have succeeded in pointing out the
numerous and weighty problems in accepting the amphictyonic
thesis as definitive, or even worse, as being the Procrustean
bed to which all future studies must be made to conform. Consider this partial list of difficulties: the dominance of linguistic and textual studies; the unstated assumptions concerning the relationships between biblical texts and archaeological data; the often simplistic assertions about the identity
of the particular culture which is responsible for supposed
remains (Franken 1976); the uncertainties and disagreements
about what constitutes cultic remains; and especially the lack
of adequate comprehensive research designs to permit the systematic use of the data coming from the excavations.

    In the light of these and other difficulties, it would
appear that what is needed is a rather thoroughgoing reassess-
ment of much of the available data based on different starting
points. At the very minimum it would seem desirable to sort
out as many as possible of those items in our treatment of
early Israelite religion as we can, in order to straighten out
some of the circular reasoning which has become entrenched in
our thinking and writing due to the dominance of the amphictyonic theory. As one step in this direction, it is the intention of this paper to focus on some suggestions from what is
happening in processual archaeology as providing some useful
heuristic models for the continuing study of the religion of
early Israel. In particular, emphasis will be placed on the
necessity of bringing more closely together the "ecological
approach" employed by anthropological archaeologists and other
social scientists and the "humanistic approach" of historians
of religion. Kent Flannery (1972: 399f.) has aptly described
the limitations of either approach when pursued in isolation
from the other:

    "The limited success of so-called 'ecological approaches'
    to complex societies has led to understandable criticism
    from humanists...Up until now, it has mainly been the
    humanists who have studied the informational aspects of
    complex societies--art, religion, ritual, writing systems,
    and so on. The 'ecologists' have largely contented them-
    selves with studying exchanges of mater and energy...Hu-
    manists must cease thinking that ecology 'dehumanizes'
    history, and ecologists must cease to regard art,

religion, and ideology as mere 'epiphenomena' without
causal significance. In an ecosystem approach to the analysis of human societies, everything which transmits information is within the province of ecology".

Flannery and other American and British processual archaeologists clearly operate within a systemic framework, specifically, general systems theory. The variant adopted is an
ecosystemic approach which concentrates on the relations which
exist between the various societal subsystems and their environment. These archaeologists also tend to accept the premise
that the given system is basically in equilibrium and that most
aspects of the system work to maintain that equilibrium, en-
couraging negative feedback and homeostasis.

Following such a lead, this paper will set forth at least
a partial outline for an ecosystem approach to the analysis of
early Israel in which the data deriving from archaeology, textual studies, and ethnographic analogies will be utilized in
the explanation of the pre-state sociopolitical organization
of Israel, and in particular, the place of religion in that society. In such an explanation, religion will be seen as but
one aspect of the culture of early Israel, so that a particular
sociopolitical organization is its necessary presupposition.
In other words, the religion of early Israel is rather the expression (albeit a very important one) of a particular cultural
identity rather than its sole foundation.

Certainly it goes without saying that one's definition of
religion is determinative of how one reads the material remains. In this regard it has been rather common practice to
follow the program of Hawkes (1954) who orders the information
available from the archaeological record into four levels of
increasingly more difficult inference. He maintains that techniques and then subsistence economies are fairly easy to infer,
but to infer to the sociopolitical institutions is considerably
harder, and to infer to the religious institutions and spiritual life is the most difficult inference of all. One of the
most important contributions of the "new" archaeology for those
who are concerned with the religious dimensions of a people's
life, is the development of research designs and methods in
which attention is explicitly given to the widest possible
range of religious impact on the material remains of a culture.
No longer need there be a religious interpretation of archaeological remains as a kind of court of last resort. As an
aside at this point, it is assumed that even the novice would
recognize that field archaeology has priority here in terms of
providing the basic data for all other archaeological endeavors; all other archaeology is of the arm-chair variety, trying
to interpret the data, seeking correlative data, etc. But as
soon as the archaeologist goes beyond the acquisition of a data
base, he or she has entered into a different realm of archaeology in which inductive logic and analogy play crucial roles
and from which one can generate testable hypotheses which can
then feed back into the acquisition process. In that light,
field archaeology by itself has no relevance for the study of
religion; but without it there could be no such study in relation to archaeology at all. So, the assumption is made here
that religion, when viewed in dynamic and holistic terms, does

make a discernible imprint on material culture. The ancient
human community resembles the modern one in that both are or-
ganismic, i.e., living systems. Religion functioned and had
meaning within a whole ideological-behavioural network of mu-
tual adaptations, or symbiotic situations.

In our attempts to understand a society such as early Israel, in which religious ideology and practice seem to have
operated as the functional equivalents to political power, more
attention needs to be given to the work of Roy Rappaport, one
of the most influential contemporary American anthropologists
who is working on religious function and meaning in such a context. Unfortunately, much of his work has been published in
sources which are often difficult to obtain, so he has not received the attention he deserves (Rappaport 1968; 1970; 1971a;
1971b). Rappaport's work begins with the assumption that the
form and structure of the subsystems responsible for regulation
and control in non-state societies are not as clearly defined
as are those operating in states. Generations of anthropologists have asserted that such institutions are "embedded" within the wider social organization of the society. Rappaport's
principal contribution, for our present purposes, is that he
shows that in many societies homeostatic mechanisms are part
and parcel of sanctified ritual activity:

> "In technologically simple societies--whose authorities,
> in the complete or relative absence of power, stand upon
> their sanctity--the sacred and the numinous form part of
> an encompassing cybernetic loop which maintains homeo-
> stasis among variables critical to the group's survival"
> (Rappaport 1971a: 39).

In Rappaport's work, the role of religion (or, as he prefers, "the sacred") in human communities and in the regulation
of social and ecological systems is approached through ritual
as the public expression of religious ideology. Operating out
of a "systems model," he sees religious ritual as a powerful
force in the homeostasis of a system:

> "Rituals, arranged in protracted cycles...articulate the
> local and regional systems, and, furthermore, regulate
> relations within each of the subsystems, and in the
> larger systems as a whole" (1971b: 60).

Religious activities are thus primarily seen as part of the
informational processes of human societies. What then are the
particular aspects of religious rituals that uniquely suit them
to function as homeostats and communication devices? Rappaport
stresses both content and occurrence. Content is particularly
important in the transmission of quantitative or more-less information, and is of significance mainly within single systems
or subsystems. Occurrence, on the other hand, is particularly
important in the transmission of qualitative yes-no information
across the border of separate systems or subsystems. The content aspect of ritual is well illustrated by Rappaport's own
field work among the Maring of New Guinea. The Maring transmit information concerning the amount of military support that
may be expected from a friendly group in future warlike endeavors via ritual. Calendric ceremonies occurring at the same

time every year, as well as longer-term ritual cycles can help
to maintain undergraded environments, limit intergroup raiding,
adjust man-land ratios, facilitate trade, redistribute natural
resources, and "level" differences in wealth (Rappaport 1970:
55f.). Some rituals are thus public counting devices and as
such they can play an important role in regulation by revealing
the states, not otherwise apparent, of important systemic variables. On the basis of such information, corrective action may
be taken if necessary or possible. Calendric rituals are of
chief importance with respect to the content dimension, while
non-calendric rituals communicate information by their very
occurrence. A non-calendric ritual occurrence may thus be a
"yes-no" signal which may have been triggered by the achieve-
ment or violation of a particular state or range of states of
a "more-less" variable and, because of the sanctity associated
with it, is a statement free of ambiguity.

In essence, therefore, the acts and interactions of ritual
are seen as rendering complex, fluctuating data into a form on
which concrete decisions and action can be taken. Ritual content, e.g., including meaning, might be used as a "program" to
keep the agricultural cycle on the right track; ritual occurrence might be used as an unambiguous signal to neighbors that
the society is ready for warfare (cf. Judg 19: 29-30; 1 Sam 11:
7). Finally, because of the sacred nature of these ritually
transformed pronouncements or proclaimed consensuses, the information and decisions are assigned truth value by their sacred context (Rappaport 1971a:69). The act and interactions
encompassed by ritual transform the ambiguous and indeterminate
into the unambiguous and believable.

In the assessment of this author, Rappaport's work provides a most important starting point for the construction of
a more comprehensive theory for explaining the ways in which
religion can contribute to the formation of social units which
transcend local kin groups. In some societies religion plays
a much more important part in such a process than it does in
others. This point might seem so obvious as to be not worth
mentioning were it not for the fact that since Durkheim and
Weber, one scholar after another has put forward a theory of
the impact of religion upon social structure. Many of these
have made little advance over a simple Radcliffe-Brown sense
that religious rites aid social integration by inculcating and
strengthening the proper sentiments of loyalty and identification with the collectivity, or by stating and resolving conflicts within the group. Rappaport's work is valuable because
it takes seriously the relationship between ideology, social
organization, and subsistence technology, a relationship which
might be diagrammed as follows (cf. Smith 1976: 496):

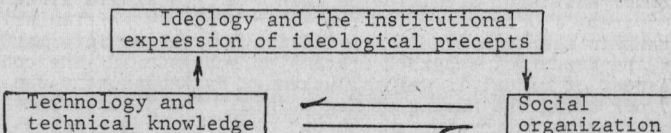

```
        ┌─────────────────────────────────────┐
        │   Ideology and the institutional     │
        │ expression of ideological precepts   │
        └─────────────────────────────────────┘
               ↑                      ↓
 ┌──────────────────────┐      ┌──────────────────┐
 │ Technology and       │ ←——— │ Social           │
 │ technical knowledge  │ ———→ │ organization     │
 └──────────────────────┘      └──────────────────┘
```

As such relationships are taken into consideration, the question arises of how to understand the particular pre-state or non-state form of sociopolitical organization found in early Israel, a form in which the sacred could and did function in ways similar to those outlined by Rappaport. If we choose from those non-state types of societies which have been described in the literature of social anthropology, it would seem that there are two possible choices: tribe or chiefdom. In making the choice, Mendenhall's advice should be taken:

"The point of the historical and religious problem is to understand, not merely label, the functioning of a surprisingly large social solidarity that seemingly had a minimum of permanent political structures or military organization and resources" (1976: 133).

Or, as Gottwald has said in commenting on the distinctiveness of early Israel:

"...the Israelite tribes were not so much unique in their basic form of segmented organization by extended families, protective associations and tribes, but decisively different in constituting a very broad alliance of such units that managed to throw off the central authority and take over its entrepreneurial socio-economic, military and religious functions at the village and tribal levels" (1976: 149).

Our problem is thus how to explain the way in which religion functioned within a given form of sociopolitical organization to maintain a non-state alliance of basically independent villages over a space of about 200 years. Can such an alliance best be understood operating from a model of tribalism or of chiefdom?

The very concept of "tribe" or "tribal society" is not one subject to ready definition in anthropological circles. In an essay, which provided the occasion for an extended discussion on the problem of tribe, Morton Fried said:

"Unfortunately, if I had to select one word in the vocabulary of anthropology as the single most egregious case of meaninglessness, I would have to pass over 'tribe' in favor of 'race.' I am sure, however, that 'tribe' figures prominently on the list of putative technical terms ranked in order of degree of ambiguity as reflected in multifarious definitions" (1968: 4f.).

Certainly there is little agreement on what constitutes a "tribe" in the essays contained in the above-mentioned volume. If agreement cannot be reached on such a cross-cultural level, what kind of situation presents itself when the referent is limited to the "tribe" in early Israel? Probably the most thoroughgoing recent discussion of the Israelite "tribe" is that of C. H. J. de Geus, in which he concludes:

"One may conclude therefore that an Israelite tribe was always a 'branch' of the whole people, and had no meaning without that whole. At the same time the tribes expressed

the inevitable territorial, linguistic, and historical
differentiation. The tribe was for the Israelite the manner in which the people functioned for him in his region,
though he remained aware that the people was more than the
tribe. That the contours of the concept 'tribe' remain
more vague than those of the clan, is due to the nature of
the Israelite tribe. This vagueness is increased by the
way the concepts mišpāḥā and šēbeṭ are used...That the
'tribe' remains so vague, therefore requires a structural
and not a historical explanation. Israelite tribes were
regional alliances of essentially independent clans. Real
power resided with the clans, or a few of them, but not at
a tribal level" (1976: 150, 156).

What is particularly telling about de Geus' conclusion is
that the tribe appears to be an unsatisfactory starting point
in the search for the development of those federations or alliance networks which made up early Israel. If, in fact, tribal
names functioned primarily as territorial indications and
tribes were regional alliances of essentially independent clans
which were the fully functional social and political units, the
explanation of the development of the larger unit must begin
with the clan. If, furthermore, clan and village often coin-
cide, archaeological tests can be proposed which can support a
developmental model. While such archaeological tests can show
developing linkages and alliance networks on the village level,
such tests have so far proved unsuccessful on the tribal level.

Certainly one of the most prominent examples of a tribal
confederacy cited in ethnographic literature is that of the
Iroquois, a seventeenth-century political organization in what
is now New York state, composed of the Seneca, Cayuga, Ononda-
ga, Oneida, and Mohawk tribes. William Engelbrecht has made
the attempt to infer the existence of the League of the Iroquois on the basis of ceramic patterning within and between
Iroquois village sites (1974). In his study Engelbrecht used
two different coefficients. One was a measure of ceramic homo-
geneity (Whallon 1968). The assumption is that the greater the
heterogeneity of ceramic designs within any site, the greater
the contact with other sites. The other measure used to infer
degree of contact between sites was the Brainerd-Robinson coefficient of agreement (Brainerd 1951; Robinson 1951). In this
case it is assumed that if a pair of contemporaneous sites
shares a higher coefficient of agreement than another contemporaneous pair, there has been greater contact between the former
pair. Engelbrecht thus assumed that if the formation of the
League is reflected in ceramic production, one would expect to
see an increase in similarity between sites in different tribal
territories within the area of the League and an increase in
heterogeneity of ceramics within the sites in the area but not
included in the League itself. For the latter, sites in the
Niagra frontier, outside the area of the League, were examined
for control. Engelbrecht's conclusion was that the existence
of the League of the Iroquois was not reflected in the ceramic
evidence.

This author knows of no similar test which has been devised and applied to early Israel in order to infer the existence of tribes as such or of a tribal league. For a later

period and on a different level of sociopolitical organization, Holladay (1976) has convincingly demonstrated that even the commonly held "northern"/"southern" dichotomy of ceramic forms, in fact represents a chronological rather than geopolitical distinction. Studies such as McClellan's (1975) might be utilized in developing an archaeological test along the lines of Engelbrecht's which could contribute significantly to the discussion of the nature of the formation of early Israel and of the level at which alliance networks developed.

De Geus' assertion that the clan/village is the basic sociopolitical unit, and the one around which alliance networks are formed, has considerable support in ethnographic literature. E.g., Gluckman's observations of the Lozi in northwest Rhodesia demonstrate the central significance of the clan/village (1959). Among the Lozi, villages are the only corporate groups of kindred. The Lozi family is thus both a political unit and a kinship group. In land-holding the village is the largest and the ultimate political unit. Inter-village linkages among the Lozi are called "vicinages" (Gluckman 1959: 71). One's vicinage is constituted by those villages close enough to his own for there to be frequent contact.

Likewise, among the Shona of southern Rhodesia, as reported by Holleman (1959), the village is primary and the next unit above the village is the dunhu, which comprises a varying number of separate and mutually independent villages. The dunhu is well-defined territorially and has a nuclear body of agnatic kinsmen who are spread over more than one village. It is the dunhu which holds the communal right over all the territory within its borders. It is also the head of the dunhu who initiates the non-calendric rituals. Holleman observes that rituals on the dunhu level are the most important ones, and that "Tribal rituals are...singularly few in number. The thanksgiving celebrations at the end of a good season do not appear ever to have been held...on behalf of the whole tribe" (1959: 377).

Edward Winter's work among the Iraqw is most valuable for our purposes, concentrating as it does on the relationship existing between ritual and social integration (Winter 1966). The three levels of organization among the Iraqw below that of "people" are those of the household, village, and "county" (an area of ca. 30-40 square miles). Social cohesion at the level of the household is obviously provided by kinship, so Winter concentrates on the village and "county." The village performs services for the households which they cannot provide for themselves and its existence is thus necessary for practical reasons of subsistence. Such practical reasons, however, do not seem to account for the existence of "counties." Why, e.g., are some rites carried out at the level of the "county" when they could be done at the village level or at one place for the Iraqw people as a whole? Winter's conclusion is that the organization of communal ritual on a "county" basis makes sense in terms of the patterns of rainfall variation (1966: 169f.). This variation causes a group of people who see themselves as facing similar rainfall conditions to cooperate ritually to solve the problem, as they visualize it, and since a group of this sort invariably involves an area larger than a village and yet smaller than the entire people, this cooperation takes place on an intermediate level. Thus the widest territorial group which acts in a unitary fashion, the "county," is defined and organized in purely ritual terms. Might the "tribe" in early Israel have been similarly defined and organized?

Turning to work more directly related to the Near East, a recent study by Diakonoff (1975) has dealt with the rural community in the ancient Near East. His observations are particularly relevant when viewed in the context of the peasant revolt model, for he insists that peasants outside of the state sector inevitably create their own organization, a communal organization:

"Communal organization was the only organization inside which a freeman could exercise the maximum of civic liberties. Among them were the liberty to possess movables, to take part in the communal proprietorship in land, and to participate in the self-government of a rural, city, or 'nome' community" (Diakonoff 1975: 123).

In the several forms of such communal organization cited by Diakonoff, two are relevant for our purposes--the 'clan,' extended family, or lineage community; and the rural community consisting of related or non-related families settling in one neighborhood. Both Jankowska (1969) and Heltzer (1976) also have dealt with communal organization in Arrapḫa and Ugarit respectively. In both cases the strength of the village as the base of the social and economic structure is evident. In both, the communal character of the village is stressed, a character which "having been formed by thousands of years of the kinship system of economics, could withstand the most powerful king, owing to its traditional regimentation of all aspects of economic and social life" (Jankowska 1969: 282).

Bringing together these examples from ethnographic studies and Near Eastern archival material, and applying them to early Israel's sociopolitical development, we might conclude that the "tribe" did not exist as a ready-made unit to provide the necessary communal organization in the face of the defection of Israelite villages from the domination of the city-states. One should not conclude, however, that early Israel consisted of an anarchical mass of individuals, but of rural communities which already possessed many of the mechanisms for self-defense and cooperation of a now free rural population which could continue to exist and prosper outside of the state sector.

Beginning then with the village community as the sociopolitical base upon which early Israel was formed, we have yet to examine the particular forms and institutions through which the sacred could operate as a functional alternative to political power. In other words, what was the nature of and locus of authority? If authorities are taken to be loci in communications networks from which directives emanate, then human societies can be placed on a continuum, from societies that are regulated in the near absence of human authorities through societies in which highly sanctified authorities have little actual power, to societies in which authorities have great power but less sanctity (Rappaport 1971b: 72). In such a context we are interested in exploring the ways in which sanctity permitted the progressive centralization of regulatory hierarchies. How did the sanctity of the leaders of early Israel make it possible for them to command the men and control the resources that eventually provided their successors with the kind of power known in the state? What kind of leaders were the šōphetîm and what was the concept of Israel in which they exercised their leadership? In what follows, it will be suggested that the social type "chiefdom" provides a useful explanatory model for understanding both the šōphetîm as religious and political leaders, and the form of society in which they functioned. Some possible archaeological tests for such a model will also be suggested.

The great merit of the work of Elman Service (1962, 1971, 1975) has been, as pointed out by Renfrew (1972: 71f.), the recognition of the failure to look closely at societies which range somewhere between the egalitarian tribal and state, and to discuss their functioning without assuming that they are only intermediate. Service has singled out "chiefdom" as a society with an identifiable degree of social integration and has presented several features which are sometimes seen in such societies but are generally lacking in those tribal socities sometimes called "egalitarian." Sahlins (1958) has observed that there is a wide variety of sociopolitical complexity within the class of societies that can be designated chiefdoms, and Goldman (1970), who examined the same group of societies as Sahlins, set forth three "types" in a sequence which can be measured by increases in power and authority--the "traditional," "open," and "stratified" (Goldman 1970: 20). Renfrew differentiates between group-oriented and individualizing chiefdoms (1972: 74). Given this variety of subtypes, what do chiefdoms have in common that differentiates them from the e-galitarian society? In egalitarian socieites ritual activities are usually organized as a network of acts and interactions for the transmission of information which all members of the society enter into as equals, except where age, sex, and achieved status are imposed as barriers. That is, at least for the duration of the ritual activity the flow of information is from all to all, and there is complete interaction among the human components of the system. In chiefdoms, on the other hand, there is a sanctified ritual separation between the chief and the remainder of the population, and ritual interaction reflects this separation. The flow of information is from all to the chief and from the chief to all. Chiefdoms, like egalitarian societies, rely on sanctified authority rather than power for regulation and control. But, unlike egalitarian societies, chiefdoms are marked by a higher level ritually-sanctioned homeostat--the chief. The complete interaction of segmentary societies has been replaced in chiefdoms by a loosely coupled two-level hierarchy (Earle 1978). Rappaport points out some of the benefits of such a shift:

> "While...ritual regulation benefits from its very simplicity it must be recognized that it also suffers from simplicity's limitations. Consensus concerning deviations from acceptable conditions forms slowly, and corrective programs are both inflexible and unlikely to be proportional to deviations...Novel challenges...might require

more flexible regulatory mechanisms, such as discrete human authorities...Chiefs, for instance, are more expensive
to keep than ritual cycles and can make more mistakes.
But they can respond to system-endangering changes in the
environment with much more sensitivity, speed, precision,
and flexibility than ritual cycles" (1971b: 66).

Furthermore, Peebles and Kus (1977) have suggested a number of
other consequences which can be realized in the change from a
network to a loosely coupled hiearchy of ritual control. Among
these are: 1) an increase in the quantity and complexity of information that can be processed by the cultural system as a
whole; 2) more numerous and larger residential groups can be
integrated into a single cultural system; 3) production can be
rationalized and part-time craft specialization can be incorporated and supported; and 4) buffering against environmental
fluctuation can be centralized (Peebles and Kus 1977: 430).

Archaeologists are now beginning to be able to identify a
number of the features of a chiefdom in the archaeological record. Renfrew, who admittedly is one of the more optimistic,
cites some twenty features and asserts that there is not one
of them which cannot be identified in favorable circumstances
from the archaeological record (1972: 73). Peeble and Kus
(1977) argue for the removal of redistribution and ecological
specialization as necessary and sufficient determinants of a
chiefdom, but still contend for a number of direct implications
for the recognition of this form of organization of regulation
and control. The demonstration of ranking, the form of regulation and control, and the spatial arrangement of settlements
are all variables cited as significantly diagnostic of chiefdoms. They go on to propose five major areas of variability
distinctive of chiefdoms for which hypotheses can be presented
and tested with archaeological materials (Peebles and Kus 1977:
431-433). These chief variables are: 1) clear evidence of
nonvolitional, ascribed ranking of persons; 2) hierarchy of
settlement types and sizes; 3) settlements located in areas
which assure a high degree of local subsistence sufficiency;
4) evidence of organized productive activities which transcend
the basic household group; and 5) correlation between those
elements of the cultural system's environment which are of a
frequency, amplitude, and duration to be dealt with but which
are least predictable, and evidence of society-wide organizational activity to buffer or otherwise deal with these perturbations. In the archaeological record, 1) can be most effectively demonstrated through the analysis of mortuary practices,
2) and 3) can be seen in settlement patterns, and for 4) there
are two areas in which the organization of tasks leaves arch-
aeologically visible traces--public works and organized part-
time craft specialization, usually coupled with intersocietal
trade. 5) is evidenced in defensive organization, a mixed
strategy of storage and distribution of foodstuffs, and the
"management" of intersocietal trade.

For the purposes of initiating discussion, I have chosen
the site of Tel Masos (Hirbet el-Mšaš) in the eastern Negev as
an early Iron I site to be used in testing the above propositions. The treatment which follows is necessarily incomplete
due to the fact that it is based on preliminary reports and

private communications with the excavators, and because of the
limitations of space. A monograph by this author on "The Israelite Village" is now in preparation and will treat items
more fully that can only be suggested here.

The site of Tel Masos is most important for any reconstruction of early Israel for a number of reasons. First of
all, it is a site whose excavation was uncomplicated by earlier or later remains. There was no Late Bronze settlement in
the eastern Negev, and because the low hills of Tel Masos were
unsuitable for the erection of a well fortified city, the settlement pattern shifted away from this site to the adjoining
mountain slopes during the monarchy, leaving the remains of
the Iron I village undisturbed by subsequent building activity.
Secondly, Tel Masos provides us with one of the best preserved
and most extensive examples of an unwalled Israelite village
of the early Iron I period yet excavated. As such it provides
telling evidence against both the conquest theory and that of
the seminomadic origins of early Israel. As Aharoni has commented:

> "Instead of the conquest of Canaanite cities we find the
> new settlement in an unoccupied area. Instead of the
> poor settlement of a semi-nomadic tribe we have the rela-
> tively massive settlement in a well-to-do village" (1975:
> 119).

Thirdly, while early Iron I is represented in this region at
both Tel Arad and Tel Beer-sheba, both of which became important central sites later during the monarchy, during the period in question, Tel Masos seems to have been the central,
large settlement in the area. The settlement from the period
of the Judges covered an area of about fifty dunams. It was
established in the late thirteenth century B.C. and terminated
late in the eleventh or early tenth century B.C. (Aharoni et
al. 1974: 7). In Tel Masos we thus have an unfortified settlement, a village, which endured for at least 200 years. The
final reason for our selection of this site for the purpose of
testing propositions is that it is in a region which has been
rather extensively surveyed and/or excavated in recent months
and years, and thus some observations can be made about settlement patterns and subsistence arrangements in its immediate
environs. In particular, another contemporary Iron I site at
Tel Esdar, some five kilometers south of Tel Masos, presents
some interesting data with regard to settlement hiearchies and
village relationships in the period.

With regard to the first of the variables cited by Peebles
and Kus, there does appear to be evidence for nonvolitional
ascribed ranking in the early Iron I society of Tel Masos. In
the northeastern sector of the site (Area A), which has been
thoroughly excavated, remains of about ten houses have been uncovered. These domestic structures form a chain of units which
encompasses a central courtyard which has been only partially
excavated. The houses are joined together to form a protective belt which, in the judgment of the excavators could seal
off the settlement from desert marauders, but was not capable
of defending it against military attack (Kempinski and Fritz
1977: 140). These houses are remarkably uniform in plan and

size. In plan they are of the one-story "four-room" house type which Shiloh maintains was an original Israelite concept (Shiloh 1970, 1973, 1978). The examples at Tel Masos are certainly among the earliest of this house type yet discovered in Palestine. In the first phase of stratum II (mid-twelfth century B.C.) the four houses whose plans are most complete (1065, 88, 2, and 42) range from about seventy two to ninety six square meters in area. Applying the formula which suggests that the number of inhabitants can be very roughly estimated as of the order of one-tenth the floor area in square meters (Naroll 1962), these houses would house on the order of six or seven persons. In no case was there more than one hearth per dwelling, nor are the individual dwellings interconnected, which suggests that there were not large extended families. There is also a remarkable uniformity in the artifactual finds in these houses, consisting almost entirely of locally-made typical Iron I pottery with only very small quantities of Philistine ware.

While the above might suggest a planned settlement made up of egalitarian small extended families, it is house 314 in area H in the southern part of the settlement which would seem to point rather clearly to a ranked society. In terms of size alone, house 314 is about 160 square meters, or about twice the size of the typical "four-room" house in area A. Size alone, however, is not a reliable indicator of the wealth or status of a household since wealthier households do not, as a rule, have more square meters per person (Kramer 1978). House 314 is also distinctive in plan, showing an arrangement of rooms on three sides around an almost square courtyard, a throwback to Canaanite structural traditions (Kempinski and Fritz 1977: 150). The inventory of finds from this structure includes hand-burnished bowls, jugs with two-color decoration (bichrome style), and red-slipped black-decorated flasks (Aharoni et al. 1975: 107), none of which were present in the "four-room" houses. This pottery is thus entirely different from the undecorated, unburnished ware found elsewhere on the site in stratum II and is certainly not made locally, but imported. Some locally made pottery was found in house 314, including jugs, storage jars, and lamps. A carved ivory lion's head was also found in this structure. Given the distinctive size and plan of this house together with the sumptuary goods found within it, the occupants of this structure would seem to be especially wealthy, having far-reaching connections with Phoenician cities and Midianite settlements in the Arabian desert (Kempinski and Fritz 1977: 150). The existence of such a dwelling in an otherwise rather uniform settlement, would seem to constitute evidence for ascribed ranking, especially so since the status of this house seems to remain unchanged throughout the early Iron I period. Unfortunately there are no further confirming data available through the analysis of mortuary practices, since the search for the cemetery was not successful (Fritz 1979). A large cemetery of the Israelite period, the first of its kind in the Negev, has recently been discovered on the eastern slope of Tel 'Ira, some three kilometers northeast of Tel Masos. This cemetery might be related to Tel Masos even though Tel 'Ira as an urban site was only developed later in the monarchy.

The second of the areas of variability mentioned above maintains that in a chiefdom there should be a hierarchy of settlement types and sizes, and that the position of settlements in the hierarchy should reflect their position in the regulatory and ritual network (Peebles and Kus 1977: 432f.). While the evidence for the area under consideration is far from complete, a two-level settlement hierarchy, which is evidenced in chiefdoms (Johnson 1973: 10ff.; Earle 1978: 2ff.; Taylor 1979), might be suggested on the basis of the relationship of Tel Masos to other sites in the area, especially to Tel Esdar. It seems clear that Tel Masos was a central site in the area in the period just preceding the monarchy. Tel Masos, e.g., covered about sixty dunams, while no other site was larger than the twenty dunams of Tel Esdar. In the excavation of Tel Esdar stratum III (second half of the eleventh century B.C.) revealed houses built on the summit of the hill in a circle of about 100 meters in diameter. Some eight houses were excavated and the remains of another two were distinguished on the surface (Kochavi 1969). All of these houses were of about the same size and plan and the pottery found in them was typical Iron I ware, locally made and showing no signs of decoration, slip, or burnish. Unlike Tel Masos, there was no distinctive structure which might indicate ranking, and the ceramic evidence confirms this judgment. The excavators have suggested that at least two ceramic types (the chalice and the storage jar) found at Tel Esdar and Tel Masos are from a single potter's workshop (Aharoni et al. 1975: 103f.). It is thus suggested that Tel Esdar was linked with Tel Masos in a two-level hierarchy of settlement types characteristic of chiefdoms.

Data for the third and fourth variables--location so as to assure a high degree of local subsistence sufficiency and evidence of organized productive activities which transcend the basic household group--are only partial, and thus our suggestions in this area should be taken as quite tentative. It does seem clear, nevertheless, that the site of Tel Masos was not selected for its defensibility, and that it was this factor which probably contributed to its abandonment in favor of a more readily defensible site in the monarchy. The location of this site, like that of many of the new Israelite sites in early Iron I, must have been made with subsistence sufficiency in mind, as suggested on a general level by Ron:

> "Settlements were established in sites less suitable for cultivation and terracing, near, but never on, the arable land itself. In all cases, preservation of cultivable area overrode in each case all other considerations in choosing the cite of settlement...This is the reason for the location of most sites at the margin of the mountain plateaus and crests of ridges adjoining it...The site of settlements, the direction of their expansion and their pattern is dependent on and adapted to the feasibility of terracing, to a great extent" (1966: 120f.)

In a growing number of studies of ancient agriculture in the Negev and elsewhere (Kedar 1957a, 1957b; Golomb and Kedar 1971; Evenari et al. 1971; de Geus 1975), the variety of methods used to extend cultivation in this difficult and agriculturally unpromising region rests fundamentally on two factors:

physio-geography (topography, lithology, exposition of the slopes, soil and the presence or lack of water sources) and the social and administrative factor (land tenure, land-tax laws, and the general economic welfare). The combination of these two basic factors has determined the specific types of land-use patterns, which is the clue to a better understanding of the economic-geographic background of a rural society (Golomb and Kedar 1971)

A detailed aerial survey of the area in question has only been completed in the last several months and the data from it are not yet available. This survey has revealed, however, that an area about one kilometer east and southeast of Tel Masos is scattered with farm houses of Iron I (Kempinski 1979). There is also evidence of at least one dam in the wadi bed of Nahal Beersheba, which was not investigated by the excavators under the assumption that it belonged to a much later period (Fritz 1979. This dam is clearly visible on Plate 16B in ZDPV 89, 1973). Those structures belonging to runoff agriculture are, however, notoriously difficult to date. De Geus maintains that agriculture on terraces in wadi beds was introduced into the Negev only in the tenth century B.C. as an extension of the techniques in the North. He does so apparently on the assumption that the state is a necessary presupposition for the planning and execution of such public works:

> "One must assume that such valuable and vulnerable institutions as the terraces, which often extend for more than a kilometer from the village, with crops left at considerable distance, presupposes political units of some significance, if not the territorial state of the Iron Age" (de Geus 1975: 69).

On such an assumption, however, it is difficult to account for the local subsistence sufficiency of a settlement the size of Tel Masos in the mid twelfth-mid eleventh centuries B.C. If, according to the model of a peasant revolt, the establishment of a site such as Tel Masos in this period represents an attempt by the settlers to maintain a subsistence cereal agriculture free from the Canaanite and Philistine spheres, then we must assume that its establishment and maintenance for nearly two hundred years outside of the state sphere, implies a form of sociopolitical organization which, while not relying on the kind of external compulsion associated with the state, could provide the necessary coordination between family groups such as that in evidence in chiefdoms which are "redistributional societies with a permanent central agency of coordination" (Service 1971: 134). The contradictions inherent in an agricultural society could be resolved by appointing a person or lineage to collect, store, and redistribute surpluses on an equitable basis. Such persons would oversee other productive and ceremonial activities as well. Thus, the potential of surplus production which would become possible with the resource drain of the city-state system eliminated, could be realized without inordinate social conflict and dislocation between the domestic producing units. Furthermore, professional specialization of productive tasks from administration through to actual food production could be organized without fears of a similar nature. The chief ruled by nature of the kinship

system and not by fiat supported by police-military specialists.
It is our contention that what took place during the period of
the Judges was that there developed a unifying ideology which
both satisfied the needs of farmers for retaining a portion of
the egalitarian structure of the chiefdom, and gave over to
priest-bureaucrats additional powers to organize production and
enforce laws. Perhaps these "theocrats" could even call upon
a citizen's army of volunteers to enforce decisions from time
to time. Perhaps they also had limited authority to enforce
labor corvées in the construction of socially-sanctioned projects.

Although the real divisive factor in agricultural villages
may more likely be increasing professional specialization than
sheer village size, it is certainly true that the growth of a
village's population, such as is indicated in additions to several houses in a later phase of stratum II at Tel Masos, produces sociopolitical change. Trigger has demonstrated that
where settlements do not exceed a few hundred people no authoritative officials are needed, but where such villages exceed
500, as Tel Masos undoubtedly did, they are necessary.

> "In the initial instance, the authority seems to take the
> form of a council of chiefs recognizing a paramount head-
> man as their spokesman. Where local groups exceed 1,500
> (which would seem unlikely in the case of Tel Masos) of-
> ficials must be able to exercise police functions" (Trig-
> ger 1974: 97).

The mechanism that maintained social solidarity and law and order on the village and inter-village level, and made possible
multi-community groupings may very well have been a unifying
religious ideology. Such groupings do not require the political integration of the state.

> "Multi-community groupings require less political inte-
> gration since, especially if the technology remains
> simple, local groups can manage most of their own affairs.
> Tribal governments are largely concerned with suppressing
> internal blood feuds and regulating relations with other
> groups. Because of this, larger numbers of people may
> come together as members of a single political entity
> without developing a state than can remain together in
> similar conditions in a single community" (Trigger 1974:
> 97).

The fifth and last of the variables maintains that there
should be a correlation between those elements of a cultural
system's environment which are of a frequency, amplitude, and
duration to be dealt with but which are least predictable, and
evidence of society-wide organizational activity to buffer or
otherwise deal with these perturbations (Peebles and Kus 1977:
432f.). At least three aspects of the environment can be explored as causal factors in the rise and maintenance of a
chiefdom: the demands of agriculture, interregional exchange
and alliance, and warfare. The very brief sketch which follows is only meant to suggest linkages rather than to prove
them, and is thus intended as a heuristic guide for further
research in this area.

One of the crucial agricultural decisions in a society such as that of early Israel would have been when and how much to plant. One would expect, therefore, that one of the duties of the chiefly establishment would include the maintenance of a calendar. In this connection, it is perhaps noteworthy that the Covenant Code (Exodus 20:22-23:33) is largely neutral in regard to the Israelite faith, yet clearly sets forth a cultic calendar (23:10-19) which contains provisions for a fallow year and three pilgrimmage festivals geared to agricultural events. Since these festivals called for the presence of all adult males, and thus had a census function, perhaps it was at these festivals that decisions were made about when and how much to plant in the context of the ritual cycle. The Gezer calendar may also reflect the connection of calendrics and cult at another level. The periodic adjustments of agricultural allottments within and among the clans may also have been associated with the pilgrimmage festivals. Ideologically of course, Yahweh, as the one who succeeded to the city-state kings as owner of the territory, was seen as the one who allotted fields to the various clans/villages, not as a possession but as a fief to be enjoyed in perpetuity so long as the vassal obeyed his obligations under the covenant (Mendenhall 1976: 138). Having said this, however, there still remains the question of the mechanics of administration. As Mendenhall has observed, the one specialization well attested in the archaic narratives is the priest/Levite:

> "It is assumed that the <u>functions</u> of prophet or 'judge'
> are not occupational <u>specializations</u>. From the story of
> Micah and the Danites in Judges 18 we can infer beyond
> doubt that religious specialists were in some demand in
> Palestinian culture of the twelfth century. The 'Levite'
> in question was merely a specialist in religious ritual"
> (1976: 149f.).

We would add that at least one of the reasons that they were in such demand may well have been because of their importance in agricultural decision-making.

Evidence for interregional trade has ben mentioned above. As we pointed out, the items of non-local materials and craftsmanship are clearly associated with the elite residence at Tel Masos.

The relationship of the "judges" to warfare has been the subject of extended treatment in recent years (Mendenhall 1958; Bess 1963; Malamat 1967; Richter 1965; Glock 1968, 1970; Ishida 1973; Hauser 1975; and Reid 1975). The consensus seems to be that along with the ritual involvement of the šōfēt or naśī the other main function which he performed was a military one, and certainly this function was one which could make possible some type of regional authority over a coalition of clans on the part of one who began as a purely local chief (Hauser 1975: 195ff.).

CONCLUSION

In an effort to clarify the role of religious ideology and practice in the sociopolitical structure of early Israel, a refined model of chiefdom is suggested which has utility for the analysis of the archaeological remains of that society. Suggestions have also been made as to ways in which ideology and environment are correlated. It is suggested, furthermore, that the situation which favors the selection for a chiefdom form of organization--i.e., which selects for a higher level homeostat--is one in which the information processing capabilities of a single-level network are transcended, and higher level controls are necessary for the maintenance and survival of the system. Following Rappaport (1971a; 1971b) it is suggested that the locus of this differentiation is in the organization of ritual within the cultural system.

SOURCES CONSULTED

AHARONI, YOHANAN
    1974   "Excavations at Tel Masos (Khirbet El-Meshash); Preliminary Report on the First Season, 1972," Tel Aviv, 1: 64-74. (co-authored with Volkmar Fritz and Aharon Kempinski).
    1975   "Excavations at Tel Masos: Second Season, 1974," Tel Aviv, 2: 97-124. (co-authored with Volkmar Fritz and Aharon Kempinski).

BESS, STEPHEN H.
    1963   Systems of Land Tenure in Ancient Israel, unpublished Ph.D. Dissertation, University of Michigan.

BRAINERD, G.W.
    1951   "The Place of Chronological Ordering in Archaeological Analysis," American Antiquity, 16: 301-313.

DIAKONOFF, I. M.
    1975   "The Rural Community in the Ancient Near East," JESHO, 17: 121-133.

EARLE, TIMOTHY
    1978   Economic and Social Organization of a Complex Chiefdom: the Halelea District, Kahua'i, Hawaii, Ann Arbor: Museum of Anthropology, University of Michigan, Anthropology Paper No. 63.

ENGELBRECHT, WILLIAM
    1974   "The Iroquois: Archaeological Patterning on the Tribal Level," World Archaeology, 6(1): 52-65.

EVENARI, MICHAEL, LESLIE SHAMAN and NAPHTALI TADMOR
    1971   The Negev: The Challenge of a Desert, Cambridge: Harvard University.

FLANNERY, KENT V.
    1972   "The Cultural Evolution of Civilizations," Annual Review of Ecology and Systematics, 3: 399-426.

FRANKEN, H. J.
    1976   "The Problem of Identification in Biblical Archaeology," PEQ, 108: 3-11.

FRIED, MORTON H.
  1968 "On the Concepts of 'Tribe' and 'Tribal Society,'" Es-
        says on the Problem of Tribe, ed. June Helm. Seattle:
        American Ethnological Society, 3-20.

FRITZ, VOLKMAR
  1979 Personal communication

De GEUS, C. H. J.
  1975 "The Importance of Archaeological Research into the
        Palestinian Agricultural Terraces...," PEQ, 107: 65-74.
  1976 The Tribes of Israel, Amsterdam: Van Gorcum.

GLOCK, ALBERT E.
  1968 Warfare in Mari and Early Israel, unpublished Ph.D.
        Dissertation, University of Michigan.
  1970 "Early Israel as the Kingdom of Yahweh," Concordia The-
        ological Monthly, XLI: 558-605.

GLUCKMAN, MAX
  1959 "The Lozi of Barotseland," Seven Tribes of Central Af-
        rica, eds. Elizabeth Colson and Max Gluckman, Manches-
        ter University, 60-74.

GOLDMAN, IRVING
  1970 Ancient Polynesian Society, Chicago: University of Chi-
        cago.

GOLOMB, B. and YEHUDA KEDAR
  1971 "Ancient Agriculture in the Galilean Mountains," IEJ,
        21: 136-140.

GOTTWALD, NORMAN K.
  1976 "Early Israel and the 'Asiatic Mode of Production' in
        Canaan," 1976 SBL Seminar Papers, 145-154.

HAUSER, ALAN J.
  1975 "The 'Minor Judges'--a Re-evaluation," JBL, 94(2): 190-
        200.

HAWKES, C. F. C.
  1954 "Archaeological Theory and Method, Some Suggestions
        from the Old World," American Anthropologist, 56(1):
        155-168.

HELTZER, MICHAEL
  1976 The Rural Community in Ancient Ugarit, Wiesbaden: L.
        Reichert.

HOLLADAY, JOHN S., JR.
  1976 "Of Sherds and Strata: Contributions toward an Under-
        standing of the Archaeology of the Divided Monarchy,"
        Magnalia Dei, eds. Frank M. Cross et al., Garden City:
        Doubleday, 253-293.

HOLLEMAN, J. F.
  1959 "Some 'Shona' Tribes of Southern Rhodesia," Seven
        Tribes of Central Africa, eds. Elizabeth Colson and
        Max Gluckman, Manchester: Manchester University, 354-95.

ISHIDA, T.
1973 "The Leaders of the Tribal League in the Pre-Monarchic Period," RB, 80: 514-530.

JANKOWSKA, N. B.
1969 "Communal Self-Government and the King of the State of Arrapḫa," JESHO, 12: 233-282.

JOHNSON, G. A.
1973 Local Exchange and Early State Development in Southwestern Iran , Ann Arbor: Museum of Anthropology, University of Michigan, Anthropology Paper No. 51.

KEDAR, YEHUDA
1957a "Ancient Agriculture at Shivtah in the Negev," IEJ, 7: 178-189.
1957b "Water and Soil from the Desert: Some Ancient Agricultural Achievements in the Central Negev," Geographical Journal, 123: 179-187.

KEMPINSKI, AHARON and VOLKMAR FRITZ
1977 "Excavations at Tel Masos: Third Season, 1975," Tel Aviv, 3-4: 136-158.

KEMPINSKI, AHARON
1979 Personal communication

KOCHAVI, MOSHE
1969 "Excavations at Tel Esdar," 'Atiqot, 5: 14-48 (Hebrew with English summary, 2*-5*).

KRAMER, CAROL
1978 "Estimating Prehistoric Populations: an Ethnoarchaeological Approach," a paper presented at the Colloque international C. N. R. S. No. 580 (13-15 June 1978), "L'Archaeologie de l'Iraq du début de l'Epoque Néolithique à 333 avant notre ère--Perspectives et Limites de de l'interpretation anthropologiques des documents."

McCLELLAN, THOMAS L.
1975 Quantitative Studies in the Iron Age Pottery of Palestine, unpublished Ph.D. Dissertation, University of Pennsylvania.

MALAMAT, A.
1967 "Aspects of Tribal Socieities in Mari and Israel," Xv^e Rencontre Assyriologique Internationale: La Civilisation de Mari, Liège: Université de Liège.

MENDENHALL, GEORGE E.
1958 "The Census Lists of Numbers 1 and 26," JBL, LXXVII: 52-66.
1976 "Social Organization in Early Israel," Magnalia Dei, eds. Frank M. Cross, et al., Garden City: Doubleday, 132-151.

NAROLL, R.
1962 "Floor Area and Settlement Population," American Antiquity, 27: 587-589.

252

PEEBLES, CHRISTOPHER S. and SUSAN M. KUS
    1977 "Some Archaeological Correlates of Ranked Societies,"
          American Antiquity, 42(3): 421-447.

RAPPAPORT, ROY A.
    1968 Pigs for the Ancestors, New Haven: Yale University.
    1970 "Sanctity and Adaptation," Io, 7: 46-71.
    1971a "The Sacred in Human Evolution," Annual Review of Ecol-
          ogy and Systematics, 2: 23-44.
    1971b "Ritual, Sanctity and Cybernetics," American Anthropol-
          ogist, 73: 59-76.

REID, PATRICK V.
    1975 "Sbty in 2 Sam. 7:7," CBQ, XXXVII: 17-20.

RENFREW, COLIN
    1972 "Beyond a Subsistence Economy: the Evolution of Social
          Organization in Prehistoric Europe," Reconstructing
          Complex Societies, ed. Charlotte B. Moore, Cambridge:
          ASOR, 69-85.

RICHTER, W.
    1965 "Zu den 'Richtern Israel,'" ZAW. LXXVII: 40-72.

ROBINSON, W. S.
    1951 "A Method for Chronologically Ordering Archaeological
          Deposits," American Antiquity, 16: 293-301.

RON, Z.
    1966 "Agricultural Terraces in the Judean Mountains," IEJ,
          16: 33-49.

SERVICE, ELMAN R.
    1962 Primitive Social Organization, 2nd ed. New York: Ran-
          dom House.
    1971 Cultural Evolutionism: Theory in Practice, New York:
          Holt, Rinehart and Winston.
    1975 Origins of the State and Civilization, New York: W. W.
          Norton.

SHILOH, YIGAL
    1970 "The Four-Room House--Its Situation and Function in the
          Israelite City," IEJ, 20: 180-190.
    1973 "The Four-Space House--The Israelite Type House," 'E-
          retz-Israel, 11: 277-285 (Hebrew with English summary,
          32*).
    1978 "Elements in the Development of Town Planning in the
          Israelite City," IEJ, 28: 36-51.

SMITH, JASON W.
    1976 Foundations of Archaeology, Beverly Hills: Glencoe.

TAYLOR, DONNA
    1979 "Some Settlement Pattern Correlates of Chieftaincies
          and Simpler States," unpublished typescript on file at
          the Museum of Anthropology, University of Michigan,
          Ann Arbor.

TRIGGER, BRUCE
  1974 "The Archaeology of Government," World Archaeology,
         6(1): 95-105.

WHALLON, ROBERT, JR.
  1968 "Investigations of Late Prehistoric Social Organiza-
         tion in New York State," New Perspectives in Archae-
         ology, eds. S. R. and L. R. Binford, Chicago: Aldine,
         223-244.

WINTER, EDWARD H.
  1966 "Territorial Groupings and Religion among the Iraqw,"
         Anthropological Approaches to the Study of Religion,
         ed. Michael Banton, London: Tavistock, 155-174.

GOLDEN GATE BRANCH LIBRARY

GOLDEN GATE SEMINARY LIBRARY